THE
COMPLETE SPORTSMAN'S
ENCYCLOPEDIA

———

Francis H. Buzzacott

FOREWORD BY DENIS BOYLES

THE LYONS PRESS

Originally published in 1913 by M. A. Donohue & Co.

First Lyons Press edition: September 2000

Printed in Canada

10 9 8 7 6 5 4 3 2

The Library of Congress Cataloging-in-Publication Data
is available on file.

FOREWORD

Somebody someplace must have an idea of exactly when it was that the American wilderness ceased to be the venue of a relentless series of bad camping accidents and became, instead, the Great Outdoors, home to happy, wholesome hikers and hunters. My guess is that, at least in America, we began celebrating Nature sometime around the turn of the century, when books like this one first began appearing in great number.

The virtue of going outdoors hadn't been an easy sell. It took a half-century or so of propagandizing by Easterners such as Thoreau before we were ready to make our peace and declare Nature noble. From the bank of a pond in Massachusetts, the elegance of a simple life lived out-of-doors must have been easy to see. But it took until 1900 or so, when America was settled from Atlantic to Pacific, before the wild places were thought of as something less than threatening. After a generation or two of farming and railway building, the wilderness was no longer the natural habitat of most Americans. If men and women in Chicago and Brooklyn and Denver and San Francisco wanted to know about life in the rough, they bought a book, went home, lit the fire, curled up and read all about it.

For men, especially, outdoors know-how assumed a symbolic value: Knowing how to catch a fish, pitch a tent, and build a fire was something every banker, broker, and barber on Main Street felt he had to know because then, as now, those things were all emblematic of the manly arts of survival. Men who were *really* men, it seemed, were first and foremost *outdoors*men, men who could get by without a roof if they had to. Teddy Roosevelt was the poster boy for this sort of back-to-nature thing, but men like Ernest Thompson Seton and the remarkable Francis H. Buzzacott were the navigators of the movement. Their books, more than anybody else's, were the guides most men used to lead them out of town and into the woods.

There was a rather pronounced difference between these two men and the books they created. Ernest Thompson Seton, a gentle Canadian naturalist, is far more familiar to most of us. Seton believed firmly that every boy could benefit from a healthful life lived in the amiable embrace of nature. He first organized something called the Woodcraft Indians as a boys' nature-crafts organization, and provided it with a handbook, *The Book of Woodcraft and Indian Lore.* In 1910, when the Boy Scouts were organized in America, Seton became the Chief Scout. Generations of boys grew up reading about "Lobo, the King of Currumpaw" and "The Cubhood of Wahb" in *Wild Animal Ways, Wild Animals I Have Known, Animal Heroes,* and other Seton books, all of which were suffused with a comfortable coziness that youngsters found appealing. (His classic work, *The Book of Woodcraft,* is now available from The Lyons Press under the title *Ernest Thompson Seton's Big Book of Country Living.*)

Buzzacott, on the other hand, operated under a different set of assumptions. As a former soldier, explorer, whaler, seal-clubber—and, as he often noted, "for forty years a trapper, hunter and guide"—Buzzacott's idea of an embrace with nature was a hammerlock followed by a full body slam. Starting in 1903, with his self-published *Complete Campers Manual—or How to Camp Out and What to Do,* Buzzacott believed that when a man went into the woods, it was to wage war with the elements, and win hands down. This approach to camping and hiking will startle some readers today. Where modern backpackers seek to enter the wilderness, then leave again without a trace, Buzzacott shows you how to chop down a tree and make a dining table out of the stump. If you follow Buzzacott's advice, you won't forget your Colt Acetylene Gas lamp. You wouldn't want to get lost on your way back to the Buzzacott Sanitary House Tent ("adopted by the World's Largest Sanitariums"), where the ladies ("who generally object to ordinary tent life") will be waiting. And that 12-ounce tent of yours? Go camping Buzzacott-style, and you'll want a porter just to carry lunch.

While Seton was chronicling the lives of cute critters and offering whittling lessons, Buzzacott was moonlighting as a mad scientist. His survey of life before Adam—*Astounding Revelations, or, Light in Dark Places*—promised to "unfold to my readers a pen and picture panorama of events prior to and since the beginning, before man even, passing and reviewing all the events, up to to-day, and even unto future years." And two of his other books—*Mystery of the Sexes: Sexual Evolution of the Human Race, Hermaphrodites, Secrets of Sex Control, Sex Predetermination and Bi-Sexual Man, or The Evolution of the Sexes* (Scientific Edition)—were rather unique arguments for the biological superiority of hermaphrodites.

Finally, where Seton aimed to promote some overarching, romantic wholesomeness, Buzzacott aimed to promote Buzzacott. The present volume is glorious evidence of his astonishing success. Each of the portions of this book first appeared elsewhere, either as a self-published booklet, or as a promotional item for sponsors, like the Gold Medal Camp Furniture Manufacturing Company, of Racine Junction, Wisconsin, for whom the "Complete Big Game Hunters Manual—or The Rifle-Man's Guide" was written. Buzzacott began conflating these booklets in 1905, issuing revision after revision of his expanding guidebook. Where previously an advertisement for a sponsor's wares had appeared, Buzzacott deftly substituted one for his own stuff. When he wrote in this final edition that this work "is different from any other volume in existence," he presumably excluded his own books. This 1913 edition was underwritten by The American and Canadian Sportsman's Association, whatever that was. (Seton's Boy Scouts did much better.)

None of this should be construed as a suggestion that this book is anything other than a masterpiece of camping, hunting, and fishing lore on an encyclopedic scale. You're lucky you found this extraordinary book. It's packed full of stuff you don't know: the speed of a game bird in flight, the proper mesh for a seining net, the cure for "mountain fever." Buzzacott didn't get all his mileage from his re-packaged, re-purposed work by being wholesome, Seton-style. He made good because he made a good book, one in which the title tells all: *The Complete Sportsman's Encyclopedia.* It's extremely complete. Definitely a big book. And it's value? Inestimable, whether you're reading it on the subway or browsing through it in some more appealing wilderness way, *way* uptown. You will love this book, as I do. But I can promise you this: none of us will love it as much, or as often, as Buzzacott did.

—Denis Boyles
Everett, Pennsylvania, 2000

Photo View of the Largest Civil Camp Ever Erected at any of the World's Great Expositions.

(During the World's Fair, St. Louis, 1904, this camp accommodated 80,000 guests.)

"A Complete Tented City," magnificently located and equipped, costing $60,000. (Built from the accepted plans of the Author.) Lieut. General Nelson A. Miles, U. S. A., pronounced this Camp, after a thorough inspection, one of the most beautiful perfect camps he ever inspected. "A series of camps" *larger even than this* is now being erected by the National Fraternal Sanitarium, at Las Vegas, New Mexico, where it is proposed to furnish tented accommodations for 5,000 patients at one time. When completed this will be the *largest Sanitarium* the world has ever seen. (The plans of this camp were also furnished by the author.)

(*Courtesy of Hon. W. R. Eidson, Prest. National Sanitarium, St. Louis, Mo.*)

"A WORD IN ADVANCE."

This volume is respectfully tendered to its readers simply as a series of practical aid and suggestions about equipment, its selection, uses and care compiled in handy form, for the purpose mostly of aiding those about to start out for a "Trip to the woods"—especially so for those who desire and contemplate using a light —(and a right outfit) which can be depended upon to smooth out the rough parts of a trip— thus contributing to its success and the resultant benefits that accrue therefrom.

It is hoped that quality not quantity will continue to be appreciated by the many who peruse its pages. I have written it as I would talk to my readers aiming to express myself

in plain, simple language, that my most humble reader can profit by its perusal, and trust it will be accepted in that same spirit, in which it is written.

It contains only facts taught by experience, and if the critical reader observes any literary imperfections, kindly pardon them, for I have confined myself to candid, earnest words, all with a view of giving you as many points as possible in as little space as I can, treating on its various subjects, with an array of simple accurate, practical facts, briefly and correctly told.

Placing in your hands as a result not a book of unhandy size, large or many pages, wasteful headings, entertaining stories or exaggerated pictorial sketches. But instead a practical volume containing much information one in the "Woods" would like, or ought to know. And last, but not least, to put in it the hands of anyone, poor or rich, in such form that neither they nor myself can object to its clumsiness, nor affect their purse, in the purchase of it, and if these things are appreciated by the reader I only ask (when you have read it) if its contents strike you as serviceable, useful and instructive, that you will increase its circulation and sphere of usefulness by speaking a good word for it to either friend or stranger, or better yet, handing him a copy and sending for another yourself, as each successive edition shall have more information than that of its preceding issue.

In conclusion I hold myself ready—pleased to hear from any brother sportsman as to observations, or to advise them on any subject pertaining to the "Craft" in all the name implies, if they will but address

"THE AUTHOR"

"
Francis H. Buzzacott
"

Copies of this book will be mailed, postpaid, to any address in the world, on receipt of $1.00

Send a Copy to your Best Friend.

"Scenes and Incidents in the Author's Career."

1	Trapping	8	U. S. Cavalry Service
2	Antarctic Expedition	9	Whaling
3	Arctic Expedition	10	Camping
4	Big Game Hunting	11	With the Indians
5	Sealing	12	Spanish American War
6	U. S. Service (Infantry)	13	Duck Shooting
7	South African Zulu War	14	Fishing

Partial Views of the "Largest Civil Camp" ever erected.

A Portion of the Toilet Pavillion.

The Hospital Pavillion Tent.

Part of the Immense Camp Kitchen.

The COMPLETE CAMPERS MANUAL

or HOW TO CAMP OUT and WHAT TO DO.

136 PAGES   200 ILLUSTRATIONS
BUZZACOTT

1

"An Exposition Exhibit of a Portable Camp and its Equipment"

For this Exhibit (the Author) received two Gold Medals and Diploma Honorable Mention.

An Exposition Exhibit of "Camp Equipment" which received an unusual High Award. (Two Gold Medals and Diploma of Honorable Mention.) It was personally inspected by President Roosevelt and party, and was the exhibit of the Author.

To Successfully Enjoy a Camping Trip

Travel light—but right—there's a deal of difference in these words—just as much as between roughing it versus smoothing it. And if you follow these pages we shall endeavor to point out clearly to you the easiest way to obtain the right outfit, and to gain therefrom the fullest amount of comfort, pleasure and benefit from a trip.

We omit nothing essential—point out plainly how, and what to provide, thus enabling you to provide for your every possible want, to live comfortably and well, and to receive from a minimum of cost and preparation, a maximum of results from an outfit, simple in the extreme, yet one that with ordinary care, will serve its purpose completely, and last you for many a long trip again besides.

Camp
Clothing Outfit

(See also article on Camp Clothing).

For each person (sufficient for a month's trip or more.)

1 Suit of Old Serviceable Woolen Clothes,
1 Extra Pair of Pants or Overalls,
2 Woolen or Flannel Over-shirts,
2 Suits of Flannel Under-wear,
2 Pair Socks,
2 Towels,
2 Handkerchiefs,
1 Featherweight Rain Cape,
1 Empty Pillow Case,
1 Pair Strong Boots or Shoes,

1 Pair Camp Moccasins or Slipper-Shoes.
1 Pair Serviceable Leggings,
1 Broad Rim Soft Felt Hat,
1 Cape Cap,
1 Mosquito Net,
1 Woolen Sweater,
1 Pair Suspenders,
1 Ditty Bag and contents. (Toilet Articles, etc.,)
1 Combination Camp Bed. Mattress, Blankets and Carry-all (four in one), (See Camp Combination)

Wear part of above—roll up balance in carry-all as shown. Size of roll, 12 x 24 inches; weight, 15 lbs.

Carry on your person these:

1 Water Cooling Canteen,
1 Reliable Hunting Knife,
1 Waterproof Safety Match Box (Filled),
1 Reliable Pocket Compass,
(Copy of this Manual in your pocket),
Pipe and Tobacco if you smoke,
Your gun or rod, if you hunt or fish.

4

The Tent

Camp Cooking, Messing Outfit, Etc., Etc.

For Four Persons.

Size and weight of tent according to your selection (see tents).

1 Tent Complete, with poles, guys, stakes, etc., 9 x 9 feet, 10 oz. Khaki Duck,
1 Tent Floor Cloth to fit,
1 Folding Pocket Axe.

1 Tent Fly, single or double (double preferred),
1 Coil Rope,
1 Coil Wire.
1 Repair Kit

1 Camp Coffee Pot,
3 Camp Stew or Water Kettles (These combined form an excellent Oven for Baking or Roasting),
1 Camp Fry Pan or Skillet.
1 Bake Pan,
4 Camp Plates,
4 Camp Cups,
4 Knives,
4 Forks,
4 Spoons,

1 Salt and Pepper Dredge,
1 Flour Dredge,
1 Flask,
1 Cook's Spoon, large,
1 Cook's Fork, large.
1 Cook's Ladle Dipper,
1 Cook's Turnover,
1 Whetstone,
1 Combination Can Opener and Corkscrew,
1 Campers Manual with all Camp Cooking Receipts.

Camp Cooking Outfit Unpacked.

Outfit Packed.

The Oven as in Use

Washing Up.

See Article on Camp Utensils.

Camp Rations

Four Men.—Five Days or More.—United States Standard Ration Scale (ample without any allowance for fish, game, etc.

Quantity and variety larger.

(Quality the very best).

20 lbs. Self Raising Flour.	6 lbs. Choice Mixed Coffee.
6 lbs. Fresh Biscuit.	6 lbs. Choice Sugar.
6 lbs. Indian or Corn Meal.	½ lb. Mixed Tea.
6 lbs. Select Navy Beans.	½ lb. Baking Powder.
3 lbs. Select Special Rice.	½ lb. Baking Soda.
5 lbs. Select Salt Pork.	4 cans Milk and Cream.
5 lbs. Select Choice Bacon.	1 Sack Salt.
10 lbs. Select Fine Ham.	6 boxes Matches, Tin Case.
15 lbs. New Potatoes.	1 lb. Soap. 1 lb. Corn Starch
6 lbs Fresh Onions.	1 lb. Candles.
1 3-lb. Can Preserved Butter.	1 jar Cheese.
3 lbs. Dried Fruits.	1 box Ginger.
½ gallon Pickles in Vinegar.	1 box Allspice.
½ gallon Preserves.	1 lb. Currants.
1 quart Syrup.	1 lb. Raisins.
1 box Pepper.	6 boxes Sardines.
1 box Mustard.	1 Screwtop Flask.

All packed in air tight or tin packages.

(*See Special Camp Ration list*).

Total weight, 125 pounds. Four Persons, Five Days.

Packed in tin lined Camp Ration Chest.

In addition to the above we suggest that you carry ready for immediate use, Fresh Bread, Meat, Sausage, or a few Eggs in case, (to last for first day or two only)—all about the size of your Bandanna Handkerchief full.

Thus stand we prepared for all things

6

So far we have shown you an itemized list of both a light and right outfit, one that will answer your every purpose admirably.

An outfit that will, in a way, later, surprise you with its simple effectiveness.

All this and more—we intend to show; how to transport and pack same, how to use it, and how your individual railroad or boat fare will suffice to carry your entire outfit as baggage, wherever you go, and how the money thus usually spent in freight or express, and what not, will partially provide you rations in plenty for your needs; tell you what rations are best: show you clearly how to prepare them. Aye, more too, besides.

Read Articles On

Camp Clothing, Etc.
Rations or Foods.
Fires—How to Build and Use.
Utensils, Etc.
Shelter, Tentage, Etc.
Portable Houses.
Camp Cooking Receipts, Etc.
Camp Furniture, Etc.
Pointers and Hints.
Camp Doctor and Receipts.
Packing and Transporting.
Etc, Etc, Etc.

This Manual is made pocket size so as to carry to camp with you.

And now be ye wise,
And take ye from ye olde garret,
Ye olde trunk that ye near forgot,
And put ye all thy party has got therein carefully,
Should ye locks aud handles be off, cord it well;
And when the Packet comes and goes,
Where ye will go, it goeth with thee;
And they asketh not its fare neither way.

Scale of Weights, for Four Person Outfit Complete.

Outfit of Clothing for four persons (*see camp clothing outfit*), - - - - - 60 lbs.
Entire Tent Outfit for four persons, including Cooking and Messing Outfit, etc., - - 100 lbs.
Entire Ration Outfit and Chests included, - 150 lbs.

Pro rata—77½ lbs. per person, - - - 310 lbs.

Divide into two packages, to be shipped as baggage for two persons.

All railroads and steamboats accept as baggage 150 lbs. per person.

(If desired an outfit of 600 lbs. can be transported as free baggage for four persons).

A Word
at the Halt

Don't elaborate—don't burden yourself with a host of "the other things" unless you wish for trouble taking care of them. Don't weary yourself with the dozens of things that catch the eye and tax the pocket of even the experienced once in a while. As an instance, don't take a camp oil stove along—the oil can will leak sure.

Men of experience and a life spent in the woods leave all these things to "the other fellow." Never mind even the other cute things that require more stove pipe room than all your cooking outfit together, for should the supply of axes run short or other things happen you'll remember the word at the halt.

We believe in every step of progression as will be evident; want to supply you with every comfort that you may actually need, but those pneumatic beds and fixings; those telescopic kettles, cups and "what nots," banish from your mind and have "ye the coin to spare and the wagon to hire" let it go to the Ration Chest, Tent Outfit, Camp Furniture, Armory or Rod for with such as these nature supplies you with other things much better and 'twere wiser so.

The Camp Fire, Range, Oven, Etc.

As much of our comforts center here, it behooves me to dwell on the "open fire we advocate," for no more interesting place in camp will we find—Truest of friends—Greatest of enemies—here can you do the most good and the least harm.

Your glowing blaze shall supply us with warmth and comfort internally and externally. Here shall weird stories be told and ruddy faces discuss the sights and pleasures of the day.

There is something about a camp fire that makes a camp seem life-like and natural; here, too, can be prepared by simplest of methods, dishes that have tempted the appetites of epicures and kings.

It matters not if you have brought a café chéf along. I would rather have a greenhorn of a week's experience in camp cooking than a Delmonico Chef without. With common sense and ordinary care most any one can surprise himself does he follow the simple outfit and rules of this Manual.

The Camp Fire Crane.

Do not burn fire wood because it is plenty, leave some for return trip. Put out camp fire before leaving camp.

How to Build
and Use Right

Select two medium thick green logs and level off with the camp axe the top as shown in the engraving. Set and brace these logs a few inches apart, only so as they will form support on which the bottom of your utensil will rest safely; scrape out a little trench underneath and with a few pieces more form the windguard or radiator shown in illustration and, lo! your splendid camp range is complete.

Here can be easily accomplished, with care, all the known culinary arts, even without utensils; take note of this fact; even Roasting, Baking, Broiling, etc., and should your outfit be such as this Manual designates, no dish known to mankind need be slighted one jot.

An improvised shelter can be made over this proof against sun or rain and which will be useful also for the preservation of meats, fish and game as these pages later show.

With such simple arrangements as these even the fire need never go out; neither will it be necessary to burn fuel by the acre nor to chop any wood; thus can you save your exertions and the axe for more fitting purposes.

Camp Pot, Hook
and Poker.

11

And Now a Word

As to the amount of fire to get the most results from: you will find it right to utilize only the flame at one end for your boiling and stewing. The hot ashes or live coals only should be used for frying, broiling, baking, roasting, etc., not so much for economy of wood as for less danger of burning, spilling, etc.

If this advice is followed very little smoke is the result. If anything looks amateur like it is to see one cooking over a big, roaring, smoky camp fire, large and hot enough to roast an ox.

If the fire is handled right there need be no more smoke than would fill the cook's hat, much less than make him choke, gasp and ——, like most do.

Camp Fire Tongs.

Let the wood smoke and the fire burn (just before you commence the cooking) then when ready your live coals will give you even more heat than you require for any small party. (Old camp cooks take out unburnt wood before they start cooking—the greenhorn puts on more wood and it makes him suffer accordingly for his ignorance.)

A Tree Full of Dry Fire Wood.

Camp Broom.

Keep wood dry by stacking it up and should rains fall your wood is fairly dry and your camp neat besides.

Camp Cooking Receipts

Camp Coffee.—(2 cups for each person.) To every cup of water allow a tablespoonful of ground coffee; then last, add one for pot. Put on in cold water and set on to boil. Allow to boil up just once; remove from fire; settle with ¼ cup cold water and serve piping hot.

Another Way.—Bring water to boiling point first; add coffee, boil five minutes, settle and serve. A good way is to put the coffee in a small muslin bag, tied loose; then boil five minutes longer and your bag of grounds can be removed before serving.

Camp Tea.—Teaspoonful of tea to each person, one for pot. Pour over fresh boiling water; set aside in warm place for ten minutes to steep, then serve. (Don't boil good fresh tea.) Boil old tea leaves three minutes for second serving and you have as good tea as the first; try it, then wash out pot and burn the leaves in camp fire. (See Hints for the Reason Why.)

Substitute for Coffee.—Parched barley, beans, rice and bread crumbs make a fair substitute; scorch a trifle and grind. You can improvise a coffee mill with a bag and stone, pounding the coffee fine.

A supply of "Horlick's Malted Milk" in chocolate tablet form is an excellent substitute for coffee or tea. It is food and drink—and a hearty and substantial meal can be made from them. 25 tablets make a good meal and a screw top flask holds 75 to 100 of them and can be used for liquids when empty.

13

Camp Yeast or Ranchman's Bread.—This is a most simple and effective way of making splendid bread or biscuit for the permanent camp and is much easier to the inexperienced than it seems. If your camp is for a week in one place we suggest a thorough trial. If you succeed you will teach the wife later on.

Take a common lard pail or any covered small bucket, and mix a simple batter of flour, warm water, a pinch of salt, and a spoonful of sugar; about a quart in all; cover this and set aside in a warm but not hot place; one side of the fire will do. When it lifts the cover of the pail (which it will surely do unless tied down) it is ready for use.

You will now note that this quart of flour has raised to the top of the kettle by fermentation and is now excellent yeast.

Take nearly all of this—saving say ¼ for next baking—and knead it into sufficient flour to make a good stiff, bread dough. This you can knead all you wish—only not too stiff—roll it out and add to it a spoonful of camp lard—sugar—and teaspoonful of baking soda. Knead again, form into thin biscuits or bread, put in oven, set in the warm until it raises to double size, then bake until done.

You now have as delicious a biscuit as your baker ever turned out.

Into balance of sour dough or yeast batter stir more flour and set aside until ready for more baking. This is genuine ranchman's bread used universally on the plains. The only essential to its success is care and warmth.

Fried Bacon.—Slice and soak half hour (if very salt) in water, if not, lay slices as cut in hot pan on the ashes of the fire. Fry until brown on both sides and serve.

Camp Biscuits.—Use self-raising flour; if not, to a quart of flour add small tablespoonful baking powder, large pinch of salt and tablespoonful camp lard (bacon fat), make dough soft with cold water and stir with a spoon, just enough to make a fairly stiff dough. Do not knead or stir too much as this makes heavy biscuits. Drop from spoon into well greased pan or kettle, biscuit size and bake in oven fifteen minutes or until well browned and done. (Note oven for roasting, baking, etc).

Biscuits, Bread, Etc., To Test When Done.—Run a dry sliver of thin hard wood into center, if dough sticks to sliver when you pull it out continue baking more until sliver will come out clean and dry then your biscuit or bread will be well done.

Don't think you must have a range or stove to have a good oven. As good an oven as can be built is made by the simple plan of taking two sufficiently large plates—common baking pans or stew kettles; one a trifle larger than the other, so as to be inverted over each other easily; fit them first so as to be sure of the right ones.

The Camp Fire Shovel.

Into the smaller set your bread, biscuits, meats, game, fish or whatever you desire to bake or roast; now make near your camp fire a flat, good

Oven from Two Bake Pans.

15

thick bed of coals (embers from the fire), on it place your pan or kettle containing the food, with the large one inverted over it. Strew more live coals on its top and you have a most excellent oven—one that needs no attention except when roasting meats and then only to renew the fire coals when burnt out or needed; otherwise it need not be

Two Tin Pie Plates.

Frying Pan and Plate.

touched until it is done; ready to serve. If roasting, basting is unnecessary. Allow fifteen minutes for biscuits; bread, fifteen to twenty minutes; meats, one to two hours according to size; beans, three to six hours, if possible.

By above plan anything can be excellently roasted, even well browned, perfect. (See also camp oven without utensils.)

Slap Jacks.—A simple batter of flour, etc., thinner than biscuit dough, so it will run thick, drop in small quantities into hot pan, well greased, fry brown, turn over. Brown and fry fairly dry. If made right they are far more substantial than cake; sprinkled when hot with sugar they are excellent and stick to the ribs on a long tramp. As a bacon sandwich for lunch they are fine.

It is an excellent plan to utilize only the embers of a camp fire for, baking, roasting, frying or broiling and to conduct these operations on one side of fire only. The direct flame of camp fire should be only used on pots, kettles, etc. (Note carefully article on camp fires.)

16

Stale Bread or Biscuits can be made fresh by wrapping in damp cloth and placing in oven for a few minutes. Very stale bread is excellent if dipped once in salt water and fried brown in hot bacon fat.

Camp Bread.—Made same as biscuit only in a loaf form. It should be flattened out to fully cover the size of oven, in either case grease well the oven bottom or dredge the bottom of dough with flour to prevent sticking.

Soda Biscuits.—Small teaspoonful soda, pinch of salt and spoonful camp lard into quart of flour, mix as for biscuits and bake. Use only one-half as much soda as baking powder or they will turn yellow and taste bitter. (See also bread without oven, etc., etc.)

An Oven from 2 Round
Camp Stew Kettles.

Broiled Small Birds:—Clean and parboil them first, then broil over hot clean embers of the fire using a split stick as shown on page 26. Excellent for Broiling any kind of meats.

Corn or Johnny Cakes.—One-half flour, one-half meal, mix not as stiff as biscuit dough; pour into pan or kettle and bake slowly thirty minutes or until done.

The tendency of most camp cooks is to have too much fire. (See camp fire observations, etc.)

17

Pork Fritters.—Slice salt pork,—soak and roll in meal or flour. Drop in hot fat and fry brown.

Fried Fish, Game, Etc.—Clean well; season and fry as above, always fry in hot fat; it sears the outside and retains the juices and flavor, while to put meats on in cold pan and fat extracts juices and makes good meat tough. Don't salt fresh meats before frying, salt in pan, when nearly done, before serving.

Fried Potatoes.—Slice and fry raw potatoes in hot fat. Brown both sides, season with salt as you remove them, serve red hot.

If sliced boiled potatoes, use but little fat, season with salt and pepper while cooking and brown in pan.

Good seasoning is one half of good cooking. Don't guess at it, season to taste.

Boiled Potatoes.—If new potatoes, don't put on in cold water; drop in boiling water instead; put in small handful of salt. When you can easily pierce them with a fork or sliver they are done. Strain well; dry a minute over fire and serve.

If old potatoes, soak for half hour, just put them on in cold water. Boil such potatoes with skins on, after washing twice, slicing piece off each end; guess what for.

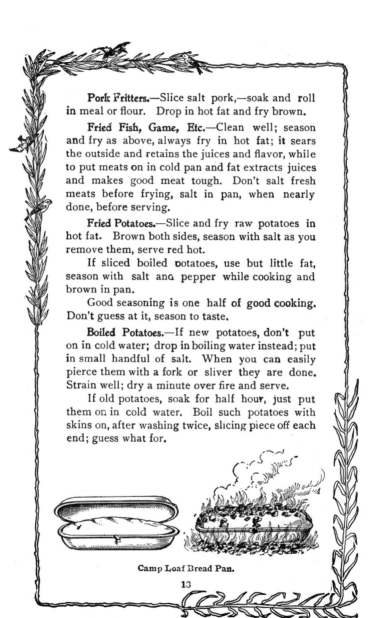

Camp Loaf Bread Pan.

Sectional View of the Buzzacott Oven in Use.

Baked or Roast Potatoes.—Wash and dry well; bury deep in good live coals—ashes of fire; cover well with hot coals until well done.

Roast Meats, Game, Etc.—Clean and prepare; dredge well with flour, pepper, etc., a little salt, add a few sliced onions and a slice or two of bacon or salt pork on top for basting qualities. Add a little boiling water to start the gravy, then it is ready for pan or pot roast. (See also cooking without utensils, oven, etc.)

Fried Mush.—Slice cold, boiled mush. Roll in flour and fry in hot pan with little fat.

Corn meal requires much cooking—boil and stir for 20 to 30 minutes.

Soups, Stews, Etc.—Crack fresh bones into pieces, add meats, scraps and a slice or so of bacon or pork, cover with cold water and boil slowly, until meat is well done; then add onions and a few teaspoonfu's rice or cooked beans. Boil until done, slowly; season to taste.

Meats for Soups, Etc.—Should be put on in cold water and simmered slowly—always. Allow boiled meats, hams especially, to cool off in the water they are boiled in—they slice better—are tender and there is a big difference all around.

19

Camp Pudding.—Have ready a large kettle of boiling water—plenty of it—and a large bag made from a piece of flour sack; dip the bag into the boiling water and dredge flour on the inside of bag. Cut into dice size pieces one cup of fat salt-pork; roll in flour to separate the mass, then to three cups of flour add one cup sugar; one cup currants; two teaspoonfuls spice. If desired dried fruit cut in small pieces can be used in lieu of currants. Add water to this and stir into good thick paste or batter. Turn this out into floured cloth—allow room for swelling of pudding to double its size; tie up tight in cloth; drop in boiling water and boil for two hours. Don't let the water stop boiiing or your pudding will spoil—better have a little extra so as to allow for boiling away. Use no baking powder or soda. Just try it once!

Sauce for Above.—One quarter cup sugar; two tablespoonfuls flour or one of corn starch ; teaspoonful of spice, cup of evaporated cream or water. Mix cold and heat over fire to boiling point, stirring well; remove from fire and stir in a teaspoonful or more vinegar to taste. The vinegar will give it a flavor like brandy sauce—just try it, following directions exactly.

Rice Pudding.—Put cup full of rice in plenty water, a little salt; don't be afraid of too much water; boil until a grain can be mashed easily between thumb and forefinger, then pour off water or strain through cloth. Every grain of this rice will be whole and separate if done correctly as above. To this rice add a cup of sugar, a spoonful of spices and a cup of currants. If possible a little condensed milk and water—say a cupful. Set aside in warm place—not over fire—for fifteen minutes ; until liquid is absorbed and you have rice pudding.

It is well to note that in this "camp cookery" we have no receipts except what conform to the contents of our Ration Chest, and if they are carefully followed we vouch for surprising results. The receipts herein have been tested for years by many thousands who have used this Manual (depended on it) exclusively.

Camp Pot Pie.—Simply follow receipts for soups or stews only leave out the bones. Fifteen minutes before serving drop in by the teaspoonful a cup of ordinary biscuit dough. Put on cover and boil until done. Boil slowly and not so as to burn. Add sliced potatoes and onions also.

Don't Boil Meat fast, it toughens it.

Smoked Herrings toasted or broiled over camp fire are excellent.

Boiled Beans.—Always soak beans over night if possible using double water and allowing room to swell (a pint of dried beans makes a quart or more) if you can't soak them put on in cold water with a piece of pork or bacon—say a pound therein; when it boils add a teaspoonful of baking soda; boil until beans are well done, adding more water if necessary. Season to taste with salt and pepper, a few spoonfuls of sugar, one of mustard. Pot beans should cook thus, three hours or more.

Baked Beans.—Simply take the above; arrange them in oven (see oven) or you can use preserve jar if empty. Score the top of bacon or pork; press into center; cover with hot water and bake from one to three hours more (an onion adds to flavor). The longer a bean is cooked the better it is. (See also cooking without utensils.)

A teaspoonful of baking soda makes hard water soft—try it when boiling beans.

21

Leaky Utensils will be better for an application of soap or a paste made of flour, salt and fine wood ashes plastered on and dried. Cracks in stoves and ranges can be cemented by the above most effectively by leaving out the flour.

Camp Meat or Game Pie.—Line a kettle with a pie crust of the following: To a quart of flour add a teaspoonful of salt, ¼ teaspoonful of pepper and a cup of camp lard, add a layer of cooked meats or game (after removing the bones) then a layer of onions, then a layer of potatoes until kettle is nearly full, over this lay a thin sheet of the pie crust and pinch the edges together, cut a slit in center of top and pour in one pint of boiling water, and bake for one-half hour slowly or until crust and vegetables are well done. Roll out crust with a bottle.

Camp Stew.—Use raw meats or game and stew slowly until very well done, then add vegetables and stew again until they are done, season to taste, thicken 10 minutes before serving with two spoonsful of flour batter.

Camp Cookies or Hot Cakes.—To a quart of flour add a tablespoonful of baking powder or one teaspoonful of baking soda and a pinch of salt, mix well, then add a cup of currants or chopped dried fruit, a cup of syrup or sugar, teaspoonful of mixed spices, two tablespoonfuls of camp lard, mix with cold water to a thick batter, roll out, cut into round cakes, using baking powder can cover as a cake cutter, and bake in quick hot oven 15 minutes; watch the baking.

Rich Soup and Gravy Coloring.—Tablespoonful burnt sugar or flour—rich brown.

Fish Chowder.—Cut small slices of pork or bacon—fry them out in kettle, then put in layer of fish cut in slices on the pork or bacon thus fried—then a layer of onions and then potatoes and biscuit and repeat in layers as above until all materials are in. Season each successive layer, cover with water and stew slowly for half an hour or until well done.

Use Meat Water.—Water that meats have been boiled in for pea or bean soups.

Corn Bread.—One quart corn meal, teaspoonful salt, one of baking powder or soda, mix with cold water to a thin batter, set to rise—when ready to bake stir your batter well, and put into bake pan or oven and bake slowly for half an hour or more until well done. In making corn mush, use a paddle whittled from a stick; stir often and cook well 30 to 45 minutes slowly.

Gingerbread.—Three cups flour, one cup of molasses, one-half cup of lard or camp fat, two teaspoonfuls of ginger, one teaspoonful of baking soda, water to make a thick batter; stir well and bake in hot oven.

Salt Meat Stew.—Take a few slices of salt pork or bacon, soak in water for half an hour, then place them in pot and partially fry them; add sliced onions, potatoes and biscuits in layers and season to taste. Stew slowly until done, adding just enough water to barely cover the stew; thicken with flour or meal if desired fifteen minutes before serving.

Fish Cakes.—Take cold fish and remove the bones; mince well and mix with equal parts of bread crumbs and potatoes; season well and fry in little fat. Brown well both sides. An onion helps it.

Always carry on a long trip a water canteen and a lunch in your haversack; a slapjack and bacon sandwich is fine. (It will not dry up or crumble to pieces).

Sample Days' Camp Menu
Bill of Fare

BREAKFAST

Hot Wheat and Corn Cakes (Flap Jacks), Syrup
Pork Fritters or Fried Bacon and Potatoes

Camp Bread   Preserves   Hot Coffee

DINNER

Camp Baked Pork and Beans

Baked Potatoes   Pickles

Coffee   Bread

Plum, Rice or Bread Pudding

SUPPER

Hot Soda Biscuit   Camp Pot Pie

Hot Tea   Cheese   Crackers

(Taken from our ration list only.)

The variety of our camp rations and camp cooking receipts suffice to give a daily change of Menu for each day in the week.

24

Cooking Without Utensils
(For Emergency Cases)

See also Utensils and How to Make.

Bread or Scones.—Can be baked by using a large thin stone well heated first in camp fire then placed on embers near fire. Flatten out dough to cover the stone, turn when under part will permit until done. Scones are equal parts of meal, bran or flour.

Frog Legs and Mushrooms—Make a dainty camp dish and are often found around camp—look out for the wrong kind: toadstools; they are poisonous. Mushrooms show a pink or brown underneath and peel easy, while toadstools are black or white underneath and do not peel easy, if you are not sure of the difference do not eat them. You may need an emetic (see Camp Doctor).

Bread, without Stone even.—Make a good, stiff dough adding a little more salt, but no lard; pull it out into a long thin strip, wrap this strip corkscrew like on a stick of wood with bark on (tree branch). Hold over very hot fire of ashes (not flame) turning constantly until done. Try this pulled fire bread—it's great!

For Large Game, wild turkeys, etc. Wrap in common mud clay and bury in pit of coals all night; in the morning take it out, break off case; feathers, skin, etc., will fall off with it and you will try this many a time thereafter.

Well Soaked or Cooked Beans—Place in bucket, kettle or pot; covered with water and buried in pit of coals all night as above, are cooked in the morning. Cover kettle of course.

Roast Meats, Fish, Game, Etc.—Without Utensils.
—Clean fish or game thoroughly, place on piece of green bark of tree. Wrap it all up in green grass; bury in pit full of red hot live coals; (no unburnt wood) red hot ashes are best, for two hours or more according to size. When done remove outside skin and serve. Another way is to roll in soaked paper, instead of dried grass.

Fish or feathered game need not have scales or feathers removed; simply wet them before covering; when done, skin. Scales or feathers will all come off together easily and the delicious flavor of the flesh will taste as you never tasted it before. Season after it is done to taste.

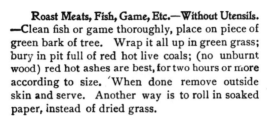

The Green Bark Oven.

Frying or Broiling without Utensils.—Use the green, thick bark of a tree, rough side down on fire. Use the camp fire tongs (as illustrated elsewhere) or make a toaster and broiler as shown, from a stick having a split end which will hold the meat over a hot coal fire. Don't pierce the meat. Always carry a small bag of salt in the haversack.

The Bark Plate and Broiler.

26

To Roast Whole Game—Open Camp Fire.—Note above spit and forked sticks; turn constantly. Large game requires two men to turn right. Excellent for rib roasts or large game.

A little charcoal (burnt wood) thrown into a pot with slightly tainted meats will sweeten them.

Scour pots, pans and kettles immediately on emptying contents before they cool off (they clean twice as easy and well). Use sand and water; It is far better than soap.

Greens.—Carefully picked spring dandelions make an excellent mess of greens for a camp. Boil in salted water (like spinach) until tender, changing water twice.

To Preserve Meats, Fish, Game, Etc.—Slice meat to be preserved in long thin slices, knead plenty of salt in and lay covered aside so as to absorb salt for four hours. Then spread out singly in the hot sun to dry for a few days, or smoke well for 24 hours over a good thick smoke, on a frame of green twigs. When properly cured they are dry to the touch and have shrunk up to one half their size. This is sun dried or smoked jerked meat, so universally used on the plains by both white men and Indians alike. Fish can be cured the same way. Turn skin side up or remove skin when removing bones.

Meats cured carefully by this method will last for a year or more; eat raw or fry.

Hints and Pointers on Camping

A Hot Sweat Bath. Can be arranged in camp with hot stones and a little water sprinkled on them (arranged by covering yourself and stones with blankets), or see Indian Quick-up, as a frame for such. This is the Indian method of curing most all complaints.

Camp Lantern. (Fish and Game Snare).—Take a piece of phosphorous (walnut size) submerge it in a saucer of water and cut into little pieces, then put, into small bottle with two ounces sweet oil, cork tightly, tie to a limb or stick. Stuck into the ground, it attracts game at night, or if tied to a string and dropped into the water where fish abound it will attract their attention and they can be caught.

A Good Camp Lamp.—Can be made by using clear tallow fat, (fat of animals), melted down and put in an old tin can. Improvise a wick from unravelled cotton or tent canvas, put one end in can and the other end on edge of can and wire.

A Good Camp Candlestick.—A safe one can be improvised from a potato with a hole in it—bottom sliced off so it will stand firmly—or an old can partly filled with dirt

A Good Camp Spoon, Knife and Fork.—Can be made from a shell and split stick. A fork can

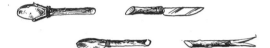

easily be whittled, and a good knife made from a piece of tin cut from an old can and inserted in a split stick; lash it tight with wire.

A Good Dinner Plate or Cooking Utensil, f r o m a piece of green thick barky tree, using smooth part for food.

Any Old Tin Can—Top carefully burnt out over camp fire, then scoured makes a good cup or small cooking utensil. Make handle of wire as shown above.

To Keep Matches Dry.—Cork a few in a small bottle. (See also waterproof match boxes).

To Correctly Ascertain the Points of the Compass.—Face the sun in the morning; spread out your arms straight from the body—before you is the east, behind you the west, to your right hand, the south, left, north, (accurately.) If the sun don't shine, note the tops of pine trees, they invariably dip to the north. (See also lost in camp).

A Reliable Camp Clock.—

A very accurate one can be improvised by making a sun dial of a piece of stick stuck in the earth where the sun's rays can cast the shadow of the stick on the ground. You can mark the ground most accurately if one of your party has a watch. Then the clock will serve you well, when the man with the watch is gone. It will not vary like a watch, and will tell the time correctly when the watch won't; don't forget that.

A Whet Stone is handier and more useful than a butcher's steel. It can be used for exactly the same purpose  any way, and will sharpen the axe and all tools when a steel will not.

Don't Spoil a Good Knife.—In opening tin cans in camp, take the camp axe. Cut a cross in the center and open the cuts afterward, but not with the fingers.

To Heat a Tent Nights Without a Stove.—Build a camp fire near tent opening, surround it partly with a radiator of logs, bark of tree or brush, so as to throw the heat to inside.

Another Way.—Throw into camp fire a lot of stones, the larger the better, let them get red hot, put into bucket and carry into tent, invert the bucket over them, and it will surprise you. With a change of stones in the fire you can renew and keep warm all night long;—or use camp kettle.

Still Another Way.—(Perfectly safe if common sense is used). Dig a pit half a bucket in size somewhere in tent. Fill it heaping full of red hot clear coals (embers) from the camp fire, taking care no unburnt or smoky wood is therein. Now cover this with the kettle or pail. With mud, plaster up the edges, and it will keep your tent and you warm all night long. Use camp pails (iron of course).

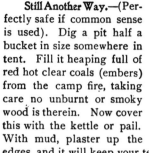

In Case of Fire in Tent.—If serious, lay hold of the bottom of the bedding and pull out, and with a blanket smother the fire, quickly. If fire is caught in time you can smother it.

Let the tent go, but save the outfit therein, if possible. You can improvise shelter but not the outfit, so save that part first.

To Find Out Correctly How the Winds Blow.—If the wind is very light, place your finger in your mouth for a minute, moisten it, then hold it in the air. The coolest side indicates the direction from which the wind blows.

How to Catch Frogs.—You can catch frogs with hook and line baited with red or scarlet rag (it's like shaking red cloth at a bull). Clean the hindquarters and roll in meal or flour and fry in hot fat. They are delicious.

A Good Fire Shovel.—Can be made of a piece of tin and split stick; it is also an excellent broiler.

Sheets of paper, or an old newspaper sewed between two blankets, equals three blankets. A thin vest lined with paper equals two.

If the seams of underwear chafe or gall the skin turn inside out. Common corn starch is a most excellent talcum or chafing preventative and cure. (It's in our ration list.) .

If Soaking Wet.—If soaking wet and no dry clothes handy take off wet garments and wring them out as dry as possible—put on again,—you are less liable to take cold, and will be much warmer besides.

Don't Sleep.—Don't sleep with the moon shining on your face, you can get moonstruck, and it's as bad almost as a sunstroke.

Burn Up All Kitchen and Table Refuse.—Even potato skins and wet tea or coffee grounds, burn out even tin cans in the camp fire, if thrown out they are fly and maggot breeders, and mean lots of flies in camp. Burnt out and thrown aside they are harmless.

To Test the Freshness of Meats, Game, Etc.—Thrust a knife blade into center of flesh—remove the blade; your nose to the knife blade will do the rest. Meat is often fresh inside when the outside is not. Your nose can't tell inside—the knife blade can.

A Good Telescope—With straps and case is the finest thing for camp and field use. (I never could see why field glasses are preferred) A good telescope is far better. (See telescopes).

For Washing Flannels and Woolens.—Don't wring out, hang them up dripping wet and they won't wrinkle up or shrink.

To Keep Fresh Meats, Game, Etc.—(See also smoked meats, etc.) By hanging in old sack, sack opening downward; secure with cord, tied to legs of game; then take a few branches of leaves and cover; the rustle of these leaves will help keep the flies away and the meat cool. Fasten the bottom opening with slivers of wood, so you can get at meat without trouble.

Do Your Part.—Let each man elect to perform certain duties in camp; one to gather wood and carry water, one to cook, one to clean, etc.

Biscuit Cutter and Rolling Pin.—The tin baking powder can cover makes an excellent biscuit cutter and any bottle a good rolling pin—even an unopened can.

To Cool Water.—Any old well soaked cloths, wrapped around outside of bottle or bucket will, if hung in the shade, help cool contents. Remove the cork. (See water cooling canteens).

A Good Waterproof Oil for Boots and Shoes.—Lay on hot mixture, one part rosin, two parts beeswax, three parts tallow. Soft and waterproof.

Water and Fireproof for Tents, Canvas, Etc.—Equal parts of alum and sugar-of-lead, quart or more of each to several buckets of tepid water, soak well, turning often, then spread out to dry. Both rain and fireproof.

To Waterproof Woolen Clothing.—"Lanoline," (pure sheep wool fat), applied to wool clothing renders it impervious to water. Can be purchased at any drug store.

A wire stretched across top of tent poles makes a good receptacle for clothing at night. (See also tent clothing hanger.)

33

A Good Camp Bed for Tents, or Tent Carpet.—
Take fine ends of any branch clippings, and plenty
of them. Commence at head of tent, lay rows of
them. butts to the rear, in successive layers. If
this is done right and carefully and ends locked
with a log rolled on so as to hold end in place, an
extremely soft bed is the result. Over this spread
your tent floor cloth and stake down (or use camp
combination).

If Thirsty and Can't Find Water.—Place a pebble or button in the mouth and keep it there; it will
surprise you with the result, and relieve that dry-
ness entirely—try it.

No Loaded Fire Arms in Tent.—Don't have
loaded fire arms in tent; a simple fall of rifle or
gun may have serious results; make this a rule.

Distress Signal.—It is generally understood (or
ought to be) that three shots in succession, another
shot a minute or so afterward, is a signal of distress.

Lost in Camp.—When you find you have lost
your way, don't lose your head—keep cool; try
and not let your brains get into your feet. By this,
we mean, don't run around and make things
worse, and play yourself out. First: Sit down
and think; cool off, then climb a tree, or hill, and
endeavor to locate some familiar object you
passed, so as to retrace your steps. If it gets
dark, build a rousing camp fire. Ten to one you
will be missed from camp, and your comrades will
soon be searching for you, and your fire will be
seen by them. (If you have been wise, read your
Manual and see cooking, etc., without utensils,
fire without matches, camp shelter, and the human
compass, etc.) Give distress signals, but don't
waste all your ammunition thus. It's ten to one
morning and a clear head, after a comfortable

night, (if you make it so) will reveal to you the fact that your camp is much closer to you than you imagined.

I have seen good men lost within rifle shot of camp. A cool head can accomplish much—a rattled one, nothing.

To locate position—note the limbs and bark of trees—the north side of trees can be noted by the thickness and general roughness. Moss most generally is to be found near the roots on the north side. Note also—limbs or longer branches, which generally are to be found longer on south side of trees, while the branches exposed to the north most generally are knotty, twisted and drooped. In the forest the tops of the pine trees dip or trend to the north; also: If you find water, follow it; it generally leads somewhere—where civilization exists. The tendency of people lost, is to travel in a circle uselessly; by all means, keep cool, and deliberate, Blaze your way, by leaving marks on trees to indicate the direction you have taken; read up on this Manual, which should be always kept in your pocket when in camp or out; it's made the right size to carry there. A cool head and a stout heart, and lost in camp is really a comedy—not the tragedy—some people make it. This is the the time a compass is invaluable.

To Make a Fire Without Matches.—Things sometimes invaluable : Such simple facts as these have saved a life many a time. Take a dry hand-kerchief or cotton lining of your coat, scrape out a very fine lint, a few handfuls, by using the crystal of your watch, compass or spectacle, a sun glass can be made that will ignite the lint, which can be blown to fire.

35

Another Way.—Sprinkle powder of cartridge, as a fuse to the cotton lint, and with the cartridge percussion cap you can easily ignite the lint, dry moss, leaves, etc.

Still Another Way.—Take scrapings of very fine pine wood, find a piece of quartz or hard ragged rock, by using your knife as a steel (a ramrod) you have a practical flint and steel. If you haven't these things, use two pieces of rough, jagged stone and by striking them together sharply in slanting blows you can ignite the lint or scrapings. (These are times when a waterproof match box and matches are worth their weight in gold.

To Dry Inside of Wet Boots, Shoes, Etc.—The last thing at night take a few handfuls of clean, dry pebbles, heat them in frying pan, kettle or camp fire until very hot, place them in the boots or shoes, they will dry them out thoroughly in a few hours, shake once in a while. Soldiers use oats or corn, but this is not available always, and pebbles are. Now is an excellent time to grease or oil them. (See waterproof for boots, shoes, etc., elsewhere).

A Tent Fly—makes a capital shelter and shade for your camp cooking and dining purposes. In an emergency it will also serve as a large shelter tent or a large tarpaulin by which you can keep your rations dry, and as an additional shelter to the tent proper when desired. By all means we advise an extra tent fly to be taken along when in camp.

A Good Compass.—Always carry a good compass to camp. (See waterproof safety compass). It's the kind you need never quarrel with, and if you do, the compass is dead right and you are positively wrong.

To make a Good Camp Lantern—From any ordinary clear glass bottle, if the bottle is long necked. Heat a piece of wire red hot, and wrap it around the part below the neck, the wide part, submerge the neck into a bucket of water and it will cut the part surrounded by the hot wire as smooth and clean as if cut to order. Now wire a bail or handle to carry it by, with a loop over the bottom, fill ¼ full with moist dirt or sand, forming a hole therein with a round stick, insert your piece of candle in this hole, cover with a piece of old tin can top (perforated with holes) and you have a good outside camp lantern. A small coil of wire is always a handy thing in camp. (See camp outfit, it's included therein). Common sheet glass can be cut with scissors if held flat under the water while cutting it—try it.

Don't Sit or Lay on the Bare Ground.—Military statistics has proven beyond question that one-half of the sickness incident to camp and field life is due to neglect of this important caution. Better sit on your hat, anything except the bare ground, even the Indian avoids this, he squats, as he knows it is harmful to even him. The United States Government now issues camp cots or beds to the United States troops in camp whenever possible, over 200,000 cots being issued to the United States troops (Gold Medal Brand). By all means avoid sitting or sleeping on the ground, is a golden rule in camp, even though it feels dry.

Limit of Man's Pack.—Don't forget 40 pounds is the limit of a man's pack, more is making a pack mule of him.

Prevent Sickness.—Keep the bowels open, head cool, feet dry and there will be little, if any, sickness in camp.

37

Hunters', Trappers' and Fishermen's Secrets for the capture of small game or fish. Take *Cocculus Indicus*, pulverize it and mix with dough, scatter a few handfuls, in still water where fish frequent, they will seize it voraciously and will immediately become intoxicated, and turn belly up on the water, when they can be gathered in. Now place them in a bucket of water and they will soon revive and be as lively and healthy as ever; this does not injure the fish or the flesh in the slightest way, and **is** positively harmless, Those you do not wish to use turn loose again, they will soon be all right, as the effects are only temporary and intoxicating only. .

Oil of Rhodium.—A few drops on your bait when fishing with a hook, and fish will never refuse to bite. Add a little of this to bait on small game traps, or oil of Amber and Oil of Rhodium mixed, (equal parts) or beaver oil, and the odor will attract them from afar, their scent of this is remarkable and they will risk anything to secure it.

These are reliable secrets of most noted trappers, and the above has been the Chinese secret of catching fish for centuries.

Bird Lime.—As it is sometime desired to capture, unharmed, for mounting, or taxidermists' collections, certain birds; the following receipt will make an excellent sticky bird lime: Common linseed oil or varnish boiled down slowly until a very thick mass; place on limbs or branches where they frequent, or near their nests. I have often used this spread on papers to rid a tent of flies, or I used molasses and flour mixed to a consistency of thick cream and put in a tin plate.

To Peel Onions.—Dip in water when peeling, they won't make your eyes water.

PART TWO

Most Modern Tent Made.
(See Tents.)

Remarks of
CAMP CLOTHING
CAMP UTENSILS

Remarks on
CAMP RATIONS
TENTS,
SHELTER
ETC., ETC.

A complete Camp Outfit for Four Persons, Packed in One Chest, so as to be Shipped as Baggage.

39

The Twentieth Century Camping Outfit

As time and things change and improve, so has camping outfits. Luxuries of a decade ago (seeming impossibilities) are only common necessities today. The man who went into camp twenty years ago went in with a feeling that "roughing it", was a necessary part of camp life. Today *"smoothing it"* is the proper term, and the man who goes in with the intention of smoothing it is the one who comes out with the greatest percentage of benefit from his trip.

We believe in and advocate roughing it as little as possible, although we admit that there is a certain pleasure in practicing the art, but when it comes to rolling ones self in a blanket, sleeping, eating, sitting on the bare ground, cooking in a cup, frying everything—cooked and grease soaked in a pan, subsisting on corn dodgers and salt pork, packing ones outfit on his back, etc., we call a halt, for there is no more need of such old flint and steel, ancient methods.

Nowadays a man can sit on a comfortable backed camp chair, eat from a practical, portable camp table, or sleep on a first-class camp cot or bed. The weight and space of these three good things adding but a few pounds and square inches to his outfit. —

Railroads now transport these things as baggage almost to the very "nick of the woods," as it were, and that 20 pounds of weight today equals what would have been 50 pounds a few years ago.

By judicious selection, today, a party can provide themselves with comforts unheard of a few

40

years ago. Folding boats, even bath tubs, a 14 oz. axe that will fell a tree, or a waterproof match box that can be carried in the hat band, and a host of more such good things, and the party who now heads for the woods will, if he be wise, see that his outfit be such as will at least give him genuine comfort.

It is unnecessary to elaborate, but we do contend that there is a common sense medium between the two "its"—"roughing it vs. smoothing it," and to such as desire home comforts even in camp we respectfully dedicate the following pages.

The Camp Combination (Five in One)

Of all things in "general camp usefulness and comfort," this is the most important, as reference to illustration shows. It comprises the following articles all in one:

Camp Bed, Mattress and Blanket.
Camp Sleeping Bag.
Camp Hammock.
Camp Shelter Tent.
Canvas Roll-Up and Safety Carry-All
and Pack.

A Wind, Weather and Waterproof Summer or Winter Camp Convenience.—First, it is an absolutely waterproof camp mattress, having a double bottom like a bag without ends; into this can be packed dry leaves, moss or twigs, forming an excellent sanitary camp mattress. The side flaps and inner bottom can be fine blanket lined, waterproof khaki covered, which equals two to four blankets. It

41

The Buzzacott Camp Combination Outfit.

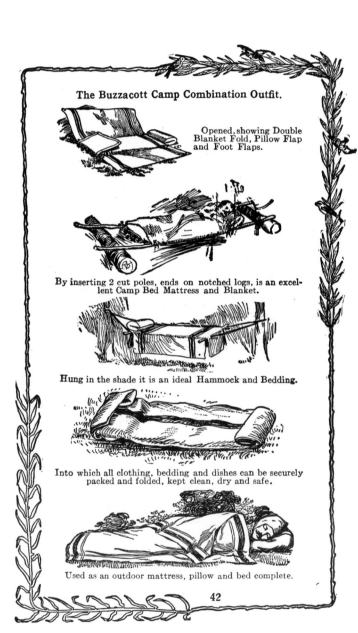

Opened, showing Double Blanket Fold, Pillow Flap and Foot Flaps.

By inserting 2 cut poles, ends on notched logs, is an excellent Camp Bed Mattress and Blanket.

Hung in the shade it is an ideal Hammock and Bedding.

Into which all clothing, bedding and dishes can be securely packed and folded, kept clean, dry and safe.

Used as an outdoor mattress, pillow and bed complete.

can be slung up as a camp hammock, or made into a cot or zeroproof sleeping bag. The pillow flaps are formed of two large pockets, into which clean clothing is kept neatly folded, and forms an excellent pillow. The foot flaps tuck in keeping the feet warm and dry, and the blanket flaps can be arranged to lay on or cover over you, converting it into a summer weather outfit or a winter one. The blanket flaps can also in very hot weather be arranged as a dewproof shelter tent as shown, if desired to sleep out in the open air. Last but not least, your entire outfit can be rolled securely, packed inside and strapped to any size bundle or pack with adjustable straps provided for the purpose, and carried as a knapsack or blanket roll on on your back, thrown into a wagon or buggy seat, or strapped to the saddle military fashion.

Its extreme size opened up covers over 9 x 7 feet, thus adapting itself to any size person, and its entire weight is but 10 pounds, while its size as a pack is but 30 x 4 inches.

Carry-All.

It is extensively used by military officers for campaign work in the field, and by cattlemen who desire an article well made and extremely serviceable, one that can be put to a variety of uses.

It can be laid on the ground and keeps the sleeper dry, even should the grass or earth be wet. As can be seen by engraving it is a combination most desirable for all round camping uses.

43

The Sportsmen's Camp in the Woods. (Read about Camp Furniture.) 44

"About Camp Furniture"—For permanent camp, portable house, lodge, log cabin, etc., I refer the reader to the various grades of camp furniture illustrated herein.

But if out for a trip of a few weeks time and you travel or equip light (and right) packing your own supplies so to speak, I do not advise any camping outfit. To lug along so-called "Portable Camp Furniture"—even be they out for a trip of a month's duration.

Even to Military men its bulk and weight becomes a serious objection (except when in permanent camp), so much so, that it is often abandoned for lack of *transportation, pack facilities or breakage.*

There is no more need of littering up one's outfit with such stuff, than there is necessity of toting along your mother-in-law to make up beds. And to substantiate this, I intend to show and illustrate how easily such things can be improvised from the materials to be found in proximity t th pot selec ed for the camp itself, which after admirably serving its purpos, can be abandoned or left, as a reminder of your ingenuity and skill i "Woodcraft" for the next sportsman wh. "'appens that way," or for your own next outing to come.

But little time is necessary to construct or improvise these things—if you must have them —and the following saving in round dollars, weight and space will perhaps lead you to cogitate and make up your mind to follow my suggestions.

A one person camp cot costs $2.50 to $3.00, weighs 15 pounds, occupies 3 feet of packing space by 8 to 10 inches width. A common camp table, *equal cost weight and space*, a back camp chair (ordinary pattern), *one-half the above.*

It is obvious to the intelligent that these three articles (simply a one man outfit) occupies 1 x 3 feet of actual space in your kit, weighs 30 to 40 pounds *dead weight*, costs $8 to $10 and

Simple Method of Camp Furniture Making
(in the woods.)

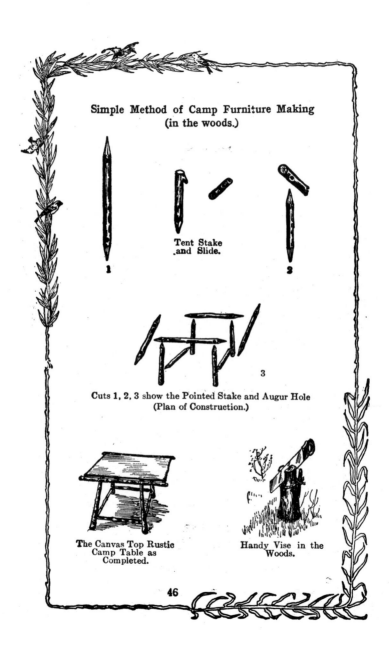

Tent Stake
and Slide.

Cuts 1, 2, 3 show the Pointed Stake and Augur Hole
(Plan of Construction.)

The Canvas Top Rustic
Camp Table as
Completed.

Handy Vise in the
Woods.

constitutes a fair-sized load alone, and should it be, that each member travels thus on the "Feather Bed Plan" you will need a pack mule, wagon or trunk to tote it around. Why, it's enough to cause mule suicide in the first muddy or quicksand creek he crosses, or at least to tempt him to kick the "Onery outfit" to kindling (where it eventually goes), leaving you to choke down cuss words and mourn the loss of the good $20 to $50 bill that the whole blooming outfit really cost you.

If, however, the party is burdened with an excess of coin, or desires to litter his pack or camp outfit with a lot of bulky "so-called necessities" in the furniture line, there is ample opportunity to blow in your hard earned coin on freight express—such fixings, and what nots, and plenty of alluring literature, advertising, which explains their desirable features but ignores the undesirable ones.

There is no more necessity of taking such things on a trip than there is of lugging the "Kitchen range along," as my articles on campfires and cooking will show, for with a few simple tools (things in that and other lines beside), can be easily improvised by the party itself. Material abundantly supplied from the woods in the vicinity of most any camp, and ample opportunity furnished for recreative exercise which will serve to while away many a tedious hour of camp life—When it's too dry to hunt, too wet to fish, or too hot to leave the shady side of a comfortable camp in the woods.

In this, as in other things, it is ridiculous to observe the good money thrown away by tyro sportsmen, who think such things essential to "smoothing it," he goes into the woods with a fair-sized mule load and comes out with mulish experience, leaving generally behind him, somewhere, a monument of such superfluous articles (really kindling), behind—.

Better far had he taken a few simple tools along instead. Then would the problem of luxurious Camp Furniture (a la rustic) be easily solved and money enough saved to pay the ordinary expenses of the trip besides.

"Wrinkles" for Camp Furniture Making
(in the woods.)

The Log Table.

Log Table with Cupboard.

Rustic Camp Table and Benches.

Canvas Top Rustic Table

(See Article about
CAMP FURNITURE.)

Board Top Rustic Table.

In nearly every camping party of say three or more, will be found one, who, while not an artisan, a mechanic, is at least handy in the use of a few ordinary tools (if brought along) *They come in handy in a hundred different ways* with them repairs to guns or fishing tackle, boats, harness, wagon, tent poles, utensils, etc., or a host of necessary camp equipage can be made; for in camp one can make few tools answer multitudinous purposes under compulsion, drawing on nature for implements and material as needed besides as they want them.

On the other hand without such tools great inconvenience, in fact absolute suffering sometimes results from serious breakdowns, especially be it to boat, wagon or gun, when, to, perhaps there is no possible means (or tools) on hand to repair it. Brought about by your lugging along Camp furniture instead, or the failure to heed my timely advice and suggestions now.

It has always been my claim that no outfit or party should take to the woods, without at least some sort of *"Kit of Tools"* not elaborate, but few and simple, and to make plain my recommendations on the subject I offer herewith a list of tools. Experience has time and time again found valuable, viz.: 1st. A piece of double width strong canvas about 6 or 8 ft. wide, 2 or 3 yards long (in which is rolled the kit of tools) suggested as follows:

A small hack saw (with rip and cross blades separate), a claw hammer hatchet, a carpenter's brace (with a one and two inch bit), a flat file, a 2 pound bag of assorted nails and tacks, a 5c coil of wire, pliers, and if not too much, a common draw knife, as illustrated. Last, a few yards of ordinary small-size rope which can be used to tie up the entire outfit; when rolled into the canvas previously mentioned, which serves as a carry-all for the entire and substantial kit—weighing in all about 10 to 15 pounds.

The Kit of Tools. (See About Camp Furniture.)

1 Flat File	1 Draw Knife
1 Combination Tool Set	1 Roll Double Width Canvas
1 Brace (1 and 2 inch Bits)	1 Tape Measure
1 Hack Saw	2 Spools Soft Wire
1 Claw Hammer Hatchet	2 Tent Needles,1 Sewing Palm
A. 2-lb. bag Assorted Nails	1 Ball Twine

(Roll up Outfit in Canvas.)

50

With such as this, by the aid of the suggestions I offer, one can improvise, construct or repair anything from a brush hut to a log house, raft, or camp furniture, galore—cots, bed (double or single), tables, stools, benches, and the hundred and one things you need, with credit to your skill in "woodcraft" and with comfort unheard of before—made by yourself in a score of substantial ways—If the hints and illustrations herein, are in any way—roughly—even crudely—followed, to wit:

To Make a Good Camp Cot or Bed take a piece of the canvas mentioned, about a foot longer than yourself, and say 40 inches wide, sew or stitch a hem 6 inches wide, along either side double seaming it if you can (this can be made before you start out if you wish)—then when you get to camp take two poles or cut saplings about 3 inches in diameter and a foot longer than your canvas, run them through the ends or loops, and lay the ends in 4 strong forks driven and braced in the ground for the purpose.

Still Another Way. Have in your outfit some old, wide gunny sacks, cut out the closed end so as to have both ends open, slide these sacks over both poles, and you will have what will make the best "camp cots" sink into insignificance.

Another Way Simpler Still. Lay the side poles on two logs, brace apart by cut notches in the logs, so as to stretch tight the canvas—now spread your blankets (The Camp Combination—or sleeping bag—on this). The side poles will spring with your weight and the result is a bed that you will enjoy after a hard tramp, more than you do your own bed at home—and equal to any $3 or $4, 15 lb. cot ever made—all at a price of perhaps 50c—and ten minutes pastime.

If neither of these are available you can make almost any fair size piece of canvas answer the purpose of a good camp bed by first strewing brush leaves, grass, etc., or browse on the tent floor and staking down over it at the ends, a canvas floor cloth as shown in the illustration. Besides this, you have an advantage in having something excellent to roll your outfit in or to "kiver" the grub supplies, in case of danger from a sudden rain storm or a leaky tent.

The Tent Carpet Bed.

"Hints" for Camp Furniture Making
(in the woods.)

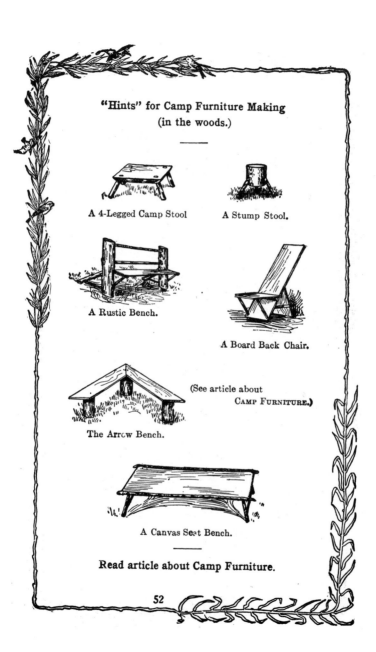

A 4-Legged Camp Stool

A Stump Stool.

A Rustic Bench.

A Board Back Chair.

(See article about
CAMP FURNITURE.)

The Arrow Bench.

A Canvas Seat Bench.

Read article about Camp Furniture.

52

An Old Bed Tick Empty will serve a similar purpose if you don't want to bother with the poles, simply fill it with grass, leaves, weeds or browse, any of which makes a bed better than the hard ground, or equal to the cot plan—

Or you can secure either of the "Camp Combinations" which I have designed for the purpose as the illustrations show, and which is the happy medium between the best Camp cots and the Sleeping Bag, by their use, as illustrated, they are adapted for all kinds of weather and uses; For instance, if the weather is warm so that all this covering is not needed by the sleeper, he may shift it to suit weather and taste, crawling in on top of as much of it as he may wish, and the less he has over him, the more he will have under him, and softer be his bed. Besides this, being water and wind proof, one can button themselves therein, as snug as a bug in a rug, leaving, if needs be only his nose out as an air hole—and no matter what horrid nightmares he may have, he can neither roll out of bed or cot, or kick off the "kivers"— nor will he catch the draft of cold air that comes along from the under side of a camp cot about the north side of his spine every time he turns over on the cold canvas of a cot, as he will surely do when sleeping on them. Neither will the "kivers" fall off—nor his feet crawl out and attract mosquitos (females) or chilblains as they are liable to do the other way—in short, he will have all of their much boasted advantages—none of their disadvantages, and if any brother sportsman wants one and cannot find an architect in his vicinity that will build it right, let him but write me and I will tell him where I have mine made, in such shape as to reflect credit on us both.

If on a canoe trip, choose the one I invented with "Tent ends" as shown, then you have the ideal and complete outfit for its tent, bed, bedding, blankets, trunk and everything else. By many it is termed "Buzzacott's War Bag," because into it go boots, shoes, clothing, rope (tools), or anything that cannot be readily placed or carried somewhere else. It is always ready and there is always room for something more besides.

The only objection to it, is that anything you want to get out is at the bottom, safe enough, but its only the work of a moment to dump the whole blamed outfit on mother earth, get what you're after, and stow the rest away again.

When rolled up rain can come down in floods and its contents are safe and dry, you can jam it into the boat, or stray corner of a wagon box anywhere, stow it on top or under a high or heavy load, where a box or trunk could never ride half as easy.

It can be knocked about at will without danger or damage. Train baggage smashers can fire it from one end of the car to the other,

or from the car to the other side of the platform
in vain. It's proof against their heathenish
instincts of Destruction, and makes them sigh
when they see it coming, because they know
they simply "Kint Bust it." You can cinch
it onto the "oneriest" cayuse, or mule that lives,
tight enough to ride for a month without fear
of his smashing it, and it stands jamming against
trees where even an iron trunk would come to
grief. Have it made by a tent-maker if you
wish, of strong canvas, and if you add to it a
coat of waterproof paint, it will last as long as
there's a feeling of camping out left in your
bones. Makers of camp furniture and tents,
however, don't like to make them because it
robs them of a sale in both tent and camp
furniture lines, and as put out by some of them,
it's a snare and a delusion. Get it made right,
pay a fair price for the work, and the stuff that
it's made of, and you, have a "dingus" that
you'll swear by for many a long trip to come.

A Modern Prairie Schooner.

As for Camp Stool or Chair what is simpler than the billet of wood with a few auger holes and pointed stakes, as shown, even if a man's "bottom anatomy" is soft through sitting on office chairs—for with a few handfuls of grass or leaves, and a foot of the canvas even the luxurious cushion pad can be tacked on top to his infinite delight, while the legs of his chair can be cut to fit his particular make up, be he spindle, straight, or even bowlegged, used to a squat stool or a high leg office chair—

Bear in mind now in speaking of things that some 25 years hard service has shown them to be in the woods the real essential to "smoothing it." For those who want to "rough it" (carrying about) such things as camp cots, tables and chairs; let them—they'll come down to "hard sense" after a while when experience teaches them a few more tricks of the trade.

A Camp Cot for Inside Tent Use.—Can be made by the simple plan of forming a rustic frame, 6 ft. long by 3 or more feet wide, on which is stretched or tacked the canvas mattress cover or the lashing to its side of the camp combination then mounted on slanting legs at both ends those of the head being a few inches longer than the *foot* for slant sake and the hygenic comforts they bestow, as is shown.

The Camp Table for Tent Us_ is made by the (plain auger hole and pointed stick principle)—or by 4 stakes driven into the ground, or by the small center tree stump support, as shown. If boards or any old provision box tops are not available, stretch taut over a small rustic frame, *well braced*, a yard or so of the canvas and you'll have a table top you can well be proud of. These same instructions apply to outside rig for table and benches that puts to shame the "Camp Furniture Fixings" men have been lugging around to their detriment the past few years.

Where "camp tables," bench or seat supports are needed for outdoor use, the simple method of inserting a short sapling of wood partly in the ground (tamping the dirt well around its base), will make an excellent foundation for a table top. (See illustration.) Or you can use forked stick uprights with a frame top, if desired over this frame should be drawn or tacked a portion of the canvas mentioned. If no boards or bark of trees is handy either will do, however, to make a most excellent table top.

Showing Plan of Construction.

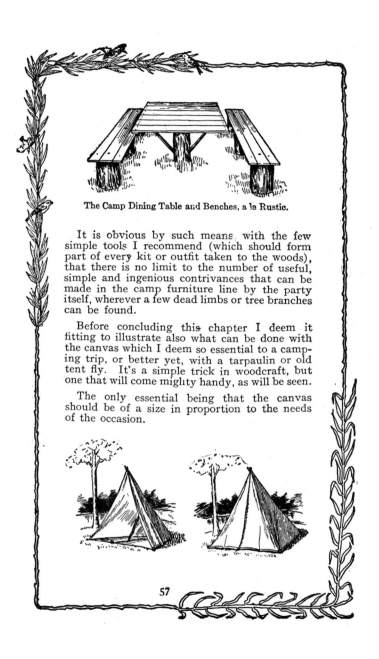

The Camp Dining Table and Benches, a la Rustic.

It is obvious by such means with the few simple tools I recommend (which should form part of every kit or outfit taken to the woods), that there is no limit to the number of useful, simple and ingenious contrivances that can be made in the camp furniture line by the party itself, wherever a few dead limbs or tree branches can be found.

Before concluding this chapter I deem it fitting to illustrate also what can be done with the canvas which I deem so essential to a camping trip, or better yet, with a tarpaulin or old tent fly. It's a simple trick in woodcraft, but one that will come mighty handy, as will be seen.

The only essential being that the canvas should be of a size in proportion to the needs of the occasion.

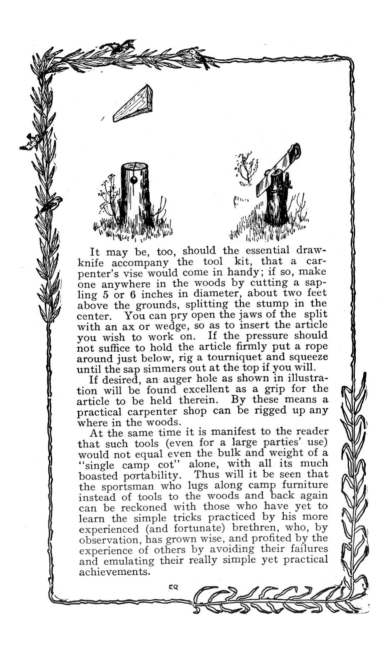

It may be, too, should the essential draw-knife accompany the tool kit, that a carpenter's vise would come in handy; if so, make one anywhere in the woods by cutting a sapling 5 or 6 inches in diameter, about two feet above the grounds, splitting the stump in the center. You can pry open the jaws of the split with an ax or wedge, so as to insert the article you wish to work on. If the pressure should not suffice to hold the article firmly put a rope around just below, rig a tourniquet and squeeze until the sap simmers out at the top if you will.

If desired, an auger hole as shown in illustration will be found excellent as a grip for the article to be held therein. By these means a practical carpenter shop can be rigged up any where in the woods.

At the same time it is manifest to the reader that such tools (even for a large parties' use) would not equal even the bulk and weight of a "single camp cot" alone, with all its much boasted portability. Thus will it be seen that the sportsman who lugs along camp furniture instead of tools to the woods and back again can be reckoned with those who have yet to learn the simple tricks practiced by his more experienced (and fortunate) brethren, who, by observation, has grown wise, and profited by the experience of others by avoiding their failures and emulating their really simple yet practical achievements.

"Buzzacott's Combined Tent and Bedding Outfit.

The following description and illustrations will serve to convey an idea of another of the author's inventions, which for some time past has been put up in practical form for those who desire such an article, excellently and substantially made. It consists of three sections of canvas of suitable length, weight and width, having at its extreme ends grommet holes, to which is fastened guy or lashing ropes, the center section is made of heavy waterproof canvas, so arranged as to be staked down to the ground over a bed of grass leaves, hay, straw or browse, so as to form an excellent and dry bed, a capital mattress so to speak, for if this is done an admirable soft, restful bed is secured over which is spread the blankets for the sleeper's use, while the end sections can be used as additional covers, according to weather or needs.

If, however, the weather is such that a partial or complete tent is necessary as *cover* from *dews* or the rays of the sun or moon, one of the end sections is thrown over 2 forked uprights cut for the purpose, anywhere in the woods, or by using boat oars or canoe paddles. This when staked out form a complete *half tent* over the sleepers the other half section remaining, serves as an excellent canvas (dew or moisture proof) covering for his blankets, while its extra width can be tucked snugly about him.

Should, however, a *"complete tent,"* a covering being needed, which will be practically storm or rain proof, all that is necessary to do is to throw over the *poles shown.* The remaining end section of canvas, and lo, a complete admirable tent is formed, even to the side walls, or flaps which can be guyed or staked out to an *angle* much wider than the bed itself, for reasons as is apparent.

It is par excellence for canoeists or two men hunting outfit who camp on the trail of same, as can be easily seen, and to those desiring same, *made right in a substantial workmanlike* manner. The author will furnish information on application or send one subject to your approval.

53

It is such recreation as this that recuperates the nervous energies, jaded from worry, care or pressure of commercial or professional life; would that the thousands of cases of heart disease, tuberculosis, brain, eye, mind and nervous troubles, insomnia, dyspepsia, etc.,——— would profit by this advice.

To such I say, cut loose awhile from your elegant homes, and its luxurious furnishings; "Go instead to the wilds," live in camp; improve the hand and mind by new channels of exercise and thought; feel that it is good to live thus away from the feathered bed plan. Men were campers before they were house livers, but, hemmed in by brick and stone walls, for generations, their hand has forgotten its cunning and craft, in the matter of outdoor home building in the "woods." Now when they would dwell in tents let them seek the simpler comforts, such as may be gleaned from the wilderness or woods wherein camp is to be pitched and made.

Then will the echo of my words, "It is good to live thus," come back to you, elaborate if you choose or must, camp furniture, there is plenty for you, but do not pass over too lightly my hints for making your own essential things as suggested in my article "Making Camp Furniture" with the little kit of tools, instead of spending your coin for them and littering up your Camp outfit—and Pack with superfluous articles (so-called necessities) in the Camp Furniture line.

The "Buzzacott" Combination Tent and Bedding Outfit, Complete.

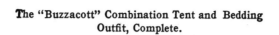

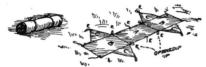

Rolled Up.   A—Bed Part: B and C—Tent Portions.

As a Half Tent and Complete Bedding.

As a Complete Tent and Complete Bed.

The Upright (Cut), Poles and Paddle.   Ridge Pole Used.

Camp or Sportsmen's Necessities

Odd to Look at, but Remarkably Efficient Articles

Safety Pocket Match Box.

Almost anything will do to carry matches in if you don't care a rap whether they are wet or dry. If you're a sportsman, your comfort certainly and your life, possibly, may depend upon the condition of your matches. The happy-go-lucky sort of fellow who crams a handful of matches into an upper pocket of his shooting jacket when he starts on a hunting or fishing expedition, with no other protection against moisture than the cloth, is mighty apt to go without a fire if he is caught out in a storm. Waterproof Pocket Match Box in all that the name implies. First and foremost it is waterproof—you can soak it in a bucket of water for a year and the matches will be as dry when you take them from the box as when they went in. It's a pocket match box—not cumbersome to carry, and of sufficient capacity to keep a man in fires and smokes for several days. It's made from brass, heavily nickeled, and is about the size of a 12-gauge shot shell. It may be carried in the cartridge belt if desired. It will last a lifetime—there's not a shoddy piece of material or workmanship in it. It's so cheap every sportsman can afford to own one—indeed no sportsman can afford to be without one. **Did you ever tumble off a log or break through the ice into the water on a freezing cold day? How much would a handful of dry matches have been worth** to you when you crawled out? Did you ever get caught out while camping? If you did you know that a dry match is worth dollars—if you haven't one. Did you ever get caught in a cold rain-storm, miles from home, and have to camp under a bunch of balsams until the shower was over? If you did you wanted dry matches, and you wanted them mighty badly. Did you ever sit on a log, wet and tired, and fill your pipe for a comforting smoke and find every dodratted match in your clothes damp? If you did, you said some awfully warm things—but you didn't smoke. Did you ever come into camp wet, tired, and hungrier than a bear, and find your partner eating raw pork and crackers, because the blankety, blank tent leaked just above where you left the match box? That's when a dry match is worth more than a gallon of snake medicine. About the only substitute for the Recreation Waterproof Pocket Match Box, is a tightly corked bottle. Bottles break. Corks are easily lost. In fact there's nothing to be desired in the way of utility, beauty, compactness, lightness and capacity. A Recreation Waterproof Pocket Match Box, with a Safety Pocket Axe, make a fire certain in any weather. It insures a smoke or a fire when most sorely needed.

Construction—The box is drawn brass shell 13-16 inch in diameter. The bottom of the box is double threaded to receive threaded collar which is attached to the downwardly extending arms of the cover. The cover has a rubber gasket firmly held in place by a brass washer with projecting tooth which prevents the cover being swung too far to one side.

Operation—Grasp the knurls at the side of the cover with the thumb and forefinger, turn the box to the left, swing cover to one side. In closing, screw box snugly against the rubber gasket in cover, when it will be absolutely waterproof.

The Handy Compass

Handy Compass. Stationary or Revolving Dials Pin it to your hat, coat, shirt, wherever you want. Guaranteed absolutely reliable.

Every military man or camper carries a compass. Most veterans do, all ought to. It's annoying to lay a course by compass at any time. If one is obliged to fish around through his pockets for the instrument and then wait to steady the needle, it's worse than annoying—it breeds profanity. With this Handy Compass it is different. To begin with the compass is accurate; this saves lots of steps. It has a deep box. This means that the needle has great freedom of action and keeps its direction all the time. It is made in two styles: Plain, that is with the ordinary dial; or similar with a marine compass, with a card which revolves with the needle, a great convenience to the inexperienced user. It pins securely to the outside of the coat or vest where it is always in sight, always in position and can be constantly consulted without halting. It is absolutely water and moisture proof. This means that the post is always free from rust and the needle works accurately. It is so made that the crystal can, with no trouble, be removed to re-adjust the post. It is neither large nor small—just large enough. (1⅛ inches in diameter). If you've ever hunted through one pocket after another for a compass on a bitterly cold winter's day, with a chilling wind penetrating to the very marrow of your bones, you've been where a Handy Compass would have been worth more than its weight in gold. If you've ever followed a ——— through miles of unfamiliar country and found it necessary to find your way back to camp by compass you have been in another position where a Handy Compass is simply invaluable. If you've ever hunted or cruised over a new region on a cloudy day, you know just how handy a compass, always level and always in sight is. If you've gone scouting and lost your way in the country where mosquitoes seem to breed under every fallen leaf, you've been in a place where you wouldn't trade one Handy Compass for a bushel of the ordinary kind. If you've carried a compass in your pocket with a knife and keys, you've wondered why the needle didn't work right. Demagnetized, but you didn't know it. If you've been in a new country with the ordinary sort of pocket compass, you know that the trouble of getting it out, opening it and stopping to settle the needle keeps you from consulting it as much as you ought. With this Handy Compass, a fairly accurate course may be laid without stopping at all. Being firmly attached to the coat, vest or belt, it is not likely to be forgotten, mislaid or lost. Equipped with a good rifle, this Handy Compass, a Pocket Axe and a Waterproof Match Box, one may cross and re-cross the continent without a guide.

Othea Forms of Compasses, Barometers, etc.

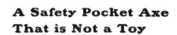

A Safety Pocket Axe
That is Not a Toy

It's a practical little axe intended to be carried
in the pocket or at the belt. It's large enough to fell
a tree in a few moments, and so small that it's never
in the way or burdensome to carry. A convincing
demonstration by the inventor has been to fell an
eight-inch Norway pine in five minutes by the

Open and Closed View.

watch, a feat that most men of average strength
and skill can duplicate, using this diminutive tool.
Every axe is absolutely guaranteed against defective material or workmanship. It is light, extremely
durable, can be carried in a coat pocket, hip
pocket or at the belt; it is evenly balanced, and is
the only axe on the market with a safety guard.
Sportsmen need it in camp and in the woods. In
camp it serves all the purposes of axe, hatchet
and hammer, and in the woods is useful in a
hundred different ways. Caught far from camp
at nightfall, the hunter can in a few moments
provide himself with a bed of boughs and the
firewood necessary to make him comfortable for
the night. Should he wish to cross an unfordable
stream, the axe and a leaning tree provide a
convenient bridge, or this failing, a raft is easily
constructed, which will float hunter and game
over river or lake. It's no sport to cut a gambrel

63

Reliable Camp or Sportsmans Specialties

Closed.   Opened.

Sportsmen's Telescope and Case.
Very powerful.

Water Cooling Canteen.

Principle of Construction.

Pocket Scales.

Pocket Safety Axe.

Safety Compass.

Waterpoof Match Box.

Hunters' Axe Belt and Sheath.

Fish Knife.

Camp Filter.
1 qt. a minute.

Hunting Knife.

Pack Harness.

Folding Pocket Hunting Knife

Articles that can be relied upon.

64

stick, or poles for carrying a big buck, with a pocket knife. A dozen blows with the axe do the business perfectly. In passing through a dense growth of underbrush, a blow here and there with the pocket axe saves a world of climbing and crawling. No one who is not a fisherman can know how exasperating it is to find one's hook caught in a branch just beyond his reach, or on a snag under the icy water of a bushy trout stream. A stroke or two with the axe and the hook is free. And so it might be enumerated scores of instances where the pocket axe proves itself "the handiest tool the sportsman ever carried." Military men, tourists, canoeists, yachtsmen, etc., find the little axe almost indispensable—it is, indeed, "the hand-iest tool the sportsman ever carried." But it's use is not by any means limited to the great fraternity of hunters and fishermen; land cruisers, surveyors, log scalers, and camp foremen find it almost indispensable, as it fulfills all the requirements of a large axe without its weight or bulkiness. No camping outfit or hunting kit is complete without one of them.

How They Are Made—They are made from the finest steel, sharpened to a fine cutting edge and protected by a patented metal guard which folds back into a groove in the underside of the handle when the axe is in use, and at other times fits closely over the edge of the blade, protecting both the cutting edge of axe and anything it may come in contact with from injury. This metal guard is lined with lead, so that the cutting edge of the axe cannot become dulled from the guard itself.

About Sizes, Styles and Weights—The axe is made in two styles, and in four weights, viz.: 14 oz. 18 oz., 20 oz. and 24 oz, There are two lengths of handles, viz.: 11 inch and 12 inch.

A Good Hunting Knife

Did you ever see a really good hunting knife? Ten to one you didn't unless you have seen a Sportsman's Ideal Hunting Knife. It's different from any other—better. In the first place it is hand made throughout, hand forged, hand polished, hand mounted, hand sharpened, and it is made and designed by the pocket axe man—that alone

would recommend it. The maker is a hunter. There is nothing theoretical in the construction of the knife. It's made on lines which constant and varied experience have proven to be essential in a hunter's knife. The blades are hand-forged from the finest razor steel by an expert, and are fully warranted. They will hold an edge under treatment that would ruin the average so-called "hunting knife." The special design of the blade (see cut) with its heavy back and bone cutting surface near the point, and its peculiar double concave surface gives it the necessary weight for heavy use and by carrying the heavy metal well down to the edge does away with thin, brittle cutting edge which renders most knives useless for heavy work. The handle is made from laminated leather set in waterproof cement, with hard rubber and aluminum trimmings, and is held to the blade by a heavy steel shank which extends through the buckhorn tip and ends in a flush ground set nut. Every knife is tested by striking repeatedly into a hard hemlock knot before packing for shipment and the slightest sign of

Marble's Celebrated Hunting and Fishing Knives.

Canoe Knife

Hunting Knife

Pocket Tool Knife

Hunting Knife

Camp Carver

Yacht Knife

Enlarged view Folding Safety Pocket Knife, Open and Closed

Dalle de Weese Knife

Skinning Knife

Fish Knife

Fish Knife

Sportsmens' Ideal Hand Forged and Tempered Knives

brittleness or softness results in its condemnation. The bone chopper at the back of the point is a feature possessed by no other knife and is invaluable, as it may be used for every kind of rough cutting, thus preserving the keen knife edge for cutting and skinning. The "Ideal" weighs about six ounces, the blade is about six inches in length and from its peculiar and original construction slides into our Special Ideal Sheath almost its entire length, rendering accidental loss from the sheath impossible.

Water Cooling Canteen

For Campers Out Generally, Soldiers and Military Men Especially—There is nothing so indispensable or important to the soldier as his canteen. Within the last quarter century the greatest improvement in the individual soldier's kit is the Lanz water canteen. No officer, soldier or camper-out should be without one.

The Lanz Water Cooling Canteen.

Military statistics abundantly prove that in every climate, the tropics especially, thousands and thousands of soldiers and civilians have contracted sickness and disease and died therefrom, the cause of which can be directly traced to impure, unpalatable water. A cool drink has saved many a man's life, and is sometimes worth its weight in gold in the field. The principal of this canteen "is the cooling of the water contained therein by retarded evaporation."

For centuries the Indians and Mexicans have been known to carry water on the march with them for days, which was found to be as cool and palatable as the day the supply was taken from the spring at the commencement of the journey. Exposure to the sun and heat did not heat or render their water unpalatable. We have improved upon their system, which for centuries have .been almost unavailed of by white men owing to innumerable difficulties which we have

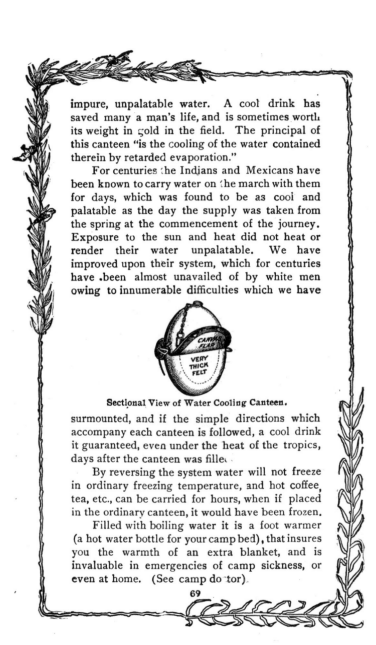

Sectional View of Water Cooling Canteen.

surmounted, and if the simple directions which accompany each canteen is followed, a cool drink it guaranteed, even under the heat of the tropics, days after the canteen was filled.

By reversing the system water will not freeze in ordinary freezing temperature, and hot coffee, tea, etc., can be carried for hours, when if placed in the ordinary canteen, it would have been frozen.

Filled with boiling water it is a foot warmer (a hot water bottle for your camp bed), that insures you the warmth of an extra blanket, and is invaluable in emergencies of camp sickness, or even at home. (See camp doctor).

A Combination Cooking Kit, Mess Kit and Water Canteen.

To those desiring an "Outfit" that includes the individual mess kit (dishes) which can be used for Ordinary Cooking Purposes, together with a complete water bottle or canteen, I refer them to the Preston Mess Kit as illustrated herewith, as can be seen, it is an ingenious contrivance, so arranged as to include all in the one package. The two plate parts form a bake pan, or when fitted, together on the handled part, an excellent fry pan, either as can be observed, also serve as plates for one or two persons, the cup forming an excellent coffee pot, and the canteen part an excellent water bottle; a knife, fork and spoon, with the bag and straps complete the outfit, which is made to carry as the ordinary canteen when all is packed together.

It is an admirable outfit for an individual canoe trip, and if each member of an hunting outfit carries one to the woods it is obvious they are thoroughly equipped with both cooking and serving utensils, and an excellent canteen or water bottle all in one in these as in any other things mentioned in this manual, information as to where to procure them, cost, etc., will be furnished by writing the author on the subject. ————

This is the Outfit Richard Harding Davis describes in his famous writings of "Kits and Outfits."

The "Buzzacott" Army Mess Kit and Canteen.

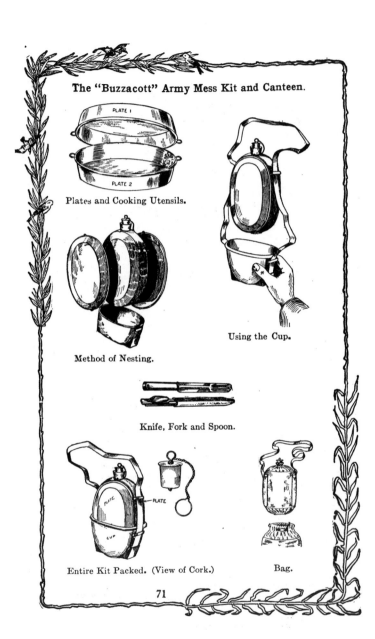

Plates and Cooking Utensils.

Using the Cup.

Method of Nesting.

Knife, Fork and Spoon.

Entire Kit Packed. (View of Cork.)

Bag.

The "Buzzacott" Combined Army Cooking Kit, Mess Kit and Canteen.

1 & 2. Cup Parts, showing lugs.

3 & 4. Plate Parts (with Detachable Handle 5) the parts united are used for Cooking, Baking, Boiling, Etc.

5. Canteen part only.

6. Entire Outfit in Case and Slings.

Entire Kit Packed in Case.

72

Tents and Shelters

A good tent is a luxury, a poor tent an abomination. Here we illustrate and make plain to the eye, none but those that experience have proven the most reliable for general camp uses.

In the selection of a tent, one must be guided by circumstances, the requirements of the party —pack—the nature of the locality and season where it is proposed to use it.

Most generally the wall tent, with fly, as adopted by the United States Government and National Guard is used and is an excellent all around tent, especially so, if an extra single, or better yet, a double tent fly, be added (see engraving).

By single fly is meant, a piece of wide, long canvas which barely extends over the roof of the tent proper, whereas a double fly extends over the roof and an equal space the size of the tent in front, also, thus securing a large shaded space which can be used as a lounging place or dining pavillion (see Wall or Munson tent), these tents all require three or more poles.

To the sportsmen and campers out, however, who desire to travel economically and light, I recommend a combination between the wall tent and others, or what is known as the single pole tents, *i. e.*, tents that require but one pole, which is easily carried along, or you can cut such a pole from the limb of any ordinary size tree, en route. These tents are roomy and comfortable, especially if a wall be provided. They give more available room or space than any tent its size or weight. Opened up or with walls lifted they shade a space equal to any tent made, are cool and comfortable and can be closed down tightly in a

Standard Types of
Practical Camping Tents

A or Wedge Tent as Used Without Poles

Lightest Practical Tent Made.

Extremely Portable.

Made also with Walls.

U. S. Army Standard Officers' Wall Tent

With Double Fly.

3 to 4 foot Walls.

Adopted by U. S. Government and National Guard.

Munson's Sanitary Tent.

The Most Modern Tent Made.

3 to 4 foot Walls, with Double Fly.

End of Fly Broken Away to Reveal Ventilator.

Above tent adopted by American, British and Canadian Governments for their Field Hospitals.

74

few seconds, storm proof and snug, and if a canvas floor cloth be used under which is strewn dry leaves and grass, an excellent tent carpet or soft bed, comfortable, restful and dry is the result, to an extreme if desired.

However, I submit and illustrate herewith all reliable tents and shelter. Leaving the selection entirely to our readers and no matter what your decision, you may rest assured of satisfactory results, unless you depart from the types we quote.

If you desire it, and it is well worth the trouble and cost, you can water and fireproof any tent by this simple receipt: Rain water (tepid), two to three buckets full; add to this 3 or 4 lbs. sugar of lead, and 3 or 4 lbs. alum (costing about 75 cents). Soak your tent over night. In the morning take it out and hang up to drip and dry; spread it out on the grass will do. It is now both fire and water proof. This is the British Government method of water and fire proofing tents—and is excellent. (Allow to saturate thoroughly and dry well before packing away.) If thoroughly dried the tent is also mildew proof.

Canvas or duck used in tents is designated according to number of ounces to the yard, for instance: 10 ounce duck means, 10 ounces to the yard; 12 ounce duck, 12 ounces to the yard; 8 ounce duck, however, should not be used in tents that are subject to severe service. If 10 ounce is used and waterproofed it is equal to the very best 12 ounce or standard army duck.

All tents should be provided with deep sod cloths, also floor cloths, stout guy ropes, and never-break malleable iron stakes or tent pins, which really occupy less space and weight than the kind

Single Pole System
of Portable Tentage

The Miner Tent.

Without Wall.

A Very Portable Single Pole Tent for All Around Camping Purposes.

The Miner Tent.

With Wall.

An Excellent Hunting and Fishing Tent.

The Bell or Sibley Tent.

Will Accommodate easily 6 to 10 Persons.

Adopted by the U. S. and Leading Foreign Governments.

76

that break—and which cost no more in the end; besides, they should be carried in a light bag, for reasons which manifest themselves.

On the Question of Tentage—One will do well to look ahead, and to keep abreast of the times. The past century has witnessed great changes, and now, the leading governments of the world, incline favorably toward the Khaki system of tentage. It has been proven by actual and most extensive tests that Khaki (drab or tan color,) is far superior to white from every point of view, sanitary or hygienic. Tents made of Khaki are found to be cool and restful to the eye and mind, far less conspicuous and glaring than the white, besides do not soil so readily. Exhaustive tests have demonstrated that the sick and convalescent thrive better under the restful influence of Khaki color and shade. The tents are cooler, and it is found that flies, mosquitoes, etc., dislike their interior. Too much in favor of the Munson Sanitary Tent cannot be said. Our own government in the Philippines, and the British army in South Africa, commend them as far superior to the old style of white canvas. In point of field and camp equipment the United States Government is admitted by all nations to be far in the lead, and the adoption of the United States system of tentage by leading European powers is now a fact.

7x7 ft.		7x7 ft.
	7x14 ft.	
7x7 ft.		7x7 ft.

Ground Floor Plan of Family Compartment Tent. (Page 69.) Thus a large tent 21x14 feet can be divided into partitioned rooms, four of which are 7x7 ft., leaving the center pavilion 14x7 ft., to be used for lounging or dining purposes.

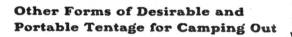

Other Forms of Desirable and
Portable Tentage for Camping Out

The Amazon Tent

With Wall.

One of the Most Comfortable Tents Made.

Extra Tent Front used as a Capital Lounging Shade or Dining Pavillion or Shelter Awning.

Square Hip Roof Tent.

High Walls, 5 feet.
Very Roomy

Front Flap used as Awning.

Family Compartment Tent.
Size, 14x21 ft.—6 ft. walls.
(See Page 68)

So constructed as to provide special separate rooms, insuring privacy. So arranged that the whole can be thrown into a large, Single Compartment Tent, when desired.

78

We commend carefully to our readers that system, and advise that your tentist only construct for you tents made of United States Standard Khaki Duck, 10 ounce double filling.

Should your tentist not keep a supply of Khaki duck on hand, it is safe to assume that he is not keeping abreast of the times. See to it also that you are provided with malleable iron tent pins, which have merits that outrank the old style wooden ones, and are superior in every way; a dozen of such pins occupy actually less space than half dozen wooden ones, weigh no more at all, and cannot be broken. As to their cost, they are less than 10 cents each, so you will do well to have your tentist supply them and no other, for if economy of space is an item, this fact together with their durability and light weight, make them the modern tent pin, that in time will displace the old wooden stake entirely.

As to Tent Poles—Innumerable devices and schemes have been tried, but so far without any marked degree of success owing to cost. Tent manufacturers and the military, which are by far the largest users of tents, confine themselves closely to poles reinforced by bands of iron at the pin point, or if ridge pole, near the socket, which answers every demand admirably, the principal objection being that the poles are of an unhandy length when carried around. The Indian offsets

(See Indian Lodge Poles, etc.)

this in using his lodge or teepee poles by lashing them to a pony's back, leaving the ends trail along the ground, behind; on the top of these poles he fastens his tent, teepee or other things. Thus does his poles serve a double purpose, and well.

Not so, however, with the sportsman, for of all inconviences when not using a tent is the poles. For the past seven or eight years I have been using a jointed pole (see cut) and found it most excellent, fully capable of withstanding the severest windstorm and abuse. I invite attention to the cut, and supplement it by stating that the ferrule is made of heavy brass tubing, so designed as to give as long a bearing on the wood as possible, then secured by brass screws thereon, the telescopic part being short. These poles are easily made, and absolutely provide a perfect jointed pole, that is most serviceable. By fitting them with an extender, as shown, having the metal cups so as to cap the ends, the pole can be lengthened or shortened sufficiently by turning the thumb nut. (To do away with the necessity of going outside of the tent to slack the guy lines in rainy weather,) These poles in any size, are now marketed and at a slight expense over the old style. One can easily secure them. They have been patented by the inventor, and those that I have seen in use at various camps, have been thoroughly commended as superior to the old style by those who were using them.

Various forms of telescopic poles have been devised and used, but generally speaking, are costly and unsatisfactory, hence I do not recommend any except the plain one piece pole, or the jointed pole as described and shown in page 71 illustrations of the Protean Tent.

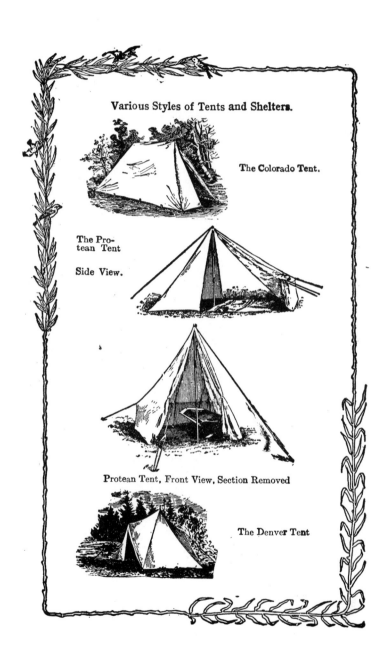

Various Styles of Tents and Shelters.

The Colorado Tent.

The Pro-
tean Tent

Side View.

Protean Tent, Front View, Section Removed

The Denver Tent

In concluding my remarks on tents, let me urge the selection of at least 10 ounce duck, double filling; do not purchase 8 ounce duck tents, and do not buy a cheap tent. If you desire to travel extremely light, select either a single pole tent, or a tent similar to the A or Wedge Tent as shown in illustration, and thus do away with the necessity of poles entirely, except such as you cut en route. A good plan is to have your tentist sew in a long ridge rope, which can be slung between two trees, or supported by cut poles. Avoid the cheap ordinary store tents, unless you want to borrow trouble. In the matter of sizes, for a party of four persons, I suggest the 9x9 size, or if possible 10x12, unless you must travel extremely light when a smaller size must suffice. If the tent is 10 ounce duck and is waterproofed as per receipt herein given, which can be done at the cost of about one dollar, it will stand anything in the shape of a flood, besides the process will make 10 ounce duck equal to 12 ounce without the weight and bulk to carry. (The United States Government tents are 12 ounce duck.) See to it if possible that you are provided with a single, or better yet, a double fly (see Wall Tents).

With tents such as we recommend and illustrate and the camp furniture as shown "An Outfit" can make themselves almost as comfortable in camp as at home under their own roof.

The Extra Tent Fly and Poles.

Various Styles of Tents and Shelters.

Tourist Tent,
Center Opening.

"Yukon Tent,"
Corner Opening.

"The House Tent."

Shelter Tent.

Trail Tent.

82

Camp Site or Location to Select in Pitching Tents

Select your camp site for convenience near wood and water. Choose a position for tent on ground having a little raise, well drained; avoiding the hollow spot. If shaded, or partly so, so much the better, but near the open preferred. Avoid the dense woods or thicket. Don't choose a spot near dead timber, for here is the breeding place of dampness and its attendant evils—better keep to the open and clear.

Stake out the bottom of your tent first evenly; insert your pole or poles; raise into position and guy out; trim and snug. I advise a small trench to be dug so as to drain off the drip water should it rain. The site selection should be free from bumps or made as level as possible, should this be necessary. Have the head of the tent on the raise so as the feet will be a trifle lower than the head when sleeping.

If correctly staked down and guyed properly a tent will shed water much better than if a bungled job be done. Many a good tent is made to leak and gets the blame when the true fault lies in incorrect pitching The sod cloth should, as its name applies, be used to weather tight its base and to conduct rains to the trench, exit of which should be at at lowest point,

Observe rules for a good camp bed and make yourself comfortable. (See camp combination.)

In breaking camp take out poles from under tent first, which should not be rolled up until good and dry especially if it is to be stored. If however it is to be used next day it matters little except that a wet tent is heavy and bulky. Don't pound loose the tent pins. With a looped rope and a pull in the direction from which they are driven they can be easily removed.

(See Chapter on Tents.)

75

The "Buzzacott" Sanitary (Insect and Storm Proof) House Tent.
(Type of House Tent adopted by the World's Largest Sanitariums.)

84

The "Buzzacott" Sanitary House Tents.

The curative and hygienic results of tent or outdoor life, are too well known to require mention here. We all know that as an instance, the successful treatment of tuberculosis calls for a strictly outdoor open air life; the largest medical institutions in the world recognize this fact. In New Mexico, Colorado, etc., are great colonies of house tents, in which are housed the year around thousands of patients suffering from the ravages of consumption and kindred other lung diseases.

It is for the securing of an ideal abode the year round that the author, at the request of the largest sanitarium in the world (National Fraternal Sanitarium), planned and built the *Sanitary House Tent,* as is shown herewith. As can be seen, the principal features are a large ventilated *double roof and wall,* so arranged that a continual current of pure air comes in at the walls and is conducted through an air chamber or screened wall up the sides of the tent, making its exit through the roof ventilator *without subjecting the occupants of the tent to any drafts* of air; the entire sides of the tent proper can be opened or closed at will, thus a current of air is continually passing between the double roofs and its sides *at the same time,* and yet in no way can the wind or draughts touch the occupants, even the floors are ventilated thus: y closing the sides in winter, using a heating stove in its centre and the substitution of glass windows in place of the screening a storm and cold proof house tent is secured that cannot be equaled by anything of a similar portable nature which is made of wood and canvas on the plan illustrated herewith The standard in size being 12 x 16 ft. interior measurements.

A study of the illustrations of the *"Buzzacott Sanitary House Tent"* can only reveal an idea of

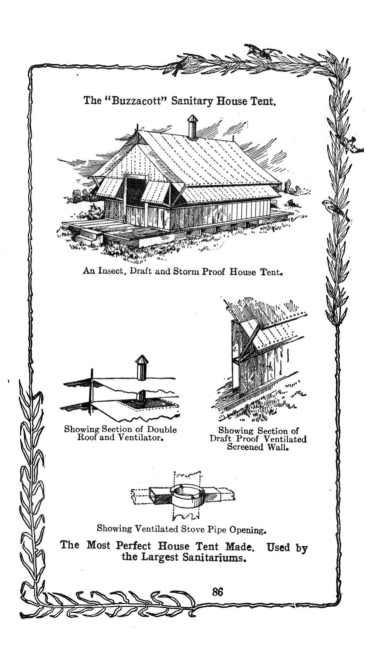

The "Buzzacott" Sanitary House Tent.

An Insect, Draft and Storm Proof House Tent.

Showing Section of Double Roof and Ventilator.

Showing Section of Draft Proof Ventilated Screened Wall.

Showing Ventilated Stove Pipe Opening.

The Most Perfect House Tent Made. Used by the Largest Sanitariums.

its many very excellent qualities. It is par excellence for outdoor uses where ladies (who generally object to ordinary tent life) are concerned. It presents a handsome appearance when erected on a lawn, occupies a space of only 12 x 30 ft. allowing for even flooring back and front porches when opened to its extreme, Absolute privacy is assured. Its accommodations are sufficient for 4 to 6 persons, the beds being arranged similar to that in the Pullman sleeper, forming when not in use a capital lounge or sanitary couch. When glass windows are inserted and the tent opened up lace or shade curtains can be employed presenting an excellent interior effect, while the wooden sides permit of library cases, shelves, folding or drop tables, seats, etc., being utilized which, when not in use, take up little *or no floor space.* Opened up the occupant has a clear view of scenery or surroundings from every side or end that is elegant for observation effect. For the summer house it is superior in both appearance, design and comfort to any portable house or cottage made. Privacy in its interior is secured by the employment of an *Adjustable Screen* which can be shifted to secure privacy to any part or portion of its interior.

It is brilliantly lighted by a hanging cluster of lights *"Acetylene gas jets"* of the Colt pattern, and for cooking purposes the *"Colt gas stove"* is employed when needed, which derives its gas from the same source as its lighting apparatus, or if needs be electricity can be employed. A front and back door screened and curtained (or glass front) presents elegant convenience and artistic effect. As a summer cottage it is unequaled by anything of its kind ever made, even the *floor being ventilated* and the entire ventilation under instant control of the occupant. There are no tent guys or ropes to manipulate, the windows or screens (side or ends) being hinged and operated from the interior. Its furnishings can be plain or artistic, presenting a really magnificent effect, while the standard size is equivalent to the largest of room, viz: 14 x 20 ft. clear, no amount of description, however, can convey an

"Tent, Light and Cooking Kits."

The Colt Acetylene Gas (Portable Outfit)

accurate idea of its manifold advantages and hygienic value from a sanitary or comfort giving standpoint.

As stated it is absolutely fly, mosquito and draught proof, cooler (by actual test) in its interior than in the shade of dense foliage in the open air, a feature secured by its admirable ventilation and *double canvas roof*. It has been personally inspected by the most eminent medical and sanitary experts of hospital and fresh air sanitariums, and is the type *adopted* after exhaustive observation and test by the largest sanitarium in the world, where it is proposed to use several thousand of t em in its treatment of tuberculosis, or such ills as require, practically speaking, *a constant life outdoors*. They are now made in any size almost, the smallest being as stated, 14 x 20 ft., the largest so far constructed being a *Complete Summer Tent Cottage of 4 rooms* as is shown and illustrated elsewhere herein.

In conclusion we illustrate herewith two other special tents designed by the author which speak for themselves.

The "Buzzacott" Special Tent.

The "Buzzacott" Extention Tent.

The Portable House Tent, or Canvas Cottage.

Sitting Room of House Tent.   Dining Room of House Tent

Bed Room of House Tent.

The House Tent Complete.

(These are made in any size: special as required.)

Improvised Camp Shelter
Brush, Bark and Log Huts, Etc.
(See also camp cooking without utensils).

Blanket Tent

These remarks would not be complete without a few practical suggestions as to making temporary camp shelter, be it for the night or season. It might perchance happen that you desire to stay over night, away from the camp proper, as an instance, ready to pick up a fresh trail of large game, etc., on the early morn, then these suggestions might not prove amiss.

But little instruction is necessary; patience, common sense and a willing hand can accomplish much, and about all the tools needed is a good sharp axe and knife.

The Indian Quick-up

(Here surely is a good article—well worth its price, the pocket axe—a thing of joy for such work.)

The Brush Tent

The supporting frames can be improvised from a tree trunk or forked branch, from which a long ridge is trailed to the ground, the larger branches serve as side walls, and the smaller ones in turn as the shingling. The only

91

important point to be observed in their uses is that the smaller clippings of the branches be used leaves down, lapping each other, so as to turn and shed the rains or dew; always work from the bottom up, as in shingling.

The Brush Lean-to

The variety shown is for the selection of the woodsman. All are simple and effective. Probably the Indian Quick-up is the simplest. It consists of light

The Bark Shanty

sapplings of any ordinary kind or length, inserted in the ground, bent over a tree or log and the ends tied with a vine, over which a blanket is thrown, or branches laid instead.

The Log Cabin

Here can one with a cheerful fire, rest dry and warm. True you may have a tent somewhere, but with the information this Manual imparts, you are independent of these things.

Portable Hunters' Cabin.

Hunters' Cabin Packed,

Remarks on Camp Clothing

In the list of clothing I could not for many reasons dwell on the quality essential to general camp wear and comfort, so in order to impress such requirements upon you I give here the following facts and suggestions.

Clothing for camp uses need not be new if in good wearing, even patched, order; in short, clean, serviceable, old clothing is best.

Unless your trip be in chilly latitudes, heavy woolens should not be used. Light weight, medium colored, durable flannels are the best.

Two complete changes are ample and if you note our list carefully you will find for example, that the overalls and sweater form a complete change of over garments serviceable in the extreme.

As to the sweater of all things and places, it is a boon in camp; light, warm, yet cool and well-fitting, it affords absolute freedom and comfort. Select a color, deep gray, tan, dead grass or Khaki, in fact, any inconspicuous color, that will not soil easy or be easily observed by game. Avoid white, red or striped colors. Take no cotton goods at all except towels, handkerchiefs and hose, even the handkerchief should be preferably bandanna, and blue, not red color and of extra large size. Your underwear need not be white, better deep gray or tan color, and canton flannel drawers are soft and prevent chafing and galls; in fact, the U. S. government issues flannel shirts, gray woolen undershirts, medium weight, and canton flannel drawers. The shirt should be tan or dark blue, single or double breasted with pockets. With such clothes

Suggestions in Camp Clothing

Tan or Blue Flannel Camping Shirt.

Type of Hunting Coat.

Campers' Rain Coat Packed.

Featherweight Campers Rain Cape.

Campaign Hat. Drab Felt.

All Wool Camping or Hunting Jacket.—Khaki Color.

Summer Helmet.

Summer Hat.

Poncho Blanket Cape.

Hunting Cap and Cape.

All Wool Camping or Hunting Sweater. Kkaki Color.

94

as these you can render yourself most comfortable under all circumstances. They are cool in the heat, absorbent, soft and warm in the cool, night air, in fact generally excellent all around, while a featherweight, extra long rain cape (pocket size when packed) will cover you from head to foot and when the rain comes down in floods keeps you dry. (See rain capes.)

As to boots and shoes, follow list, especially a good moosehide mocassin is comfortable and warm, restful and most excellent. Keep shoes soft and waterproof by using receipt herein for the purpose.

Don't pass over even toilet soap. Select either a good tar, cuticura or arnica soap. Their cleansing, and healing properties make them most desirable tar soap especially. Mosquitoes are less apt to annoy or bother you. (See Mosquitoes, Ointments, Etc.)

The hat should be medium weight, broad rim, so as to shed sun and water. Drab or khaki color; the U. S. campaign Hat is excellent (see hats); while a soft cap with soft pliable peak is a welcome change, most comfortable about the tent or camp.

When a change of clothing is desired the soiled clothes should be immediately washed and dried. If camp washing is dreaded, simply rinse out three or four times in clean water, dried and aired well will suffice, spread not on the ground but on the bushes or a stick, and if the pillow case mentioned in outfit is used as a receptacle for clean, dry, neatly folded clothes (all not in actual use) it provides an excellent, soft pillow that is comfort giving, but don't jam in the clothes any way, but keep them as above clean and dry.

Suggestions in Camp Accessories

Hunting Vest

The Army Shoe.

Hunting Boot.

Moose Hide Moccassin Shoe.

The Army Boot.

Mosquito Hat and Netting. Folding Pocket size.

The Puttee Leggings.

Campers Leggings, Tan.

Folding Toilet Case.

Pocket Medicine Case and Medicines.

Camper's Ditty Bag.

The Canvas Bedding Roll-up.

96

If you take (which you should) a Camp Combination along you are excellently provided with both bed, mattress and blanket (hammock-cot, all in one) and sufficient for summer or winter use, besides it forms a most complete receptacle for your entire outfit when through with it, and is without exception the most important item in your outfit. (See Camp Combination.)

As for mosquito net—it assures against night attacks, should they come; if not, it weighs but a few ounces and the cost and space it occupies is practically nothing.

A note book and pencil is handy for observations and receipts, while a package of postal cards sends your orders and wishes to your friends or family. Don't carry stamps, envelopes, ink or pens along—heat and moisture gum them together, ruins them, or the ink spills, and generally these are the first things thrown out in camp. Fountain pens and pocket ink stand are O'. K. if preferred.

A good stiff military clothes brush; a pocket comb and case, tooth brush, folding mirror are conveniences productive of cleanliness, while a pack of cards is a pleasant diversion; pipe, tobacco and water proof match safe, scissors, needles, thread and bachelors' buttons all packed in the camp ditty bag—see it—while the pair of tan army leggings keep the legs well protected, warm and dry.

As for the whiskey flask for medical purposes (snake bites, etc., this old excuse) cut it out. More camps are spoilt over it than snake bites cured with it. Very few snakes ever infest any camp. Seldom do they bite anyone unless cornered, besides the snake bite, receipts in this Manual are twice as effective as whiskey which takes quarts to cure such things and it is often the case that if the snake don't kill the whiskey will. The writer has had experience in this even too. In India, Africa and Texas; has personally seen men bitten and by the prompt and simple methods quoted in this manual has never yet known a single failure except when whiskey alone was used. (See Camp Doctor.)

If you object to sleeping in camp in your underclothes, I suggest an outing flannel suit of pajamas, medium color, (tan color is excellent) which are are now made expressly for that purpose, "military style."

Have your guns or rifles treated by the Gun Bore Process, and thus prevent rusting, pitting, etc., entirely and do away with the necessity of cleaning and cleaning rods.

Do not go to the dense woods unless you have a waterproof match box and a safety compass.

The Military Camp.

Do not forget it took time, experience and money to complete this book. If you do not value it make a present of it to those who do—in other words pass a good thing along.

Remarks on Camp Utensils for Cooking

In the selection of camp utensils one must consider many things, *i. e.*, portability, bulk and weight, general adaptability to many and varied requirements and emergencies. Coffee pots, fry

Entire Outfit Unpacked.   Packed.

pans, stew kettles, etc., that give splendid results at home will not do for the camp and many an appetizing dish has been spoiled because of poor camp utensils; they tip over, the lids, spouts, handles, etc., melt off or are too short and the unlucky camp cook thinks of Shadrach, Meschach and Abed-nego as he rubs his hands and —— as he tries to rescue his victuals from the fire and dirt.

All this is obviated when using proper camp utensils. Handles, lids, spouts, everthing, is doubly riveted; lifters are provided for handling and removing every utensil or oven from the fire. Such things as these keep your disposition sweet and greatly contribute to success in camp cooking generally.

More than this, these utensils serve a variety of purposes. The kettles can be used as water pails, fry pans, oven or pots, and if you note carefully the rules laid down in this Manual you will see how they can be utilized for your camp bake or, roast oven and even as a tent heater. All these things are essential to smoothing it. Note weight, size, cost, etc., and do not omit the fact that they are generally excellent and to be found with the Arctic Expedition which lasts for years or the summer camp of a few days only, and last but not least, can be used in the home kitchen as well.

Ordinarily, good heavy block tin is most desirable for camp purposes, but care should be taken to avoid the lighter and cheaper grades, whenever possible stamped or one piece utensils only, should be selected; those with handles and bail-clips, etc., securely riveted thereto. A camp fire plays havoc with soldered parts, which drop off, from the intense and exposed ·heat of the camp fire, almost the very first time they are used. The very best coffee pot is known as the Miner Solid Lip Coffee Pot, which we illustrate herewith, it being made expressly for camping out. This coffee pot, as its name implies, has the body and lip all in one piece; the bottom is rimmed on; the lid, bail and handle are all double riveted. The material is serviceable and yet light, and its shape peculiarly right for camp fire uses.

In the matter of camp stew kettles, care should be taken that they are not top heavy, as these tip over very easily; in their make the same rule applies, as above stated. By far the  best is of heavy steel, with straight, not flaring

The "Buzzacott" Complete Camp Cooking Outfit.

The Most Practical, Portable and Complete Camp Cooking Outfit Made.

Outfit Unpacked.   Part in Use.   35 Utensils and Dishes.

Washing Up.

The Oven in Use.
Roasting.

The Entire Outfit Packed.

Size packed, 12x15, 8 inches,
weight 25 lbs.

A Simple, yet Complete Outfit, which contains all the kit complete for the cooking for a party of Sportsmen or Campers. Outfit even including Dishes, Knives and Forks, Spoons and Cups. It is made in any size.

sides, so constructed, that two or three of them will nest together into the largest one, the smallest should be at least, three quart size, into which the Miner Solid Lid Coffee Pot should nest, as shown in engraving. If this is done you have in the space of one utensil, four good ones, sufficient

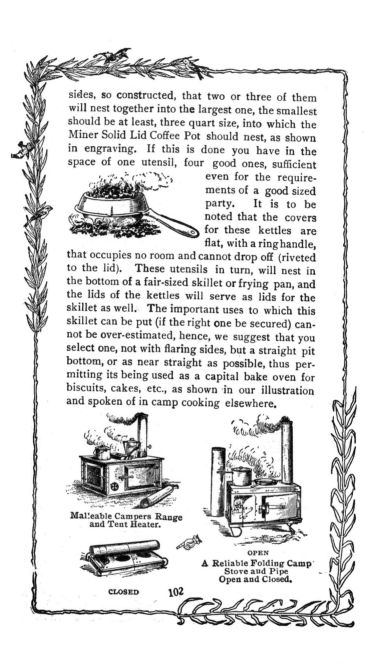

even for the requirements of a good sized party. It is to be noted that the covers for these kettles are flat, with a ring handle, that occupies no room and cannot drop off (riveted to the lid). These utensils in turn, will nest in the bottom of a fair-sized skillet or frying pan, and the lids of the kettles will serve as lids for the skillet as well. The important uses to which this skillet can be put (if the right one be secured) cannot be over-estimated, hence, we suggest that you select one, not with flaring sides, but a straight pit bottom, or as near straight as possible, thus permitting its being used as a capital bake oven for biscuits, cakes, etc., as shown in our illustration and spoken of in camp cooking elsewhere.

Malleable Campers Range and Tent Heater.

OPEN

A Reliable Folding Camp Stove and Pipe Open and Closed.

CLOSED   102

Such utensils as these, cost no more than other good articles, and are equally suited for home uses, in fact, a set of these kettles have been used by my own family, for several years, and show but little sign of the wear and tear they have been subjected to; such utensils however must be obtained from the

The Rover Camp Stove

better class of dealers who make a specialty of procuring only the correct grade of goods

In this connection I must say, that most stores

A Camp Oil Stove

that handle ordinary goods, positively refuse to handle the durable and expensive kind, they cost too much and last too long. Such utensils as we speak of, are to be found at any first class dealers in hotel and restaurant supplies, being used by the class, who demand the very best, and most lasting grade made, not found in the ordinary stores.

I am reminded by this to caution the inexperienced, against the cheaper grade of camp cooking contrivances, for sale by some sporting goods dealers. Their only claim to recognition, lies in their cheapness.

I was once present at a large gathering of military officers, at an encampment of the Illinois National Guard, and one of those much Catalogued

Stoves" was inspected and as quickly condemned, —sent back to the maker in disgust. There are meritorious outfits, that truly deserve recognition, and are recognized, but if those imposed upon sent back to dealers these frauds, it will soon have most telling effect, and be productive of the better kind. I wish also to speak of a so called "Tent Heater," which is nothing more than a thin sheet iron box, no thicker than the square oil can, and which serve the purpose about as well.

For the purpose of tent heating, there is no better tent heater made than what is known as the "Sibley Tent Heater," adopted and used exclusively by the military forces of the United States Government for thirty years past. (Tens of thousands of them,) under every condition of field and camp service; and for the benefit of my readers, I illustrate herewith, the same. It can be easily made and positively has no equal as a tent furnace, or it would not have been used so long by our government.

The Sibley Tent Heater

A Folding Camp Stove

As to camp stoves, there are many good ones, that combine both cooking and heating qualities, and can be either used, in or out of tent, the objection, however, being that they are bulky, and they require stove pipe, and the man who adjusts the two or three lengths of pipe in camp, is apt to remember the experience long after he has gotten rid of the soot and dirt. In an experience of some fifteen years, I have used and seen used about all the schemes for camp cooking and stoves, and for the benefit of my readers, I illustrate the most satisfactory grades. They really merit attention, and in order to cover the field properly, are illustrated herewith, quoted in various grades and styles.

As to the mess or dining outfit, I suggest as in utensils, heavy stamped and retinned ware, not pieced. About a nine inch dinner plate, deep, and commend to our readers the coffee cups and plates shown herewith. Both are stamped tin, the cup having a spring clip handle, which permits its being nested so as to pack closely. Six of these cups can be placed inside the three quart coffee pot, with the cutlery, and if right selection of plates is made, these in turn, will nest inside frying pan. The whole outfit can be placed and carried in a bag, as is illustrated elsewhere, forming a package less than a foot square, weight in all, twenty pounds, and sufficiently complete to answer admirably every possible requirement of any party for "Camp Cooking" in all the name implies; besides this, they are equally serviceable at home also.

If objection be made to tinware, I recommend pure white enameled ware, yet this is expensive and heavy besides. The best of enameled ware, however, is subject to chipping off. Aluminum is an ideal ware, but is very expensive, It is remarkably light and durable, in fact, excellent all around, yet its cost is too much by far. If however you must travel extremely light and to such places where your outfit must be packed by yourself or guides, then is aluminum well worth its price.

The Outfit of Utensils

The United States Army Malleable Field and Camp Range, 100 Men Size.

The 100 Men Army Range and Outfit Packed for Transportation

In concluding my remarks I deem it fitting to illustrate the "Camp or Field" Range, as is used by U. S. troops for campaign service, nearly ten thousand of them being purchased by our own and other governments. They are made in various sizes and forms, and can be readily purchased from the manufacturers or dealers, as are the various other kinds shown elsewhere herein.

Remarks on Camp Ration Outfits

The ration list is ample (without any other foods such as game, fish, etc.) for the entire wants of four persons for five days—three full meals per day. Allowance is even made for waste and the scale given in table can be absolutely relied upon, being prepared from the United States Army standard field and camp ration list now recognized by the leading governments of the world as the highest and best, as U. S. Standard means Highest Quality.

I have even elaborated on this as regards variety and quantity and in a few, very few, cases in quality.

The amount given you is ample for the given number of persons and time and should you frequent a location where your larder can be replenished at times, there is no need of even this amount (yet we advise taking no chances).

If, however, you can obtain other supplies, as game, fish, etc., it is obvious that this list will be ample for a larger party or a greater length of time. It is plain to be seen also that the very quantity we list will form a correct basis for computing the necessary amounts for any party large or small, for any length of time, hence is invaluable.

Absolutely nothing perishable is quoted, except by fire and water, and is withal composed of the very choicest of foods, put up in Waterproof ration bags, tagged and tied, secured with double draw strings and tags. The variety is such as to satisfy the most exacting taste and with such items as is usually to be found within the vicinity of most settlements or camps (fish, game, etc.), your party can fare sumptuously even.

As to preserved food, desiccated, evaporated vegetables, etc., leave them out, if possible, unless your trip takes you away from civilization for months at a time. Confine yourself to fresh, solid foods that will last for any ordinary trip, even of a month's duration. Steer clear of coffee tablets and such "what-nots," and in the purchase of canned foods; let your selection be confined to the very best grade of goods, which contain the most solid and nutritious of foods and the least dead weight of liquids and water.

If you can purchase these goods en route do so; don't stint or overload, but be sure you can obtain these things and not trust to luck. (See list of Scale of Camp Rations, etc.)

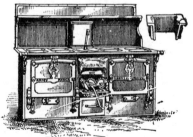

U. S. Army Barrack Double Range for **200** Men

Don'ts and Ifs

Don't forget that "we smooth things" for you; point out the way—designate the tools—show you how to use them—where and how to obtain them.

Don't hesitate to go camping because your not experienced. Every man has his first trip and the immense army of them that follow it year after year is evidence that they enjoy and benefit by it.

Don't think it expensive—no trip can be made more economical than a camping trip. Nature supplies most things free—wood—water--food—privacy is there for you—no rent to pay.

Don't hesitate because of poor health—that's the very time to go—that run down, worn out system craves fresh air, change and healthful rest. Follow the simple rules of this Manual. Throw away drugs—try it—you'll thank me for this advice later and the doctor will lose a customer.

Don't think it necessary to go and travel far to find an ideal spot, most like ten miles away from your side now is an ideal spot if you think it over.

Don't think it necessary to be a hunter or fisherman to camp out. Thousands go every year for the pure air, change and rest. It works wonders to that tired spirit, mind and body.

Don't overlook the fact that by our system a camping outfit complete costs *pro rata* of only one to two dollars per day, entire outfit; tents, clothes, rations, everything for a person. Thus is a camping trip, the most economical vacation that can be made.

Don't hesitate to take the wife and children along; they enjoy it as well as you.

Don't omit to read every line this book contains, there is something to learn on every page.

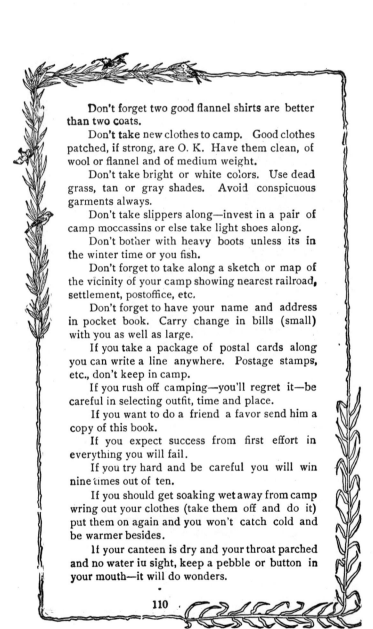

Don't forget two good flannel shirts are better than two coats.

Don't take new clothes to camp. Good clothes patched, if strong, are O. K. Have them clean, of wool or flannel and of medium weight.

Don't take bright or white colors. Use dead grass, tan or gray shades. Avoid conspicuous garments always.

Don't take slippers along—invest in a pair of camp moccasins or else take light shoes along.

Don't bother with heavy boots unless its in the winter time or you fish.

Don't forget to take along a sketch or map of the vicinity of your camp showing nearest railroad, settlement, postoffice, etc.

Don't forget to have your name and address in pocket book. Carry change in bills (small) with you as well as large.

If you take a package of postal cards along you can write a line anywhere. Postage stamps, etc., don't keep in camp.

If you rush off camping—you'll regret it—be careful in selecting outfit, time and place.

If you want to do a friend a favor send him a copy of this book.

If you expect success from first effort in everything you will fail.

If you try hard and be careful you will win nine times out of ten.

If you should get soaking wet away from camp wring out your clothes (take them off and do it) put them on again and you won't catch cold and be warmer besides.

If your canteen is dry and your throat parched and no water in sight, keep a pebble or button in your mouth—it will do wonders.

The Camp Doctor

(See Camp Medicine Case and Medicine Therein.)

Keep the bowels open, head cool, feet dry and there will be little, if any, sickness in camp.

As a rule there is very little need for the use of drugs but as it is well to be prepared for any emergency the few simple rules herein will not prove amiss. Generally speaking we can cure here almost anything in a most unique way.

Should, however, any very serious accidents happen we advise the preliminary precautions and rules of the manual and in the Meantime send one of the party to the nearest settlement for a physician or transport the patient there at once.

How a capital stretcher can be improvised: "See camp-bed."

Constipation.—Give doses compound cathartic pills, eat freely of preserves; drink often.

Diarrhoea.—Apply warm bandages to stomach; fire brown a little flour to which two teaspoonfuls of vinegar and one teaspoonful of salt is added; mix and drink. This is a cure, nine cases out of ten. A tablespoonful of warm vinegar and teaspoonful of salt will cure most severe cases. Don't eat fruit. A hot drink of ginger tea is good. Repeat every few hours the above.

Cuts and Wounds.—In bleeding from wounds or recent amputations press the finger or hand over the bleeding point, pressing on the main

The 1st Aid Packed (Illustrated above) is made for just such emergencies.

111

artery supplying blood to the wound. If this is not possible, apply a bandage as tightly as possible above the wound. By tying a handkerchief loosely around the limb, thrusting a short stick through it and twisting it tightly an excellent tourniquet may be improvised,

The blood from an artery which has been severed is a bright red, and comes in spurts with each beat of the heart. The color of the blood from an ordinary cut is of a dark purplish shade, and flows in a steady stream. All cuts should be washed out with warm water, to which one or two drops of carbolic acid has been added. The edges of the wound should then be brought together and held in position by strips of plaster, then bound up tightly with clean bandages.

Cramps and Chills.—Mix pepper and ginger in very hot water and drink. Give dose of cramp tablets.

A hot stone makes a good foot warmer.

Fevers.—Give doses of quinine tablets; loosen bowels if necessary; keep dry and warm.

Sore Throat.—Fat bacon or pork tied on with a dry stocking; keep on until soreness is gone then remove fat and keep covering on a day longer. Tincture of Iron diluted; swab the throat.

Pocket Medicine Case and Medicines.

Burns.—Use common baking soda, dry flour, camp fat or oil, or mix as a paste.

These Simple Receipts are prepared from articles in your camp outfit. The others with pocket medicine case and contents we quote in this Manual; note the fact.

Scalds.—Relieve instantly with common baking soda and soaking wet rags—dredge the soda on thick and wrap wet clothes thereon. To dredge with flour is good also.

Colds.—Put on warm, dry clothing. Drink freely of hot ginger tea; cover well at night; give dose of quinine every six hours.

Toothache.—Warm vinegar and salt. Hold in mouth around tooth until pain ceases, or plug cavity with cotton mixed with pepper and ginger.

Poultices.—Common soap and sugar, mixed; stale or fresh bread, mustard and flour, equal parts mixed with vinegar or water.

Ivy Poison.—Relieved with solution of baking soda and water; use freely as a cooling wash. Keep the bowels open.

Poisoning.—Give strong emetic of warm water, mustard and salt. Cause vomiting by swallowing small piece of soap, tobacco, etc., if by no other means.

Poisons.—In all cases of poisoning there should be no avoidable delay in summoning a physician. The most important thing is that the stomach should be emptied at once. If the patient is able to swallow this may be accomplished by emetics, such as mustard and water, a teaspoonful of mustard to a glass of water, salt and water, powdered ipecac and copious draughts of luke warm water. Vomiting may also be induced by tickling the back of the throat with a feather. When the patient begins to vomit, care should be taken to support

Twenty-Four Bottle
Medicine Case
and Medicines.

the head in order that the vomited matter may be ejected at once, and not swallowed again or drawn into the wind pipe.

Poisonous Snake Bites.—Suck the wound instantly and thoroughly (it is perfectly safe if no sores are in the mouth); sear with red hot iron; cut out wound if necessary and with red hot iron burn it out so as to destroy entire surface. It requires nerve but a life depends on it. Act at once. Keep cool. Ammonia is one of the best antidotes for snake bites known. Apply externally.

Insect Bites, Wasps, Etc.—Common mud is excellent; use plenty of it. Crushed penny royal weed keeps mosquitoes away.

Earache.—A piece of cotton sprinkled with pepper and moistened with oil or fat will give almost instant relief. Wash with hot water.

Insects in Ear.—Use warm oil or fat. Wash well in hot water.

Mosquito Ointment.—Solution ammonia or camphor or tar soap. Apply bruised penny royal.

Another One.—3 oz. tallow, 1 oz. camphor, 1 oz. penny royal, 1 oz. creosote or carbolic acid solution; mix. Cork tightly in bottle and anoint face, hands, etc., when needed.

Another One.—2 oz. pine tar, 2 oz. castor oil, (olive, sweet oil or melted tallow will do as well) 1 oz. of penny royal; simmer slowly over slow fire and cover tightly in six ounce bottle.

Cuts, Bleeding, Etc.—Wrap with common paper use mixture of flour and salt. Bind on until it stops bleeding. In extreme cases tie a handkerchief over part nearest the body and with a stick twist up good and tight, then dress the wound and gently remove.

Ointment for Bruises, Etc.—Wash with hot water then anoint with tallow or candle grease.

Sprains.—Apply cold water application and cloths.

Sore and Blistered Feet.—Wash in warm water then bathe well in cold water to which a little baking soda has been added—wipe dry and anoint with tallow from candle or fat. Keep the feet clean. Dirty feet and socks make sore ones. Soap well the stockings (using common soap) until the feet harden—this is an excellent method.

To Quench Thirst.—Don't drink too often, better rinse out the mouth often, taking a swallow or two only. A pebble or button kept in the mouth will help quench that dry and parched tongue.

Inflamed Eyes.— Bind on hot tea leaves or raw fresh meat. Leave on over night. Wash well in morning with warm water.

Keep Head Cool.—By placing wet green leaves inside of hat.

Convulsions.—Give hot baths at once; rub well the lower parts of the body to stimulate; keep water as hot as possible without scalding, then dry and wrap up very warm.

Struck by Lightning.—Dash cold water on body continually; if severe case, add salt to water; continue for hours if necessary. If possible submerge body in running water up to neck.

Drowning.—Handle the body gently. Loosen any clothing. Carry the body face downward, with the head slightly raised. No time should be lost in following out the instruction given below, which should be continued for hours without ceasing, or until a physician, who should be summoned immediately, shall arrive. The body should be stripped of all clothing, rubbed dry and placed in bed in a warm place. Warmth should be supplied to the body by hot water bottles or some other appliance. Cleanse the mouth of any dirt or mucous that may be in it, and draw the tongue forward with a handkerchief, holding it with the finger and thumb. This is most important, as it opens the windpipe, and should not be neglected. The patient should be placed upon his back, with head and shoulders slightly elevated. The operator standing behind his head, should grasp the arms just above the elbow and draw them steadily and gently upward until they meet above the head, then bring them down to the side of the chest slowly and persistently at the rate of twenty times to the minute. These movements imitate expiration and respiration. The trunk and limbs should be rubbed when breathing commences, and a stimulant or warm drink given.

Bathing.—Be careful bathing in strange places, Don't dive; weeds may be at bottom or sharp rocks. Water that looks inviting often is full of treacherous, slimy weeds in which once caught it is almost impossible to get free. Look out for deep unseen mud holes. Better splash water over body than to take big risks.

Choking.—If possible force water down the throat or push down substance with spoon handle. Hearty slapping on the back is also effective. Getting on all-fours will help matters.

Freezing.—At all hazards keep awake. Take a stick and beat each other unmercifully; to restore circulation to frozen limbs rub with snow; when roused again don't stop or fall asleep—it is certain death. Remember this and rouse yourself.

Snow or Sun Blindness.—Smear the nose and face about the eyes with charcoal.

Use raw onions for insect bites and stings.

116

About Canned Goods—These are O. K. for any permanent camp, but if you pack your outfits and transportation is limited don't carry too much canned stuff, especially those of the delusive kind, that are two-thirds water   The chances are you'll find better water where you are going to camp, and save the freight.

Fruits, etc., are dried or evaporated in such excellent style nowadays that there is little need of carrying them about, put up in or with two-thirds tin and water.

Have your provisions put up in canvas bags with strings to secure them (ration bags) don't risk paper ones. If you do you are apt to find things sadly mixed at some stage of the trip.

In Winter Time—If freezing cold—Campers, Hunters, etc., should never remove snow from ground on which they pitch Camp, better heap up more snow—(inside and outside) to dig down to the ground would be to dig up cold and discomfort—snow is a warm and soft bed—compared to hard frozen ground.   Artic Explorers always choose the protection of the biggest snow banks they can find. even animals, birds, etc., burrow holes into them to secure warmth.

For Frozen Fingers, Nose, Ears, etc.—Never rub with snow, the one who recommends rubbing such tender members with snow is a fool. Instead clasp the frozen member with the warm hand firmly so as the warmth of the hand will thaw it out, to rub such a member already frozen with snow is to break the skin and do much harm—suffer much pain, common sense tells a man you can't thaw ice by making it colder.   A good way (if it can be done) is to dip the member into cold water, then pour in warm water gradually until of a good blood heat.

The Winter or Ground Hut.

117

Packing and Transporting the Camp Outfit

The Modern Complete Camp Outfit and Chest Packed

In these days railroad transportation enables a party to ship and check as baggage a complete camp outfit, to any part of the world, the only requirement being that it is boxed and the box or chest be provided with handles or roped well; such can be easily made or purchased, and as railroads now carry one almost any where, the question of transporting the complete camping outfit thus is a simple one.

Should, however a trip be unusually or necessarilly migratory and where no such transportation exists, in the very heart of the woods so to speak, it will have to be carried on the backs of the party as a pack, each member having an equal share of the bulk and weight which can be proportioned off be-

Pack Harness.

fore starting; for this purpose pack or breast and shoulder straps are employed, which are adjustable

Carry-all Bag

to any size or bulk (the Alaska Pack Straps made for the purpose, being all desired). If the outfit exceeds forty pounds per man (which is the limit a man should burden himself with) either packers should

Rubber Specialties for Camp Uses

Folding Rubber Toilet Case.

Folding Rubber Bucket, Open.

Closed.

Rubber Poncho Blanket Cape.

Folding Rubber Wash Basin.

Folding Rubber Bath or Wash Tub and Packing Case.

Feather-weight Rubber Rain Cape.

Rubber Bag. Used in Packing.

Canoe Folding Drinking Cup.

Rubber Tumbler.

Rain Cape Packed. (Pocket size)

Tobacco Pouch.

Rubber Poncho Tent.

118

be employed or a pack mule and saddle used, same as adopted by the United States Government; the load of a pack mule is from two to three hundred pounds, and a good pack mule can be easily lead or driven wherever it is possible for man to travel afoot; on this, however, we shall dwell but little, as such service necessitates both an experienced mule and packer and to state our experience or to take up the subject properly, would require a small volume in itself.

A plan very much followed at the present time is to hire a light servicable buckboard wagon and with a team of country broke horses, transport the entire outfit to the limits, where the main or headquarter camp is established and maintained; from here the party starts out, equipped light, for several days or more (especially in big game hunting) returning periodically to the main camp or rendezvous proper, to replenish or disgorge, as the case may be. Some people who indulge yearly in hunting trips, travel with a wagon fitted out for the purpose, while others hire them for a suitable period of service.

As to the rations they can be packed and carried in waterproof heavy canvas bag, made now for the purpose, or carried in a special Ration Chest as illustrated on this page, either of which are put up by Specialists in camping outfits.

In the matter of packing up, it is a good plan to roll blankets, bedding, clothing and all such articles in a roll of canvas, the ends and sides of which are doubled inward, so as to prevent articles from dropping out

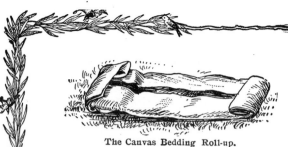

The Canvas Bedding Roll-up.

of roll or getting wet; for this especially the "Camp Combination" with its other good points, is the best thing ever devised. T h i s permits you of forming the whole, into a roll about twenty-four inches wide, the proportion of height or bulk being according to the amount of clothing or articles therein, it is then strapped with adjustable straps provided for the purpose, and can thus be thrown about with other supplies, packed or carried easily.

Bedding and Clothing as Packed

The tent should be packed in a canvass bag w h i c h is made for the purpose (see article on tents), pin-stakes rolled inside in a small bag, so as not to soil or mar the tent. The poles, (if jointed poles are used) can be carried likewise, in the tent pack, thus making a package of tent, fly, poles, guys, and stakes (everything), say a 9 x 9 tent, 36 x 24 inches.

The cooking and messing outfit combined and complete, can be nested together as described elsewhere (see article on camp untensil, etc.) in a stout canvass bag, or if the Buzzacott Camp Cooking Outfit be used, the utensils all of them, plates, cups, etc., etc., nest easily into the very complete Practical Bake or Roast Oven furnished

with it; thus we have the complete camp cooking outfit for four to six persons reduced to convenient size and shape to pack or carry easily, entire weight being only twenty pounds, and space occupied, one foot quare.

These parts can in turn be placed in the box herein described, and shipped to nearest railroad, point or destination as simple baggage, the weights of the respective parts being equally divided as follows, assuming t h a t the party is four persons, "travelling right."

If an outfit of suitable camp furniture and other convienences be added, it can be packed in a small compass and shipped likewise. The weight of a camp table complete for four persons being but fifteen pounds, and the chairs or stools two pounds each, or less according to grade.

Thus, can it be easily computed that a most modern and comfort giving camp outfit can be provided, which, from a minimum of space and weight would give a maximum of most desirable comforts which contribute largely to the p l e a s u r e s and

The Buzzacott
Complete Camp
Cooking and
Messing Outfit
Packed.

benefits of an outing, anywhere, and yet the entire weight of an elaborate outfit, everything complete for four people would not average over 100 lbs. per person, transported s a f e l y in the two chests described.

Camp
Cooking
Outfit
Unpacked

Tent Pole Conveniences

In Use.

Clothing Hanger.

Such little articles as these contribute largely toward the neat and cleanly appearance of a camp. It insures dry clothing, and safety for such equipment as ought to be hung up instead of laying around the tent.

The weight of these articles are but a few ounces and occupy but a few inches, they are very popular with the Military, and from a sanitary point of view alone are invaluable. They are made to adjust to almost any size Tent Pole, there is no necessity of marring the poles with unsightly lines, ropes or nails which are apt to splinter the wood and later tear the canvas of the tent. The hooks are of twisted steel wire, plated so as not to rust, and the hooks permit of nearly all clothing to be hung thereon, aired and out of the way. They will support any weight you choose to put thereon, or your rifle can be hung handy and out of danger or dampness, a feature alone that speaks for itself. It is known as the Warnock Tent Pole Hanger, and is now sold by all reliable dealers in camp equipments.

If a more portable or flexible leather tent pole clothing hanger is required get the "Buzzacott" pocket size. It fits any size tent pole or sapling —can't break style; or send for special circular.

122

The "Buzzacott" Tent Pole Specialties.

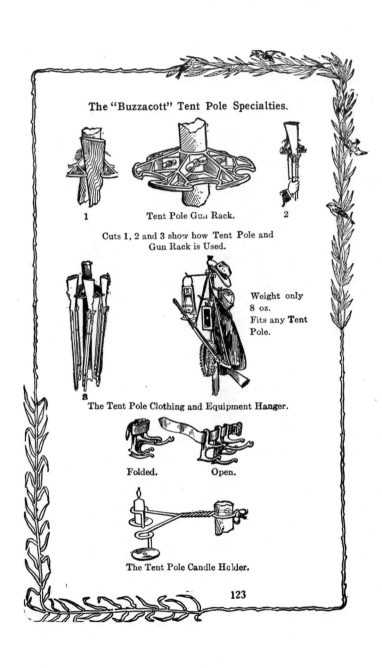

Tent Pole Gun Rack.

1   2

Cuts 1, 2 and 3 show how Tent Pole and
Gun Rack is Used.

Weight only
8 oz.
Fits any Tent
Pole.

3

The Tent Pole Clothing and Equipment Hanger.

Folded.   Open.

The Tent Pole Candle Holder.

Portable Hunters Cabins
Summer or Winter Cottages

American ingenuity has made possible the construction of a simple Hunters Cabin, or the elaborate cottage, at points distant from civilization, and already American made portable houses dot the earth from Alaska to Africa. They are fitted together in our factories and shipped in sections, one or more of which represent an entire building that can be easily transported and put up in a few moments, or at the most a few hours time according to size, not a hammer or nail or sharp tool of any kind whatever being needed. The only tools essential being a pocket screw driver and wrench. A room of full size with floors, roof, walls and windows weighing only 500 pounds. As they are made in any way and style desired, for any purpose or needs, they range from a child's play or doll house to an elegant six room modern ranch, mining headquarters or a summer home having all the comforts and luxuries of the city residence. The doors, windows, roof, walls and flooring can be made double, absolutely wind, water and draught proof. Interior walls can be lined with tapestry, linen or paper, making a handsome interior capable of withstanding the rigors of an Arctic or Tropical climate. Such houses can be put up in a very short space of time—taken down and moved as may be needed. Folding wall beds with spring mattresses which occupy only wall space when not in use are with our camp furniture used in these buildings.

Our own government now uses them as portable barracks for our troops both in the Philippines and Alaska which is sufficient endorsement of

Portable Houses, Barracks, Cottages, Etc.

Style 1

Portable Hunters Cabin
Complete
Put up in 15 Minutes

Style 2

Complete Summer
Cottage,
Sportsmens Club
Headquarters
Family Resort.
Put up in Three
Hours Time

Hunters' Cabin Packed.

A Complete
8 Room House.

Portable
Automobiles
Houses

Put up without a
tool other than a
pocket screwdriver
and wrench.

their merits. One of these portable houses will cost less than the freight on the lumber. A six or seven room cottage can be erected in a day ready to occupy, avoiding all loss of time, trouble, and expense of labor, building, etc. As the parts are interchangeable you can remodel your house any time. As to cost, one hundred dollars per room is a fair average. Fitted out with Folding Camp Furniture renders them equal to the modern constructed frame house that can be occupied as the family home or the head quarters of the Millionaire' Sporting Club in the heart of the forest. Some idea of the extreme uses to what they are put can be formed when it is known that they are extensively used for the following purposes as mentioned and illustrated herein:

Portable

Army Barracks.
Military Hospital.
Railroad Waiting Rooms.
Restaurant's Annex
Golf Link and Skating Houses
Sporting Club Headquarters.
Ranch or Mining Houses.
Army Officers' Quarters.
Contractors Offices and Homes.
Shooting and Fishing Clubs.

and a host of other like purposes. Thousands of them being erected in South Africa, South and Central America and Alaska. In this as in other like things American Product excels, and export shipments show that our make is by far superior to those of foreign grade.

In Hunting, bear in mind that game has unusual power of scent, sight and hearing, As you tramp (noiselessly you may think) thro the brush and w o o d s, you w o u l d be astonished if you knew that the very game you s e e k has perhaps time and time again seen and a v o i d e d you. The keen-eyed and eared rascals are seldom c a u g h t napping, a n.d are ever alert to t h e slightest sound or noise.

Equipped for a 5-days' trip.

If you be wise, select s o m e good spot in the woods where the game you seek abounds, at a point where your observation commands as large a vicinity as possible, select a log or comfortable seat and sit still. Watch and wait. You'll find this plan far more successful than tearing through the brush, unconsciously scaring away anything that otherwise would afford you an opportunity for your skill.

The Indian, master of the art that he is, moves silently, hardly disturbing a twig or a leaf, and rarely does he return empty handed as the r e s u l t of such careful studied woodcraft, which h i s white brother will do well to imitate.

Haversack

The Coquina Outfft

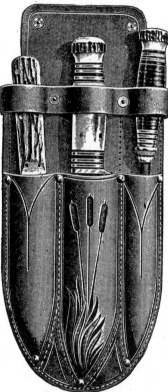

A first class combination for the use of large game hunters, that can be depended upon, one that is especially put up for those who desire to be prepared for any emergency, from the skinning of a coon to the carving up of a moose or grizzly. Fastens to waist or cartridge belt. With such an outfit as this, one can blaze a trail or cut their way through a jungle of small brush, or build a good brush hut or shelter and shingle it. With such an outfit and a folding axe one is equipped with cutting and chopping apparatus that will for a lifetime serve every possible purpose awoods or astream. The illustration shows a hand forged, hand made, hand tempered, hand sharpened Hunters Skinning Knife, heavy Hunting Knife and Chopper and select fine Sharpening Steel, all in a compact dependable leather sheath, the whole arranged to be there and kept there safely, until time to use it, without danger of loss, no matter how hard you tear through the brush in the pursuit of game.

Reliable Weather Signs

Pale yellow sky at Sunset indicates wet weather

Red Sunrise indicates Rain and Wind

"Red at night, Camper's delight;

Red at Morning, Camper's warning."

"Rain before seven, quits before eleven."

Rain with East Wind is lengthy

Red Eastern Sky at sunset means bad weather to come

Sudden Rain, short duration

Slow Rain lasts long

When Beetles Fly expect a fine to-morrow

Busy Spiders mean fine weather

Flies bite harder on approaching storms

When Dogs sniff the air frequently look out for a change in the weather

Morning Rains make clear Afternoons

Birds flying high indicate good weather

Birds and Animals travel away from water in the morning, toward water at night

Hiding Spiders or Breaking Webs indicate Storms

Heavy Dew means Dry weather to follow

When Birds ruffle or pick their feathers, huddle together, look out for changes in the weather

Low Clouds swiftly moving indicate coolness and rain

Grey morning sky means good weather

Soft looking clouds mean fine weather to come, moderate winds.

Hard Edged Clouds, light winds

Rolled or ragged clouds heavy winds

A strip of Seaweed, in tent or house, in fine weather, keeps dry and dusty-like in coming rains it gets wet, damp and sticky

To tell the Points of the Compass with a Watch.—When the sun is to be seen—(for men do even get lost in sun-light) put down your watch with the hour hand pointing directly toward the sun—half way between the hour hand and figure twelve is south.

Do not kill more game than you need or can use; don't be a hog.

Do not fire at an object until you are sure it is not a human being.

129

THE COMPLETE FISHERMAN and ANGLERS MANUAL
OR
HOW TO CATCH FISH

136 PAGES   200 ILLUSTRATIONS by "BUZZACOTT"

WEATHER TABLE

For Foretelling the Weather Throughout all the Lunations of Each Year—Forever.

This table and the accompanying remarks are the results of many years actual observation, the whole being constructed on a due consideration of the attraction of the Sun and Moon, in their several positions respecting the Earth, and will, by simple inspection, show the observer what kind of weather will most probably follow the entrance of the Moon into any of its quarters, and that so near the truth, as to be seldom or never found to fail.

If the New Moon, First Quarter, Full Moon, or Last Quarter, happens	In Summer	In Winter
Between midnight and 2 o'clock	Fair	Frost, unless wind South-west
" 2 and 4 morning	Cold and showers	Snow and Stormy
" 4 and 6 "	Rain	Rain
" 6 and 8 "	Wind and rain	Stormy
" 8 and 10 "	Changeable	Cold rain if wind West, snow if East
" 10 and 12 "	Frequent showers	Cold and high wind
" 12 and 2 afternoon	Very rainy	Snow or rain
" 2 and 4 "	Changeable	Fair and mild
" 4 and 6 "	Fair	Fair
" 6 and 8 "	Fair if wind North-west	Fair & frosty if wind North or North-east
" 8 and 10 "	Rainy if South, or South-west	Rain or snow if South or South-west
" 10 and midnight	Fair	Fair and frosty

130

"Where the Fish Hide," 130

Various Modes of Fishing

"Casting"

There are three different modes of fishing, each requiring slightly varied equipment and methods.

1st comes **"Still or Bait Fishing"** which means that you offer fish an acceptable food, using a common, ordinary rod, line, float, hook and bait and place it before them, usually in mid or deep waters.

2nd by **"Trolling or Trailing"** either natural or imitation fish or objects representing such, as revolving spoons, spinners, etc., etc., or by using either live or dead baits trolled near surface, mid or deep waters, and by movement (usually trolling is carried on from a moving boat or line) attracting the attention of fish and so deceiving and luring him into the belief that it is a thing of life as to tempt them to bite at it and be caught. For this purpose many excellent "revolving or spoon baits" are used, having concealed about them one or more hooks, both open and weedless, for use in various waters, used with and without foods attached to them.

While the 3rd is by **"Bait or Fly Casting"** or tempting and deceiving fish with apparent or natural dainty morsels, either insect or other form, deftly thrown or lightly tossed on the surface of the waters, that which represents what the fish is known to be fond of or antagonistic to, and by skillful manipulation, imitating life, and of all sport, requiring knowledge and skill, that experience only can master, this, of all, stands pre-eminently alone, for fly or bait casting holds the same relation to other fishing as *"poetry does to prose."*

131

In bait fishing the game is all yours, while in fly fishing its evenly divided between the angler and the fish. This is explained by the fact that in bait fishing the fish is usually allowed to swallow or gorge the bait and hook, and this hook being partially down the fish's throat, his chances of shaking it out, in the struggles to follow, are decidedly against him; while in fly fishing, the hook being usually fastened in his mouth, or edge of it (where there are few, if any, nerves of pain) no great torture is inflicted, while its strength and breathing faculties being thus uninjured, leaves him all strength and ability to resist your efforts at capture, thus both contributing to and prolonging the sport and skill required to land him.

Bait that is to be used in still or bait fishing must always be fresh, alive if possible. If not alive so hooked and handled as to deceive by its natural appearance, scent or movement. If, as before stated, dead bait is used, it must positively be fresh, otherwise fish will avoid and refuse it. It is, therefore, apparent that the all important lies in the possession and use of proper and not improper bait; such too, as is most liked by the species you set out to capture. Bearing in mind that it is not the costly tackle, but the most fitting bait and knowledge in knowing how and where to put it that contribute towards being the successful fisherman. Thus it is wise to secure absolutely fresh, appropriate bait, even at the expense of your other equipment, be your still fishing especially.

A fine outfit of rod and tackle will lessen your labors, add to ease and enjoyment in handling it, but its the bait that gets the fish. *"So jot that down."* (See articles on baits.)

When breezes are soft and sky's just fair,
 Steal a few hours from worry and care,
And wander away to yon babbling brook
 With your **rod**, your **lines**, your **baits** and **hooks.**

A Few Species of American Game Fish

Brook Trout
4 oz. to 4 lbs.
Northern
States and
Canada

Lake Trout
3 to 20 lbs.
Northern lakes

Spotted Sea
Trout
1 to 5 lbs.
Atlantic coast

Black Bass
1 to 6 lbs.
Northern and
Western rivers
and lakes

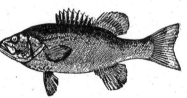

Striped Bass
1 to 20 lbs.
Northern,
Western and
Southern coast

Average weights only are given.

133

The Successful Fisherman

Is the one who familiarizes himself with the ways of fish, he who studies out a n d observes the peculiar traits, habits and haunts of the various fish he sets out to capture, who acquaints himself with facts as to their sense o f sight, scent and hearing, their mode of existence, foods, likes, seasons, etc., thus qualifying himself to better understand them, so as to take advantage of their ignorance, avoid their ready perception of things, and fool their cunning.

Thus enabling him to better seek or locate them, then to tempt or deceive, to that point where they will strike at a proffered or attractive bait, either to satisfy their hunger or to rid themselves of its tantalizing presence about them. Very few who start out "a fishing" have any such conception or proper ideas concerning these points, and yet nothing is more conducive of success, and be he bobbing for eels or whale fishing, the one familiar with such things, is mighty apt to be the most successful at the end of the trip.

He should become familiar with the fishes natural foods, their methods and time of procuring it, the places they frequent, those they avoid, and why they avoid them; with such knowledge one can often turn failure into success, and yet strange to say, very little is generally known of these things.

The sight of fish is unusually acute and they are possessed of the faculties of both hearing and feeling sound. They breathe the air that is dissolved in water, and do not as is generally supposed, derive that air or oxygen from the chemical constituents of the water, but from the very air we breathe; when they exhaust the air as in the use of bait pails, they suffocate; yet if a supply of fresh air be forced into the water of even a bait pail, the fish will revive. Their eyes are peculiarly placed, rendering it somewhat difficult to see on a level or directly under them, they can however, see plainly anything that is above or about them, and for an unusually long distance in clear or shadier waters, especially so, be it still waters. Their sense of smell and hearing is well developed and it is certain that they possess the faculties which enable them to perceive and distinguish odors, also that various scents attract or repel them. In most cases fish like snakes, see motion only. As they have no (or but little tongue, their sense of taste is poor) and they rely mostly on sight and smell in the choosing of their foods. Not a few fish feed on vegetable matter, or mud which contains ailimentary matter in a living or decomposed state, and while they are mostly carnivorious, yet they will subsist on vegetation should other or live food become scarce; most fish are however extremely voracious and the rule eat or be eaten, applies to them with unusual force. Whatever the prey, in most cases, it is swallowed whole, and they show but little choice in its selection, devouring their own offspring or kind indis-

A Few Species of American
Game Fish—Continued

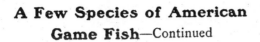

The Salmon
6 to 40 lbs.
Pacific, Atlantic and Canadian rivers

The Pike
2 to 12 lbs.
Northern and
Western rivers
and lakes

Wall Eyed Pike
1 to 12 lbs.
Northern,
Western and
Southern inland waters

The Pickerel
2 to 8 lbs.
Eastern, Western and Southern waters

Muskallonge
8 to 30 lbs.
Western and
Canadian
waters

See chapters concerning these fish

criminately with others; living to fight and fighting to live, from the very earliest stages until that time when age renders them but fitting to the attack of the turtle undertaker.

Owing to lack of nerves, it is safe to say that many fish experience but little pain, and it is well known that a Pike whose mouth has been lacerated by a hook, will continue after it with eagerness, while larger fish such as shark will allow itself to be repeatedly cut and stabbed, without noticing it or abandoning its prey, especially so, be it hungry. Fresh water fish can go for weeks or a month without food entirely, while to salt water fish one-half that time would mean starvation. In all fish, teeth are shed and renewed at intervals during the entire course of their life, and at such times they invariably are active, yet do not seem to either need or care for food; same in spawning, and in winter time when owing to inaction certain species often cease to feed entirely, laying still in deeper waters and where owing to this inaction they require little or no food. On the other hand those of the pike species are less inclined to feed during the hotter months, but in colder weather are both active and hungry. In most cases the females exceed the males in size, while they take on the colorings of their surroundings, and science has proved beyond doubt that fish-like the salmon, for instance, who feeds largely on "crustaceans" and which the stomach's process of digestion turns red (as in boiling) seems to impart into their flesh the well known pink or salmon color. When out of water fish suffocate easily, yet there are species notably eels, carp, catfish, etc., that possess such powers as to enable them to live for hours even days out of water entirely. Big fish usually prefer solitude and inhabit the deepest, choicest portions of the waters they dwell in, usually the deeper, cooler spots. Especially those where winds and currents carry or drive floating or other foods about them. When feeding they are usually alert to any sight or sound about them and invariably hide behind projecting rocks, banks, stumps or weeds or in shadier waters, where they can observe and be hid from their prey, thus able to locate, dart out and seize all those of food that come within their reach, and if hungry or provoked they will not hesitate to devour even a fish of their own species and size, which they swallow head first, and if there be no room for the tail part it remains almost in its captors mouth until that portion inside is sufficiently digested to bring the balance in. Often in cleaning one is amazed at the large size of fish found thus in the stomach of a captured one. When they have gorged themselves thus with food, fed their fill, so to speak, as they invariably do when feeding if they can, they retire to deeper, darker and cooler waters and here they sleep and remain inactive.

Peculiarly enough in the heat of summer the cooler waters are in the deeper spots while in winter the order is reversed and the deeper portions are the warmest.

Usually it is well to avoid fishing in the middle of a hot day, although in some kinds of fishing and places, it seems to make no difference, especially be it their feeding time.

It is a good rule, however, to go, either in the early morn (after an early breakfast) or late of an evening, before dark, or at night and the cloudier the weather the better are your chances of success especially be it before a storm or rain, for at these times fish are unusually active and alert and if the surface of the waters be ruffled or stirred by a breeze or mild wind then is it still better, for in calmer or still, smooth waters they usually remain inactive, necessitating much deeper fishing, if you desire to reach or attract them

There can be no set rules specifically laid down for fishing, unless conditions are considered with them. Conditions of the weather, season, time

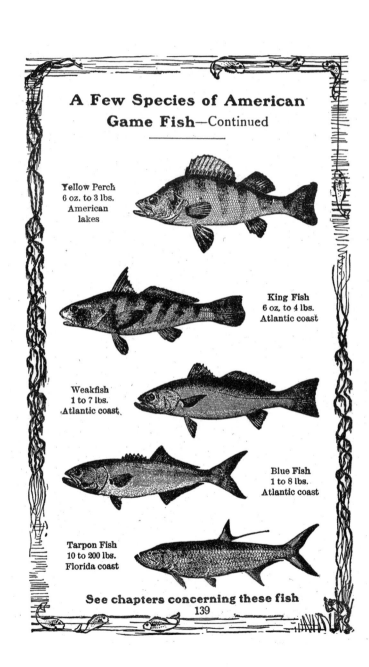

A Few Species of American Game Fish—Continued

Yellow Perch
6 oz. to 3 lbs.
American
lakes

King Fish
6 oz. to 4 lbs.
Atlantic coast

Weakfish
1 to 7 lbs.
Atlantic coast

Blue Fish
1 to 8 lbs.
Atlantic coast

Tarpon Fish
10 to 200 lbs.
Florida coast

See chapters concerning these fish

and waters. Today fish may bite well almost anything you offer them, yet few are to be seen. Yesterday plenty was in evidence, yet for some reason they absolutely refused to bite. Here they take any fly, every one you offer them, an hour hence they refuse all but one, and that the last one you tried. Today all small fish, with one specie biting only; others not to be found. All these are conditions. Adapt yourself then not to set rules, but conditions. Rules are all right, but if you want to be successful you must acquire the knack of adapting conditions with and to the rules, for, truly can it be said *"that the ways of fish no man knoweth."*

It is also best to studiously avoid not only being seen, but heard by fish you are after. Water is a sound conductor, and the lesser the chance of any fish seeing or hearing you the greater the chances of success. Again water magnifies. This is proven by articles therein which to the observer often appears larger when submerged than they really are, and such a monstrous affair as yourself reflected on the surface of water is not calculated to invite fish to your vicinity or to even stay there and especially is this so while angling for that most wary fish the trout.

Of all senses possessed by fish none is more acute than their sense of smell and no fish can be lured by an ill-smelling or putrid bait. It has been proven by experiment that fish that rushed and fought for fresh foods flung to them refused to even rise to putrid or ill-smelling food, even blind fish avoid it. Hence it is obvious that it was a powerful sense of smell that guided them aright. Neither will they accept an unnatural looking or uninviting bait, (in still fishing) their sharp sight enabling them to quickly detect an unnatural bait unless it be hid by movement, rendering it less liable to be observed by them. The choicest spots for fishing are usually found in the most difficult places to get at. Often where the deeper, cooler waters and unfrequented spots exist, near bottom springs or brooks. Here is where the larger fish are to be found. On the other hand, the smaller ones frequent the more shallow, difficult waters, where they are, in a measure, safe from the rushes of the larger ones. Again, small ones school together, while the big ones prefer solitude, except in spawning season or when they mate, and frequently large fish hover about extremely shallow water hiding at some point ready to seize such as pass their way. Again, fish bite well before rains, seldom well after; simply because rains wash foods in plenty from earth and soil, bringing with it and stirring up other life, at the same time, hence they are busy seeking food in such places (unknown to you) where past familiarity with the waters have taught them nature sends food to him in a more plentiful, easier way.

All fishes conform to the laws regulating activities, and become more sluggish as their surroundings become colder.

At such times they remain quiet seemingly lifeless and because they exert so little energy they require but little food, and it is during activity only that they consume quantities of food.

It is the inclination to go into deeper and consequently warmer water in the fall, that has doubtless been the factor in developing that migrating instinct in the species that run "down stream in fall" and "up stream in spring."

Read also the Art of Angling, Bait Casting, Splashing, Sputting, etc.; Trolling, Trailing, etc. About fishes and fishing for them.

The Midday Rest.

When About to Fit Out

Or outfit for a fishing trip don't imagine that the amount of success depends on the dollars and cents expended in your kit.

That country boy with the green cut pole, store cord and penny hook, might beat you all holler, does he but use judgment (fish sense) in its manipulation. A few paltry dollars or cents, if judiciously expended and correctly handled, is as conducive of success as the more costly equipment in the hands of the careless, indifferent or ignorant.

If needs be you must economize, select but a simple, yet correct outfit. In fact, I strongly recommend the inexpensive outfit to the new beginner. There is time enough to invest in the higher, better grades when one has acquired sufficient practical experience to render him reasonably proficient in the art of correctly judging and handling it. No amount of nickel parts, fine rods or reels catches fish. See then not to its looks or fineness at first, but to your all-round capability of handling it correctly, and to place on the wet end the right article before the fish in a fitting way. Then will most any reliable fair priced tackle serve its purpose well and if you start out thus equipped, with a good supply of patience, a determination to try hard and put up with repeated failure and go with a light pack, prepared to meet disappointment and failure, to get wet and hungry and to wait patiently, for hours perhaps, without a single bite (except from a blood thirsty mosquito) you will, I warrant it, not only meet with *"glorious success,"* but live to grow both an old, wise and most enthusiastic angler, reaping much pleasure, health and enjoyment from many a long trip, in the time to come, for there are many other benefits to be gotten from a fishing trip, besides fish.

Read Articles on Various Equipment.

142

Did you
Ever Observe

The experienced "fisherman guide" the man who has perhaps spent the most of his life "a-fishing and showing others how," who possessed an elaborate fishing outfit. I say no, for in my travels (and I have come across some pretty old hands) I have yet to find one who used anything but the simplest kind of an outfit, and who did not care for or deem essential anything else, and while you put in time on your fine tackle; he busied himself with his baits and hooks.

Hence I repeat see not to the fine tackle or the abundance of it, but to its appropriateness. Give more consideration to your baits and the right places where fish abound. This with other proper methods of luring them is what counts, then will the simplest outfit suffice your needs, especially so, do you use judgment; and study both conditions as well as rules in the use and employment of it.

"The Experienced Fishermen"

If Your First Trip "A-Fishing"

"If even a boy, one who has been there."

If possible choose for a companion (if even a boy) one familiar with the waters and place you go, "one who has been there." The longer he has been at the game the better he can serve you; a few pratical questions (even if taken from a book) diplomatically made and a few ready answers, will, in a measure, convince you of his sincerity and experience in fishing matters.

If an experienced guide (can you afford it) or a friend of yours, so much the better, as nowadays the successful man is the one who acquires experience the quickest—he who learns by observing others, by emulating their achievements, and avoiding their failures. Life is too short for personal experiment, and should your choosen companion be experienced so much the better can he serve you.

When you have acquired sufficient practical knowledge to render you familiar with the employment of the various kinds of tackle, how to assemble and use it, the selection of the various baits and places, then it is time to strike out for yourself, and go alone, at least far enough away from your companions, as to be unmolested by their movements or discouraged by their success or failures, for let me impress the fact that it's the *"lone and quiet fisherman"* that's the successful one, so jot that down, too.

The Fishing Outfit

Depends entirely on circumstances, your pocket, the time and place you intend to go; the kind of fish that's there; whether it be a pond, brook, stream, river, lake or sea; fresh, brackish or salt water; whether you go for a few hours, days, weeks or a month and the season of the year.

First you must decide just where to go. This done, to post up on the kind of fish that's there and the most successful methods in vogue of capturing them; then as to the time you intend to stay, for the kind of outfit you need depends largely on these things. The rest is a simple matter, at least, until you get down to fishing proper.

And in order that my readers will better understand these conditions, I will further on go into details as to the proper selection of equipment as well as suggestion for the care and use of it all further on.

See chapters on baits, rods, reels, lines, floats, leaders, snells, hooks, creel, landing nets, gaffs, wading. Articles on various species of fish and other things.

"The Lone and Quiet Fisherman on the Outskirts."

146

To the American Woman

American girls are noted the world over as participants in all kinds of healthful, enjoyable, outdoor sports. Hence it is not amiss to venture the remark that of all sports, to the lady, angling is the choicest. By all means girls, insist on going along; take your last summer's dresses and cut them off to just below the knee, (woolen or flannel is best.) Take a pair of ladies fine rubber boots and a broad rimmed hat, sweater jacket, rain cape, a light pair of high shoes, under bloomers, and a pair of ladies thigh leggings, and you have an ideal outfit. Two changes all around is ample; a light waist or two, extra, a woolen traveling dress, a suit of ladies pajamas for sleeping; towels, soap, etc., (leave powder at home) and come back with the tan and rosy cheeks of health instead. Thousands and thousands go every year and revel in the pleasures of camp life; fishing, hunting, gathering wild flowers, long walks and boat rides, fresh air, camp appetite, health happiness, and genuine pleasure awaits you if you leave behind luxuries, and go with a common sense outfit; prepared to revel and enjoy the plainer, more substantial life and living that your great-grandmothers enjoyed and profited by before you. Let me say, try it once; you'll have less doctor bills, and will thank me on every trip you take thereafter, for the advice now.

THE AUTHOR.

About Baits

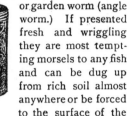

Of all fish baits 'none is more tempting than the common earth or garden worm (angle worm.) If presented fresh and wriggling they are most tempting morsels to any fish and can be dug up from rich soil almost anywhere or be forced to the surface of the

Preserved Baits

ground by a liberal drenching. The best time for their capture is after a heavy rain and if put into a small porous, earthen jar (small flower pot) partially filled with wet moss, and the pot kept cool and in a dark place, they will keep for days. Don't put them in a tin can filled with soaking wet mud, as most do, for this kills them.

Worms are most fitting bait to most any fish and this is why fish seldom bite during or immediately after rainy weather, as they are then busy seeking them; those that every downpour of rain washes from the earth and soil into the creeks, streams, brooks and into lakes or waters where fish abound, hence they are busy seeking such foods, not dangling from a hook but in places where past experience has taught them nature sends them in a more plentiful, easier way. When, however, you use worms for bait see to it that they are impaled well covering your hook, passing the worms from *head to tail* and leaving just enough dangling to show a wriggle of life or movement and when thus placed in the water it will rarely be missed if fish abound there too.

Next to this and of equal worth is the minnow, the fish's actual food. Grasshoppers. Even the

148

considered repulsive (but excellent bait) the maggot, Helgramite or Dobson, caterpillars, beetles, wasp, bees, larvae, palmers, crickets, moths, snails, gnats, bugs, insects and flies of all kinds, raw liver, beef, the little mouse, fat of pork, or for salt water, shrimp, shedder, crab, clams, (hard portion) sand worms, small eels, or even the white skin or belly meat of the fish itself, can be used to advantage all of which should be cut and hooked so as to as cl sely represent some living article as possible.

For live bait nothing can beat the small, live minnow or very small frog, both of which are excellent, hence I deem it fitting to go into details concerning both.

In choosing frogs the angler should remember that the smaller ones are best. This is true even of frogs no larger than the first joint of a man's thumb. Some contend that these are too small to attract attention and that bass, for (frogs are best bait for bass fishing) cannot see them a sufficient distance away, but it's a mistake. In fair bass waters any bass will see a frog of that size a distance of 20 feet and hit it every time if he is hungry. Again the small frog casts better going out well with the line and striking the water with little splash to alarm the fish, and what is more important a bass will take it at one gulp, permitting an almost instant strike instead of swimming and toying with it for a few seconds, only to spit it out if the point of the hook is felt. Hence the small frog an inch or two in size hooked through both lips just behind a small spoon makes the most fatal of baits in July and August bass fishing.

In color the frog should be green with a white belly, with a tinge of yellow about the throat. The frog with the brown back and yellowish belly being not so good.

The meadow frog either green or brown is of

right size but its color is too faint. The bright green tree frog of slender shape is an excellent lure, but is a poor swimmer and soon drowns, hence the best rule is to get them as small and green as possible. In keeping frogs for long trips and for days after the fishing ground is reached many make the serious mistake of giving them too much moisture, and while it is true that marsh frogs live in water, yet they thrive better *without it* in captivity.

Frogs will live longer and remain strong if kept in a dry- basket, wet thoroughly two or three times a day. They should not even have wet moss or grass under them Frogs will live surprisingly long piled on top of one another four or five deep in a basket and kept dry.

A very good method to keep them in captivity is to set the basket with a stone in it on the edge of the water so that one end barely touches the water, two-thirds of the basket being on the shore. Thus they can have as much or as little water as possible and by looking into the basket as often as you will, you will find them invariably huddled together on top of each other, always in the dry end. Frogs do not need food in captivity. They will live comfortably enough without it for two weeks and seem to be at the end of that time as strong and fat as when first caught. On a good lake, bass fishing a man will need two or three dozen frogs a day, unless he fastens them to his hook. A frog that has died in the box should be used first and is just as good as a live one if used at once so don't throw any away.

As to minnows for all *general* purposes these are the best of baits. The one great difficulty being in securing and keeping alive a sufficient quantity, as when captured they require no end of care to keep them healthy and alive. To this end a multitude of folding, telescope, and other novel minnow buckets have been made and marketed. Yet of all these there is but one that is made on the right principles necessary to really keep them alive. The trouble with all minnows is that being unusually delicate, they cannot well survive the frequent rough handling or jolting they are subjected to when carried around in a bait pail. Again they soon exhaust oxygen necessary to sustain life which is so small, in a bait pail, necessitating a frequent changing of the water and its temperature, and despite the greatest of care, they soon succumb to the necessary rough handling, when they turn up on their backs and die.

All this has been changed by the construction of a bait pail, built on scientific principles, the same as that adopted by the U. S. Fish commission, in its successful methods, by which fish of all kinds are transported for many thousands of miles —on journeys that consume often a week or more of time, and for the benefit of my readers I illustrate herewith the principles employed. A glance at the illustrations plainly showing the essential features necessary for the keeping of imprisoned fish or minnows alive for any reasonable length of time, by an arrangement which steadily supplies the water with air as fast as the fish exhausts the supply so necessary to its existence. By reference to illustrations of the *Aerating minnow pail* it will be noticed that under the water compartment, separated from it by a water tight bottom, is an air chamber or retort made of sheet steel, so riveted together as to be very strong (to withstand the air pressure.) A brass air pump is attached to the outside of the pail and connected with the air retort or chamber, into which the air is compressed by the pump. From this retort the air is released into the water (at the bottom) in

151

small bubbles, through a tube; two tubes being furnished, one for free flow, the other for a lighter flow of air. In operation it is so simple that its success is obvious almost at a glance. The pail proper is 12 inches high, 10 inches in diameter and has a water capacity of about 2½ gallons, weighs 7½ lbs. Fifty good sized minnows or 150 small ones, can be thus kept alive, without pumping or change of water for days; and if kept in a fairly cool place, out of the sun, and pumped up occasionally, say twice a day to keep the chamber full of air, *minnows can be kept for weeks* by feeding them. No changing of water even being required except it be once in four or five days and then it is necessary only to do this in order to clear the water of its excretions or dirt.

Care must be taken, however, to set no pail in the heat of the sun. It should be shaded and covered with a cloth. Thus can minnows be safely kept day and night and be as lively as ever when needed mostly, in the early morn, (these rules, of course, applying to points away a distance from waters.)

If a change of water is not possible, by pouring off and repouring back frequently the same water from a good height will restore the water with a supply of air again. Yet it must be done a dozen times or more to charge the water with sufficient air. Even a simple rubber bulb and hose connected to any bait pail will be better than those absurd creations without it.

Recently, however, a prepared minnow bait has been marketed by which they are put up whole so as to literally last a life time. They are put up in bottles (frogs also) packed carefully and immersed in a preparation like so many sardines. All being necessary is to take them out of the bottle, soak them in water for a few minutes and they are ready for use—ready to do their full share of luring others to swallow them and be caught.

This bait is at present receiving much attention from fishermen, it being claimed that they are just as plump and shiny as the day they were caught and that they can be carried any distance without sun or weather affecting them in the least. In my estimation they are well worth a trial especially to those who cannot well secure *live bait,* and is daily gaining devotees from all classes of fishermen, who must necessarily make hurried trips, and even by those who have hitherto swore by their favorite make of artificial bait.

For Trolling or Trailing—Various revolving and glittering spoons, spinners, etc., are used which by their action or movement (revolutions) in the water, glitter and attract, thus alluring and deceiving fish into the belief that it is both living and moving and rarely will a larger fish fail to perceive, rush and strike at them, should they happen to notice it, and as these are often supplemented by either living or fresh foods, and one or more hooks, concealed here and there about it. Woe to the fish that savagely strikes at them. Yet care should be exercised that they troll naturally as even fish can quickly detect and avoid an unnatural, suspicious or bungling bait, and more especially so in "still fishing."

Before concluding my chapter on baits let me invite the attention of the angler to that excellent, yet rarely used bait, the maggot. (Trout love them.) A piece of meat or fish exposed to the sun, heat and flies (at a safe distance away) will insure all the bait a man can use in a week, in 24 hours time almost. A full grown maggot has great tenacity of life in the water, while their color is attractive and the size just right, if several are used. As to offensiveness, keep them in a small box of corn meal, bran or even bread crumbs and there is nothing about them, that is any more objectionable than the dirty, slimy worm, that you handle with impunity. Don't be prejudiced. Try them alongside of other bait and judge for yourself.

"See also Wrinkles and Kinks"

Luminous. and Non=Luminous Baits.

(Casting and Trolling Baits, Spoons, etc.)

These remarkably efficient and peculiar baits, have for twenty years, been before the fishing or angling fraternity, and to those unacquainted with the merits and peculiar properties of the most fitting luring kinds, it is necessary to enter into details concerning them. Luminous. baits are artficial lures now made in every conceivable form and shape of insect and small fish life, used in the successful capture of larger fish, which when placed in the waters emit a **phosphorescent glow** and the luminous properties of this glow, together with the artificial appearance of the bait, attract fish to them from unusual distance. The shine is not a brilliant one, but just enough to represent the unusual glittering scales of a live fish in the water, and when applied to trolling or other baits gives out an extremely alluring effect, especially at night (when invariably the best fishing prevails.) They are unequalled for day use and are more successful than any other baits for night use or for darker, deeper or roilly (stirred up) waters. These are put up of flexible yet strong oiled silk, linen, wood and metal form, in every conceivable shape of appropriate fish or insect life; any size from the common midge or house fly to the five or six inch large chub; and it may be well to add that although "phosphorescent" in nature or appearance, they do not contain phosphorus. The process being a secret which has with the success and merits of the lures, brought fame and riches to its inventor, and built up the largest manufacturing plant for

SEE DESCRIPTION ELSEWHERE.

For Casting, Trolling, Spinning, Etc.

the manufacture of artificial baits in the United States.

At the same time there are many other grades and styles of non-luminous baits and spoons that possess universal and meritorious alluring and killing qualities, being made by experts in their line, who have studied most carefully all the known conditions, and used practically by millions of fisherman and anglers in almost every fishable waters. Most of these are highly or brightly plated, and the glittering and spinning effect of them when used in the waters, serve to attract and decoy fish from afar, that would not have been able to either see or hear the ordinary kinds. Hence the only essential in choosing them is to select those most suited to the fish you set out to capture, be it the small or large Trout, Bass, Pike, Pickerel, Salmon or Muskallonge. Among the most reliable brands being Pfluegers, Skinners, Shakespeares, Burtis, American, Buels, Hendryx, P. & S., Delavan, Hastings, St. Lawrence, etc., every one of which can be counted A No. 1, and intending purchasers or users can make no mistake in their selection provided they confine themselves to those that are genuine, and not those varieties made and sold in cheap imitation of the more popular and meritorious kinds. (See illustrations.)

"A Fine Trout Stream"

"Fishermen's Favorites."

"Which do you use and like best?"

See chapter on Angling.

Casting, Baits, Spoons, Flies, Etc.

Were one to give due consideration to all the most fitting variety of Baits, Flies, etc., it would need a book many times the size of this volume, yet as it is considered by most anglers that fly or bait casting is the most sportsmanlike method of fishing, a few remarks on Flies will not be amiss. It is a well known fact that in season when flies of all kinds abound, they are often most frequent near and about woods and water, and most fish have learned that they are especially good eating, hence for years anglers choose to capture live flies for use as baits; this in time led to the manufacture of artificial insects, which were found to equal the luring qualities of the natural fly, and to last ten times longer. Hence anglers now invariably prefer artificial flies to the real bait of any kind, and as most fish seem to consider flies as equal to any other food, rising to the surface to grasp them, it affords far greater sport than any other methods where fishing or angling is carried on for sport, instead of mercenary ends. Hence almost every conceivable form of insect or bug life, has been made ready for the anglers use; to each of which concealed and securely fastened is the treacherous hook, on which the biting fish impales itself at almost the faintest grab. These are called "flies" and to each one has been applied either the name of the fly they mostly represent, or some other name to better distinguish it from the others; some of them resemble closely the living article of life, while others resemble no possible living creature, yet all of them possess at times remarkable luring and tempting qualities, that serve every purpose.

157

The question why fish take these bunches of colored silk, wool and feathers is unanswered, except that they imagine that alike the others that form a part of their menu, they are good and do not stop to cogitate on the kind or taste, until too late to realize their error or mistake.

In the selection of flies much has been written, and rules have been laid down and specific flies put up for every kind of fish that will take them, for every season (as shown further on) yet, one must as in other things be guided by conditions as well as rules. It is a good rule to follow and use the flies that are in season at the time; yet there are times, plenty of them, when a decidedly different fly will take better. It is conditions one must study, conditions of light, shadows, wind, weather, and last but not least, the likes of the fish in the matter, changing as often as is necessary to secure one that the fish will strike at; one should use bright flies on dark days, dark flies on bright days and gaudy flies when the fish refuse to rise to the surface for the plainer ones.

Many anglers carry a hundred or more flies and no two hardly alike, yet I think this overdoing it. My book contains at the most four dozen, and when I have frequently changed a dozen or more times without success, I invariably prefer to seek other waters instead. At times these flies are supplemented by small spoons or spinners as shown by illustrations; and for the employment of them, see articles on Fly or Bait Casting and fishing elsewhere.

In the use of Flies the tendency is to use *too large ones,* hence it is wise to select the smaller ones, and not those of too large a size.

About the Rod

The Rod and Form Case.

It is no easy matter to select a fine rod, you can take all the advice you can get on the subject with benefit perhaps, but when it comes right down to selecting one, you have just got to know something about them, to do it right. Bear in mind that I am speaking now of "fine rods." For ordinary purposes however, a fine rod is unnecessary to the new beginner, so don't bother with them, if you do, you are apt to find that later its too long, too heavy, "well just don't suit anyhow" necessitating the purchase of another fine rod.

By all means let the new beginner select a good well made Lancewood rod, and put the difference in cost between that and the finer article (the Split Bamboo) in his supply of other tackle. Then when you know more about rods, through experience with your Lancewood, strike out boldly and buy the finest guaranteed hexagonal Split Bamboo rod that American skill and your money can produce; and if you patronize the right kind of specialists or makers of them, you will make no mistake, and get one you can forever after swear by. Don't ever invest in the articles put up especial for "cheap store" bargain sales, unless you want to borrow trouble and get stuck.

There is much to be considered in the selection of a good rod. It should balance correctly, be neither too limber or stiff, of good flexible action, and particularly suited to your individual strength of arm muscle and grip, and last but not least, it

159

should not weigh an ounce more than is necessary for the work for which it is intended. The handle grip had best be of cork, avoid the hard wired or corded rubbered ones, unless you work with your hands and they are real tough. It should be provided with drawn seamless "serrated" ferrules, free running agate guides and tips, and if wound with silk, (like the Silkien invisible two-joint rod is) *it will never stick, throw apart, or break at the joint,* like a ferrule rod will; and if you patronize and bestow your patronage on some reliable dealer, who can aid you in the selection of your first rod, it is evident that if he values your future patronage, he is apt to do the right thing by you in the matter of an exchange if necessary; and when you succeed in getting a good rod, don't lend it to the boys, or leave it around uncared for and neglected when through using it. (See hints as to care of rods.)

It is not essential to lay in a variety of rods, at least until you become a crank on the subject of fine tackle and angling. For all around purposes, for general use on various kinds of fish (except Salmon) but including Trout, Bass, Pike, Pickerel, etc., and fish up to medium good size and weight, for stream fishing, etc., an 8 or 9 foot rod weighing about 5 to 8 ounces, in my estimation comes very near to holding its own with any (even a supply) of them.

If a fine Split Bamboo, let it be of the 6 or 8 strip, square or hexagonal edge about the same size, but an ounce or two less in weight, and it will be found as fine a rod to cast a fly or handle a fish with as any.

If a trolling rod is desired, that of about 6 to 8 feet will suffice, weighing about an ounce or two to the foot. If a Salmon rod, let it be about 15 ft., weighing about 20 ounces; and for the better information of my readers I include a table of the most appropriate woods used in the manufacture of reliable rods, in the order named.

Spiral or twisted Bamboo, Split Bamboo, (Calcutta,) Steel, Lancewood, Snakewood, Greenheart, Bethabarro, Ironwood, Maltese, Indian Bamboo, Japanese Bamboo, Hickory, Ash.

The cost of these rods range from $50.00 to $5.00 although there are some good ones ranging from $3.00 up; but as I confine my remarks to the better class of goods, deem it unnecessary to waste time and space on the other kind. If cheapness is the only consideration, why not select the common Bamboo pole, costing but 15 cents up and weighing 2 or 3 pounds, and which is cut to fit and done with it.

Among the well known popular makes or rods can be mentioned the following excellent grades: Kosmic, Silkien, Special, Gogebic, Divine, Burtis, Henshall, Bristol, Gunnison, Degame, Pelican Lake, Taylor, Rodgers, St. Lawrence, Hendrick-Kalamazoo-Cooney, etc., and for further reference note illustrations accompanying this chapter, or Hints and Pointers, elsewhere. These rods when not in use, should be kept in handy rod forms and cases, of which various styles are made and sold for the purpose, of either canvas or leather.

About the Reel

The reel is a small clockwork l i k e device composed of numerous side cogs and wheels all joined to a suitable light skeleton frame, so arranged as to be easily and securely fastened to the rod or pole.

161

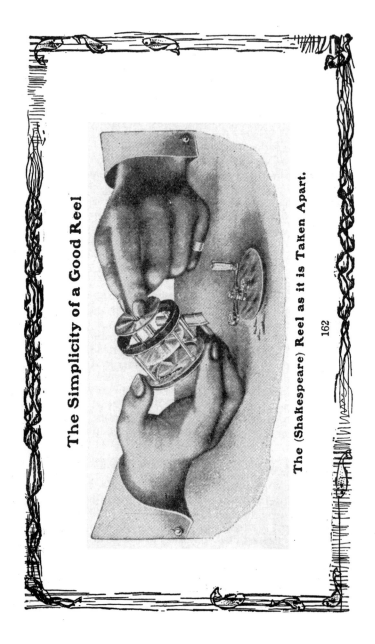

The Simplicity of a Good Reel

The (Shakespeare) Reel as it is Taken Apart.

In angling it plays a very important function, its uses and action requiring its operation to be in perfect accord or correspondence to the movement, of the line, when playing a fish, all under control of the angler.

To meet these requirements, clicks and multipliers are employed; the click acting as a brake, checks or retards the line from running out too freely, while the multiplier gathers in that slack with increased speed, a single revolution of the handle reeling in a foot or more of line. Formerly the great difficulty in ordinary reels was the tendency of the line to spool unevenly in winding in, but now even automatic spooling devices are employed which distribute the line evenly on the spool; and if a less expensive reel, it can be even provided with an automatic spooling device, as is shown in illustration, which can be applied to any ordinary reel.

Good reels can now be purchased for a few dollars, although the very fine grades range in price from $3.00 to $50.00, depending largely on its size, grade and movement. They range from 1 to 24 ounces in weight and vary in size accordingly, holding from 40 to 1,500 feet of line.

The purpose of a reel is to accommodate and hold the line, and to give (unreel line) or to take (reel in) when necessary, for casting or playing a hooked fish.

For fly casting, a single action click reel is used, while for bait casting a multipyling or automatic reel is preferable, and if the latter, 60 or 70 feet of line can be given or taken by simply pressing a button. This action is done by spring power and is so arranged that it can be changed from automatic to free running or vice versa, by simply pressing a button or slide thereon. I illustrate various and most desirable kinds for the information of my readers, and as I include none but those of the highest standard of perfection, the fortunate possessor of either of them will find both ease and simplicity in their use, for their action is truly remarkable. The metal used in these reels is unaffected by water, while the pinions (revolve as in a watch) on jewelled bearings.

When a game fish takes the line he usually does it with a rush, and with the proper reel can be either met by a free line, or by applying the click or drag, it takes the strength of the fish to secure line; while in the forward rush slack line can also be taken up quickly. At times these reels revolve with such speed as to keep running after the strain has ceased; this avoided by using a brake or by thumbing the line when on the spool, as in casting. (See Bait Casting.)

All good reels are provided with clicks and drags, either or both of which can be quickly brought into service, causing the spool to revolve with difficulty; bringing a strain on both the fish and line, thus the question of playing and exhausting a large and fighting fish, is a simple matter.

One of the most confusing things to select to the inexperienced, is a reel, and let the amateur go into any store or consult a catalogue on the subject, he is often amazed if not confused by the endless variety placed in front of him. In the use of them that of a bait rod should be on the top side in *front of the handle*, while on a fly rod, on the *under side* below the handle. Among first class reels the following are standard grades:

Julius Von Hofe, Shakespeare, Kentucky, Gayle, Milam, Blue Grass, Hendryx, Pennell, Berger, Meisselbach, Talbot, Orvis, Yawman & Erbe, Automatic, etc. When through using a good reel, it should be detached from the rod, cleaned and dried, oiled with good clock oil and put in a *Reel Case*, safely away. (See also Wrinkies and Kinks elsewhere.)

About the Lines

Trolling Line

In the selection of these, points to be considered are size, weight, etc., of the fish you set out to capture, the necessary and most suitable sizes and strength of the line most appropriate to your mode of fishing. For the line par excellence I recommend for casting, the very best silk casting line, braided and waterproof, for other purposes choose the braided silk line waterproof and enameled. The material used in the construction of such lines being twisted strands of pure silk, afterward treated with a preparation of parafine and a superior quality of linseed oil, which not only renders them waterproof, but adds to their strength and flexibility, besides they are less apt to kink. Such lines can be purchased in almost any necessary size or length.

In the purchase of lines see that they are of uniform thickness, avoiding the tapered line, if you desire hard service, as the ends of these being finer soon lose their strength and give out at the critical moment (when the strongest part is on the reel.) In going on a trip the addition of an extra line or two is a wise precaution, guarding against the unforeseen, and enabling you to perhaps help out a less provident, yet worthy brother angler, if not yourself.

As the best of silk lines can now be purchased at a few cents per yard according to weights and sizes, mounted ready for use either on spools, boards, coils, or in hanks, ranging in lengths from 25 to 1,000 feet, the question of a plentiful supply of the best lines is an easy matter.

Average Size and Strength of Various Fishing Lines.

(Braided, Linen and Silk)

6 or **H** ▬▬▬▬▬

5 or **G** ▬▬▬▬▬▬▬▬

4 or **F** ▬▬▬▬▬▬▬▬▬

3 or **E** ▬▬▬▬▬▬▬▬▬▬

2 or **D** ▬▬▬▬▬▬▬▬▬▬▬

1 or **C** ▬▬▬▬▬▬▬▬▬▬▬▬

Above illustrations are made as near correct as a cut can be made from the almost invisible line.

6 or H—Tests	10	to	12	to	20	lbs
5 or G—Tests	12	to	15	to	25	lbs
4 or F—Tests	18	to	20	to	30	lbs
3 or E—Tests	22	to	25	to	35	lbs
2 or D—Tests	30	to	35	to	40	lbs
1 or C—Tests	40	to	45	to	50	lbs

Raw Silk Lines—Are made from raw silk containing all the natural gum of the silk worm.

Finished Silk Lines—Have all the natural gum boiled out, reducing the size of the line, yet *still preserving its full original strength.* For instance a size 5 finished silk line is slightly smaller than a No. 5 raw silk, yet fully as strong. (This treatment adds to its cost.)

Oiled Silk Lines.—A raw silk line which has been soaked in oil, rendering it *practically waterproof* and as strong as the raw or finished silk line.

Enameled Silk Line.—A line which has been treated with a preparation giving it a hard and glossy surface, which becomes flexible when used in water.

Tested Strength.—The tested strength given above is for wet lines (as in use;) when dry a line will test from 20 to 25 per cent more (unless thoroughly waterproof) so bear that in mind.

Tests of course vary according to whether lines are of first quality or not.

166

If however a still cheaper, yet serviceable line is desired for trolling, etc., select those of hard braided Irish linen or flax, costing one cent per yard, and for the better information of my readers, I append herewith a table of illustrations and sizes, correctly given, of both silk and linen llnes, with data as to their strength.

All lines should be colored either water green or pale grass color, and stand a test of about 1 to 2 lbs. to each twisted thread on the braid Thus in a twelve thread line, the breaking tension should be about 12 to 20 lbs., steady weight; and the careful angler should occasionally test his lines before starting out on a trip; and by reversing the ends so as that part on the spool can be used and dried; occasionally wiping them with a rag or sponge dipped in linseed oil, the question of how to keep lines both soft and waterproof is easily answered.

When through using them, they should be drawn through a soft cotton rag or sponge, unreeled and allowed to dry well before putting away,—"Reel Dryers" being made for the purpose.

In addition to those mentioned, there is a braided Metal Line. It is composed of sixteen flexible wire strands braided over a core of strands composed of silk or cotton, thus giving great flexibility and strength. The line is rustless, and stands use in salt water exceedingly well. It is intended to be used without a sinker, and for that reason in trolling a shorter length is required than if a cotton or linen line is used. It will not rot when reeled wet, runs well on reel, goes through guides smoothly and does not kink. The line is intended especially for catching large fish, which usually seek deep waters, especially trout, lake trout, pike, pickerel, muskallonge, etc. The line comes in 10, 25, 50 and 100 yd. lengths on spools, ready for use.

The Leader, Snell, Etc.

These are sometimes improperly called "cat gut," yet are an imported product of the silk worm, coming to this country in bundles from Spain, and put up 100 strands to the hank, or 10,000 strands to the bundle. The lengths of these strands range from 9 to 13 inches; only, when several of these strands have been properly fastened together in lengths of 3, 6 or 9 feet, with a loop at each end for securing line and hook theron, they are termed "Leaders." They are also made of single, double, treble or 6-ply twist, by either hand or machine, all with a view of securing greater strength when so required. Ordinarily however, single leaders are generally used in lengths of 3, 6 or 9 feet as desired. Leaders are also made of Gimp and wire, especially adapted for heavy trolling, etc. To the hooks is also fastened pieces of the gut, gimp or wire, usually looped and whipped on with fine silk or wire, the latter being proof against being cut off by the sharp strong teeth of larger fish. "Called Snells."

In the selection of Leaders, 3 to 6 feet will be ample for ordinary uses, usually 6 feet for Trout, Bass, etc., or 9 feet for Salmon; the question of length however, being confined to the individual likes of the anglers, whose tastes in this respect varies, many using lengths of 12 feet; personally however, I think those of less length than my rod, ample.

In color they are of a pearly transparent white, rendering them when in the waters almost invisible, especially so be they dyed the favorite mist color. They should have a round smooth surface, and in testing them should be drawn between the thumb and forefinger and if rough spots are detected, should be rejected as they are apt to be fractured, and will easily break at the fractured part when you least expect it. In the purchase of them insist upon best quality, as they are classed and sold in three grades, good, medium and best.

When going on a trip leaders should be carried in a box made for the purpose; kept between several pieces of dry or moist felt. Never use them when dry, lest you fracture them; soak well before using, and if it is desired to render them extremely soft and pliable for joining, etc., vinegar will render them softer still.

About Floats

Very little need be said of these, the split cork with the line forced to its center, answering every purpose and being the equal of any. They are mostly used in bait fishing, being so attached to the line, as to suspend the bait at any desired depth of water. By their use the least little nibble is instantly detected, while a bite causes it to bob under the water, thus giving a signal preparatory for the strike.

They are also very effective in using hand or drift lines, and bait can be often sent down stream to promising waters, that could not be reached otherwise, and by keeping an eye on a series of them, some really good fishing can be enjoyed. They are made of cork, light bass and other woods and are easily attached, raised or lowered to any desired length of the line. In still fishing and using floats, the depth of the waters should be first determined by the aid of a line and sinker as a plummet, and the float fastened at the proper distance, in order that the bait may be kept off or just touching the bottom or mid waters as the case requires. They range in price from 1 cent to 25 cents and in sizes from 1 to 4 inches; one grade being so arranged that the line can run freely through its center whenever it comes in contact with the top of the rod, when reeling in the line, and termed the "automatic float."

169

Various Styles of Fish Hooks

(Cuts about one-half size)

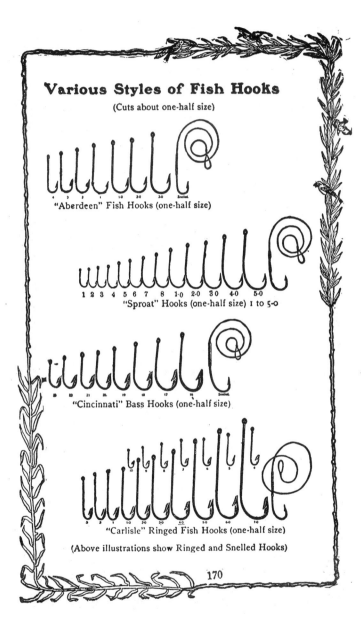

"Aberdeen" Fish Hooks (one-half size)

"Sproat" Hooks (one-half size) 1 to 5-0

"Cincinnati" Bass Hooks (one-half size)

"Carlisle" Ringed Fish Hooks (one-half size)

(Above illustrations show Ringed and Snelled Hooks)

About the Hooks

In the selection of Hooks I advise those already snelled, together with a good assortment of various well known popular killing flies tied on, a few assorted sizes without flies so as to be used for bait fishing, as illustrated elsewhere. There are many forms and styles of hooks, among them being the Sproat, Limerick, O'Shaughnessy, Sneck, Kirby, Aberdeen, Carlisle, Cincinnati, Kendall, Pacific, etc., which come in single, double, treble, or gang form.

To my mind however, the Sproat hook leads them all, it has a scientific barb and shape, is tempered on correct principles and can be relied upon to pierce the toughest mouth and stay there; and as any of these hooks are now furnished with every conceivable sort, kind and size of a fly, insect, beetle, bug or fish in artificial form, it is only necessary to select the most alluring kinds and sizes, such as are most appropriate for the fish you are after. Hence to aid you in their selection I have compiled a list of the most suitable sizes, for your information. (See illustrations.)

About Fly Books, Tackle Boxes, Etc.

To the careful angler these commend themselves, as they furnish a compact portable case in which an outfit of Flies, Hooks, Leaders, etc., and other things which form the basis of an angling kit can be conveniently and safely carried, clean and in order. These come in assorted styles and sizes with partitioned metal spaces and removable trays so as to carry a simple or elaborate outfit, or anything else you desire to carry in it. Usually these are supplemented by a Pocket Fly and Leader Book, and the more complete Tackle Box left at some near by camp or lodge, and a suitable day's outfit carried thus, in a handy pocket. As there are many good styles and grades, the principle feature being size and capacity. I illustrate those of standard pattern, leaving the selection entirely to the angler.

Standard Tackle Outfit Boxes for Complete Fishing Outfits.

No. 1.

No. 2.

No. 3.

No. 4.

No. 5.

No. 6.

No. 7.

No. 8.

No. 9.

Metal and
Leather
Patterns.

No. 10.

All Sizes,
Grades
and Styles.

Angler's Favorite Patterns and Grades

Landing Nets, Gaffs, Etc.

For small fish (when desired) and for the purpose of landing large ones. Are provided with various plain dip or landing nets, made of either cotton, fine silk or linen, large or small mesh, the whole fastened to handles of various patterns, solid folding or telescopic, ranging in size from 2 to 6 feet. For fly fishing the short handle having a looped cord so as to be thrown and carried over the shoulder (when not in use) is used, while others prefer those of a long handle, so as to meet varied requirements. These nets range from 18 to 24 inches in diameter at the mouth and about 24 inches in depth.

They are unncessary except for the purpose of making sure a catch, and many disdain to use them entirely. However as in fly fishing the hook is at times barely fastened and apt to tear out, and as fish invariably make their hardest and most frantic efforts to escape, usually before landing it is well to add them to an outfit, for it usually happens that the fish lost *was the biggest one I ever saw.*

For larger heavier fish, large steel hooks secured to a stout handle is employed, called "gaffs," both single hook, plain or automatic as illustrated. In their use a heavy cord should be secured to the handle, lest it be wrenched from the hands and both fish and gaff be sacrificed.

Very large fish such as Muskallonge or Tarpon are either shot, clubbed to insensibility, or towed to shore before landing.

Automatic Sure Grip Gaff.

The Fish Basket, Nets, Creel, Etc.

Folding Creel

This is used mostly in Trout fishing and wading, where the angler must necessarily be on the move. It is secured and carried firmly against the body by breast and shoulder straps as illustrated. It is either of light or dark color, ranging in size from 7½x10 inches to 10x16 inches, holding from 7 to 35 pounds of fish. To the straps should be also fastened the "Fisherman's or Angler's" Featherweight Cape, and rolled up therein a light lunch or a supply of pipe, tobacco, etc., separated by its folds; as in wading there is no telling when a misstep will send the angler floundering in the waters and drench his clothing. In the basket should be strewn a few green ferns, so as to keep the fish from bruising each other, and looped in a convenient place a "Hook Extractor." For the question of dry matches, the angler should provide himself with a Waterproof Safety Match Box; which insures a warm fire or a smoke at the end of a long journey or successful battle, no matter if he has fell in and been swimming. I myself have floundered more than once and invariably I consoled myself, and others who were less provident, with a dry match afterward; hence no angler should fail to carry one along.

As to the "Featherweight Cape" it covers the entire body almost to the feet, while the sleeves are provided with flexible rubber bands at the hand holes, as illustrated, keeping the arms dry, and is so small when packed as to carry conveniently in creel if desired; and as cloudy threatening weather is generally the most successful fishing time, a sudden rainstorm sends the angler home happy and dry—for by the way, usually fishing ends with a rain any how.

Last but not least, don't disgrace yourself or creel with small fish, unless absolutely necessary, gently unhook them and quietly return them again to their native waters. Honestly better luck will attend you (or some brother angler) if you do this sportsmanlike act.

As to keeping fish, use either a fish bag net, 24 to 36 inches in size, or the common fish stringer as is illustrated elsewhere (if still fishing.)

Wading, Etc.

For wading in the cooler, deeper waters of brooks and streams (for older anglers especially) it is advisable to use Wading Pants, either with or without boot feet; an article made of rubber or canvas waterproof material, covering if desired, the lower extremities of the body, or reaching in the one continuous garment nearly to the arms.

These are made in various styles ranging from the good old Baptist minister's baptismal pants, (sometimes used by enthusiastic pastoral anglers) to those of either stocking or heavy boot feet, by the more ardent lovers of the sport.

They should not be worn however, out of the water, as they are thus unusually heating and uncomfortable, and if only woolen drawers and socks are used inside instead of pants and all, I have always found them not only comfortable but cool.

The young hardy angler however can dispense with these, if this advice is followed. Take a pair of heavy, solid, old, well fitting congress or side elastic shoes, and have them filled (and clinched) with malleable iron hob nails, so as to prevent slipping off slimy rocks; put on a suit of medium wool underclothes and socks, and over all draw a pair of canvas overalls; lace over your legs and upper part of shoes, a pair of stout army canvas leggings with straps passing under the shoe center. Thus equipped take to the water, and in a few minutes the disagreeable chill will leave, as soon as the heat of your body has assimilated the temperature of the water next to the skin, and provided you keep fairly on the move, there is no fear of a chill. I myself prefer this rig to any wading outfit, and as such a dress is my ideal hunting or fishing costume (and I am invariably supplied with a dry change in camp) I have yet to suffer any inconvenience or after effect. Don t however permit yourself to sit down for any unreasonable length of time, out of the water, as this is harmful; besides I have found that the knowledge of clean clothes without washing, resulted thus. As soon as my dry change was on, and the wet ones dried and folded away, a feeling of comfort and satisfaction of killing two birds with one stone, pervaded my system throughout.

I have seen many follow my advice, some of which thought they improved on my plan by cutting slits (to, as they termed it, let the water out of their shoes) but as sand and small pebbles invariably got in, no matter where the slits were made in the shoes, they often regretted the error of not wholly following my simple and inexpensive plan.

"A Trout Stream.

Preserving Fish and Other Things

American ingenuity and science has come to the aid of the angler or sportsman in many ways, lending assistance even to the preservation of the choicest specimens of his catch or skill; be it the tiny or monster of the water or earth, keeping it either as food or for the taxidermist, all without ice or laborious methods, and absolutely without affecting its quality, taste, or smell, by the use of an article termed "*Preservaline*" which has been found to keep anything during the hottest weather, for a week or more, thus enabling a shipment home or ample time to bring the choicest specimens of a catch along home with you, that otherwise time and heat would spoil.

It is put up in small packages, each of which is ample to preserve 50 to 100 pounds of fish or game and being as easy and simple to apply as common salt, while its cost is but trifling compared to the excellent results that attend its use.

As to preserved baits, the article on Baits covers this I trust satisfactorily, and I append herewith for the still better information of my readers, a most excellent device used by many anglers, and known as the "Ideal Fisherman's and Angler's Refrigerator Basket," one of the toughest, smoothest, lightest, neatest articles ever put up for a short though pleasant trip. It is constructed of fine basket material, closely woven, with zinc and metal linings, together with a combination

This is It.

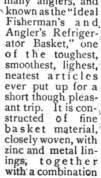

177

of compartments, lined and made air tight with metal, felt and asbestos filling, so arranged that a very small amount of ice will positively refrigerate its entire contents for at least 24 hours. A blessing for that Sunday, or any other day and night single trip, which means for the party and occasion, cool butter, ice cold milk, (in bottles of course) cool salads, etc., and after its all eaten and enjoyed it serves to bring home, cool, fresh and clean, your fish, when the trip is ended; and if traveling afar, by boat or rail, a jolly to the chef" or a good cigar to the porter or storekeeper fills it with its small supply office again (only a few handfuls being needed) for an extra 24 hour jaunt again.

Think of it—a practically refrigerator for boat, buggy or automobile use, which is only a market basket in form and appearance, a basket to buy or carry stores in, and a refrigerator when coming to camp or home. It weighs but a few pounds, costs but a few dollars, is rain and dust proof, and just the thing for that park picnic, outing, office or down the bay trip, just as much as for the fisherman's camp. It is neat enough to look right anywhere, and a blamed sight more practical than anything of its kind in existence—that was ever devised for that "short though happy trip," with cool things on tap.

Angler's or Sportsmen's Portable Out Door Dining Outfits

For You and Me

Before concluding chapter on the conveniences of out door life, I also deem it fitting to illustrate and describe in connection with other good things what is known as the above, and which for twenty years past has been the favorite with that class of anglers and sportsmen who believe in traveling right, "smoothing it"

178

so to speak. These are made in endless variety of sizes for 2, 4, 6, 8, 10 or 12 persons and are completely equipped with unbreakable dining equipment, even to the smallest detail; the whole compactly arranged in an extremely stout, light and portable wicker basket, and including air tight compartments or vessels for foods; cutlery, plates, cups, saucers, butter and other dishes, liquid bottles, and can't-break glassware, absolutely nothing being omitted, from can opener to corkscrew, lemon squeezer to carving knife. Such an outfit as this is a treasure to those epicurian dainty ladies who in this 20th century, invariably accompany the automobile, fishing, camping, hunting or traveling trip. This might bring a smile to the pessimistic old fogey, who believes and always will believe in roughing it, but to those who like to enjoy life (and there are tens of thousands of them) such an article is essential to solid comfort, and I doubt not that there is hardly anyone who would not gladly change from the tin plate and cup idea, to the use of this compact and modern outfit, with the basket table and clean linen thereon, did they but try it once. Cleanliness, and neatness is conducive to any ones, even a camp appetite; and as they are fitted when desired, with even folding table thereto, even chafing dish and fuel, it is obvious that practical as they are, the fortunate possessor of one is to be envied.

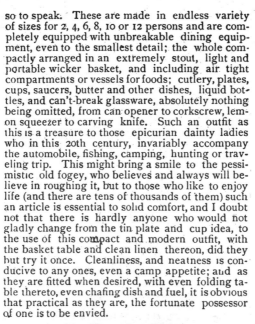

For the Six of Us.

The Art of Angling

The school boy who comes home for his midsummer vacation, usually commences his apprenticeship to the art by fishing for some of the finny tribe in waters adjacent to his home, either from the banks of certain ponds, lakes or rivers, or about the piers and wharves of city waters, usually for some of the Carp, Perch, Catfish or Bullhead species. For this purpose he provides himself with a long bamboo or cut pole, 8 to 12 feet long; 10 to 20 yards stout line, a small cork or quill float, (perhaps a yard of silk worm gut) and a hook or two, of 1 to 8 size, and can he afford it, a small light reel.

With this elaborate outfit and a can of worms, he is the envy of every boy his age, who "favors" to go along to tote the pole, or usually to carry home a good sized string of fish.

If he is a wise boy he first plumbs the depth of the waters, adjusts his float so that the hook barely touches the bottom or remains suspended in mid-waters as the occasion requires. On his hooks he threads or fastens a good size red worm, casts his lure into the water and patiently waits for a bite.

By the float a nibble is instantly detected, while a bite causes it to bob under the water; when he jerks up the rod, and either yanks the hook out (nearly jerking off the fish's head at the same time) or sends his fish flying into the air behind him, and forthwith he ranks as an expert, with all the boys who accompany him.

Later on he observes the older hands and imitating them, uses more judgment, and after a few losses, when he hooks a big one plays it somewhat until nearly exhausted, when he carefully brings it to hand, raising it into a safe place.

This constitutes his first lessons, but there are other things to learn, hence this Manual, intended to cover generally all subjects not only for instruction, but information of those not too familiar with the varied methods of luring or capturing different species

In Still Fishing

Some anglers use what is known as "*Ground or Buoy Bait*," for the purpose of luring fish to the vicinity of his tackle. An excellent one being a mixture of bran, oat meal, bread, boiled rice and small cut worms, maggots, or raw liver, lights, etc. A few handfuls of either or all, being cast in still waters some few hours or a day before fishing that spot, thus attracting fish to that vicinity, so as their capture can be more easily effected.

If this is done in a likely spot in the early morning—toward evening one is apt to find good fishing right there, especially so if he uses for bait that same food or meat, which previously was used as ground bait. Care must be taken however, not to feed them too much, and necessary time allowed for fish to find it, and be seeking for more about the time you get there. When this is done at two or three likely spots, dividing your time between these places, is often very successful in results.

Trolling, Trailing, Etc.

This is a very successful method employed for the capture of many species of larger fish; Bass, Pike, Pickerel, Lake Trout, Muskallonge, etc., and consists of drawing along through mid-waters, certain baits or bright glittering spoons or artificial lures, disposed on one or more hooks, and by motion revolving and glittering, attracting the attention of various fish, causing them to bite and be hooked; when it is either played or drawn to boat and captured. Usually boats are employed, lines being trailed from the sides or stern; if however, no boat is available, a long weighted line is coiled and thrown far out into deep waters and slowly hauled in. Another method is by the "trolley rig" which is operated from any convenient bank or wharf, either live, dead or spoon bait being used.

The proper kind of tackle to use for trolling, varies according to weight and kind of fish trolled for. In a general way there are certain kinds of lines, rods, reels, etc., that afford the best results, if a rod is used it should be made in two pieces, the whole measuring from 5 to 8 feet, the butt being made with a grasp below and above the reel seat, and care should be taken (if using a rod) that it is not too stiff, as a fairly flexible rod will exert a more steady strain, and when fish leave the water, it will not straighten out and leave the taut line.

The Reel should be large enough to hold 100 yards of good braided silk or linen line, a double multiplier; and the leader, a treble or six-ply twisted gut, gimp or wire cable leader, usually six feet long, used with two or more swivels so as to avoid twisting. The Baits or Spoons used are simply endless in variety, and are either natural fish bait or artificial, ranging from the murderous gang to the single trolling hook, that is more sportsmanlike to use. In trolling from a boat, often two lines are used, or a single heavy line with two or more swivel-connected leaders, each fastened and arranged so as to troll deep, mid or surface waters at one and the same time, thus giving fish, by reason of their varied lengths, a first, second or third chance, and if the main line is properly sinkered so as to touch the bottom, and the bait lines made of different lengths and distance from each other, there is no fear of their coming together. For marshy, weedy waters, weedless hooks and spoons should be used. Row slowly and keep your lines well in hand, feeling the bottom with your main line sinker, raising or lowering the main line according to the conditions and depth of water, and the fish you are after. In lake trolling go deep, 50 to 75 feet, in other waters accordingly.

Assortment of Trolling Baits.

Lake Fishing

Lake fishing differs in its practice materially from that of stream fishing, and though some flies which are used on streams will also kill on lakes, yet, for the most part, there is a fancy repertoire in this respect which differs wholly from that employed in streams. Lake-trout flies, particularly those made in Scotland, are made with wool bodies, the prevailing colors being red, claret, orange, yellow, green, and black, with a light spiral up the body of gold or silver tinsel. The hackles are chiefly either black or red, or red with a black center; the wings are either of teal, mallard, or woodcock. Here and there the white tip feather in the drake's wing is a favorite wing for flies. They are usually dressed on 7, 8, or 9 hooks; the same flies a size or two larger do equally well for sea-trout flies.

Lake-trout fishing is conducted either from a boat or from the shore. The best depth of water in which to fish for trout varies from 6 or 8 to 12 or 14 feet, and in trolling in hot months do so near the bottom in about 50 feet of water, and between these depths the best sport is obtained; and the angler should therefore fish over them for choice, though occasionally fish may be caught in both deeper and shallower water. In lake fishing it is always desirable to have a good ruffling breeze, as the fish do not rise or take well in a calm. The best places are in sheltered bays, by rocky points or islands or where foods flow in; drifting along by these, and casting ahead and shorewards, the angler watches every break in the water. While drifting along in his boat, it may

happen that, the wind being high, he drifts too
fast to fish thoroughly and properly over the
ground. To obviate this a stone or an anchor is
cast over and allowed to drag along the bottom, so
as to check the way of the boat, and to give time
to the angler to fish. A good boatsman and nets-
man is here a great desideratum, and much of the
chance of sport depends upon him. The great
fault of most boatsmen is that they go too quickly
over the casts; and it requires a man with a knowledge of the lake, as well as experience in managing the boat, so to conduct matters that the angler
has the best chance of sport. When rowing to his
ground, or from point to point, the angler shoul always put out the spinning minnow and troll deeply, and thus he may take one or two of the best
fish. As fish do not always lie in the same places,
wind and weather have to be sedulously consulted.
In fishing from the shore the angler seldom gets
the best sport, and often has to wade to reach fishable water, while best casts are often beyond his
reach; and therefore, whenever a boat can be employed, it is to be preferred for lakes.

Art of Bait Casting

This of all methods requires practice, and such practice always had best be confined to natural waters, thus adapting your efforts to various conditions that actually exist. It is not difficult to master, patience and perseverance being only essential.

The Secret of It All.

For this a fairly stiff rod is required, 5 to 7 feet only, (some anglers prefer only 5 feet) and for this purpose a good Lancewood rod is all to be desired, although the split Bamboo is better. The Reel should be a level winding, quadruple multiplier; for here it has work to perform, thousands of revolutions being necessary in casting and retrieving the bait; it should be provided with 40 to 50 yards of good all silk casting line, with a breaking tension of 10 to 20 lbs. Assemble together your rod, reel and line, arrange your bait and wind up the line, until your bait, an artificial or natural frog, bucktail or casting spoon is at or near the tip of your rod; set your line to free running and take position for the cast. Place the thumb of your rod hand on the center of the spool, so as to use it as a brake and thus control the reel, and cast the bait by an upward then forward movement of the rod (just as though you were throwing an apple from a pointed stick;) allow the line and bait to go forward as far as you can; diminishing the pressure of the thumb on the reel while doing so, yet never releasing control of

"In the Depths where Silence Reigns Supreme."

it under the thumb, whose action is essential in regulating the speed of the reel.

As the greatest difficulty is in managing the reel great care should be exercised to always keep it well under thumb control, lest it overrun, thus subjecting you to the annoyance of what is termed "backlashing. The instant the bait touches the water, stop the reel, and raising the tip of the rod by a backward and upward movement, draw the line back for the recast. When casting aim not to allow the bait to fall on the water with a splash, but as lightly as possible, and when it touches the water, start the bait back towards you again, winding the line in position to repeat the cast.

To do this, place the butt of the rod against the body, grasping it in front of the reel with the left hand, using the right to wind the reel and line into position again. Repeat these operations for a few times until the knack of thumbing the reel and line in making casts is accomplished, and when you can thus place your bait within a foot or so of the spot aimed at, you are ready to try and catch fish. For all practical purposes, 40 to 50 feet is sufficient in casting; greater distance will come with time, and while long casts are showy and at times necessary yet the distance mentioned will serve its purpose and well.

If necessary and water is unavailable, the novice can take his first lessons by simply placing a sheet of paper on the ground, adjust his tackle and aim away at it, thus in a measure mastering the first rudimentary efforts as to controlling the reel and line, in making the cast, if no more. If your reel is not provided with a level winding device (note the automatic spooler) illustrated elsewhere.

When you have acquired proficiency in the forward cast, change your position in order that you may better familiarize yourself with the right and left; remembering that the great secret of casting is to always have complete control of the reel. Practice the back right and left casts, and in a short time you will be able to cast all around yourself, covering a space or circle of 150 feet or more.

However, it is not distance that counts in catching fish, but in so manipulating your casts as to permit the bait to alight naturally and be lifelike, not as though it dropped from the heavens, with a splash that would be heard by and scare every fish fifty yards away.

As for bait in casting, use either live or artificial frogs, minnows, or any of the better class of casting baits, Shakespeare Weedless Expert, Bucktail, or any of those I illustrate elsewhere.

Splashing or Sputting, Whipping, Etc.

Often called "skittering," a very successful method, usually practiced in very shallow waters, in and about grassy, weedy places, among banks, lily pads, etc.; at this one should provide themselves with an extra line, flies, weedless hooks, etc. and small or appropriate baits for the work, a bucktail weedless making an excellent bait for this work.

Begin by casting into the pockets of weeds, rushes, etc., twitching the bait towards you and allowing it to rest an instant in every likely spot you find, dropping it into every pocket, and to every side of you, always in a different spot, as close to weedy places, grass and shore that you can, keeping your bait on the move. If in a boat, as soon as you receive a strike, have your partner pull for both open and clear water; avoiding slack line and aiming to keep your fish from running among the weeds and rushes, and thus entangling your line. Pike, Bass, Pickerel, etc. are ever alert toward the more shallow waters hence it is well to always cast from the boat toward shore, being careful not to splash the oars or make any unuusal noise on the bottom of the boat.

A Word in Behalf of the Small Fish

Always return to the water while alive, any game fishes that are too small for your creel, or your table, and never carry away from the water more fish than you need. Fish as long as you like, catch and land all you want, but return to their native haunts, alive, all you do not need, especially the little ones. Put these back, even if you do not fill your basket. Let them grow to a decent size, and take them at some future time, or let some brother angler do so.

The true sportsman fishes for sport and not for meat. If you hook a big fellow, who makes a royal fight, and if you do not need him for the table, release him gently from the hook and return him to the water for nis bravery. The chances are you will not have hurt him seriously. It is not necessary to lacerate a fish in taking the hook out of his mouth, unless he has gorged it.

We frequently hear of men who catch great strings of fish, who take them to camp, weigh them, count them, perhaps have them photographed,

"A Quiet Spot on the Outskirts."

mores the shame, and then throw the fish away to rot. Such men are not sportsmen. They are low down pot fishermen, and should not be allowed to camp or associate with gentlemen.

It is only by the practice of self denial and a proper regard for the rights of others, that even the best stocked waters in the country can remain so.

Quit when you get enough. That should be the motto of every true sportsman in the world.

The League of American Sportsmen has done a great work in educating the public along these lines, and in protecting the game and game fishes. The laws of nearly every State in the Union reflect to-day, the wisdom and the hard work of that organization. There are selfish men everywhere who denounce this organization and the founder of it, and who attempt to belittle the work of the League, but the motives of such men can generally be traced to the fact that they have felt its power.

To the intelligent sportsmen, however, this League appeals as a most worthy institution, and all such men know that without its splendid work the forest and the waters would soon become as barren of life as the Desert of Sahara.

No honest man can do otherwise than admire that well known writer, G. O. Shields, editor of the best Sportsmen's Magazine in America, "Recreation," for his untiring efforts on behalf of the game and the game fishes. He organized the League of American Sportsmen five years ago, has built it to a membership of over 9,000, and it is the duty of every sportsman in the United States to join this League, and to aid him in his great work.

The Sportsman's Grip. 190

Surface or Fly Fishing

This method is conducted with both the natural and artificial fly, the first being termed "dipping or dapping," consists of using a long light rod 7 to 9 feet in length; about 6 feet or more of strong fine gut of mist color, (some anglers use even 12 feet) to the end of which is fastened a No. 6 to 8 Sproat Hook and a live fly, beetle, grasshopper or insect of some kind fastened by transfixing the thorax of the insect on the hook. The angler having watched fish rising at some spot, (where he is hidden from view) creeps softly to some nearby point, and keeping himself out of sight, pokes the po nt of his rod through some open spot in the bushes and allows his insect or fly to drop gently near or a little above where the fish have been seen to rise; probably he will not be able to see well, then he must trust to hearing and touch, and he will hear a slight "plop" like a bubble from a submerged bottle, or feel the fish.

A gentle strike then is required, and a tight hand on the fish, as such places are usually near old roots or boughs, in which the fish will try to shelter himself and entangle the tackle. The best fish are frequently taken in this way. Another method of using the natural or living fly or insect is by casting it. In this case a single-hand fly-rod is used, and it requires great care to avoid whipping the insect off the hook. Having cast the bait to the extent required, the line and bait rest on the surface, and the bait floats down quite naturally unchecked, and the fish rises at it in the ordinary manner. What is called the blow-line is another favorite method of using the fly. A length of light floss silk is fastened on to the running line with about two feet of fine gut and a light hook at the end. Baiting the hook with a fly, the angler turns his back to the wind, holds the rod (a long light cane one) upright, allows the wind to blow the light floss line as far out as it will go, when he gradually lowers the rod and guides the fly till it touches the water a yard above a fish, when he floats over it. A little wind is required for this kind of fishing. Some insects, beetles, creepers, or lavæ of the stone-fly, etc. are used in mid-water as already noted. A word or two as to the method: a couple of shots being fixed on the line, the bait is cast with an underhand swing, as in minnow fishing, down stream, and allowed to travel away from where the angler stands. At every stop or check of the line it is necessary to strike, for the bait being tender, whether it be a twig, mud or fish that arrests it, it will be spoiled; therefore the angler must always strike on every suspicion of a bite.

"Taking the Fly"

Some anglers fish up stream, but this is hard work (yet at times has its advantages.) The best way however is to fish down stream, and still another good method is to fish diagonally up and across the stream. The angler pursues one of two systems. He either waits till he sees the fish rise and fishes over them, wasting no time on intermediate water when he sees no rises; or he fishes the water out thoroughly, searching every hollow, bank, weed and stone, that may hide a Trout. In fishing for small Trout, the latter method is generally the one adopted. In larger rivers, where the fish are heavy and few, the former is more often preferred. When a good fish is hooked it will often resist strongly, and rush violently about, seeking to hide itself under weeds and roots, which are dangerous to the tackle. The angler must guide the fish as well as he can until it is tired, letting out line from the reel when resistance becomes too severe a strain on the tackle, and winding it in again when opportunity serves, but always keeping a tight line on the fish, as a slack line frequently loses it. When tired the fish should be towed gently to a favorable bank, and the landing-net quietly slipped under him. There must be no dashing or hasty movement with the net, lest the fish be frightened and make another effort to escape, as fish frequently do, and successfully, as it is a dangerous moment in the struggle. In fishing with double-handed rod the rod is longer and the line a little heavier; in other respects there is no difference. The rod will vary from 10 to 15 feet if Salmon fishing. The left hand grasps it below the reel and the right hand above; though, if the angler desires a change, or necessities of stream or wind require it, the hands can be reversed. The double-handed rod has several advantages over the single, having more power with big fish, and keeping the line and flies higher above obstructions.

"Rushing It."

Artificial Fly Fishing or Casting

"Trout Fishing"

The Rod used should be a good one, preferably a Split Bamboo, 7 to 10 feet in length and weighing 3 to 7 ounces (although many experienced anglers prefer still a shorter and lighter rod) yet in this as in all fishing, conditions must guide. In open waters when there is plenty of room, a larger rod can be used, but when difficult casts must be made owing to dense growths of nearby vegetation, a short rod is essential.

A light, single action, click reel, and 50 to 75 yards of silk casting line, hard braided, but not enameled. A 6 to 9 foot good leader and an assortment of the very best Flies you can buy, those appropriate for the fish you are after, tied on No. 8 or 12 Sproat Hooks for brook fishing, and No. 6, 7 or 8 hooks for rivers or lakes. To a 6 foot leader, attach two of your best flies, Tail and Dropper, unreel about 20 feet of line, toss your flies gently into the stream and let them float down with the current. When your flies are down stream, lift your rod quickly until the tip is up and back of your body, carrying your line and flies with it, and as soon as your flies swing straight behind you, send forward your rod lively, and allow your flies to light on the waters "just as a natural fly would," raising the tip of your rod so as to keep them moving on the surface, like the thing of life it is supposed to be; always trying to avoid letting your lines touch the water, in either the backward or forward cast.

The moment you see a rise and feel your fish, strike gently, but not too quick, as fish often rise

Double Pleasures.

"Doing the Work."

"Telling All About It."

to inspect a fly, and if your line is fairly taut (as it always should be) the chances are that the fish will hook itself. If not, a simple twist or upward movement of the hand and rod only will suffice. It is unnecessary to move the entire arm and body, as I have seen many do. If you have hooked a fish play it well, and allow your rod to do most of the work; (if a good one) it will respond nobly, yourself simply guiding your fish into smoother, deeper waters, giving line only as the fish fights for it, and taking it when you can. Don't be in a hurry to land your fish, wait until such time as the exhausted fish can be led to net, and look out then for his final flurry when getting him, for he is apt to make a most desperate effort to escape, at the last moment; and for the better information of my readers I append herewith a few suggestions (not rules) to be used in fly casting, emphasizing however that these suggestions must always be subject to existing change of conditions, always conditions, first, last, all the time, conditions.

The question of why fish take bunches of feathers tied on hooks, and what they mistake them for, has often been asked; and it is now pretty generally allowed that they take them for flies in the majority of instances, though in others they mistake them for water beetles, lavæ, or spiders, of which latter insect there are several that inhabit the water. Now, there are two classes of disputants on this matter: one which holds altogether to the fly theory, and therefore strives to imitate each fly that comes out closely; the other, which inclines more to the general insect theory, and merely gives a few flies of different colors, not caring to imitate anything in particular. Probably the best fishermen recognize both theories, but bind themselves exclusively to neither.

Fish like brightest colors, and every fisherman knows that gaudy flies will attract fish when the more modest ones will not lure them from the depths.

Now for myself I thoroughly believe that fish see and also that they like bright colors. I have seen fish refuse all kinds of live bait and do nothing but watch it and swim around it, yet when a bright piece of tin happened to be thrown into the water, they immediately made a rush for it. Of

196

course, some will say that the tin had motion, but so did the bait, and the only reason that the fish dashed for the tin was that it had a bright color and attracted their attention.

Suggestions in Fly Casting

Aim to let your flies touch the water lightly, just as a natural fly would alight.

Try to keep them there for an instant or two, give them a trifle of movement, as though it were struggling on the water.

Keep a fairly taut line so as the fish can hook himself, or so as to be ready to strike when needed.

Don't strike too quick, often fish rise and do not take the fly; give him another chance, but still keep your fly moving just a little.

When you strike don't jerk his head off, a simple turn of the wrist will suffice to send the hook home (if its a good one.)

Play your fish well, letting the rod do most of the work, let the fish get excited but keep cool yourself.

Don't be discouraged by repeated failures (we all experience them,) fish often rise yet refuse to bite; cast repeatedly in most likely spots, not omitting what you think are unlikely ones; change your flies often if needs be; think of conditions. Don't be impatient, you might angle for hours and all at once strike the right fly or place and fill your creel.

Again, if you fish for sport alone and have caught a worthy but small antagonist, and need not his flesh for your table or food, consign him back to his haunts again, for if the hook has not penetrated his gills or throat you have neither hurt or pained him seriously.

Only by such sportsmanlike methods as these that can solve the question of leaving well stocked rivers, streams and lakes full of fish, instead of fishing them out of all life therein, and wasting one-half a catch. Millions of fish are caught only to be thrown back later into the waters (or on the shores) dead and useless, when by the exercise of a little judgment and true sportsmanship they could have been turned free again, to live on, grow or propagate their species time and time again.

197

Trout Fishing

Of all fish sought for more dilligently than others, is Trout, which inhabit a greater range of waters than any other fish known; more has been written about them than any oth-

"A Trout Stream".

er fish; while the family has been divided and added by professors, into scores of various species, and classified with the most ridiculous jaw breaking names; yet after all the Trout is not a Trout, but just plain Charr Fish.

It has a long body with markings of brown on a deep greenish back, with blue, yellow and red spots distributed thereon; a large and leathery mouth; and though small, is a most wary and difficult fish to capture; yet the choicest morsel that ever graced a broiler. It is becoming scarce in lakes, rivers or streams in close proximity to large

Brook Trout.

cities, owing to the vast number of anglers who go in search of them. But in the waters of Maine, Colorado and Canada, they are still in plenty. Despite their fear of man they are the gamiest of fighters, and their hunger for food (or anything resembling it) is not exceeded by any fish that swims, and if hungry they will not hesitate to devour even their own offspring. Peculiarly enough they inhabit only the purest and coolest of waters; ranging in size from one-half to ten pounds, it is a fact however, that rarely does an angler catch them above the average of two or three pounds.

In fishing for Trout use a 6 to 9 foot, 4 to 6 ounce rod is the popular favorite (a fine split Bamboo) a light common click reel, G or F silk line with a 6 foot gut leader (some anglers use more), No. 4 to 6 Sproat hooks, with a split shot for sinker, so as to sink the bait when needed.

For bait use either "Trout Flies," the very best money will buy, angle worms, maggots, or small live minnows. (See chapter on Baits, Wrinkles and Kinks, etc.) and list of Trout or Bass Flies. If bait fishing, the action of the waters soon tears the bait to pieces; besides the use of flies have become far more popular for Trout fishing. Always fish down stream, as Trout lie head up stream; while the water takes the bait or fly naturally away from you, and when hooked, Trout invariably run down stream, knowing full well it cannot battle against you and the currents at the same time, until you force it to at least.

If wading keep well to the middle of the stream, go slowly and extremely quiet, lest you frighten them, remember they can both hear and see well, and a monstrous animal such as yourself is not go-

The Spotted Sea Trout.

ing to attract fish to your vicinity. Keeping your bait or fly moving so as to represent a thing of life, casting your lure into every likely nook and crook of the stream, behind, in and around every appropriate spot, weeds, stumps, overhanging bank or projection, letting such things get between yourself and line so as to avoid being seen; go slowly and quietly, (resting occasionally, sitting down if you can,) then try again most likely places; and if fish abound you are apt to get a good sized string.

If fly fishing, two or more flies can be attached to your leaders, and often two or more Trout can be hooked, as they are as quick as a wink, and will surprise you how quickly they can take the fly. In such cases I advise that you allow them to play against each other, directing your line to

199

shore, and by a quick movement, not a jerk, run them upon the bank to secure them.

Often Trout can be seen yet will not rise to the fly, no matter how hard you tempt them with an assorted menu, then it is well to sink your fly a trifle under water, or to make a radical change from those you have been using. It is inexplainable why at times Trout refuse to take the fly, and often have I experienced just such luck, although they rose freely about it, when a little further away they took it with eagerness. In such cases I usually took note of the spot, and later on met with success, even though it were a day or so after.

"Truly the ways of fish no man knoweth."

If your casts average 30 to 40 feet you are doing well; long casts look nice at "sportsmen's expositions," and may win records, but they don't catch fish, where the surroundings of natural waters and streams are different. Such shows are imposing, but its like hunting in a shooting gallery far different from the real thing; and the angler who can cast skillfully 30 to 40 feet, will perhaps land more fish than he who can swish away 30 to 40 feet further.

Experience will soon prompt the uninitiated and as this article pertains mostly to Trout fly fishing, I append herewith illustrations of various flies used together with a very complete list of flies, and approximate size and weight of Trout, which may be considered as a safe estimate at all seasons.

Approximate Weight of Trout from Actual Measurements.

8 inch Trout weighs	4 ounces.
9 inch Trout weighs	5 ounces.
10 inch Trout weighs	7 ounces.
11 inch Trout weighs	9 ounces.
12 inch Trout weighs	1 lb.
15 inch Trout weighs	1½ lbs.
18 inch Trout weighs	2½ lbs.
24 inch Trout weighs	6 lbs.

Styles and Sizes of Various Flies.

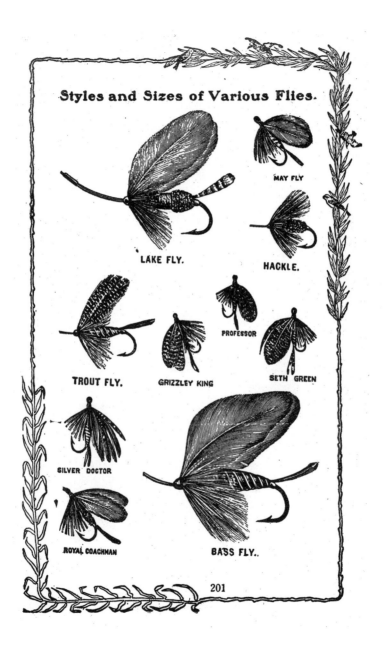

MAY FLY

LAKE FLY.

HACKLE.

TROUT FLY.

GRIZZLEY KING

PROFESSOR

SETH GREEN

SILVER DOCTOR

ROYAL COACHMAN

BASS FLY..

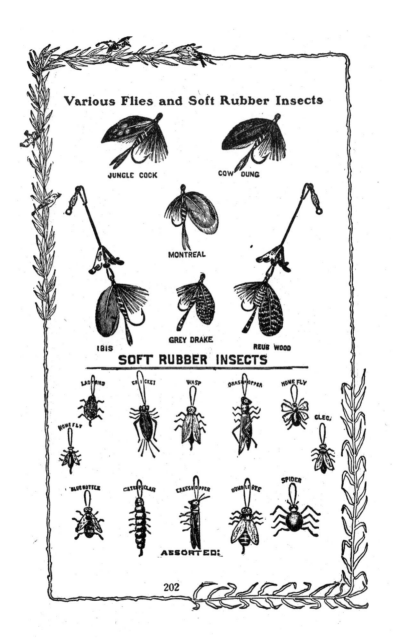

Various Flies and Soft Rubber Insects

JUNGLE COCK

COW DUNG

MONTREAL

IBIS

GREY DRAKE

REUB WOOD

SOFT RUBBER INSECTS

LADYBIRD

CRICKET

WASP

GRASSHOPPER

HOME FLY

HOME FLY

CLEG

BLUE BOTTLE

CATERPILLAR

GRASSHOPPER

BUMBLE BEE

SPIDER

ASSORTED:

List of Artificial Wing Flies Suitable for Trout and Bass.

Alder
Adirondack
Academy
Abbey
Alder
Alexandra
August Dun
Beauty
Bee
Black Prince
Beaverkill
Black Gnat x
Black Drake
Black Moose
Black Ant
Black Hackle (2)
Brown Ant
Brown Hen
Brown Hackle x
Blue Jay x
Brown Alder
Brown Coflin
Bright Fox
Blue Dun
Blue Blow
Blue Miller
Blue Bottle
Blue Professor
Captain
Cinnamon
Cocktail
Claret
Cahill
Canada
Coachman (3)
Royal Coachman
Cooper
Cow Dung (2)
Caldwell
Coch-Y-Bou Dhu
Critchely
Caddis
Dark Fox
Dusty Miller
Deer Fly
Downlooker
Evening Dun
Eptin
Frank
Fern
Ferguson
Furnace
Fox Light
Fox Red

Fox Gray
Fox Dark
Grannon
Green Drake
Gray Drake
Gray Dun
Great Dun
Grey Alder
Grizzly King x
Golden Rod
Golden Spinner
General Hooker
Governor
Grouse
Governor Alvord
Guinea Hen
Ginger Hackle
Gravel Bed
Golden Doctor
Gold Stock
Henry x
Hares Ear
Humble Bee
Hawthorn
House
Ibis
Iron Blue Dun
Jungle Cock
Jennie Lind
Jennie Spinner
June Spinner
King Fisher
King of Waters
Little Egg
Lowery
Lottie
Last Chance
Lord Baltimore
Lake George
March Brown
Magpie
Martin
Montreal Dark x
"   Light
March Brown (2)
Orange Coachman
"   Black
"   Miller
Olive Gnat
Oak
Oriole
Parmachenee Belle
          x
Polka

Poorman
Plum
Professor (3) x
Post
Quaker
Queen of Water x
Dr. Quack
Red Ant
Raven
Royal Coachman x
Rube Wood
Red Spinner
Red Fox
Red Hackle
Red Ibis
Scarlet Ibis x
St Patrick
Seth Green
Silver Docter x
Silver Black
"   Fairy
"   Brown
"   Jungle
"   Stork
Shoemaker
Soldier
Spider
Stone Brown
Shad
Turkey
Tootle Bug
Thistle
Tuxedo
Van Patten
Von Holt
White Miller x
Willow
Widgeon
White Hackle x
"   Moth x
Willow Drake
Wrentail
Woodduck
Wichham Fancy
Yellow Dollie
"   May
"   Sallie
"   Hackle
Zulu
Zulu Chief

X—Means Special Good Flies.

In Choosing Flies–Buy the very best "Reversed Wing" quality.

203

Hackles and Palmers

The difference between a Palmer and Hackle Fly is that on the Palmer the Hackle is tied from the head of a hook and extends the full length of the body, while on the Hackle Fly the Hackle is tied only around the head of the hook.

Black Hackle, Green body.
Black Hackle, Peacock body.
Black Hackle, Black body.
Black Hackle, Red body.
Black Hackle, Yellow body.
Brown Hackle, Green body.
Brown Hackle, Ostrich body.
Brown Hackle, Peacock body.
Brown Hackle, Brown body.
Brown Hackle, Red body.
Brown Hackle, Yellow body.
Green Hackle, Green body.
Gray Hackle, Ostrich body.
Gray Hackle, Peacock body.
Gray Hackle, Red body.
Gray Hackle, Yellow body.
Gray Hackle, Green body.
Grouse Hackle, Peacock body.
Partridge Hackle Orange "
Red Hackle, Red body.
Yellow Hackle, Yellow body.

Black Palmer, Green body.
Black Palmer, Black body.
Black Palmer, Red body.
Black Palmer, Peacock body.
Black Palmer, Yellow body.
Brown Palmer, Brown body.
Brown Palmer, Ostrich body.
Brown Palmer, Red body.
Brown Palmer, Peacock body.
Prown Palmer, Yellow body.
Green Palmer, Green body.
Gray Palmer, Green body.
Gray Palmer, Peacock body.
Gray Palmer, Ostrich body.
Gray Palmer, Red body.
Gray Palmer, Yellow body.
Ginger Palmer, Yellow body.
Grizzly Palmer, Orange body
Red Palmer, Peacock body.
Red Palmer, Yellow body.
Red Palmer, Red body.
White Palmer, White body.
White Palmer, Red body.
Yellow Palmer, Yellow body.

Never economize in the purchase of **Flies**, "they catch the **Fish**." Buy the very best.

"Good Fishing Here About."

"Wa'al I'll be Durn."

"You kan't ketch nothin' with them thar things,
With yarn fer bodies, an' feathers fer wings,
You must think Trout is terrible fools
To be ketched with such outlandish tools.

"An' look at that pole—why, that won't do;
A good, big Trout would bust it in two,
An' never think nothin' ov what he did,
As quick as lightnin' away he slid."

"Well, I'll be durn, you can shoot me dead
Ef here ain't a windlass filled with thread,
An' ther littlest sort ov thread at that—
Why, man, that wouldn't hold a gnat!"

"You'll find a good place over here,
Under ther rapids deep and clear,
You'd better take worms an' er hick'ry pole,
Or you won't ketch nothin', 'pon my soul!"

Sixteen beauties, speckled bright,
The basket bore ere the fall of night,
He counted them o'er on the bank of fern,
And all he said was, "Wa'al—I'll be durn."

ROYAL COACHMAN

The TURKEY BROWN

CAPTIN

Other Favorite Flies.

205

The Lake Trout

This Trout is of gray color, with deep brown spots, and owing to the delicate pink color of its flesh, is often called Salmon Trout. Unlike the Brook Trout, it attains a size and weight from 2 to 20 lbs. The usual method of capture being by trolling, yet it will often take the fly. They take freely a large bait, up to a 4 or 5 inch fish, chub or trolling spoon often secured to a double or treble hook, usually attached to a heavy leader having a

The Lake Trout.

single hook several inches above the gang; this hook passed through both lips of the bait, the others at other portions of the body, and one gang allowed to trail behind; the whole being connected with a strong swivel between the line and leader, in order that no twist of the spinning bait will be communicated to the leader or line. A short fairly stiff rod is often used, preferably a Lancewood or split bamboo, 7 or 8 feet in length and weighing about 8 or 9 ounces. A multiplying reel and 75 to 100 yards of braided silk or linen line, size G or F and if preferred, any of the many trolling baits or spoons. In trolling the boat should be moved slowly; and if you are after murdering the fish, use the gang hook, but if you desire to be sportsmanlike, use only the natural bait and single trolling hook on which is impaled a chub, minnow, small fish or other natural lure.

All devices with gangs of hooks should be discarded as barbarous and unsportsmanlike. Possibly you may kill more fish with the "grappling irons," but if fish is all you are in pursuit of, why not purchase them at the nearest market and thereby save the expenses incident to a trip to angling waters? There is not much enjoyment in the easy achievement of anything; therefore when fishing use tackle that will call for good judgment and

careful manipulation, so that when your fish is finally landed, after a hard struggle, you can men-
tally converse with yourself in thise wise: "Old
fellow you put up a plucky fight and resorted to
all kinds of tricks for liberty, but you have been
fairly beaten and outwitted in a contest wherein
the slightest error on the part of your antagonist
would have given you the liberty."

If this noble fish had been hooked with a double
or treble hook, thereby reducing his chances of
escape to. a minimum regardless of how awkward
ly handled, wherein would be the skill? You might
as well shoot a woodcock or a dog on the ground
and call it sport. Any country boy could do the
same. Having provided yourself with the necessary and suitable tackle the next point for consid-
ation is how to use it, and where are the fish most
likely to be found. It is indispensable to successful trolling that the boat move very slowly, just
fast enough to make the bait spin. A strike at an
artificial bait should be returned immediately so
as not to give the fish time to discover and eject
the lure before hooking him. After he is hooked
a taut line is absolutely indispensable to success.
Let your fish run when he wants to and reel in
when you find him coming towards you; do not
give him slack line for an instant. When he is
sufficiently tired out to give up the fight, reel in
and use your landing net to lift him into the boat.
Be sure he goes into the net head on. In the early part of the season when the water is cold look
for the fish in shallow water, or near the surface of
deep water. When the season advances and the
water grows warm, they will be found in deep water, and to get down to them it is necessary to use
a sinker sufficiently heavy to carry the bait to within three or four feet of the bottom.

Notwithstanding the writer decidedly prefers fly
fishing to any other mode of angling, he is not
averse to trolling, with a single hook, when his efforts to induce the fish to rise to his fly have prov-
en unsuccessful. I know there are anglers who
deem it sacrilege to take trout or salmon otherwise than with fly, and claim they can do this any
month of the open season.

If what I am about to say, should perchance
come to the notice of one such honored member

of the brotherhood of anglers, let him know that it is not for him, nor is it for the angler expert in trolling, but to the uninitiated I would offer a few humble suggestions, with the sincere hope that they may serve, in some small measure at least, to add to the enjoyment of his angling hours. With a proper outfit, trolling is by no means to be despised, as it requires, after the fish is hooked, all the good judgment and careful manipulation necessary in fly fishing. Do not be led astray by the erroneous idea that any kind of a "pole" is good enough for trolling. Your outfit for this way of angling should be selected with just as much care and attention to detail as that used by the fly fisherman. Bargain Counters and cheap John stores are not the places to purchase fishing tackle, and no angler, who fishes *con amore*, should allow the temptation of economy to influence him in his selection of an outfit. Do not misunderstand me, I am not advocating an extravagant expenditure, nor the purchase of fishing tackle at fancy or exorbitant prices, but as the artisan's tools should be made out of good stuff and fashioned to suit his work, so should your fishing rod be manufactured out of the best selected materials, be nicely

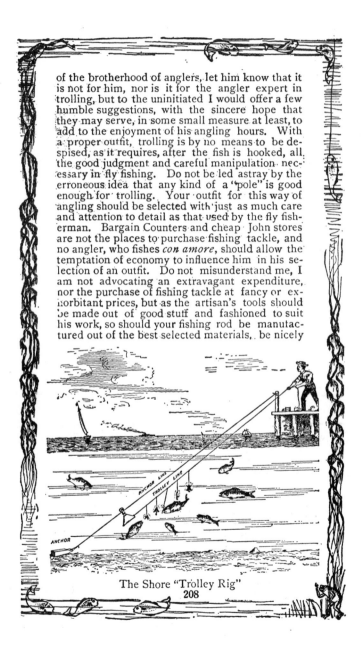

The Shore "Trolley Rig"
208

balanced, of suitable length and weight, and so fashioned to embody all the requirements that go to make up a weapon that will give the best results and not disappoint when put to the test of exacting service.

The Salmon

This magnificent fish be well named "King of Fish" for it is one of the noblest and strongest on which the angler can essay his art. It is bred in waters or rivers in close proximity to the sea. Has a blue black color, silvery sides and a white belly. It can be caught with either bait or spoon, but is considered far more sportsmanlike to be caught with the fly.

In the month of August they ascend the rivers and wallow by a movement of their bodies, a hole in the gravel of river beds, where the female deposits her spawn; the male then covers it with his milt, and after covering them deep with the pebbles and sand, desert it; early next spring these are young "smolt" and the following year are good large fish and fine eating; when they thus attain a weight of 2 to 6 lbs. they are termed "grilse."

After depositing its spawn the adult fish later hastes to the sea, before winter sets in, returning periodically year after year in the spring to the same waters.

By a peculiar gift of nature they can by bending their bodies, like a cane bent to a circle and suddenly let go; after a sudden rush, by the rebound leap high into the air, over obstacles, and clear of water falls, to a considerable height; and the fortunate observer of these "salmon leaps" are amazed at their sagacity and perseverance, for often a dozen trials are necessary before success crowns their remarkable efforts. The growth of young Salmon is rapid, probably increasing its weight twenty to thirty times the first summer, it is then termed a "smolt' and is ready to go to sea; when they return.in spring from the sea, as stated before they are termed "grilse." Some ideas of the immense number of them can be formed when it is known that in the Columbia river alone, millions of them are taken every year, and the supply is still on the increase.

Salmon are fond of deep waters and usually swim near the bottom, yet they will readily rise to the surface and take any spoon or fly deftly offered or observed by them; and a single day's good Salmon angling with the fly, furnishes enough to talk about for a year; as to forgeting it, if ever fishing made a man talk in his sleep, Salmon fishing will do it.

Reader if you have ever caught on the fly and played a fighty three pound Trout or Bass, just magnify and think what it would be had it been a 10 or 20 pounder, and you have it in a nutshell; and those that have mastered the art can be reckoned in Fish Freemasonry as Past Grand Masters of the art. For equipment nothing short of the best is needed, both hands and all the brains nature has given you; for the rod, the best split Bamboo is none too good, it should be double-handed and measure from 13 to 15 feet, weighing from 15 to 20 ounces. The reel should be large(4½ inch disk), the line hard braided strong silk, 100 to 125 yards, size C, B, or D, leader extra strong, 9 feet in length, and the most guady, brightest colored flies you can find in a well filled Salmon fly book.

In taking the fly, Salmon do not rush at it, and if the angler strikes as promptly as in Trout fishing, he is apt to pull the hook away and his chance for Salmon meat is gone, for rarely will they rise twice to the same. When then he takes the fly give him time to go head toward the bottom, (which they invariably do) then strike easily so as to hook him good, bearing in mind that perhaps 10 to 20 pounds dead weight is below the hook, and you need your tackle for subsequent proceedings. The instant he feels the hook look out for a panic, for he suddenly remembers a date way down stream, and like a flash goes to make the date good. Often he dashes through the water for a distance of 60 to 90 feet, compelling the angler to reel out the bulk of his line; leaping out of the waters, in a vain attempt to rid himself of the hook, and finding that force and swift running will not do it, he often has recourse to cunning, and will endeavor to rub or drag it out by rubbing his nose on the sharp rocks at the bottom. When these leaps are made the angler should give slack line, taking it in as quickly as he touches water again, and keeping whenever possible a fairly taut line, until by sheer strength the fish has exhausted himself. When unable to resist any longer, he is led toward shore or rock, where the attendant or guide stands crouched with the gaff, waiting for an opportunity to land him; and as the fish is near him, the hook is carefully extended and gripped, when he is dragged to terra firma. A blow on the head between the eyes usually ends his life.

In Salmon fishing there are certain spots in rivers called casts, where Salmon are known to rest or feed; these may be a simple ledge, or they may extend for 20 to 50 feet or more. Often too they can be seen sporting or jumping about; but where for some reason they never feed or take the fly; and the angler who studies or knows these casts has a great advantage, as he can thus avoid these barren spots. In fishing a cast the angler casts across or down stream, drawing the fly up stream toward him, raising or lowering the tip of his rod so as to check and loosen the fibres of the fly alternately, so as to properly counterfeit fly life. When the Salmon rises to the fly he usually makes a big bulge or boil on the water, or if he is eager and hungry throws his head and portion of his body above the surface, rolling over like a porpoise in his endeavor to grasp it; and the worst the angler can do is to pull it away from him, by imagining it is time to strike. If he misses it, give him a second chance, as they invariably turn around and angrily make the second snatch at it that rarely fails. In Salmon angling no two casts are alike, so each angler must fish to suit conditions; long casts are generally unnecessary, 40 to 50 yards being ample.

Grilse and Salmon Flies

Black Dose x
Black Fairy x
Brown
Bob Sweep
Brown Dog
Butcher x
Donkey x
Dusty Miller x
Durham Ranger x
Canary x
Brown Fairy x
Fiery Brown x
Green Grouse
Green Parrot
Green King
Green Well
Gray Monkey
Harlequin x
Helmsdale
Hopdog
Hornet
Indian Crow
Jackers
Jeanie
Jockie
Jock Scott x
John Ferguson x
Judge
Kate
Killer
Lady Caroline
Lascelles
Laxford
Lemon Monkey
Lion
Lhanover
Logie
Mallard Silver

Major x
Murderer x
Marquis of Lorne
Mohair Yellow
Mcrgan
Murray
Mystery x
Nicholson
Niger
North Lynne
Orange & Grouse x
O'Donoghue
Old Blue
Olive (4)
Owen More
Parson x
Policeman
Poynder
Pointer
Popham x
Powell's Fancy
Prince William x
Pride of Aberdeen
Prince of Wales x
Princess Louise
Priest
Purple King
Rainbow
Red and Blue
Sapper
Scottish Chief
Shrimp
Shannon
Silver Bell
Silver Doctor x
Silver Gray x
Joch Scott x
Sir Archibald

Sir Frances Sykes
Sir Richard
Snow Fly
Smoky Dun
Smith
Spey Dog
Spring Grub
Salmon
Stevenson
Stunner
Switching Sandy
Tartan
Tait's Fancy
Thunder x
Thorney Dyke
Tom Tickler
Troi Camps
Tyne Doctor
Water Witch
Welshman
White Wing
White Tip
White Doctor x
Wilkenson.
Yellow Prince
Romeo
Juliet
Countess
Amazon
Gipsy
Rooster
Raven
Pyramid
Cock Robin

Those being marked x being considered unusually good killing flies.

Outfit for Salmon or Grilse, Etc.

13 to 15 ft. Salmon rod 15 to 22 oz.
Quadruple multiplying reel (Salmon size.)
100 to 125 yds. fine silk hard braided or linen line.
3 doz. assorted fine Salmon flies (special) and book.
3 9 ft. Salmon leaders (fine gut.)
3 assorted Salmon spoons, 1 gimp or cable leader.
150 to 200 ft. Salmon line No. 9 (on reel.)
1 marble automatic gaff.
1 tackle box.
1 doz. hooks Sproat assorted sizes swivels and sinkers.

About Bass. (The Black Bass, 1 to 6 lbs.)

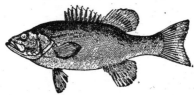

Dr. Henshall in his famous work on these fish, entitled the "Book of the Black Bass," and his other equally famous work "More of the Black Bass," call these the "King of Game Fish" or the "Bulldog of the Waters." Certain is it that it can be classed with the "best of them." (Yet there are others.) It is an unusually finny fighter, as many a pickerel twice its size has found out to its cost. It is one of the most greedy fish known, and, like the proverbial Irishman green enters chiefly into its color, in various localities of its body, with a white belly, and in form is short and chunky. There are two varieties, small and large mouthed black bass, either of which can put up a "battle royal." They invariably take the bait with a rush and when it finds itself hooked, it will rush a little more to get rid of it, and will spring out far and clear into the air, and shake himself fiercely in his vicious effort to jerk out the hook. Even at the last moment, like the ingenious possum, it will feign death and make a final and terrific rush for liberty at the moment of landing requiring much skill of the angler to prevent it from accomplishing its purpose, hence it is called a tricky fish. As stated before they take almost any bait readily either natural or artificial.

For live bait use Helgramite, frogs, (small green ones) crawfish or minnows; a 9-foot rod, multiplying reel, F size silk line, hard braided, 6-foot strong leader and No. 1 or 2 hook.

For Trolling—What is known as the Revolution bait. Evolution or No. 4 spoon baits are excellent, or the bucktail or bass spinners, any of these are most remarkable baits, provided they are well made on scientific and fish principles; and for the benefit of my readers I illustrate the most desirable and well known styles only.

It is, however, well known, that bass take freely any bait, and it should be remembered if live is used, as in minnow casting, that as fish take live bait head first, time should be given for the fish to stop and swallow the bait. Then and not before should the strike be made. Don't strike the instant you feel the bite, lest you yank the bait from his mouth and sacrifice it. Give him time to gorge it first, then do your strike skillfully. If using minnows keep them in deep water near the bottom. If using crawfish keep them on the bottom just as they live, as its natural.

If Bass Runs—Under your boat strike its bottom with your foot. The sound magnified largely in water will soon drive him away and quickly.

In Fly Fishing for Bass—Occasionally allow you flies, which should be shotted, to sink a trifle under the surface when desired and select the most gaudy flies—the brightest in all your book and in fly fishing strike the instant you note the bite. Let it tug and earn hard very inch of the line you give him. If it leaps into the air lower the tip of your rod, so as to slack the line a trifle, while it is in the air, retrieving the slack with the rod tip the instant it reaches water again. This is the critical time and must be met promptly by the angler or "lost fish" or something else will surely result.

In Fly Casting for Bass

Cast so as the flies will light on the waters as quietly and life like as possible, then skip them along the surface zigzag way, letting them once in a while, sink a trifle below the surface, especially in the most likely spots. If the waters are running swift, let your flies float with it, then skitter them on the surface back again to the recast, casting over the same spot several times so as to coax them to rise. When Bass bite eagerly, whip the stream, by repeating the casts rapidly, first one side then the other, allowing the flies always though to light easily, never however permitting slack line, as with a fairly taut line the fish will invariably hook himself when he strikes. Cast below rapids and ripples, over pools and eddies, along the edge of weeds, grass, under projecting banks or near drift wood, off shoals or long points of land; don't fish long in long deep reaches of water. The best time is from sundown to dark or on moonlight nights, on streams an hour or two; after sunrise of warm weather is good, if dark, cloudy days, any time is good. Bright, hot sunny places and times should be avoided. When you see or feel a rise strike at once, lest he spit it out or reject it, as fish often will, and lead your fish to deeper waters so as to play him. Don't hurry to land him, the harder and longer he fights the more sport there is in it. When he breaks water, lower the tip of your rod and assume that taut line the moment he strikes water.

In Bait Fishing for Bass—Use a bright small minnow, and don't strike until he has the bait well in his mouth, feel him first, and when he has had time to gorge the bait, then strike. If still waters, sink your minnows near to bottom, in rapid waters nearer the surface.

Fishing for Bass—In any waters is best attended with success when the surface of the water is ruffled by breezes. This is so in any fishing, but especially so in bass waters. It is poor time to labor for bass in smooth or very still waters unless they are unusually hungry.

Among Bass Flies the Most Successful Are—Scarlet or Red Flies, Tipperlin, Bucktail, Ferguson, Henshall, Cheney, Seth Green, Jungle Cock, Grizzly King, Oriole, Baltimore, Premier, Blue Bottle, Imperial, Black and Gold, La Belle, Montreal, Coachman, Manchester, Professor, Black Maria, Henry, Frank, Epting, Gray Hackle, Queen of the Waters, Royal, Silver Doctor, White Miller, Fitzmaurice, Black Prince, Polka, Yellow Sallie, Kippe, Reuben Wood.

It is to be noted that one dozen of each flies makes an ample assortment, although by many a well filled fly book often containing three to six dozen is carried, yet it is doubtful if those fortunate possessors of six dozen or more, catch any more fish than the more prudent angler whose book contains "just the dozen and no more" of good bass flies.

In fishing for bass look out for a partner. When you catch one, as during the summer they mate and two then usually travel together, hence it is wise to cast again over the same spot or thereabouts for still another one.

Size and weight of Black Bass, in inches.

9 inches	1 lb.
10 inches	1 lb. 2 oz.
11 inches	1 lb. 6 oz.
12 inches	2 lbs.
14 inches	3 lbs.
15 inches	4 lbs.

The Pickerel

This fish is usually found in grassy streams, ponds and marshy waters, It is yellow and green in color, long flat head, formidable jaws and teeth and is extremely rapacious. · For its capture skittering and trolling are most successful, but should be given time to swallow the bait if skittering method be employed. It usually gives a spasmodic effort when first hooked or hurt, but allows himself to be brought easily to the boat, before making any serious attempt at

escape; when up to the boat or after capture, it awakens to a sense of activity when too late to be of service. Spoon bait trolled from a boat is the common method used in its capture; yet it will take anything presented to it that is of an eatable form. It preys on its own specie and is always hungry for more; it is an enemy to everything that swims, is a most destructive fish, and not to be even classed as the best of eating, owing to its bony condition.

Midsummer they are in their worst form, but later especially during winter they are excellent; in the spring they go to spawning near the banks and bogs, especially where a deep, muddy bottom is found. At this time a favorite method of catching immense quantities of Pickerel is by night spearing, in a boat provided with a light or fire of some kind, spearing them when seen. In winter a dark tent or house box is placed on the ice ponds and the interior darkened; a hole is then cut in the ice so as to observe the fish, which is lured to within spear point by means of a decoy minnow.

Pickerel Spearing in Winter

The Tip-Up.

As illustrated above or by a simpler method called the "tip up." A number of these contrivances being used through the ice at various points, bait being used, either live fish or meat. When the fish bites or is hooked, the weight tips up the pole and signals the catch. Another method for various species, being to have a bright fire of pitch pine near the bow of a boat on some suitable iron or heavy wire frame, when the fish are speared as they show themselves. Brook and lake Trout are by both methods, caught in large quantities; but the method is unsportsmanlike, and is referred to here simply as I desire to illustrate the various methods in catching fish.

They are also taken by "bait casting" as described elsewhere, a method often practiced in fishing for

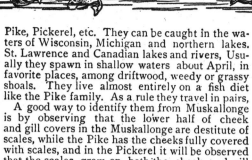

Pike, Pickerel, etc. They can be caught in the waters of Wisconsin, Michigan and northern lakes. St. Lawrence and Canadian lakes and rivers, Usually they spawn in shallow waters about April, in favorite places, among driftwood, weedy or grassy shoals. They live almost entirely on a fish diet like the Pike family. As a rule they travel in pairs,

A good way to identify them from Muskallonge is by observing that the lower half of cheek and gill covers in the Muskallonge are destitute of scales, while the Pike has the cheeks fully covered with scales, and in the Pickerel it will be observed that the scales grow on both the cheek and gill covers.

In early spring they are particularly fond of sunning themselves, but as the summer heat increases they seek bottom waters and stay there. The best bait for Pickerel is a chub, at least four inches long and a fat one; and let me say here, that of all baits, chubs can live about as long as any bait known if handled right; hence they are a most desirable bait. In hot weather the Pickerel takes the bait lazily, but in the spring or fall it goes after it with more of a rush. The weight of these fish range from 1 to 5 lbs. (average.)

They spawn early in spring and frequent the weeds about shoal waters.

Almost any tackle will do for Pickerel fishing, and almost any bait—a piece of skin of fat pork, minnow or frog, small mouse, or large gaudy flies allowed to sink a trifle beneath the surface, or skittered over them (large Bass Flies are excellent.) When hungry they will grab at almost anything that is bright or has motion, a good bait being a small lively green frog, or a bucktail; the moment it hits the water it should be kept on the move, and skittered around about rushes, grass, etc. from boat to shore always. They will often bite for pure viciousness. (See Art of Bait Casting, etc.)

In Trolling Deep Waters

Weight the end of your main line with a heavy weedless or snag proof sinker (egg shape;) at different intervals attach by means of swivels, your trolling lines and baits, several feet or more apart, so as to troll bottoms, deep and mid-waters, (See illustration) at one and the same time.

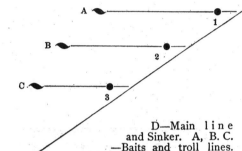

D—Main line and Sinker. A, B. C. —Baits and troll lines. 1, 2, 3.—Swivels and troll lines attached to main line.

The Pike

Much the same methods are to be observed in Pike and Pickerel fishing as for Muscallonge, and is usually caught by trolling or skittering, using either a bright spoon or any other baited hook. Even a white and red rag will suffice, as they are

extremely ravenous, hence are termed the fresh water wolf and will bite at almost anything offered them from a piece of China crockery to bright pieces of jagged tin or colored rag. So extremely rapacious are these fish that they have been known to swallow fish of its own kind so large that a portion of it remained in his mouth while that in his stomach was digested. I, myself, have seen time and time again, in their stomach those of a size but a few inches less. It loves extreme solitude and fears not to be seen even; while their bite is more or less poisonous. They mate and spawn early in spring only, and often can be seen thus in shallow waters in the mud to sun themselves where they are at times caught by spearing in large numbers. They usually inhabit or frequent the weedy grass spots, where Pickerel weed is plenty and are extremely fond of young frogs.

The Wall Eyed Pike

So named owing to the peculiar dead or white appearance of its eyes. It is best taken with trolling spoons; live baits, minnows, frogs, crawfish or white fish meat, etc. Use about the same tackle as for large Trout or Bass or any good

spoon of proper size for trolling. It is a wandering fish and is usually to be found any place. It puts up a good, stiff fight and is to be reckoned a good fish all round. It is a bottom feeder and is extremely voracious. They are usually trolled for in waters 30 to 40 feet deep, the lines being weighted by sinkers. Best time for fishing May and June. Usually found in deep waters, mouths of creeks, inlets and oftimes in shallow waters.

The Muskallonge

This is the largest and handsomest of the Pike family, and is often captured 4 to 5 feet in length, weighing over 30 to 40 lbs. In color it is silver gray, while its back and sides are dotted with brown spots. It has a very large mouth filled with unusually long and sharp teeth, hence it is often called the Shark of fresh waters. The early spring and fall months are best for its capture, May, June and September especially. It is by nature one of the hungriest and most vicious fishes that swims, attacking anything that may come within its reach, that can be swallowed and used for food. Its favorite places are usually in the grass or at the edge of reeds, rushes, etc. For their capture a short trolling rod, 100 yards of strong E or No. 3 line and a No. 7, 8 or 9 spoon are used, to which is attached live bait or a strip of meat, or a fine chub 4 or 5

inches long, being unusually successful. Direct your boat, and spoon or bait around, deep, dense growths of reeds, banks, grasses, etc., fairly deep in the water, letting out sufficient line to keep the bait moving or spinning, 75 to 100 feet behind the boat. When the Muskallonge sees it, he will invariably sieze the bait and go down to swallow it. Give him a little time to gorge the bait then strike, and have your boat pulled for deeper waters. When a Muskallonge is hooked it feels as though a Whale was on the line, for he pulls with the strength of a Sampson, and thus failing to dislodge the hook, he will often rush and shoot out of the waters in his efforts to get away; struggling, jerking, jumping, pulling and fighting until exhausted. The faster the boat is rowed the better the chances of drowning or exhausting your fish, as he swims and fights when hooked, with mouth wide open. The favorite method of finishing these large fish is to shoot them before gaffing, as they are a very heavy strong fish, and can at the last moment like all fish, make a terrific effort to escape.

Bullheads, Catfish

An excellent pan or table fish called a bottom fish, very common in most waters; easy to catch. It clings to life more than any other fish and as it lives on the bottom the baits used must be sunk deep. I do not desire to go deeply into the subject of them as their habits are most generally well known. They bite freely, almost anything and swallow the bait; their peculiar horn projections close to the mouth, often making unhooking them a difficult matter unless a hook extractor be used. They are capable of living a long time after being taken from the water. It is also a vegetarian fish and frequents muddy bottoms, taking almost any hook or bait offered them. Average size 1 to 3 lbs. up to the 50-lb. Catfish of Ohio and Mississippi water. Raw liver or worms is excellent bait for Catfish. A splendid time to catch them being at night.

White and Yellow Perch

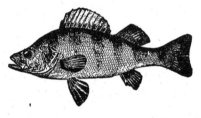

One of the easiest fish to capture. It is an unusually bold biter and peculiarly enough, are good free biters at all times of the day; and no matter how many are caught in the one spot, they can be hauled out one after the other with impunity, as they are in no way timorous. I have myself seen a boy fall overboard in the vicinity of good Perch fishing, and despite the floundering, good fishing went on just the same but a few minutes after. They usually swim in large shoals, and when Perch are biting, swarms of people in the neighorhood of large cities, invariably get all good size strings. Worms being the usual and most fitting bait, and a simple 10 cent outfit of tackle is as good as the best. Usually a light Bamboo pole about 10 feet long, and 20 to 30 feet of line is used, with a small float and a No. 2, 3 or 4 hook with a small sinker a few inches above the hook, so as to keep the bait heavy and about a foot from the bottom. Yellow Perch are often fished for in the winter, by cutting holes in the ice. It is a bony fish but good eating.

SALT WATER FISH

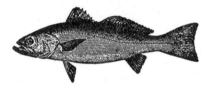

Weakfish

These fish are the most timid of salt water fish; the least noise will scare them off. Keep away from other boats so as to avoid their noises. Weakfish are not bottom swimmers, although at times they run deep. Use a good flexible rod, and as their mouths are tender, don't strike hard. Any light tackle will do, as used for Trout, Bass, etc. They bite hard and usually with a rush, hooking themselves they then pull hard· and rush about, but only at intervals. If they nibble don't strike until you feel your fish.

In weakfish "chumming" is essential. This is done by chopping up fine mussels, crabs, clams, shrimp, porgies and casting a handful over the boat occasionally. (Shells and all) this will draw all kinds of fish about you and usually you can never tell what you will get—a shark, dogfish, skate, sea bass, blackfish, rock crabs or flounders, porgies or menhaden. June to October is the best season, but the hottest months are best. Find big fish on the surf or open ocean, smaller fish in channels and flats of bays, creeks, inlets, etc. Use leaded or pearl squid and fish near the surface, using No. 4-0 Sproat hook, 1 to 2 ounce sinkers for trolling or deep waters and split shot and float for light tide fishing. Half tide is best or ebbing tide in deep waters, flood tide· in shallow water. Use any light tackle.

The Sheepshead

A rather homely fish, but excellent eating; usually found around old wrecks, shell covered docks, spiles, reefs, etc. Clams, Hermit Crabs or Shedder Crab is good bait; send your bait to the bottom and twitch slowly your bait to keep it moving and resting on and off the bottom alternately; best time July to October. Use No. 1 or 2 Sproat hook and sinker. When hooked they invariably allow themselves to be drawn to the surface, then make a terrific plunge and struggle, as though they then realized their danger, and keep up the fight until played out and landed. They weigh 2 to 8 or 10 pounds.

Bluefish

"Chumming" for Bluefish is essential to success to a marked extent, as in Weakfish they are ravenous biters and it is well to wire the hook lest he bite and sever the leader and line from the hook. Fish near the surface water, using a float or allowing your bait and hook to drift with the tide.

If using floats let them be about 3 or 4 feet from the hook. Very strong tackle should be

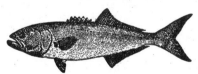

used and No. 3-0 to 5-0 Sproat Hook wired. Use a large piece of menhaden squid or moss bunker for bait and fish in the "oil slick" of your chumming, drifting with it. Season June to November. Open sea, surf or bays. Flood tide best in bays or surf. Always keep a taut line. If fishing for small fish about 3 to 5 lbs. use a No. 3-0 or 4-0 hook. If still fishing "chumming" must be kept up. Bluefish run heavy and pull unmercifully so wear gloves. It is an unusually savage fish and has powerful jaws and teeth. In trolling the pearly squid trolling hooks and a copper wire swiveled leader is best. It rushes with fury and a line in an ungloved or soft hand will cut deep into the flesh if you are not careful. If possible engage a small catrigged boat and seek deeper waters.

In the winter months they migrate to the south and appear in eastern waters about June. If a rod is used choose a 7-ft. fairly stiff one, 120 yds. of strong linen line and a good multiplying reel, with a good gaff to land your fish. Young Bluefish (snappers) bite quickly and any light ordinary tackle will suffice. A glittering small spoon or small piece of tin or tin foil attracts them. They are surface feeders, thus bait should only be sunk a little below the surface. For bait use killies, shedder, crab or their own flesh with shiny skin left on. It is an unusually destructive fish.

The King Fish

This is a bottom fish peculiar to the eastern coast waters. Although a small fish it is a splendid fighter, hence its name. It is usually captured in the summer months in eastern salt waters; feeding on Shrimp, Crabs, etc., and it is obvious that this is excellent bait for use in its capture. Almost any light tackle will suffice.

Flounders

Choose rich mud bottoms, in February, March, April, October, November months, avoiding hot weather; as they often lie imbedded in the mud, in cold weather, it is necessary to stir them up, using an oar or rake (oyster or garden rake) and scrape them from the bottom, around the boat. A good way is to fish near oystermen; when thus disturbed they fall to feeding. Sand worms, clam bait or angle worms are excellent bait. When you feel your fish, strike, but as they at times only suck in the bait, be careful not to yank it out of the mouth. If using sand worms for bait, keep them in dry seaweed moistened only. Use No. 6 to 8 Sproat hooks, and line with sinker. Flood tide in shallow waters and ebb tide in deep waters is best.

Blackfish (Tantog, Bergalls, etc.)

These fish are bottom feeders. Their choicest food being barnacles or shell fish that cling to piles along wharves, rocks, wrecks, etc. In such places care must be taken not to let the fish run so as to entangle him among the old dead timbers. They have a tough mouth and it is necessary to strike hard. Use a fairly stiff, common rod, line and sinker so as your line will rest on or close to the bottom. Use No. 3 to 5 Blackfish hooks and for bait sand or angle worms, clams, (hard portion) and fiddler or shedder crabs are excellent. Fishing at flood tide is best. They range in weight from 2 to 20 lbs. Season from April to November.

It has a large eye, big head, abundance of fins, large scales and a small mouth, and can both tug and pull with gusto.

Striped Bass

A most cunning and wary fish, easily frightened. In trolling, a bright spinner spoon is effective if played a few feet under the surface of the waters. Night fishing time is best; season, April to November in bays, August to October in surf. At times they refuse any baits, and will often swim or

school together on the surface, at other times will feed there; again often running near the bottom. In creeks, bays, inlets, etc. fish close to banks. In trolling use a No. 3 or 5 spoon and let your bait be carried along by the tide so as to strike all cross currents. Use No. 1-0 to 2-0 Sproat hooks; large 2 or 3 oz. sinker for surf casting; 2 oz. sinker for bottom still fishing and split shot for creeks. If surf fishing, long casts are essential from 100 to 150 feet, using for bait, Shrimp, Shedder, Crab, Menhaden, small Eels or worms securely fastened to hooks.

if fly fishing use bright, gaudy colored flies and sink them below surface; try the edges of shoals, over flats that rising waters have covered, near the junction of fresh and salt waters, in shallow bottom places, and is useless to try fly fishing in very deep waters.

Sea Bass

Another bottom feeder found in open sea, bays, inlets and creeks; favorite haunts near mussel bottoms, banks, reefs, around wrecks, etc. Use No. 3 to No. 2-0 Sproat hooks, at first and last of ebb tide or flood tide, using Shrimp, Shedder Crab, Mossbunker or Clam bait, or Killies. They often play with or feel the bait, and again at times take it with a rush; give them time (unless they strike hard at your bait) to gulp it. Like the Weak fish their mouths are very tender, hence it is unnecessary to strike hard. A little red or scarlet flannel tied to upper shank of hook is attractive to them, or use a Pearl Squid. Fish for them a few feet from the bottom, always fishing deep. They haunt also the banks of creeks and inlets. It is found that the point of the hook exposed is good in Sea Bass fishing. Best months, August to October. They like to frequent the borders of very shallow and deep waters; they rarely come to the surface, so always choose the deeper waters.

Fluke Fish

The Pickerel of salt water fish; extremely voracious and always hungry. Like the Pike he seizes the bait and lies still to swallow and enjoy it. When you feel your fish handle the line gently so as the fish fearing he will lose the bait will snap at it and thus take the hook. For bait use live killies, shedder and crab fastened to No. 2-0 or 4-0 Sproat hook. If killies are used fasten them through the lips and allow them to swim about near the bottom or to float off with the tide. June to November are the best months. Try the Bottoms of sandy bays, creeks, or in the surf or open ocean waters.

The Tarpon or Silver King

The fame of the game-fishes of the State of Florida extends throughout America, and beyond. Wherever there are anglers and rod and fishing clubs, the prowess of the "Silver King" is known and talked about. The one great hope of every angler is that he may go to Florida and kill a Tarpon before his fishing days are over. But while

the Tarpon or Silver King is the king of game-fishes of this state, it is by no means the only game-fish. Some of the largest Black Bass known have been caught in Florida waters. The Sunfishes are the largest of their kind. The Ladyfish and Bonefish are thought by many to equal their relative, the Tarpon, in game qualities. Trolling for Kingfish, Jack, Crevallé, Bluefish, Spanish Mackerel, and Spotted Sea Trout, at Indian River, Lake Worth, Key West, or Biscayne Bay, furnishes sport of the most exciting kind; while still fishing for Sheephead and Mangrove Snappers at Indian River Inlet; for Chubs, Porgies, Porkfish, Yellow Tails, Snappers and Grunts at Key West; or for Red Snappers, Red Groupers, and others of their kin on the Snapper Banks, furnishes sufficient variety to please any angler, in whatever mood he may chance to be.

There is no other place in the United States where one can study live fishes so satisfactorily as at Key West. Fishing boats are lying at the fish wharf at all times and in their wells may be seen specimens of numerous species, many of them of brilliant coloration; and by going out with the fishermen upon the bars and coral reefs one may, by the aid of a water glass, spend many hours observing and studying a multitude of fishes and other interesting forms as they disport themselves in the clear waters beneath the boat.

As the Tarpon is one of the largest and best of game fish I deem it fitting to give it mention. Yet there are 500 species of other fish in Florida waters.

This large fish often reaching 100 lbs. in weight and 3 to 6 ft. in length is a native of the Florida waters and is possessed naturally of great strength and fighting qualities, despite the fact, however, those of immense size are caught with rod and line by enthusiastic anglers or fishermen. It is covered with large scales, which owing to their silvery color has given the fish the name of Silver King.

For their capture a strong 6 ft. rod is often used. Several hundred yards of very strong line and a Tarpon hook, baited with fish or small mullet. Owing to its immense strength and agility they are permitted to tow the boat around when hooked and to carry off unusual amount of line. Often they will leap from the water and rush in every conceivable direction until finally exhausted or killed. When fishing for Tarpon, however, in these waters one is apt to secure on the line everything except what they are after as Shark, Red Drum, Sheepshead, Skip Jacks, as these all frequent the water in abundance.

In fishing for Tarpon allow them to run with the bait, so as to gorge it before striking.

"Playing the Fish."

230

Sailors, Anglers and Fishermens Knots, Hitches, Etc.

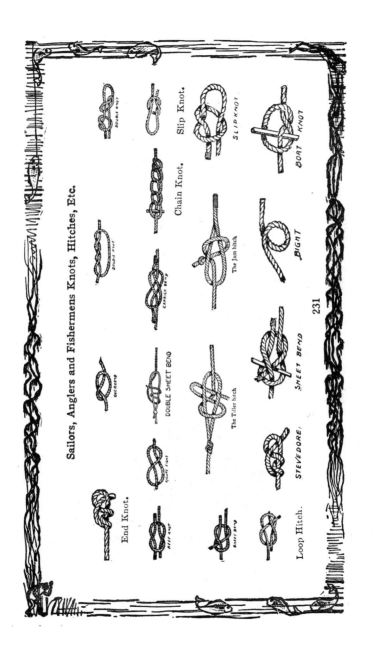

End Knot.

Chain Knot.

Slip Knot.

DOUBLE SHEET BEND

Loop Hitch.

STEVEDORE.

SHEET BEND

The Tiller hitch

The Jam hitch

BIGHT

SLIP KNOT

BOAT KNOT

DOUBLE KNOT

REEF KNOT

BOAT BEND

OVERHAND

CARRICK BEND

231

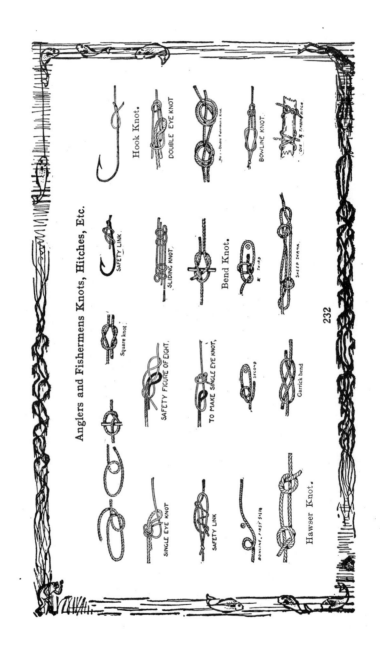

Anglers and Fishermens Knots, Hitches, Etc.

Hook Knot.

DOUBLE EYE KNOT

No. 1.—Double Fisherman's Knot.

BOWLINE KNOT.

OUR BIG TIMBER HITCH

SAFETY LINK.

SLIDING KNOT.

Bend Knot.

IT TIRED

SHEEP SHANK.

Square knot.

SAFETY FIGURE OF EIGHT.

TO MAKE SINGLE EYE KNOT,

SECOND

BOWLINE, FIRST STEP

Garrick bend

SINGLE EYE KNOT

SAFETY LINK

Hawser Knot.

232

Splices, Hitches and Bends.

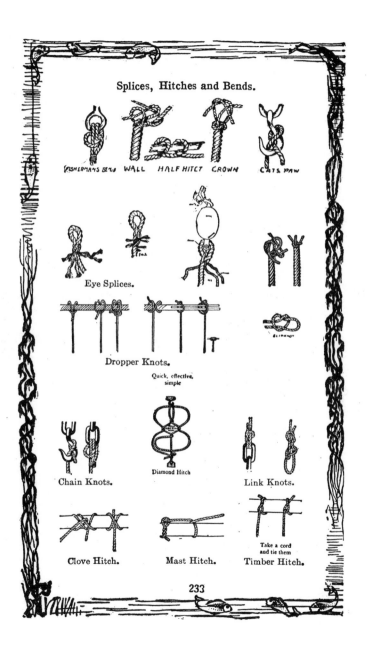

FISHERMAN'S BEND   WALL   HALF HITCT   CROWN   CATS PAW

Eye Splices.

Dropper Knots.

Quick, effective, simple

Chain Knots.

Diamond Hitch

Link Knots.

Clove Hitch.   Mast Hitch.   Take a cord aud tie them   Timber Hitch.

233

Wrinkles and Kinks
for Fishermen, Anglers, Etc.

Keep Angle Worms, (not in a Tin Can) but in a small porous earthen jar (very small flower pot) fill it not with mud or dirt, but green moss. wet. If fed with the white of a hard boiled egg, placed therein, or a teaspoonful of cream or bruised celery, they will assume a pink color, live long and be attractive. Don't drown them in mud as most do. Cover hole in bottom with a piece of the pot.

A Splendid Bait—Are live maggots taken from meat that is fly blown. Anglers will do well not to despise the hitherto considered repulsive maggot, if kept in a small box, with corn meal; there is no more objection to handling them, than any worm or other slimy bait; try it once and be convinced.

In Early Spring—Use very small Midge flies, when trout fishing.

Carry and Dry Your Flies—By sticking them under your hat band, or around it; a few dozen can be accommodated thus, keeping them safely and drying them when needed.

Don't Use too Big Flies or Hooks.—Better small than too large; big fish will take a small hook, but little ones can't take a large one.

Fish Scent or Lure—A little assafoetida, oil of anise or sweet sicily; a drop pinched in your bait, will attract fish, to it.

Don't Blame the Fish—For not biting, or taking the fly. Perhaps you're to blame. Think over conditions and inspect your bait or tackle.

The Difficult Places—To fish are just where the fish are.

Old Fish—Like new flies. Young fish take old ones.

234

Fish Wardens—When you catch thieves cut off all their pants *buttons*. They can't run well and hold up their pants at the same time.

Kill Every Water Snake—You find. They eat millions of fish eggs every year.

To Keep Fish Alive—Use a fish bag, even a gunny sack, with small slits on its top and centre.

To Find Worms—Choose a manure pile or after a heavy rain, when they crawl to the surface of the ground.

Take Your Wife—Along on your fishing trips. She will surely enjoy it, or else take ——

Choosing Flies.—Choose the smaller ones every time.

Fly Blown Meats—Suspended over a trout or fish hole drops the maggots continually in the water. This attracts fish to that vicinity.

Oil Reels—With good clock oil, *not* watch oil.

Red Chubs—Or black striped minnows are excellent bait.

To Attract Minnows—Throw fresh meat bones refuse in shallow waters or likely places, it keeps them hovering around it.

Fishing at Night—Is fishing right. Fish'ng midday hardly pays. Dark days are best, they say.

Clean Utensils—Used in cooking fish (when hot using sand and water), scouring it hard before you cook meats, vegetables, etc.

Frogging at Night.—Take a very bright light, locate your frog, and turn the light on him squarely. It dazzles him and you can pick him up like a potato. Don't think he'll jump away; the light confuses him and he forgets himself.

In Casting for Bass—Choose the edge of lily pads, weeds, rushes, etc. Pickerel also.

Fish Scratches or Wounds.—Use common salt and vinegar, or suck them well and put a chew of tobacco around it and bind it on.

Never Let Your Shadow—Be observed by fish you are after. Get behind a tree, bank, or cut a few branches so as to hide yourself behind them, or lay in the high grass and crawl to the most likely spots, especially in trout fishing.

Never Use Pork Rind.—Except in trolling. Use the white fat meat instead and shape either as near to a minnow or frog as possible.

A Complete Camp Cook Book.—Have you a copy. If not send 10c. for the "Complete Campers Manual." Covers all subjects. 136 pages, 200 illustrations, by "Buzzacott," Chicago, Ill., U. S. A.

If Wading or Your Clothes are Wet.—Keep moving and there is no danger of a chill.

Always Carry a File.—A small one to sharpen the barbs of your hooks. Examine them often to see that they are sharp.

Keep Your Spoons Bright.—Revolving spoons can be scoured with tobacco ashes or wood ashes, polish them with a dry rag and elbow grease.

Brass or Copper Spoons.—Vinegar and salt will instantly clean and brighten them if rubbed hard with a rag dipped in above, then polished with a dry one.

To Kill Fish.—Hit them between the eyes with a club, stick of wood, knife handle, etc.

Fish Killed at Once—As soon as caught, keep better, and the flesh remains firmer and better all around.

Catch Frogs.—Use hook and line, and piece of red or scarlet rag. Keep only for bait the little ones, the large ones, use their hind quarters and fry and eat them. Excellent.

Keep Frogs—In a perforated box, with a little moist grass, they need no water at all, and will keep in a cool place without food or drink for a week or more, simply drench them once or twice a day only.

Keep Shrimp.—Put them in wet saw dust, moss, water grass or seaweed.

To Preserve Fish—Use Preserveline. 1 lb. will preserve 50 to 100 lbs. of fish. Its all right.

To Feed and Keep Worms Fat—And alive, use the white of a hard boiled egg, a small part of it.

Smear Rod Ferrules—With tallow before jointing them and they won't stick when unjointing them. If they do, apply the heat of a match so as to expand the metal.

The Man in the Boat—Should keep still, and aid the angler, not retard him.

To Soften Leaders—Soak them in vinegar and water.

Never Use Dry Leaders.—You are apt to fracture and ruin them.

To Keep Leaders - Moist and ready for use, use a leader box.

To Color Leaders—Soak them in strong green or black tea or very strong coffee.

Always Test—Your lines, leaders, snells, etc., before starting out on a trip.

In Purchasing Flies—Always buy the best, even if you must economize elsewhere.

Always Have—An extra rod tip along with you on a trip.

On Cold Days—Trout are sluggish and unless hungry or feeding, refuse to bite.

On Hot Days—They usually await the cool evening or morning before biting well.

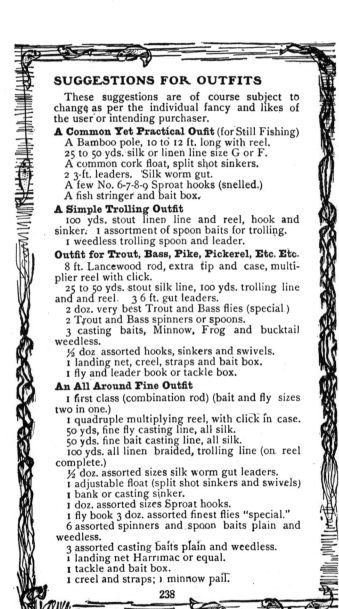

SUGGESTIONS FOR OUTFITS

These suggestions are of course subject to change as per the individual fancy and likes of the user or intending purchaser.

A Common Yet Practical Oufit (for Still Fishing)

A Bamboo pole, 10 to 12 ft. long with reel.
25 to 50 yds. silk or linen line size G or F.
A common cork float, split shot sinkers.
2 3-ft. leaders. Silk worm gut.
A few No. 6-7-8-9 Sproat hooks (snelled.)
A fish stringer and bait box.

A Simple Trolling Outfit

100 yds. stout linen line and reel, hook and sinker. 1 assortment of spoon baits for trolling.
1 weedless trolling spoon and leader.

Outfit for Trout, Bass, Pike, Pickerel, Etc. Etc.

8 ft. Lancewood rod, extra tip and case, multiplier reel with click.
25 to 50 yds. stout silk line, 100 yds. trolling line and and reel. 3 6 ft. gut leaders.
2 doz. very best Trout and Bass flies (special.)
2 Trout and Bass spinners or spoons.
3 casting baits, Minnow, Frog and bucktail weedless.
½ doz assorted hooks, sinkers and swivels.
1 landing net, creel, straps and bait box.
1 fly and leader book or tackle box.

An All Around Fine Outfit

1 first class (combination rod) (bait and fly sizes two in one.)
1 quadruple multiplying reel, with click in case.
50 yds, fine fly casting line, all silk.
50 yds. fine bait casting line, all silk.
100 yds. all linen braided, trolling line (on reel complete.)
½ doz. assorted sizes silk worm gut leaders.
1 adjustable float (split shot sinkers and swivels)
1 bank or casting sinker.
1 doz. assorted sizes Sproat hooks.
1 fly book 3 doz. assorted finest flies "special."
6 assorted spinners and spoon baits plain and weedless.
3 assorted casting baits plain and weedless.
1 landing net Harrimac or equal.
1 tackle and bait box.
1 creel and straps; 1 minnow pail.

In Fishing for Black Bass—It is next to useless to cast on perfectly smooth water.

Use Small Spoons—When trolling for bass.

Black Bass Go in pairs all summer. If you catch one look out for his mate.

In Trolling for Bass—Row about three miles an hour only, the tendency in trolling is to go too fast. Row only to keep good motion of your bait, and, if you twitch it often so as to make it spurt or swerve, so much the better.

Where to Go—The author will be pleased to inform readers where is the best to go, and also furnish printed matter describing routes and dates. On writing enclose postage for replies and matter 4 to 6c., and state kind of fishing desired, time of prospective trip, and how far or to what state you intend to travel to; whether your trip is for waters of your own or other territory. This advice is free.

In Fishing With Live Bait—Allow time for the fish to turn and swallow or gorge the bait, as fish invariably swallow bait fish, head first. If using minnows keep them well under water. If rapid waters, it will by its own force unless sinkered keep the minnow near the surface, which is the proper way.

A Little Red or Colored Rag—Fastened at the head of spoon bait often makes a more attractive lure.

Use a Fish Scaler—For cleaning or scaling all fish.

For Weak Fish—Use a pearl weak fish squid bait.

For Large Bass or Trout—Use a good spinner fly.

239

Fish in Spawning Season—Are less apt to be scared, yet there are many who absolutely refuse any food at these times; before or after they will eagerly take anything offered them.

The Largest Fish—Can oft times be found in most shallow or unlikely waters, in search of foods.

Always Buy—The very best flies that money can purchase, and provide yourself with abundant select bait, even if you must travel third class to do it, for first class fishing will result.

To Use Frog Successfully—Keep it moving so as to resemble life, a twitching movement is best, (as a frog swims.)

Brook Trout—In autumn (spawning season) take no food.

Good Bass Flies.—Jungle Cock, Silver Doctor, Montreal, Frank, Henry, Coachman, Epting, Seth Green, Ferguson, Lord Baltimore.

If a String—is in a knot, patience will untie it; patience does most anything if you will but try it.

March.—This is the earliest time for fly fishing, and can only be practical when the snow water is all out of streams. The earliest fly found on waters is the February Red, Blue Dun, March Brown.

April.—Red Spinner, Cow Dung, Red and Black Hackles, Iron Blue and Yellow Dun.

May.—Stone Fly, Sedge Fly, Alden Fly, Black Gnat, Evening Dun.

June.—(Best month for trout.) Green Drake or May Fly, Grey Drake, Coch-y-bon-Dhu, (try it,) Brachen, Shorn Fly, Light Colored Duns and Spinners.

July.—The (**Worst Month.**) White and Brown Moths, Red and Black Ant Flies and Small Midges.

August.—August Dun and Cinnamon Whirling Dun and Willow Fly, bringing up the angler's season for fly fishing for trout.

Use Cork Handles—To your rods. They are softer, cooler to the hands.

Be Cautious.—More caution is required in fly fishing than in bait fishing; objects beneath the water, do not scare fish so easily as those on the surface.

Fish Take Live Bait.—When fish seize smaller fish, they always swallow it head first, so give it time to turn and gorge it thus, before you strike.

To Extract Hooks—From flesh or clothing, push back the upper end so as to bring point out where it went in.

Best Bass Fishing—Is at night or on a cloudy day, or early morn or evening.

Strew Ferns—In your fish basket or creel, to keep trout separate, clean and moist.

For Fly Casting—Use a very light elastic or flexible rod, strong and servicable, 6 to 9 feet in length, not over six ounces in weight.

For Bait Fishing—Use a medium weight, fairly stiff rod, about 9 feet long.

For Trolling—Use a short stiff rod, extremely stout and strong, 6 to 8 feet long, weighing 12 ounces or more.

For Salmon Fishing—Use a double handed rod, 15 feet long, about 15 ounces.

The Eyes of Fish—Are peculiarly placed rendering him incapable of seeing plainly objects on a level or directly under him. They can, however, see plainly all that is going on above, and for a long distance about him, say 40 to 50 feet.

Fish Don't Bite—Always to satisfy hunger only. They often strike at a glittering or attractive bait for pure viciousness or greediness.

241

Always Breakfast—Before starting out mornings "a-fishing." Don't start out on an empty stomach, or *too early*.

A Fish Decoy.—Take a dozen bright minnows, and cork them up in a bottle (a clear glass one) of water with a small hole in the cork; suspend them midwater, in a very likely spot; when the bottle is submerged, it is hid by the color of the glass and water, and the imprisoned but moving minnows attract other fish to that vicinity.

Keep Minnows Alive—By providing or attaching to your minnow pail, a rubber tube and air bulb. Fill the bulb with air and force it through the tube into the water, thus "erating it" or supplying air to the water. Thus you have the most expensive minnow pail, at a cost of a few cents.

In Bottom or Still Fishing. Plumb the depth of the water first, so as to be sure of its depth; then act accordingly.

Excellent Bait for Bass—Young carp, very small green frogs, live grasshoppers.

In Fastening Frogs—Pass the hook through both lips and use the smaller ones.

For Carp Fishing—White maggots smeared with honey, stale doughy sweetened bread, potatoes, etc. Wait until he swims away with the bait before you strike.

The Best Time—For trout fishing is at night; then large fish are active. Select a quiet spot near a deep hole, and leave it for a night trial. Cut a few branches and group them around so as to hide yourself behind them, Do this the day before you fish the spot. Cast over and draw your bait or fly quietly over the top of the water. If big trout are there you'll quickly get a rise.

Don't Fry Trout.—Try broiling it over the camp fire.

242

Bait Casting—Use a short rod 5 to 7 feet long, a fine, smooth line, free running quadruple reel. Wind the line until the bait is close to the rod, then cast as you would throw an apple from a pointed stick. Cast the bait 50 to 60 feet or more from the boat, which should be in deep water, and casts made toward shallow water. Cast to the edges of rushes, weeds, etc., then trolling the bait to the boat for the recast.

Repair Kit—For anglers containing awls, brads, Shellac mending silk, wax, cement, etc., should be taken on long trips.

For Cold Weather—Use a chamois shirt; light and warm as a coat. They are flannel lined.

A Splendid Fish Bait—Maggots from meat that has been fly blown.

Lead Your Hook—Well to the head of live fish bait.

To Preserve a Landing Net—Immerse it in Linseed oil. Shake it out well, stretch it open and dry well.

Yellow Perch—Like gay colored trout hackles if sunk below the surface. Use one or more flies at the same time.

Dead Sand Worms—Are useless for bait in salt water fishing.

In Trout Fishing—If you can't hide behind places, cut a tree branch or two and make a blind. Do this the day before you fish that spot.

Hide From View.—I have seen a dozen fish leap to take the fly, but the moment they caught sight of me they refused everything later offered them; a few hours later I took care to hide myself and crawling cautiously near that spot, the finest fishing I have enjoyed, resulted from that care.

In Your Tackle Box—Should be a stick of angler's wax and ferrule or rod cement, a few connecting links, split buck shot, a weedless floating meadow frog, for casting; a spinning fly for casting or trolling; other trolling baits, spoons, etc.; a gimp leader, a bucktail bass fly and spoon; a double and single swivel, a foul tackle clearing ring, a bank sinker, a cork float, and a fisherman's file and pliers, and if possible a line dryer, leader box and fly book and you have an outfit that is complete.

Consult Your Guide—If possible, follow his recommendations, treat him with the same respect as you expect from him, insist upon his doing his duty thoroughly and well, always take a receipt for money paid.

Double Barb Hooks—Can be purchased any size, and is used for fish that nibbles instead of biting.

Don't Strike too Hard.—Approach likely waters carefully and fish the nearest side first; when you rise a good fish and fail to hook him, give him a little rest before casting over him again.

Notice What Flies—Are on the waters you are fishing and what the fish seem to be taking, and imitate it.

Open the Stomach—Of your first fish and see what they are feeding on, and follow the "tip."

Use a Smaller Fly—Than the natural one, the larger the imitation the easier fish can observe the fraud.

For Trolling.—Troll close to the edge of rushes, lily pads, etc., just between deep and shallow or light and dark waters. Morning, evening and after dark is the best time for trolling.

Using Spinners—Go slow and deep for success and big fish.

On Wet Days—Fish often fail to bite because food is washed into the waters in plenty.

In Bait or Fly Fishing—Always fish down stream. There are times however, that up stream has its advantages, but its hard work.

Fish Cannot be Caught—While snow water is in streams.

Grub Worms—make good bait.

Change Your Flies—Often if fish refuse to rise; fish that oftimes refuse seasonable flies, will strike eagerly at a most radical change.

Keep the Sun—In front of or at the side of you when fishing.

It is Said—Fish bite better between the new moon and first quarter.

On Cloudy Days—Use bright flies, dark days use white flies, bright days use dark flies.

A Nest of Very Small Mice—Make excellent large trout or bass bait.

Fish Decoy.—Cut up small fish, meats, etc., and scatter in likely still waters the day before you fish there. It will attract them to that vicinity.

Salmon Leaders—Should be 9 feet long. Trout leaders, 6 feet long.

Bobbing for Eels.—Take a piece of stout darning worsted and a needle and thread it full of angle worms; the longer the string the better. Wind it up in loops, tie your line to it, and sink it to the bottom, where the eels are, (do this at night) When they bite their teeth get caught in the worsted and holds them fast; or take a piece of raw meat and sew it full of worsted, cross and recross, and it will answer the same purpose.

Good Salt Water Bait—Shrimps, shedder, crabs, sand worms, clams, (hard portion) small crawfish, etc.

A Tangled, Kinky Line—Can be unravelled by towing it behind a boat or trailing it in running water.

Raw Beef or Raw Liver.—Especially hog's liver is excellent spring bait.

To Skin Eels.—Pin with a fork his tail to a tree stump, split the skin around a few inches from the fork and pull it over its head. *Fry or stew them.*

Assafoetida—Or camphor put in bait box is said to attract fish by its scent.

In Fly Casting—Have the wind at your back, the sun before you and do not let your line touch the water, that's the place for your fly only.

Keep Minnows Alive—Or revive them by adding a spoonful of salt to the water.

A Live Chub—Makes good bass bait, or use the Dobson or Helgramite. Find them in brooks and rivers under large stones.

The Best Time—For trout, the month of June.

When Bass or Trout—Refuse to rise to the surface for a fly, try sinking it a foot below the surface.

Use Shakespeare—Sure lure weedless bait for bass fishing, its excellent.

Fish in the Water—Can see plainly out of it. Things in the water are magnified out of it, just as they are magnified in the water to you.

When Wading—Tie strings to articles in your pockets, lest they fall out in the water and *be lost.*

Tie Your Hat—To your back shirt collar with a piece of cord, (out of the way) for windy days.

Fish Early—And fish late. It is a good plan midday or hot noons to take a *rest* or choose shady spots and deep waters.

Carry a Mosquito Hat.—Its worth its price, in an hour at times. Get it folding and pocket size.

No Fisherman or Angler—Should fail to provide himself with a copy of the Fish and Game Laws of the United States. Price 25c. postpaid.

Don't Wash Fish—When desired to keep them any length of time; simply draw and wipe them dry. Illustration shows how to clean and draw fish.

For Stream Fishing—Use size G or H line; for lake fishing use F or G line; for still fishing use G or H line.

In Fishing From a Boat—Use adjustable rod holders, which can be adjusted to any angle on side or seat of the boat.

Bucktail Bass Flies—Are made from the hair of a deer (buck) tail, the hair of which *does not mat when wet.* Bodies are of pure silk ribbed with tinsel, tied on hollow Sproat hooks.

Good Trout Flies.—Brown Hackle, Parmacheene Belle, Montreal, Silver Doctor.

For Tarpon Fishing—Use a stiff rod 6 ft. long (double handed.)

For Bait Fishing—Use a rod 6 to 10 ft. long, 5 to 10 oz.

For Fly Fishing—7 to 9 ft. long, 5 to 8 oz.

For Bait Casting—6 to 9 ft long, 5 to 8 oz.

For Trolling—(If a rod is used) 6 to 8 ft. long 12 oz. or more.

All Round Rod—A combination (2 rods in one) a 2 piece bait or trolling rod and a 3 piece fly and casting rod making both, a 7 ft. and 9½ ft. rods.

When desired steel telescopic or jointed rods can be furnished. Valise or trunk rods of any well known woods used in the manufacture of standard rods. Lancewood, Greenheart in 2-3-4-5 or 6 piece rods (any length, any weight) or 6 or 8 strip hexagonal split Bamboo (finest rods made) made, if desired, especially to your order. Spiral or twisted split Bamboo or Silkien invisible rods made to order.

Build a Large Bonfire—Where the reflection can be cast upon and about the waters. It will attract fish at night to that vicinity.

South and West Winds—Are said by fishermen to be the best winds for fishing.

A Pocket Fish Scales—Will correctly tell the weight of your capture. Weigh as soon as removed from water, as they lose weight after.

Bass, Pike, Pickerel—When feeding, are alert toward shores or shallow waters.

In Trout Fishing—Use a lively grasshopper. Get behind a tree or bank or crawl unseen to a very likely spot. Drop it in gently and move it on the surface (as if alive) and you will have sport, if they abound there.

Practice Fly Casting—In natural waters. Aim not for distance, but perfection.

Dye Your Leaders—Mist color, using one drachm of logwood, 6 grains copperas, boiled in one pint of water. Immerse leaders for 5 minutes or until correct color is obtained.

Wipe Your Lines—With a sponge or cotton rag so as to absorb the moisture when through fishing, or unreel and dry them when you get to camp.

Mosquito Dope.—Annoint the face with mosquito paste, or make preparations yourself as per receipts in the "Complete Campers Manual" (have you a copy?)

Port and Starboard.—"Port" is the left hand side of a boat (looking forward;) "Starboard" to right side; "Windward" the side the wind comes from; "Leeward," the other side; "Ahead," in front of the boat; "Astern," in rear of the boat; "Abeam," off the center of boat; on the "Quarter," either side of the stern of boat, for instance, Port or Starboard Quarter; "Amidships," center of boat.

248

Boats, Canoes, Etc.

To reach deeper waters and for following the course of new streams, rivers and lakes, or for trolling, bait or fly casting, skitting. etc., for long and pleasant excursions and trips over water and for transporting outfits (into less fished or better angling waters) various portable, folding, telescopic, canvas or steel boats, canoes, skiffs, etc., are employed, ranging from the Birch Bark Indian canoe, to the highest type of canvas, metal, alluminum or wood boats, capable of carrying from one to three or a party of one half dozen enthusiastic anglers or sportsmen all in a bunch.

Often it is that waters too grow extremely shallow and unnavigatable, necessitating a "portage" or carrying of these boats over difficult places, meaning hard and laborious work, were it not for the fact that even boats have been made for just such cases. For on long trips one must remember that there is not only the boat, but "duffle" (provisions and outfit) to be hauled likewise "to boat water", before the trip can be resumed, hence for such work and the glories of sport and fish beyond, boats are required that are not only extremely light and portable, but lasting and durable besides.

As thousands and thousands of anglers flock to the nearby brooks, streams and lakes adjacent to cities, it behooves those who have the time to own their own craft and set out on wondrous journeys afar, where oftimes they are not only recompensed or repaid by the magnificent stretches of scenery, but which yields them record catches, that go far to make them famous. Often the natural currents of running waters too suffice to propel such tiny crafts for a hundred mile trip or more, to where perhaps the foot of man rarely touches, and on the return trip all that is necessary is to hug close to either shore or side (usually they go up one side down the other) to have equal pleasure and ease on the return trip, thus avoiding the current, which they took advantage of a while before.

Boats for these purposes are made sectional, folding of light canvas or steel ranging in weight from 35 to 150 lbs., while the dimensions vary from 8 to 15 ft. and costing $15 to $50. Very many thousands being used in not only the waters of this immense country, but in the waters that dot the earth. Here we illustrate and make plain to the eye, those that have for years been the favorites of prominent sportmen and anglers, and our readers make no mistake in the selection or purchase of either. Among the most noted makes are the following: Osgood, (canvas) Mullins, (steel) either of which can be used for any and every kind of fishing, hunting, exploring, pleasure or business purposes; and before concluding this chapter let me say no man or woman who has ever taken a canoe or boat ride on any richly bowered lake or stream for the first time can ever forget the joy and pleasure of such a trip. Under slow, easy strokes of the paddle or oars the graceful craft skims swiftly over the water with scarcely a ripple. At times the woods seem to feel the spell of silence. Onward, onward, new scenes fill the very soul and eye with delightful inspiration. Even the most cold blooded money lender or matter of fact man, cannot help but feel grateful for taking such a trip, and its memory will ever live green and fresh to him, and should perchance he possess a camera, scenes suffice to keep the button going in regular gatling gun fashion, for there are many other pleasures from a fishing trip besides catching fish.

Portable Boats, Canoes and Skiffs
Continued.

Ideal Steel Boat.
Flat Bottom Steel Fishing Boat, 12 ft. long; width 41½ inches;
Depth 12 inches: weight, 115 lbs. 3 persons.

Steel Sectional Boat.   Packed.
14x3 ft. 3 in.   Depth 14 in.   Weight 103 lbs.

Steel Family Boat, 16x4 ft.; depth 15 and 25 in.; weight 160 lbs.
For Six Persons.

The King
Folding
Canvas Boat

8, 12, 15 foot
Sizes.

All Steel, Canoe Shape, Hunting Boats.

Duck Hunter's Favorite.
Any Size for Individual, Party, Outfit or Club Uses

Portable, Canvas, Steel Boats, Etc.

Ready for Use.

The Osgood Pattern.　　　Lightest Boat Made.

For 1 to 4 Persons.　　　30 to 75 lbs.

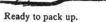

Ready to pack up.　　　The entire boat and chest
　　　　　　　　　　　　(shipped as baggage)

The Double End Sectional Fishing Boat with Fish Tanks.

Closed.

Steel Trunk Folding.

(Pack Outfit therein.)

Length 11½ ft.　Width 30 in.　Depth 10 in.　Weight 120 lbs.
Holds Entire Outfit.

Boats of Canvas, Steel or Aluminum. Any Size.

Lake and River Seine.

About Seining

The forms of Nets used vary according to the manner in which they are intended to act. This is by either entangling the fish in their folds, as in the *tramnel* net, receiving them into pockets as in the *trawl*, suspending them by the body in the meshes as in the *Mackerel net*, or imprisoning them within a labyrinth like partitions or spaces as in the *stake net*, or drawing them to shore as in the *seine net*.

The parts of a net are the "head" along which floats are strung on the supporting rope and the "foot" on which lead is coiled and weighted thereon.

The Fyke Net and Wing

The mesh of these nets vary in size from the minnow seine ⅛ inch square mesh to the best cotton or linen sea, lake, or river seine or gill net, with a 2½ in. mesh as per (half size) illustration herewith stretched measure, these in square measure are one-half the size given and are made of

¼	⨯⨯
5-16	⨯⨯
⅜	⨯⨯
½	⨯⨯
⅝	⨯
¾	⨯
⅞	⨯
1	⨯
1⅛	⨯
1¼	⨯
1⅜	⨯
1½	⨯

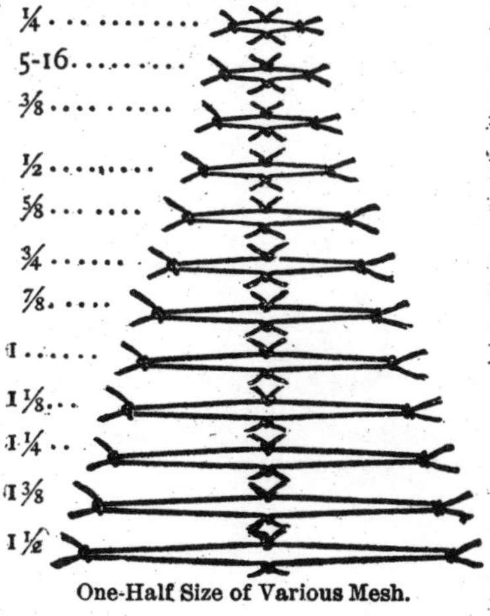

One-Half Size of Various Mesh.

253

single selvedge, double selvedge or double mesh, as is shown and illustrated elsewhere; and all that is necessary in ordering them in these days, is to mention the kind of fish you want to catch, and the way you propose to fish for them; the size, depth and length you desire, whether single sel-

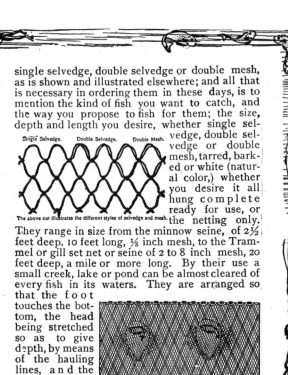

Single Selvedge.   Double Selvedge.   Double Mesh.

The above cut illustrates the different styles of selvedge and mesh.

vedge, double selvedge or double mesh, tarred, barked or white (natural color,) whether you desire it all hung complete ready for use, or the netting only.

They range in size from the minnow seine, of 2½ feet deep, 10 feet long, ⅛ inch mesh, to the Trammel or gill set net or seine of 2 to 8 inch mesh, 20 feet deep, a mile or more long. By their use a small creek, lake or pond can be almost cleared of every fish in its waters. They are arranged so that the foot touches the bottom, the head being stretched so as to give depth, by means of the hauling lines, and the seine or net forcibly dragged from deep to

The Trammel Net

shallow water, when a half circle is made, covering as great a water space as possible and thus hauled ashore. The proper handling of the head and foot ropes so as not to let the fish escape from either bottom or top, being the important qualifications; for in a well handled net, the fish are gradually forced to the swelled or bellied center of the net. These seines vary in size from those small enough to capture a few minnows, to the Shad seine of several miles in length, worked by steam power, which sweeps 1,000 acres or more of river bottom.

Much more was written concerning their use, but space, unfortunately, is too small to publish it at the present time.

PISCATORIAL SELECTIONS

"The Salmon Leap"

And when the Salmon seeks a fresher stream to find,
Which hither from the sea comes yearly of his kind;
As he tow'rds season grows, and stems the watery tract
When Tivy falling down, makes an high cataract,
Forc'd by the rising rocks that there her course oppose,
As tho' within her bounds they meant her to inclose;
Here, when the laboring fish does at the foot arrive,
And finds that by his strength he does but vainly strive;
His tail takes in his mouth, and bending like a bow
That's to full compass drawn, aloft himself doth throw,
Then springing at his height, as doth a little wand,
That bended end to end, and started from man's hand.
Far off itself doth cast; so does the Salmon vault
And if at first he fail, his second somersault
He instantly essays. and from his nimble ring,
Still yerking, never leaves until himself he fling
Above the opposing stream.

"The Old Bass Ground"

Our boat was a clumsy, leaky scow, made from an old barn
door;
Our poles were long and springy cane, bought at the village
store;
And the bait? Well sir, there's nothing that Bob and I ever
found
To equal a lively meadow frog on the Old Bass Ground.

I recall the whopping "Bronzeback" I hooked after dark one
night.
He pulled like sixty, thrashed about, and after an awful fight
Got off! Gee! What a big one! I knew by the pull and sound
But we couldn't coax him out again from the Old Bass
Ground.

You don't mean it, Bob! The bass is still there? In that same
quiet spot?
The bend of the little river, down by the old back lot?
Tomorrow is June? Hang business! I'll go with you, for
I'm bound
To find that grizzled "Bronzeback" I lost in the Old Bass
Ground.

"When the Bull-Heads Bite."

Been thinkin', last few days,
Of the times of long ago,
When we youngsters went a-fishin',
And it makes me feel as though
I would like to try once more,
With a bent pin for a hook,
Just to catch a mess of bull heads,
In some good old-fashioned brook.

255

In a pool 'neath shadowy elms,
  Where the water is at ease,
And the mud is deep as blazes,
  All along a row of trees;
I would bait the hook with worms,
  Just as day was turnin' night,
And I'll bet in half a minute,
  I would have a bull-head bite.

Bobber floatin' on the water,
  Quickly starts and sinks from view,
And the willow pole is bendin',
  Got a bull-head—pounder too;
Swallowed hook, and bait and all,
  Never left a bit of worm,
Golly! ain't it fun a-fishin'
  When the bull-heads bite and squirm.

"That Trout."

I've watched that trout for days and days,
  I've tried him with all sorts of tackle;
With flies got up in various ways,
  Red, blue, green, gray and silver hackle.

I've tempted him with angle-dogs,
  And grubs that must have been quite trying,
Thrown deftly in betwixt old logs,
  Where probably he might be lying.

Sometimes I've had a vicious bite,
  And as the silk was tautly running,
Have been convinced I had him quite;
  But 't wasn't him—he was too cunning.

I've tried him when the silver moon
  Shone on my dew-bespangled trousers,
With dartfish; but he was "too soon"—
  Though, sooth too say, I caught some rousers.

I've often weighed him (with my eyes),
  As he with most prodigious flounces
Rose to the surface after flies.
  (He weighs four pounds and seven ounces).

I tried him—heaven absolve my soul—
  With some outlandish, heathenly gearing—
A pronged machine stuck on a pole—
  A process that the boys call spearing.

I jabbed it at his dorsal fin
  Six feet beneath the crystal water—
'Twas all too short. I tumbled in,
  And got half drowned—just as I orter.

Thou piscatorial, speckled wonder,
  Bright be the waters where you rise,
And green the banks you cuddle under,
  Adieu, oh, trout of marvelous size!

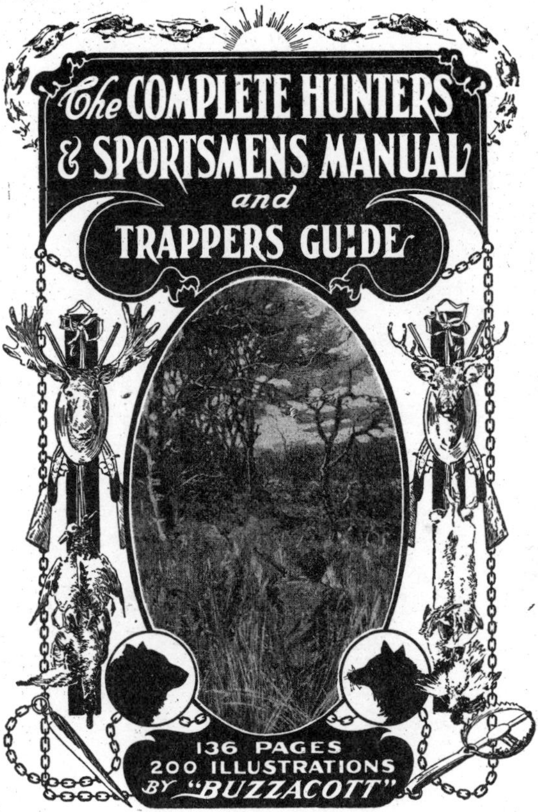

The COMPLETE HUNTERS & SPORTSMENS MANUAL and TRAPPERS GUIDE

136 PAGES
200 ILLUSTRATIONS
BY "BUZZACOTT"

Say--This is Sport. 258

"A Chip of the Old Block."

Shot Gun Shooting Outfits

The kind of outfit needed for sportsmen using the shot gun, depends chiefly on the kind of sport indulged in, season of year and shooting ground. It is obvious that different equipment is needed where the hunter's route brings him about marshy waters or low lands, as to that needed by those who frequent the brush, high wooded dry localities, or the open field. **No one outfit can be made to suit all occasions.**

If duck hunting in a boat, where one must keep a portion of the body perfectly still for hours at a time, a different outfit of dress will be required than were one to choose a tramping route around the shores or borders. About marshy, shallow waters, it is essential that the hunter if afoot should be provided with waterproof, light and easy fitting leather boots, so as not to tire the feet. Rubber boots would be apt to render him most uncomfortable, where much tramping around is necessary. On the other hand if little walking is to be done, and that in wet and muddy, oftimes deep places, rubber boots of the hip variety would be essential. To cover all these requirements I deem it best to divide this chapter on outfits into three portions as follows:

Outfits for Boats; Outfits for Low Lands, Marshes, Etc. and **Outfits for Field and Brush Shooting,** taking them up in the order named.

We will assume that the first is an outfit for the duck hunter, who usually starts out to his favorite grounds in the fall of the year, and who intends to remain in his boat, or blinds constructed by him, for perhaps hours at a time, here warm, dry foot gear, clothing impervious to moisture will be needed; heavy woolen underclothing, woolen sweater and gloves and heavy hose; in addition a warm canvas, leather or oilskin jacket should be taken along, so as when chilled by a long wait, he

can receive additional protection; warm wristlets
and an extra pair of dry woolen socks can be carried in a handy pocket. If decoys are used, a pair
of waterproof rubber gloves will come in handy
when handling them or wet birds. Stowed in the
boat somewhere, should be a small coffee pot and
cup with a pocket stove and fuel (all packed inside) and a little coffee and sugar, so as to refresh
himself by a warm cup of coffee when needed; for
these things, with a bite to eat, enables the sportsman when shooting is good, to spend the day
profitably and pleasantly.

If blinds have to be built, a pocket axe, a heavy
knife, cords, etc. are essential. If time is to be
spent in them, a grass colored rubber blanket will
come in handy; and in your shell box plenty of
cartridges, a ball of string, and a few weights, etc
so as to anchor and manipulate your decoys, or assist you in setting out dead ducks as additional
ones. It is essential that **your footwear be both
warm and dry,** as of all things cold feet in a boat
or blind is distressing. Let the clothes be of dull
grass color, always avoiding anything like black
as too conspicuous. Even the boat had best be
painted yellow so as to resemble the natural color
of the grasses, or if winter time when snow and ice
prevails, white is better. By all means strive to
take along the essential things to make yourself
comfortable, for it all contributes to the pleasure
of a trip and the success of it.

**For the Outfit when tramping around marsh-
es** or wet low lands, the footwear is the all important item, and the condition of the locality you frequent should decide what is best to be worn. Personally, except for wading, I dislike rubber boots,
(yet there times when they are invaluable.) I prefer a good waterproof leather boot, (water repel-
lent and well oiled) light in weight, easy fitting. A
good, heavy woolen sweater with pockets, underneath of which is worn a **shell vest;** this keeps out
the cold equal to a leather jacket, and the pockets of the sweater enables one to carry sufficient
shells handy, without inconveniently loading them
down. **A Bedell Game Skirt and Holder** (see illustration) is a handy article for carrying both
game and shells. For headwear a slouch hat or

cap should be worn (the former only in the rainy season) and the cap should be provided with ear flaps for use if necessary. Remember I am speaking now of fall or winter dress; it is unnecessary to dwell on what should be worn at other seasons, as it is an easy matter to divest oneself of superflous clothing if too warm.

If for Brush or Field Shooting—About the edges of thickets or woods, on dry ground, the boot can be dispensed with entirely (unless you are used to them), for this I would advise if boots are desired at all, those of the three-quarter boot size, but what I prefer is a good stout shoe and a pair of leggings—for this the "hunter's garb" mentioned in chapter on big game hunting is all to be desired. A sportsman should aim to be so appareled so as to make as little noise as possible; **the more quietly you can pass through the stubble or underbrush,** without disturbing the feathered game you seek, until you are **within range** the better; many a sportsman has been annoyed by the noise his canvas clothing has made, when **trying to steal within range** of a covey of birds that he has located. If hunting with the aid of a good dog, it don't make much difference, but the less noise your clothing renders, the nearer and quieter you can approach out of range birds **before flushing them.**

The leggings should be of woolen cloth, preferably to canvas, yet if the canvas be covered with cloth or buckskin it will not only be noiseless, but keep out the wet of moist dews or rain on the grass should such conditions prevail. Here the **hunting sweater is again an all important item.** Its color should be as before stated, tan, or if snow has fallen and covered the ground, white is equally as good if not better. One should aim to have his clothing in keeping with the surroundings; usually action keeps the body warm, and such an article as a canvas or leather coat can be dispensed with even the coldest of weather. A good flannel shirt covered with a light vest, if warm underclothing is worn, is **sufficient for even the coldest of weather.** It is unnessary to lug around a weighty or heavy coat; **the secret is to travel light but right,** and be clad in such garb that will absorb, moisture or heat of the body; and no argument can be brought in favor of canvas, corduroy or leather clothing as being essential, where **activity is indulged in**; where one has to sit in a boat or blind for hours, it is different. Here either canvas, corduroy or leather clothing is eminently satisfactory, but where constant traveling or moving about is possible and necessary, it is vastly different. One of the best arguments in favor of such clothing is the variety and size of pockets, so conveniently placed and distributed about it, forming as they do, a veritable game bag. But as the Bedell Game Skirt (before mentioned) has all these conveniences, the up-to-date sportsman can use his own judgment in the selection of either. In the matter of other equipment needed, note the various chapters under their respective headings—such as Boats, Blinds, Decoys, Shot Guns, etc. mentioned elsewhere.

For other Sportsman's Equipment read our other books, each 160 pages, over 300 illustrations. (See title page.)

The New 5 Shot Automatic Shot Gun (12 Gauge)

As a "Take Down."

The Trap Gun.

The "Messenger" Gun.

263

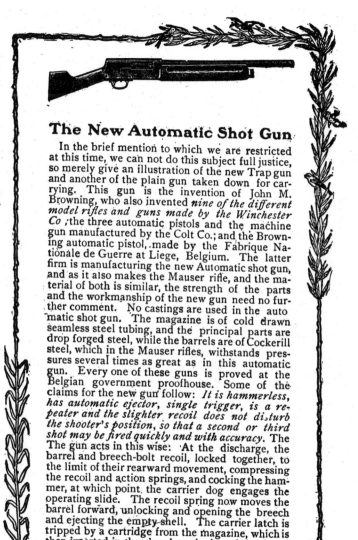

The New Automatic Shot Gun

In the brief mention to which we are restricted at this time, we can not do this subject full justice, so merely give an illustration of the new Trap gun and another of the plain gun taken down for carrying. This gun is the invention of John M. Browning, who also invented *nine of the different model rifles and guns made by the Winchester Co;* the three automatic pistols and the machine gun manufactured by the Colt Co.; and the Browning automatic pistol, made by the Fabrique Nationale de Guerre at Liege, Belgium. The latter firm is manufacturing the new Automatic shot gun, and as it also makes the Mauser rifle, and the material of both is similar, the strength of the parts and the workmanship of the new gun need no further comment. No castings are used in the automatic shot gun. The magazine is of cold drawn seamless steel tubing, and the principal parts are drop forged steel, while the barrels are of Cockerill steel, which in the Mauser rifles, withstands pressures several times as great as in this automatic gun. Every one of these guns is proved at the Belgian government proofhouse. Some of the claims for the new gun follow: *It is hammerless, has automatic ejector, single trigger, is a repeater and the slighter recoil does not disturb the shooter's position, so that a second or third shot may be fired quickly and with accuracy.* The The gun acts in this wise: At the discharge, the barrel and breech-bolt recoil, locked together, to the limit of their rearward movement, compressing the recoil and action springs, and cocking the hammer, at which point the carrier dog engages the operating slide. The recoil spring now moves the barrel forward, unlocking and opening the breech and ejecting the empty shell. The carrier latch is tripped by a cartridge from the magazine, which is then inserted in the chamber, the breech is closed and locked by the action spring, and the gun is again ready to be fired by a pressure on the trigger. The magazine holds four cartridges, which, with the one in the barrel, makes five shots at the shooter's command. Cartridges remaining in the magazine while any number of shots are fired do not become headed at the crimp so they will not enter the chamber freely. The gun has two extractors which withdraw the shell positively, even if the head be broken on one side. The hammer is light and quick; the trigger pull is smooth and easy. A safety catch, conveniently located in the trigger guard where it can not be moved accidentally, securely locks the trigger, and as the trigger is also the sear, there is no possibility of the cartridge being discharged by a jar. Then, too, the trigger is so balanced that it can not be jarred off even when not locked.

The gun is as safe as any on the market and in many respects it is the safest, but in addition *to all this there is the solid breech. The receiver is solid on top, which keeps* rain, dirt, rain, etc., from falling in; but a point of far greater importance to the shooter, and one to which we wish to call especial attention, is the *fact that it is perfectly solid in the rear.* The breech-bolt does not slide out, nor is there any opening of any kind in the rear; consequently *it is impossible*, no matter what might occur, for gas, grease, firing-pin, breech-bolt, bursted head of shell or anything else to fly back through the receiver into the eyes or face. But three models are made. They are, a plain gun, a trap gun and one for messenger or riot service. All sorts of extras may be had, however, and barrels of different length or boring can be interchanged quickly. The gauge will be 12, and the standard length of barrel 28 inches. The standard gun takes five cartridges, but the company also makes one taking two cartridges.

The take down feature of this automatic shot gun permits the use of *interchangeable barrels* by which the owner can change the gun from a *full or modified choke bore* for field, duck, or trap shooting to a *cylinder bore* for, snap, brush shooting etc., thus having a variety of weapons practically with the one arm by this remarkable weapon.

Types of High and Medium Grade Shot Guns.

Automatic Ejector—"Hammerless" Shot Gun.

The Repeating Shot Gun.

High Grade "Hammerless" Shot Gun.

Medium Grade "Hammer" Shot Gun.

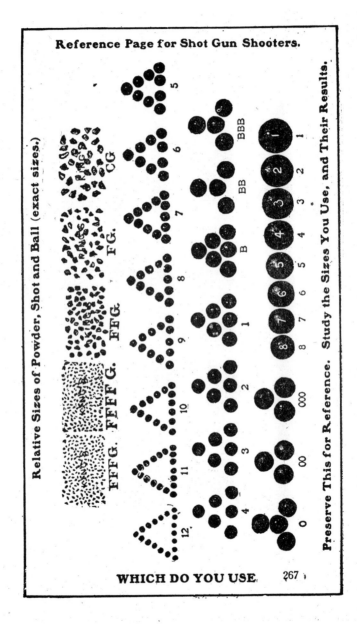

Reference Page for Shot Gun Shooters.

Relative Sizes of Powder, Shot and Ball (exact sizes.)

Preserve This for Reference. Study the Sizes You Use, and Their Results.

WHICH DO YOU USE. 267

About the Shot Gun

For the *best all round shot gun* I advise the selection of the 12-gauge, weighing about 7 to 8½ lbs. Such a gun as this will be capable of rendering excellent service for almost any purpose for which a shot gun can be used. If possible choose a "Hammerless Ejector," barrels 30 inch either full choke bored, or if you prefer, right barrel modified choke, left full choke. If for duck shooting choose that of the 10 bore variety, about 9 lbs., both barrels full choke.

Choke boring consists of restricting the interior of barrels *near the muzzle* in order to bunch or crowd the shot, securing thereby greater force and penetration for long distance shooting. When this is done away with the bore is termed "cylinder," which for close shooting is excellent; but as the choke bore can be easily made to scatter shot, at the same time carrying it closer and further, greater killing qualities is secured, making it by far the better gun. The popular plan is as stated before, right barrel modified (about half choke more or less) so as to be used for close range; left full choke for long range, thus securing a combination that is considered most effective. With such a gun the shooter by using ammunition of varied charges, can secure almost any results he could possibly desire. Many good shooters select a 32 inch barrel, but like everything else these things are a matter of personal selection, left to the user.

In selecting a shot gun, personally I advise those of American make (of which there are many good ones) or such as L. C. Smith, Parker, Lefever, Ithaca or equal; all excellent weapons, any of which will do the trick of filling your bag, if you are capable; personally I see no great necessity of patronizing the costly imported grades. I will admit their qualities are good, for the merits of such guns as Greener, W. & C. Scott & Sons, etc., are not to be disputed, yet I believe honestly that the money can be put to better advantage in providing shot and shells for practice, so as to render one proficient. No man's abilities are to be judged by the name and grade of the weapon he carries, and American guns can hold their own with any of them, if handled right. Some of the best shots in the world are using them, and the way they shoot holes into European records with them, should convince anyone of their effectiveness and sterling worth.

By gauging your loads (charging them) according to old and time tried principles, they will be right for any size of game or shooting for which a shot gun can be used, About the next important matter *is in the fit*, it should be brought to the shoulder and aimed at some object, *and if it admits of your bringing it into position without discomfort or stretching your neck*, is light and comfortable, natural like, when to the shoulder, enabling you to sight with ease, this is about all that can be done until you test its shooting qualities by firing practice or use. Many a good gun is blamed, because the purchaser chose the one *the salesman liked the best*. If its too heavy (for you might be a diminutive man) *choose a lighter gun*. All these things are essential points and should not be lost sight of; shooters, like guns vary, so act accordingly; and if you consult a specialist in such things giving him data concerning yourself, experience with other arms, and describing your wants, you will be surprised how well you can be served. If you are a crank on heavy loads let me advise the addition of a good recoil pad, which will lessen considerable the effects of recoil; another little essential to some shooters is a shot gun sight (as illustrated) even the ivory bead being superior to the ones with which they are usually provided.

After selecting these things, about the next important matter is to find out by practice the best loads, adopting and holding to the standard in all cases, until by experience you are enlightened and rendered yourself competent to vary from them, then when you have mastered that knowledge you can adjust matters to your exact requirements by *loading and making your own ammunition* if you choose.

To those about to select a shot gun I advise patronizing some responsible dealer, who has a fair sized stock on hand to select from, thus enabling him to choose for you a weapon exactly as you need it; no responsible dealer will object to your

269

returning a gun several times until you are thoroughly satisfied, provided you do not use the weapon or abuse his wares; and if you send with your order the necessary amount covering the cost, even a half dozen could be sent you at any distance enabling you to thoroughly satisfy yourself in its selection at your leisure. Too much care cannot be given these things, and mention of the fact should be given as to your size and weight, for it is obvious that a strong, long armed shooter, *requires a different fit*, than the small and more delicate formed person, so act accordingly, take your time and secure the right weapon, and do not decide on your purchase until you have the article in your hands, and can in every sense say to yourself, this is just the *gun I have been wanting*, for it fits me right, and with such satisfaction as this, confidence will enable you to secure results that could never be obtained from a weapon that **did not just exactly suit you.** It is an easy matter to please those who know what they want; the greatest difficulty is experienced from those who do not, and my advice to those is in all cases to consult some person whose experience in such matters (as the selection of guns for other and all classes of people) qualifies them to give you the benefit of such experience.

NOTE—Many first class dealers allow shot guns to be targeted before final acceptance.

(See also Points for Shot Gun Shooters.)

"The Duck Hunter's Camp."

270

Reloading Shot Guns

The quantity of paper shells that are used in a year by shot gun shooters in this country is astonishing; it runs well up into millions, and until of late they were considered as worthless, and were cast away after being once shot. Now, however, the economy of reloading is becoming the universal practice by shooters, for they can now purchase implements *made especially to aid them in that line.*

Economy, however, is not the only consideration. It is an instructive, pleasurable pastime for shooters who like to experiment. Loading and reloading of their own shells enables them to ascertain for their own individual benefit, what may be done with this or that kind of powder, this or that combination of wadding, shot, etc.

While some are contented to have everything done for them, there are those who prefer to do for themselves. The latter are generally those who will know the whys and wherefores, and to such the making of one's ammunition is as interesting and pleasurable as the shooting of it. When black powder was universally used, there was but one style of paper shells, and one size and quality of primers for them, and if a charge varied from one to twelve grains, it did no particular harm. All this has been changed with the coming of smokeless powders, *which will not permit of such a variation.* Therefore, the first and greatest consideration is measuring powder accurately and uniformly. Uniformity in the charge begets uniformity in shooting.

What is a drachm? There has been considerable controversy as to what the standard drachm measure for measuring powder is. Of course, all recognize the fact that a drachm, correctly speaking, is a weight; sixteen drachms make one ounce Avoirdupois, etc., *so a drachm is one-sixteenth of an ounce Avoirdupois (or when converted into grains, Troy or Apothecaries' weight, one drachm Avoirdupois equals 27 11-32 grains Troy.)* When the drachm powder measure was originally made, it was supposed to be of the proper capacity to measure, in bulk, one-sixteenth of

271

an ounce by weight of black powder, and sporting black powders were nearly all of the same density. This, however, is not the case with the *various smokeless* powders, the specific gravity of which vary very much.

The original Dixon drachm measure, No. 1105, was intended to hold drachms and fractions thereof in weight, of Curtis & Harvey's T. S. (British) No. 4 black powder. This measure has been generally accepted as the standard. The uniformity of the results when using this or any other dip measure, however, depends upon the uniformity of the action of those using them.

The old-time dipping with a hand measure, and striking the measure off flush, is not regular. Tapping the measure to settle powder, and then striking it off is not uniform. You try to dip at the same speed and depth, through a sufficient quantity of powder, and try to tap always exactly the same number of times, with exactly the same force, yet your own results are variable, and others may not secure the same results that you do.

For our own satisfaction, we carefully tested a Dixon No. 1105 measure, set at *three* drachms, with results as follows:

We first used Hazard's F. F. G. black powder *dipped* from a receptacle holding *sufficient quantity* to insure uniform dipping, and *and without hitting or jarring the measure, but striking it off flush*, we secured 82½ grains, which is within one-half of a grain of the correct weight in grains Troy for three drachms Avoirdupois.

(See the table reducing drachms Avoirdupois weight to grains Troy or Apothecaries' weight.

Going through the same operation again, and hitting the measure *once* with a common lead pencil, then striking it off, the weight was 84 grains. When hit with a pencil twice, weight was 85½ grains. When hit with a pencil three times, weight was 88 grains, and when jarred by hitting the measure with a knife, which jarred the powder below the edge of the measure, then filling the measure up again and striking it off we secured 92 grains, which you will please note is 9½ grains in excess of the standard weight. Going through the same operation with the New "E. C." smokeless

272

powder, we secured weights as follows, in their order: 33, 33½, 35½, 36½, 37½ grains.

Now please note that with the Ideal measure set at three drachms, and using Hazard's F. F. G. black powder, the weight secured was 82½ grains, which is identical with the weight secured in the Dixon measure, using the same powder, when the latter is not jarred. This shows pretty plainly that the Ideal measure and the Dixon measure are of the same capacity. We prove this over again, when with the New "E. C." smokeless powder, the Ideal measure when set at three drachms, will be found to throw 33 grains, which is the same as that thrown by the Dixon measure, when it is used by simply dipping and striking off, without any hitting or jarring.

With the Ideal Universal Powder Measure there is no hitting or jarring required. With a simple movement of the handle back and fourth, which all persons can do alike, the quantity delivered will be found regular and uniform. As to which should be the standard, each one must decide for himself. We, however, recognize no standard other than the *Apothecaries' Scales*, to which all manufacturers of powder and ammunition refer when testing for scientific and accurate results.

As most of the tables of charges published by the powder and ammunition manufacturers, in which they state that so many drachms and fractions thereof are so many grains, were obtained by using the Dixon measure, which was jarred one way or another, we would say in reference to such, that with the Ideal measure not being jarred in any way, results possibly may be found slightly under the weights designated in the various tables; all of which, however, is on the safe side, and *positively obviates all danger of overcharges*, which is very essential when using some of the dense high pressure smokeless powders.

As to the fact of how many grains weight of this or that kind of smokeless powder, there may be in one, two or three drachms measure or fraction thereof, we do not say, but we are pleased to state for the benefit of those who desire to secure the grains weight by measure of the various smokeless powders as tabulated, that they can do so by setting the Ideal measures in accordance with the tables on the following pages. These tables are

273

Comparison of Weight (by Grains) of Bulk Measure of Black Powder, with the weight of the same Bulk Measure of Smokeless Powders.

The figures in the first column are the graduations on the Ideal Loading Machine, Model 1899, which are for grains weight black powder only The other columns are comparative weights for same bulk measure.

	Graduations on Measures for Black Powder.	DuPont's Smokeless Shot Gun.	HAZARD'S Blue Ribbon Shot Gun.	PEYTON KING'S Semi-Smokeless F. F. G.	BALLISTITE KING'S Smokeless Shot Gun.	WALSRODE Gray Shot Gun.	WALSRODE Green Shot Gun.	Wolf Smokeless Shot Gun.
	GRAINS.	GRS.	GRS.	GRS.	GRS.	GRS.	GRS.	GRS.
SMALL MEASURE	16 equals	6½	7	13½	10½	12	12½	7½
	17 "	7	7	14½	11	13	13½	8
	18 "	7	7½	15	11½	13½	14	8½
	19 "	7½	8	16	12½	14½	15	9
	20 "	8	8½	17	13	15	15½	9½
	21 "	8½	9	18	13½	16	16½	10
	22 "	9	9	18½	14½	16½	17	10½
	23 "	9½	9½	19½	15	17	18	11
	24 "	10	10	20½	15½	18	18½	11½
	25 "	10½	10½	21	16½	18½	19½	12
	26 "	11	11	22	17	19½	20½	12½
	27 "	11½	11½	23	17½	20	21	13
	28 "	11½	12	23½	18½	21	22	13½
	29 "	12	12½	24½	19	21½	22½	14
	30 "	12½	13	25	19½	22	23	14½
	31 "	13	13½	26	20	23	24	15
	32 "	13½	14	27	21	23½	25	15½
	33 "	14	14	28	21½	24½	25½	16
	34 "	14½	14½	29	22	25	26½	16½
	35 "	15	15	30	22½	25½	27	17
LARGE MEASURE	40 "	17	17	33	24	28½	30	20½
	45 "	19	19	37	27	31½	33½	22½
	50 "	21	21	41	30	35	36½	24½
	55 "	23	23	45	32½	38½	40	27
	60 "	25	25	49	35½	41½	43½	29½
	65 "	27	27	53½	39	45	47½	32
	70 "	29	29	57½	42	49	51	34½
	75 "	31	31½	61½	45	52½	55	37
	80 "	33½	33½	66	48½	56½	59	39½
	85 "	35½	35½	70½	51½	59½	62½	42
	90 "	37½	37½	74½	54	63½	66	44½
	95 "	40	40	78½	57	66½	70	46½
	100 "	42	42	82½	60½	70	73½	49

Comparison of Weight (by Grains) of Bulk Measure of Black Powder, with the Weight of the same Measure of Smokeless Powders.

The figures in the first column are the graduations on the Ideal Loading Machine, Model, 1899, which are for grains weight black powder only. The other columns are comparative weights for same bulk measure.

Graduations on Measure for Black Powder	E.C. SMOKELESS No. 1 Shot Gun	New "E.C." and New SCHULTZE	VELOX Smokeless Shot Gun	C.P.W. Smokeless Shot Gun	ORIENTAL Smokeless Shot Gun	Robin Hood Smokeless Shot Gun	LAFLIN & RAND "Infallible" Smokeless For Shot Guns
GRAINS.	GRS.	GRS.	GRS.	GRS.	GRS.	GRS.	GRS.
SMALL MEASURE							
16 equals	7½	6½	19½	8½		10	9½
17 "	8	6½	20½	9		10½	10½
18 "	8½	7	22	9½		11½	11
19 "	9	7½	23	10		12	12
20 "	9½	8	24	10½	9	12½	12½
21 "	10	8	25½	11		13	13
22 "	10½	8½	26½	11½		13½	13½
23 "	11	9	28	12		14½	14
24 "	11½	9½	29	12½		15	14½
25 "	12	10	30	13	11	15½	15
26 "	12½	10	31½	13½		16½	16
27 "	13	10½	32½	14		17	16½
28 "	13½	11	34	14½		18	17
29 "	14	11½	35	15		18½	17½
30 "	14½	12	36	15½	13½	19	18½
31 "	15	12½	37½	16		19½	19
32 "	15½	13	38½	16½		20	19½
33 "	16	13½	40	17		20½	20
34 "	16½	13½	41	17½		21	21
35 "	17	14	42	18	15	22	21½
							22
LARGE MEASURE							
40 "	18½	17	47	21	17	27	24½
45 "	20½	19	53	24	19	29½	28
50 "	22½	20½	58½	26½	21	32½	30
55 "	25	22½	64	29	23	35½	33½
60 "	27½	24½	70	31½	25	38½	36½
65 "	30	26½	76	34	27	41	39½
70 "	32	29	81½	36½	29	44½	42½
75 "	34½	31	87½	39	31	47½	
80 "	36½	33	93½	41½	33	50½	
85 "	39	35	99½	44	35	54½	
90 "	41	37	105½	46½	37	57	
95 "	43½	39	111	49	39½	60	
100 "	46	41	117	51½	41½	63½	

compiled from samples of powders given to us by the manufacturers, and are changed or approved by them for each issue of our Hand Book. We, however, do not hold ourselves responsible for any changes in the powder that may be made after the tables are printed.

All of the various powders on the market have friends, and all have their own particular merit. It is not for us to advise one as superior to another. The different manufacturers of powder, have by a long series of experiments, demonstrated to their own satisfaction the proper loads of their various powders for the different gauges, so we would advise following the instructions that usually accompany each canister of powder.

Many have an idea that to get strong shooting, they must use a larger wad than the regular sizes that they are loading, and that they must ram the powder and shot as snugly as possible; we believe this is wrong and we would not advise using wads larger than the regular gauge that is being loaded, and in no case should a shell be enlarged beyond its normal size, by using large wads or by excessive ramming. Good elastic wads of the regular gauges are far better as a gas check, than hard wads that are one size larger; elastic wads expand in the gun at the time of discharge, thus preventing any loss of pressure by gas escapement, and they are not so apt to expand the shell when being loaded, unless they are rammed too hard, which would cause trouble at the time of inserting the cartridge in the chamber of the gun. We receive requests occasionally to make the loading chamber a tight fit, to prevent the shell from swelling when large wads are used. To such, we would state that as soon as a large cartridge is expelled from a tight loading chamber, it immediately expands and causes trouble as above. *If the shells are not expanded in loading, there will be no trouble.*

There are almost as many ideas about wadding as there are shooters. Our experience would say that there is no necessity for wads to occupy more than ⅜ to ⅝ of an inch of space in the shell. The quantity of wadding that may be required

276

must be determined by the space to be filled. If dense powders are being used, which take up but little space in the shell, high base shells, that are made especially for those powders, should be used. If shells are to be loaded and kept long before being used, we would advise a field wad on top of the powder. This is placed next to the powder to avoid the possibility of grease destroying the powder if left in a warm place. If cartridges are to be used soon after loading, one good ¼ inch pink edge or black edge wad will be all right, followed by a good ⅜ inch felt wad and a cardboard, on which is placed the shot. If shot is placed on a wad that is too soft, the pellets will sometimes sink deeply into the wad, causing it to keep company with the shot, which is not beneficial. For shells that have been cut off short to be reloaded, we would recommend two ⅛ inch pink or black edge wads, and a cardboard before the shot. Remember to leave ¼ inch for crimping in every case. Hard cardboard wads of large sizes should be avoided, as there is nothing that will destroy the choke in a fine barrel sooner.

Whether shells are loaded by yourself or at the factory, it is well if using a repeating shot gun, to test the cartridges, by inserting them all in the chamber of the gun before putting them in the magazine. This may prevent a jam at a time when it would cost more than the time it takes to gauge them.

Cartridges will sometimes upset in the magazine being jumped together by the recoil of previous discharges. Loaded cartridges should be kept in a dry place, for dampness will cause them to swell.

Cut "O" illustrates the Ideal Loading Machine Model 1899. It is provided with triple graduations, which are as follows: One for drachms and fractions thereof, from ½ drachm to 5 drachms. Another is for grains, from 40 to 140 grains, in marks 5 grains each, for shot gun and larger rifle charges. Still another will accurately measure from 1 to 35 grains, 1 grain each mark; thus the smallest and largest charges desired can be secured. *When the weather is humid and heavily charged with moisture, the cold metal of which*

277

a measure is composed, may condense the moisture on the inside, and cause the powder to adhere to the sides, therefore at such a time extra care must be exercised in keeping the measures thoroughly dry on the inside. These Loading Machines are made for 10, 12, 14, 16 and 20 gauges only.

For those who desire to load *and reload* their shells

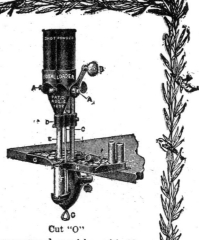

Cut "O"

we recommend machine with No. — Shell Receiver, for after paper shells have been crimped and fired, the muzzle is left soft and out of true, so that it is impossible to seat proper size wads on the charges, without tearing or distorting the muzzle of the shell.

The cone-shaped fingers of No. 2 Shell Receiver (See cut "P") are made of light spring brass and extend downward within the shell, and the wads can slip easily on the metallic surface thus afforded, and be seated on the charge as required. This improved Receiver No. 2 has detachable screw top, and will operate on varying lengths of shells from 2½ to 3 inches in length.

No. 2 Shell Receiver for the Loading Machine has proved so successful for *reloading* paper shells, that we have been requested by many shooters, who do not load in sufficient quantities to warrant the purchase of a Loading

Cut "P"

Machine, to fit them up a cheaper portable hand implement embodying the same principles. Responsive to these requests, we here illustrate our Straight Line Hand Loader (see cut "Q") It may be used by being fastened to a bench (which is preferred) or not, as desired. They will be made for 10, 12 and 16 gauge only. Parts "A" and "B" are different for each gauge; the part "C" is the same for all gauges. Those having an Ideal Loading Machine, desiring a portable hand implement to take with them on a trip, may purchase the parts "A," "C" and "D" only, and use the Receiver that is with the Loading Machine, as the part "B" in the "Straight Line" Hand Loader is the same as Receiver No. 2 in the Loading Machine

Cut "Q"

The Ideal Pocket Powder and Shot Measure is the smallest adjustable dipper made that is graduated for shot and powder. It is graduated from 1 to 1½ ounces of shot, and from 2½ to 3¾ drachms (black powder measure.) There are no screw threads or notches in the adjustments. It can be set instantly to a fractional part of a grain. The illustration "R" shows the handle broken off.

Shells that have been fired and are to be used over again, should be re-sized and de-capped as soon as possible, and kept in a dry place. If the primers are allowed to corrode in the pockets of the shells, they can not be easily expelled, and the pockets will be weakened. If shells are allowed to get wet after being fired, the hardness and toughness of the paper will be destroyed. The waterproofing, which contains a lubricant, is some-

Cut "R"

what extracted by the heat at the time of discharge, thus moisture operates more quickly, causing the shells to swell and the laps of paper to separate, leaving the shells larger end weaker than when they were first withdrawn from the gun. Reject all shells that are torn, *stripped lengthwise, or frayed on inside.*

We do not find the highest price metal lined shells as good for reloading as the medium grades, such as the U. M. C. Smokeless and Nitro Club, Winchester Repeater, Blue and Yellow Rivals, Peters New Victor, etc. If shells expand so they will not enter the chamber of gun freely, they must be resized. It will be found best to resize them before other operations, on account of the metal forming the head and reinforcement in some shells being so thin and light that they are not strong enough to be pushed out of the resizing die without bulging the head. *Such shells are useless.*

Cut "S"

Be sure that all shells will enter the chamber of your gun before reloading, and it is well to be sure that all loaded cartridges will chamber freely, especially if you use a repeater.

We find there is a difference in the sizes of the various shot gun chambers. For some guns the shells require to be sized smaller than for others. The Ideal Shot Shell Resizing Die (see cut "S") is a double-ender. If the shells are first driven in the end marked "1," they will be found correct for most guns; if, however, they are still tight, drive them in the other end after being first resized in the end marked "1." Shell Resizing Dies are made for 10, 12, and 16 gauge only.

One of the seemingly insignificant things about reloading paper shells is the re-capping and de-capping.

There is a great variety of forms and shapes of the inside base, each designed by the manufacturers of the shells to meet the requirements of the various high and low pressure, dense or bulk, smokeless powders with which they are to be loaded. To properly ignite these various powders there has been a great variety of primers manufactured; they have been specially designed to hold the proper charge of the different compounds, and are of different shapes, lengths and diameters, so that to meet the present requirements the simple old style re-capper and de-capper is of no use whatever.

Heretofore, the shells have been held by the outside rim or head with no inside support, and the force required to insert or seat the primer concaves the head of the shell, *thus carrying the top of the primer beyond the proper reach of the firing pin, and causing misfire.* The great variation in the shape and the thickness of the base, together with the variety of lengths and diameters of the primers, makes it impossible for the old style hinged lever, with an inserting punch moving on a circle, to reach the varying heights of the top of the primers, which should receive the pressure centrally on the top, and should be pushed into the pocket of the shell on a straight line.

There is only one part of the shell that has not been changed, and that is the outside dimensions; that part can not be changed very much and fit the various standard chambers of shot guns.

Therefore, the outside of the shell is used for a guide only, in both operations of re-capping and de-capping. The inside stud or pin is small enough to escape all of the various shapes and sizes of the base of the shells, and all shells rest on and are supported on the top of this inside stud, the end of which is small enough to permit either the solid paper base or metallic pocket to rest upon it, and all of the pressure exerted is received on the top of the pin or stud. There can be *no concaving of the head* or receding from the pressure applied on the lever.

The Ideal "Straightline" Re and De-Capper (see cut "T") is claimed will re and de-cap any and all shells with central fire holes whether of domestic or foreign manufacture, brass or paper, from 10 to 28 gauge, without any extra parts, excepting a a bushing for each gauge. It makes no difference what the shape or size of the shell may be on the inside, or what the thickness of the head, or what primer may be required.

We would advise expelling the old primers as soon as possible after being fired, or corrosion will weaken the primer pocket, and the old primers will stick as if they were soldered in. If pocket of shell has been corroded, all of the corrosion *must* be scraped out before seating a new primer for the soft copper primers cannot be forced into this corrosion without upsetting.

Cut "T"

Ironing
Attachment

WILL CUT THEM
ANY LENGTH

Cut "U"

When reloading shells that are to be used again the same length as they originally were, without cutting them off, they should be rolled or ironed at the muzzle. This operation hardens and solidifies the soft portion that has been previously crimped. It also straightens out the wrinkles, and leaves the muzzle in better form to receive the wads. If the muzzle of shell is ironed before being inserted in the No. 2 Shell Receiver, it will prevent injury to the springs which is liable to occur by forcing in shells, the muzzles of which are left ragged and doubled up. At every club shoot there are quantities of shells of various kinds used and cast away, most of which may be used again two or three times. The longer ones may be cut off to any length desired, and they will be found as good as new. The Ideal Shell Trimmer illustrated (see cūt "U") is a very satisfactory implement for this purpose. With it, shells may be cut off any length, from three and one-quarter to two inches. These Trimmers are made for all sizes from 10 to 28 gauge.

Last, but not least, is the operation of crimping. There is as much depending upon the uniformity and perfection of the crimp, as there is upon any other one thing in loading or reloading paper shells.

Many have an idea that to get strong shooting the whole charge must be rammed very hard, and the powder, shot and wadding crimped as snugly as it is possible to force the loaded shell up against the crimping head, the shortness of the lever on the crimping tool alone preventing the cartridge

| Imperfect Crimp. | Square Crimp. | Round Crimp. |

from being crushed. Occasional complaints are made that the crimping tool spoiled the shells, and samples of work done have been sent us, as per illustration of end of imperfectly crimped

The same thing may be caused by using too large wadding, or ramming so hard that the body of the shell is enlarged or distorted. Remember that the shot shells are only paper, and that they are made correct in size at the factory. If they are enlarged so that they can not enter the crimping head properly, results may be expected as per illustration "E." A crimping tool that will operate perfectly on an empty shell, should do the same kind of work on one that is loaded, if it has not been distorted in wadding or ramming, for forced too hard in crimping. *Forcing will roughen and spoil a good crimp.*

To insure a perfect crimp, at least one-quarter (¼) of an inch of the shell must be left without wadding, the cartridges should be forced up slowly, and the crank or crimping head revolved rapidly. Do not force shell faster than it is crimped, and when the end of the shell is turned over firmly upon the wadding, *stob,* and results will be similar to illustrations "C" and "D," showing perfect square and round crimp. *Continued pressing after shells are sufficiently crimped, results in injury.*

Until the coming of the repeating shot guns the square crimp was universally preferred. The users of the repeating shot guns find that the square crimp will at times catch on entering the chamber when being inserted by the mechanism; therefore, the round crimp is required to obviate that trouble. All heads for Ideal crimpers are furnished with one set of pins each for turning the round and square crimp, as per illustrations "C" and "D."

To properly crimp shells that have been reloaded, especially those that have not been cut off, but have the soft muzzle, we would advise a straightline crimper, such as Star Crimper No. 1 (See illustration "V" With such an implement the shells cannot be bent by being cramped.

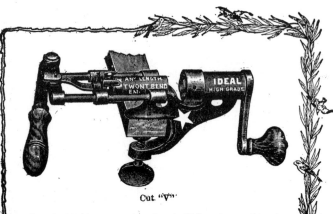

Cut "V"

shell. This shows that the shell has been forced so hard that it has been upset or enlarged while in the crimping head.

Crimping shells that have been fired, is very unsatisfactory on account of the muzzle of the shell being left dry and without lubrication, which has been extracted by the heat at the time of discharge. This deficiency may be supplied by dipping the end of the shell about one-sixteenth of an inch into hot beef tallow, which penetrates into the fibres of the paper. This may be done after the shells are loaded, before being crimped; anyone trying this will be surprised at the great improvement. When old shells ate so treated the crimping on them will be found equal to that on new shells; in fact, it improves the work on many new shells, as some of them have not as much lubrication in the woterproofing as others, and this tIllow treatment supplies the deficiency and injures none.

Shells that have been fired and the soft muzzle not cut off, must be forced into the crimper *very slowly*, and the head revolved as *rapidly as possible*.

A head that is correct in size for a new shell, may be too small for a shell that has been fired. An expanded shell can not be reduced in size at the muzzle by forcing it in a small head. The paper will crinkle or fold on one side every time. In such cases, we would advise an extra head that is larger, for the shells that have been fired. When ordering such special head, select several shells that are of the largest size that will go in the chamber of your gun freely, and send them to the manufacturers for special heads to fit

The Ideal Star Crimpers are the only ones on the market that work positively on a straight line, that will permit of interchangeable heads, followers, and pins, and that will turn the various crimps as shown in illustrations "C" and "D" Only one Star frame is required for 10, 12, 14, 16, 20, 24 and 28 gauge. A different grip is required for the 24 and 28 gauge

If the few suggestions given in the preceding pages are found of interest or value to the beginner or inexperienced, my work is well done and I am satisfied. If can I be of further service to any of the readers, I will be pleased at all times to answer correspondence, or to supply you with either of my other manuals, as is mentionted on the title page; each of which will be mailed on receipt of your order and 10c in stamps or coin, by addressing the author.

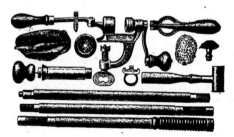

Reloading and Cleaning Set.

Marsh Shooting for Water Fowl.

See Hints for Shot Gun Shooters, Etc.

287

Powder Flasbes

Hints to Amateurs.—Use care in filling shells, to obtain uniform loads powder and shot should be accurately measured; try and get them all alike. Don't break the grains by pounding the powder (*and never compress Nitro powders.*)

For Trap Shooting—At inanimate targets the following is a popular load for a 10-gauge gun, 4 drachms *Hazard's Trap Powder No. 2;* two No. 9 and and one No. 10 black edge wad (spilt) in order named; one and one-fourth ounces (dipped measure) chilled shot No. 8; one-half of a No. 10 black edge (split) or shot shell crimped. Many shooters prefer three and three-fourths drachms of powder, and this quantity of Trap No. 2 is sufficient. It is desirable to have a light paper wad next to powder to prevent the grease from wads affecting it.

Charges for Breech Loaders—For guns under 8 lbs. in weight, 12 bore, 3 to 3½ drachms *Hazard Powder,* 1⅛ ozs. shot. 10 bore, 3¼ drachms powder, 1⅛ ozs. shot.

Guns Over 8 lbs. in Weight—12 bore, 3 to 3½ drachms Hazard powder, 1⅛ ozs. shot. 10 bore, 3¾ to 4 drachms powder, 1¼ ozs. shot.

Exact Amounts—To give satisfactory results can only be determined by repeated trials—Guns like shooters vary. The distribution of shot can be increased either by decreasing the quantity of powder, or increasing the charge of shot. To produce better penetration, increase the powder, decrease the shot.

Hazard's Trap Powder.—No. 1 (fine), No. 2 (medium), No. 3 (coarse). No. 2 is popular for both trap and field shooting, being slightly quicker than F. F. G. Kentucky.

Duck Shooting Powder.—No. 1 fine to No. 6 coarse; finer size for field shooting, the coarser for water fowl.

Look Out For Accidents.—Never compress *Nitro* powders. Black powders require compression, but to do this on Nitro powders might lead to serious results (a funeral perhaps.)

For Dupont Smokeless Powder.

Shells.—Use shells adapted to bulk smokeless. powder.

Powder.—The best loads for a 12-gauge gun are 2¾, 3, and 3¼ drachms, standard measure filled and struck. The smaller loads give slight recoil, high velocity, and very close pattern, and are well adapted to general shooting. For a quick, far-reaching load, 3¼ drachms is recommended. With this charge a close pattern is maintained and the necessary lead on quartering birds greatly reduced.

Wads.—In general, one trap or field wad, two or three black edge wads, and a thin cardboard wad over the shot will give excellent results. One cardboard, one white felt, with black edge wads to fill, will be found equally satisfactory for use over the powder. Wadding ought to be chosen of a thickness that will leave from a quarter to three-eighths of an inch for a tight crimp and the wads should be seated firmly on the powder charge.

10 gauge guns, 3 to 4 drachms and 1¼ oz shot.
12 gauge guns, 2¾ to 3¼ drachms and 1, 1⅛, or 1¼ oz. shot.

New Schultze Smokeless.
"E. C." No. 1, "New E. C." and "New Schultze" are Bulk Powders.

1 Drachm measure "E. C." No. 1 weighs 14 grs. avoirdupois. 3 drachms measure "E. C." No. 1, weighs 42 grains avoirdupois, etc., while 1 dram measure "New Schultze" or "New E. C." weighs 12 grains avoirdupois, 3 drachms measure "New Schultze" or "New E. C." weighs 36 grains avoirdupois.

Proper Loads of These Powders are

20 Gauge guns, 2   to 2½ drachms by measure.
16 Gauge guns, ¼ to 2¾ drachms by measure.
12 Gauge guns, 2¾ to 3½ drachms by measure.
10 Gauge guns, 3½ to 4½ drachms by measure.
8 Gauge guns, 4½ to 6¾ drachms by measure.

Always use paper shells adapted to Bulk Nitro Powders, and place enough tight fitting wads over powder, firmly pressed down, to leave about ¼ in. of paper for a solid crimp

The Perfect and Imperfect Crimp.

E—The *imperfect* crimp.   C—The *square* crimp.
D—The round crimp.

C and D are correct crimps.

Walsrode Powders.—New Green for shot guns
.12 gauge, 30 grains; 10 gauge, 38 grains. *Wolf
Smokeless*, (the new Walsrode) 12 gauge, 32 to 36
grains or 2 drachms; 10 gauge, 48 to 52 grains or
3¼ to 3½ drachms.

Loads for Rifle Powders—(Dupont Smokeless
No. 1) 45, 70, 405, 28 grains. 38, 70, 255, 25 grains;
for high power rifle use 30 caliber annular smokeless rifle powder; 303 Savage, 29 grains; 30-30
Winchester or Marlin, 26½ grains.

Laflin & Rand (Lightning Smokeless—30-30
Winchester, 23 grains or 1⅛ drachms; 303 Savage,
27 grains or 1¼ drachms; 303 British, 28 grains or
1 and 5-16 drachms.

Walsrode High Pressure Rifle Powder - 30-30
or 303 Savage, 25 grains.

Two good loads for Trap work. No. 1—3 drams
Hazard Smokeless. 1 No. 12 trap or field. 1 No.
12 white felt, ⅜ in. 1 No. 12 black edge, ⅛ inch.
1¼ ozs. No. 7½ chilled shot. Space for good
crimp.

No. 2—3 drachms Hazard Smokeless. 1 No. 12
card. 2 No. 12 black edge, ¼ in. 1 No. 12 black
edge, ⅛ in. 1⅛ ozs. No. 7½ chilled shot. Space
for good crimp.

Still another one—3 drachms Hazard Smokeless.
1 No. 12 top shot wad. 3 No. 12 pink edge, ¼ in.
1⅛ ozs. No. 7½ chilled shot. Space for good
crimp.

290

Grass Hunting Suits, Shore and Boat Blinds, Calls, Decoys, Etc.

14—Decoy Duck.

13—Decoy Ducks.

6—Shore Blind.

8—Hunting Grass Suit.

7—Hunting Grass Suit.

1—Duck Call.

9—Hunting Grass Suit.

2—Dog Call or Whistle.

3—Snipe Call.

4—Allen Duck Call.

5—Goose and Crane Call.

10—Wading Boots.

11—Boat Blind. 291

12—Wading Boots.

About Blinds.

(For shore, wear, or boat uses.)

The Grass Suit.

In these days it is unnecessary to go into details as to the methods of *constructing blinds, stands, etc.*, for the reason that the sportsman or duck hunter can obtain them at slight cost, put up in *portable form* for either *wear, boat or shore*, as occasion requires, as a glance at the page of illustrations (which accompanies this article) shows; Grass Hunting Suits being now extremely popular for *wild Goose, Duck, or all kinds of water fowl shooting.* These are made ready for immediate use, of dry, long, tough marsh grass, into suits (cape, coat and hood) convenient to *wear and shoot from;* weighing about 4 lbs. and really making good *snow and rain proof* garments as well. Hunters appreciate these, as it really does away with the *thankless, difficult work of building* blinds or bough houses, so necessary before these were introduced. They fit practically any person, really converting them into a semi-natural *growth of rushes, hay or wheat stack.* If shore blinds are desired, they are made in standard *lengths and rolls* of 6x3 feet, by which a shore blind can be made of any length, size or shape desired; giving ample room for a seat, and supplied even with "stocks" or supports, to be fastened and set up anywhere. *Usually two of these lengths* construct an admirable, roomy sized *"shore blind."* On the other hand if a *"Grass boat blind"* is desired they are made in lengths of 5 ft. 10 in. by 27 inches, made to resemble wild rice, rushes, marsh grass, etc.; rolling compactly *in a small roll*, each piece being supplied with sticks which fit into screw eyes screwed in rail (or gunwale) of boat, making *them easily adjusted.* Usually four pieces are sufficient to go around an ordinary boat, while if desired one side of the boat only need be used for a blind. In the methods of use, or construction, the illustrations convey an accurate idea; while their price is such that many thousands of sportsmen choose to use them in preference to the long and arduous task of building them from material on the grounds, which is a very difficult and sometimes impossible task.

In the arrangement or construction of blinds, it is always best to locate them in such position that the ducks or fowls will not have to first pass over the blinds to reach the decoys, or come within range. No matter how carefully you arrange blinds, ducks can perceive them and are able to distinguish the fraud, (hence they are apt to avoid them.) Again, in arranging your decoys, when ever possible, set them as far out in open water as possible (within range) and to *leeward* of your blinds; although at times to windward is the better plan. This depends greatly on surroundings, for at times conditions are such that one has to tax their ingenuity to do either. The whole secret however, is to so locate and erect your blinds *so as they can not be seen by fowl approaching on the wing*, and to arrange your decoys (head to the wind) in such a way as they *can not be hidden, but are to the contrary in plain view from all directions.* Let them drift off, and with a cord occasionally bring them to your vicinity, as though it were a living flock of ducks moving about from place to place; feeding and resting.

About Decoys, Duck Calls, Etc

The value to the duck hunter of **good decoys** when shooting from shore or boat blinds, cannot be **over estimated**, as by their use many a flock of birds are deceived into approaching, and **even settling amongst** what appears to be a cozy and safe retreat or feeding grounds; not realizing the fraud until the sportsman has thinned their ranks, by quick and deadly shooting. These are now considered as a most **important part of the duck hunter's outfit,** and are made in infinite variety of forms; so deceptive in appearance as to often get shot at by the sportsmen who are using them, who at times can barely distinguish them from the **real thing.** They are made of wood (folding) in imitation of Mallard, Canvas Back, Red Head, Blue Bill, Pin Tail, Widgeon, Sprigtail, Blue Winged Teal, etc (even with glass eyes) weighing when packed, from **7 lbs. per dozen to 30 lbs.** Again they are made of **waterproof cloth over wire frames,** with anchors complete, each being a size of 16x14x7 inches; being very compact and weighing about 1 lb. each; a dozen of which packs into the **handy box shown in illustration which heads this chapter.** Others of canvas, all painted, durable and lifelike, weighing 7 to 14 lbs. per doz. according to grade and kind.

If geese decoys are desired, these are made so as **to be set up on land for field shooting,** weighing from 14 to 24 lbs. a dozen, according to grade and price. In the matter of **"Calls"** many sportsmen of long experience can imitate and send forth calls with a degree of marvelous imitation, while others cannot even pucker up their lips and whistle. For this all sorts of excellent calls are provided, among which the **"Allen Duck Call"** has won its way to the heart of the most **skeptical sportsman** or duck hunter. By their means **Snipe, Turkeys, Ducks, Geese, or Cranes** can be perfectly imitated, if the well known kinds be selected. The sportsman should however, use care in the selection of those that have not been found by extensive use, to be perfect. The most well known grades being illustrated in connection with the Blinds and Decoys shown elsewhere

In the setting out of decoys, many sportsmen **make the mistake** in arranging them in such position that the ducks must necessarily pass over the blinds before they can observe them; this is wrong. Decoys should be always placed so as the ducks will observe the decoys first; otherwise they will surely observe the blinds and detect the fraud; thus they will swerve away. Generally speaking, always set your decoys to leeward of your blinds, well into the open waters, where they can be very plainly observed by ducks that are on the wing. Never set them on the edge of, or in close proximity to your blind, but well out into the opening or clear water, where they can be easily observed and plainly kept in sight. In short the whole secret is in arranging your blinds, so as they can not be observed; and in arranging your decoys so as they can. The more you can conceal your blinds and the more **prominently you can display your decoys,** the better success will attend your efforts.

Broiled Duck and Coffee.

About Boats

One of the most essential things for the duck hunter in particular, sportsmen in general, is the possession of a staunch *yet light and portable boat.* These are made in infinite variety of aluminum, s h e e t steel, c a n v a s or wood. It should be capable of carrying a good load safely and require but little water, so as to slide safely over shallow places; beside this it must be capable of being easily lifted on the shoulders and carried from point to point, be a sea or rough water boat and capable of standing lots of hard knocks—in short have *the carrying capacity of a scow,* all the ease of propulsion so noticeable in the clinker boat, and *without its crankiness.* It must be a safety so as not to sink, safe on treacherous streams and rapids, capable of not being damaged by snags or rocks. The birch bark canoe has all these points *except for durability.* Hence a score of manufacturers vie with each other to produce an all around boat. To those desiring to purchase, I advise a perusal of the various grades illustrated herein or in the *"Fisherman's Manual,"* recommending particu larly those that can be packed in small, conven ient compass, and stored in a chest, so as to be *shipped as baggage.* Some of these boats (not ably the Clark-Devine) are so arranged as to form a packing case for tent and other portions of a sportsman's outfit; or if a still more portable boat is required, *the Osgood Foldiug Canvas Boat* is all that is to be desired. Another excellent boat extremely popular is the *Mullins Steel Boat;* or

STANDARD TYPES of (Portable) HUNTING and FISHING CANOES

Oskosh.

Portable Double End Hunting Canoe. (Bent's Model.)

The Portable Hunting Skiff. (Oskosh.)

The Duck-Hunter's Favorite.

For Other Styles of Portable Boats—See Fisherman's Manual.

Combined Oar or Paddle.

297

The "Clark=Devine" Portable Sectional Boat and Oar.

A Trunk when shipped.

An ideal fishing or hunting boat.

For other kinds of Boats, see Fisherman's Manual.

Depth 13 inches

Weight 100 lbs.
Size 12x3 feet.

For three persons.

Can be shipped as baggage and will hold a 300 lb. camp outfit besides.

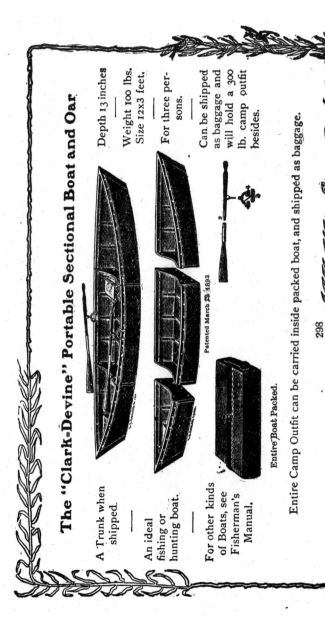

Patented March 28, 1893.

Entire Boat Packed.

Entire Camp Outfit can be carried inside packed boat, and shipped as baggage.

298

in fact any of them illustrated herein or those mentioned in the "Fisherman's Manual." Many of these boats are supplied with air chambers, rendering them practical life boats.

These steel boats are built of heavily galvanized "Appollo" steel. Each strip is cut from a special pattern and made to conform without strain to the beautiful curves that distinguish this line of boats from all other craft, and gives to them that graceful poise in the water that is distinctive, and draws forth praise from all who see them. The lapping, seaming or grooving of the steel strips is by a new process, used only in these boats. By its use leakage is absolutely impossible. The steel boat will last forever. It cannot rot. The heavy galvanizing protects it from rusting, and it is so staunch that a blow from an axe that would fell an ox will hardly dent a good steel boat. They have been severely tried out in stumpy water where wood boats had been stove in numerous times; they have been taken down rocky rapids in trout streams and came through uninjured, where a wooden boat of equal dimensions could not have been made strong enough to stand the knocks and jars. They will not check or crack nor get out of shape, because there is no strain anywhere, all the pretty curves are natural, and they have a much handsomer, cleaner appearance than the wooden boat that must inevitably become water-soaked and rotten.

The Sportsman's Favorite Boat.

FIRST AID BANDAGES
A Boy Scout Who Has Been Used as a "Subject"
by His Comrades.   Note the Sling
for a Broken Arm or Wrist

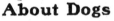

About Dogs

The prevalent belief at the present day regarding the origin of the domestic dog, is that it is the result of the crossing of various species of wild animals, notably the wolf and jackal, which the Savages were wont to capture when young, confine and train for their own uses. Darwin has shown us **that the fear of man in all animals** is an acquired instinct, for it is a well known fact, of which the writer can testify to from personal observations in the Arctic regions, that both **birds and animals** at times, in interior portions of that country, were so unused to man, that they permitted so near approach that they could almost be caught by hand.

The Savages have been known in all parts of the world, to cross their captured or tamed semi-wild dogs with wild animals, to improve the species. The American Indian's dog or that of the Esquimaux is known to be a species of the wild wolf, and it has been said that the species of stag-deer or sheep hounds, have been crossed with the animals they have been named after. The wolves of Hungary, India, even America are hardly distinguishable to-day from the dogs of these countries; and there are tamed wolves, that in their gentleness, love of their masters, and intelligence shows the true dog-like capacity. Their period of gestation (63 days) agrees; and wolves and jackals when tamed evince the same points, when carressed or petted by their masters; jumping about for joy, wagging their tails, lower their ears, and lick the hands, crouch down, and even throw themselves on the ground belly upwards; or carry their tails between their legs, and howl when hurt or frightened. The habit of barking however, is more or less cultivated, and appears to be capable of being lost and again acquired. The Egyptians, Greeks and Romans bred their war dogs thus; and like the wild animals mentioned, the dog of to-day is mostly carnivorious, preferring for foods, flesh that is slightly putrid. In drinking it laps with its tongue and never perspires, except by a hanging tongue, and fluid that drops from it

By the attention of man, dogs have by careful selection and intercrossing, been moulded into infinite variety of forms; retarding certain senses, and increasing others, there are few **human passions** not shared by the domestic dog; many of which has been taught him by his master; for like him it shows anger, jealousy, love, envy, hatred, grief, gratitude, pride, generosity and fear. It is known to sympathize with man, and numerous instances can be cited of its sympathy with other animals. It remembers, and is thus assisted by association of ideas; it is imaginative, which is proven by their dreams of pursuing game in its sleep. It is subject to shame and seems to know when it has done wrong, for it will oftimes submit to punishment. It shares with man fear of unknown things, and a courageous dog will oftimes become startled and tremble at the rustle of a leaf if sudden.

In the selection of a dog for sporting purposes, it is an easy matter for the sportsman nowadays to choose the best.

For a water dog—duck hunting, etc., a retriever is essential; a cross between a Newfoundland dog and a setter being a good choice. **If a smaller, yet** efficient animal is preferred, a cross between a **Setter and Spaniel** is desirable, or a Retriever and Spaniel. The choice of the American Duck hunter being that of the Chesapeake dog.

For Deer hunting, the Deer or Stag Hound is best. For the sportsman away from waters, choose the **Setter or Pointer**, or a cross between both. For the trapper, the **Beagle or Terrier Dog.** For the watch dog, the Mastiff or Bull dog; although the Terrier is equally as good.

It requires much patience and honest work to train a good dog. If you can afford to purchase one, do so slowly; first satisfy yourself that those you purchase from are **reliable in every sense of the word**—otherwise buy a young puppy of the specie mentioned, and train him yourself, or have him trained especially for you by a specialist in that line. In all cases try and select a dog of a good **liver color;** and if you start out with a liberal supply of patience, firmness and kindness, you can soon possess an excellently trained animal, that time will render very nearly perfect.

One cannot commence too early with a puppy. First see to it that you gain its good will and confidence; get him to like you, to greet your coming, and to grow fond of you Don't try and commence the training part **too quick;** rather confine your efforts to a participation in its romping, playful innocence; and reward its efforts of play with a few choice bits from your own hands. If it is sullen, deceitful or morose, discard it for a brighter, better one. When its age is such **that it can reason and think,** then teach it little things, like laying down at the word of "down," and when it understands, **insist that it does what you tell it to do.** Enforce obedience. Teach it to pick up little articles and bring them in play; first to pick it up and let you take it from him easily; then to **go and get it.** For a like purpose use the same **words,** always, such as fetch, bring, carry, lay down, look, etc. Punish him only when you must, and do not tax his patience with too long lessons. Better still, if you emphasize your lessons with a certain—**always the same movement of your hand,** of the different lessons you teach him, so as he can recognize that hand signal in lieu of your voice of command **when in the field.** The fewer the words you speak the better. **If a water dog,** never throw him into the water after an object; take and put the object a few steps in first, then throw it farther and farther out, and encourage him by words of praise and petting when he does it. Don't choose cold days at first, harden him gradually, and he will soon be only **too eager** to do **your bidding,** in ice cold waters.

Try and convey to him your meaning by illustration, take for instance teaching him to "down," if he fails to grasp your meaning, force him to lay down by pressing him down—don't be too hasty; it takes time to teach a child—years of it; and you cannot expect to train a good dog in a few weeks. Teach him to put things he brings you into your hands. Keep him around the house, don't let him

303

wander off with other dogs; punish him when he deserves it, and let the punishment count—don't kick him; and soon he will learn to **obey you.** Teach him to carry your paper, a parcel or package, then to find where it is hidden, and soon he will take pleasure in hunting things you have hidden in almost unheard of places. No animal living has greater intelligence than a dog, and if you have gained his good will and affection he will **die for you.** No human friendship is akin to that of a canine friend; he will stick to you through adversity; bring his bone to share with you if necessary; no matter what happens he will stand by you. Cold, wet or hunger will not tempt him to desert you. Poor faithful beast will make his bed at your grave, refusing food and shelter, to be nigh you—no friendship on this earth can equal it; and in concluding this chapter on the faithful beast, let me give space to the following facts which speak for themselves, which happened in my own great city, Chicago, and which was published in the local papers, extensively, and mentioned in various magazines, books, etc.

Those who have nothing but curses and kicks for, **and who have no use for dogs,** would perhaps be better citizens, did they but possess the same attachments and friendship often exhibited by the dog; particularly by a large, black Newfoundland dog, a few days ago in excessively bitter cold winter weather. For days he was noticed by the **Lincoln Park Police,** intently watching the water; every now and then he would go to the ice and scratch as though trying to dig up something. **All through the bitter cold weather, night and day** he faced the storms of the lake, and the piercing, icy blasts, and could not be coaxed away. The park police finding all efforts to get him away failed, brought him food and shelter, **which he refused.** One morning he was found **dead, frozen stiff.** The supposition was that his master had fallen and was drowned or committed suicide. He was only a dog, yet how many human beings could be found like him. Hence the following poem in commemoration **still lives.**

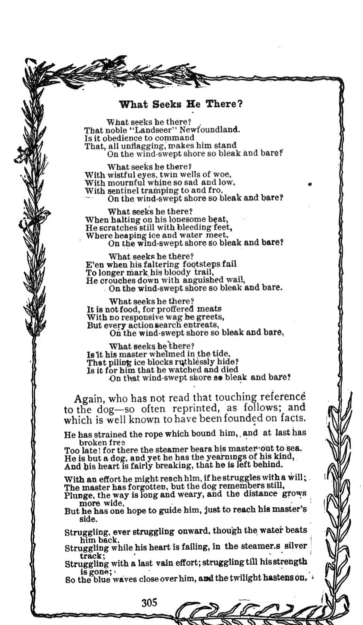

What Seeks He There?

What seeks he there?
That noble "Landseer" Newfoundland.
Is it obedience to command
That, all unflagging, makes him stand
    On the wind-swept shore so bleak and bare?

What seeks he there?
With wistful eyes, twin wells of woe,
With mournful whine so sad and low,
With sentinel tramping to and fro,
    On the wind-swept shore so bleak and bare?

What seeks he there?
When halting on his lonesome beat,
He scratches still with bleeding feet,
Where heaping ice and water meet,
    On the wind-swept shore so bleak and bare?

What seeks he there?
E'en when his faltering footsteps fail
To longer mark his bloody trail,
He crouches down with anguished wail,
    On the wind-swept shore so bleak and bare.

What seeks he there?
It is not food, for proffered meats
With no responsive wag he greets,
But every action search entreats,
    On the wind-swept shore so bleak and bare,

What seeks he there?
Is it his master whelmed in the tide,
That piling ice blocks ruthlessly hide?
Is it for him that he watched and died
    On that wind-swept shore so bleak and bare?

Again, who has not read that touching reference to the dog—so often reprinted, as follows; and which is well known to have been founded on facts.

He has strained the rope which bound him, and at last has broken free
Too late! for there the steamer bears his master out to sea.
He is but a dog, and yet he has the yearnings of his kind,
And his heart is fairly breaking, that he is left behind.

With an effort he might reach him, if he struggles with a will;
The master has forgotten, but the dog remembers still,
Plunge, the way is long and weary, and the distance grows more wide,
But he has one hope to guide him, just to reach his master's side.

Struggling, ever struggling onward, though the water beats him back,
Struggling while his heart is failing, in the steamer.s silver track;
Struggling with a last vain effort; struggling till his strength is gone;
So the blue waves close over him, and the twilight hastens on,

Pointers

On the Care of Dogs and a "Tribute to the Dog"

To those who are possessed of a good dog 1 will give a few suggestions as to the care and treatment of them necessary to keep them in good condition:

Keep them clean. Wash them in cool water, never hot water. Don't over feed them. Let their meals be given them morning and evening only (unless working in the field hunting.) The best food is clean scraps from the table or well boiled soft mixtures of meats scraps and vegetables, with a meat bone (fresh) uncooked occasionally so as to keep his teeth in trim. Rice, wheat flour, etc., can be used to thicken the stews. In hunting seasons when they work hard give them a liberal allowance of raw meats, so as to build up their strength. Use for bedding fresh straw, burning the old and adding new say weekly. Exercise him often and note carefully any changes in *his condition* which indicates *irregularities or sickness.* Occasionally disinfect his sleeping quarters. Keep his bowels open, his stomach free from worms, clean quarters and regular feeding and you will have but little trouble. Treat him according to his age—as though it were a human being, using even the *same medieine* and you will seldom need a veterinary surgeon's assistance. The most frequent ailments of the dog (common) are distemper, worms, colds, diarrhoea, constipation, mange and fits. These can be treated successfully by the owners (if not allowed to run on) until severe, the *greatest difficulty being in determining the nature of them.* To aid you thus, it is only necessary to write for little *free books* of the dog and its care, diseases of it, published by the following specialists and to act accordingly. Better still if you would write them a personal letter giving forth the following facts: Breed, age and weight; condition as to flesh, skin coat, appetite, bowels and urinary organs; positions and actions of the animal, symptoms and how long noticeable. This will be answered *without cost*. No man deserves a dog if he permits an animal to suffer for the trouble of letter or a *few cents* for treatment. In writing these specialists send a stamped envelope for reply and you will not fail to receive *good advice and attention*. Address, Spratt's Patent, Newark, N. J., for book (Dog Culture;) H. C. Glover, 1278 Broadway, New York City, (Diseases of the Dog, How to Feed, etc.;) Polk Miller, Richmond, Va., (Dog's ailments, How to Treat Them,) you can rely on receiving much information of value and conscientious treatment for the reliability of these firms are only too well known. Many a poor brute has been allowed to *suffer needlessly*, and often the cry "mad dog" raised on some poor dumb animal, suffering only from fits, pursued by an excited and blood-thirsty mob; whereas all the poor beast required was a little medicine or treatment to restore him to his natural condition; and if these few lines can ever be the means of doing good for the *greatest friend of man* I shall consider myself well repaid for including them here. In conclusion let me again cite another truthful tribute to the dog.

A Tribute to the Dog

"Treat a dog like a man, and you will have a noble animal, treat him like a dog, and you will have a dog that knows more than you do. Proof: He understands your lauguage; you do not understand his.

The best friend a man has in the world may turn against him and become his enemy. His son or daughter that he has reared with loving care may prove ungrateful. Those who are nearest and dearest to us, those whom we trust with our happiness and our good name, may become traitors to their faith. The money that a man has he may lose. It flies away from him, perhaps, when he needs it most. A man's reputation may be sacrificed in a moment of ill-considered action. The people who are prone to fall on their knees to do honor when success is with us may be the first to throw the stones of malice when failure settles its cloud upon our heads. The one absolutely unselfish friend that man can have in this selfish world, the one that never deserts him, the one that never proves ungrateful or teacherous, is his dog. A man's dog stands by him in prosperity and poverty, in health and in sickness. He will sleep on the cold ground, where the wintry winds blow, and the snow drives fiercely, if only he may be near his master's side. He will kiss the hand that has no food to offer; he will lick the wounds and sores that come in encounter with the roughness of the world. He guards the sleep of his pauper master as if he were a prince. When all other friends desert he remains. When riches take wings and reputation falls to pieces, he is as constant in his love as the sun its journeys through the heavens.

If fortune drives the master forth an outcast in the world, friendless and homeless, the faithful dog asks no higher privilege than that of accompanying him, to guard against danger, to fight against his enemies. and when the last scene of all comes, and death takes the master in its embrace, and his body is laid away in the cold ground, no matter if all other friends pursue their way there by the graveside will the noble dog be often found.

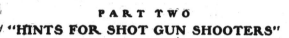

PART TWO
"HINTS FOR SHOT GUN SHOOTERS"

(READ ALSO "HITS AROUND THE BULL'S EYE"

Something Wrong.

A Series of Suggestions as to
LOADS, CHARGES, WADS, RELOADING, SIGHTING, GUNS, SHOT, POWDER, SHELLS,
Miscellaneous Information, Etc.

Points for
Rifle Users

Hints for
Hunters and
Campers

SEE ALSO "TRAPPERS TRICKS'

309

Hints for Shot Gun Shooters

The Best Boat for Duck Hunting—A scull boat with cockpit. The Mullins duck boat (steel) painted dead grass color. (See Boats.)

Best Dog for Duck Hunters—Cross between a Newfoundland and Setter, or a Retriever and Water Spaniel, or a cross between the Setter and Spaniel; best color, liver color.

Best Blinds for Duck Hunting—The natural grass or rushes that abound in the vicinity; use plenty of them.

The Best Rifle for Small Game—Or for target practice is of course largely a matter of choice. Either the Stevens, Remington or Winchester are accurate guns. A good choice is the Winchester, 25-20, either single shot or half magazine repeater, equipped with Lyman combination rear sight. Lyman leaf in lieu of the regular rear sight on the barrel and Lyman ivory bead fore sight, it is satisfactory for either smokeless or black powders.

The Best Ammunition—For rifles is that made by Union Metal Cartridge Co., or Winchester Repeating Arms Co.

The Best Shot Gun—Is hard to determine, there are many good ones. The Greener being a splendid weapon; following close comes the L. C. Smith, Parker, Ithaca (American make.)

When Using a High Power Rifle—Fit to the butt of it, a good recoil pad, and have your rifle fitted with a Lyman leaf sight; fold down the crotch, raise the bar and use the ivory bead for front; these are better for shooting trim than any globe peep or crotch sights, which are good for target uses, but not for game killing.

The Best Repeating Shot Gun—The Winchester shot gun is probably the best of its kind, its action is reasonably smooth and reliable. It can be used as a large ball gun, and if proper loaded ammunition is used, is a most satisfactory arm.

The Best Book on Reloading—The Ideal Hand Book for Shooters. Ideal Mfg. Co., New Haven, Conn. (Send postage.)

Try Using the Right Barrel—For objects passing to the left, left barrel for those to the right on long ranges.

A Wire Scratch Brush—Will not scratch the interior of barrels and is invaluable for cleaning a shot gun. Rust can be removed by a rag dipped in kerosene if not pitted in. Wipe well dry and oil afterward or vaseline.

Gun for Brush Shooting—Right barrel cylinder left modified choke bored. For field shooting right barrel modified left full choke. Trap shooting both barrels full choked or first barrel modified choke.

Don't Change—Your gun or rifle if it is a good one. Stick to it. Change your methods which is most apt to be at fault, if faults exist.

Choke Bore Guns—Insure close shooting and good penetration. For shooting at close range a cylinder bore is preferable. Such a gun will shoot spherical bullets up to 50 yards.

Auxiliary Rifle Barrels—Can be placed in temporarily and used in the barrel of a shot gun of 10 or 12 bore.

Chilled Shot—Is better than soft shot in many respects.

To Scatter Shot—Place one wad on the powder, two wads between the shot, over the whole put a thick wad. Never use poor home made wads.

Quick Shooting—is essential when using a shot gun. Shoot the instant your gun points as closely as possible without taking second aim.

Velocity of Shot From a 12-Gauge Gun.

Powder	Drams	Size of Shot	Ounces	Range in Feet	Mean Velocity in feet per second
H	2½	2	1¼	50	1013
H	2½	2	1¼	100	865
H	2½	2	2¼	100	854
D	3	7	1⅛	100	776
D	3	7	1¼	100	783
D	3	7	1¼	50	855
H	2½	2	1¼	50	995

Plant Wild Rice.—If the sportsmen will do this in the fall of the year, he will be amply repaid for his pains later. Ducks will not linger in waters devoid of food. It is to your interest to plant wild rice.

For Duck Shooting—Use a 10 bore shot gun, 8½ to 9½ lbs., full choke, or a 12-gauge. Best time October and November.

To Scull a Boat—With one oar, place oar over the stern or rear of the boat in a rowlock secured there for the purpose, and thrusting the blade in the water deeply, move it so as to describe as near as possible a series of turns similar to the capital letter L, allowing the blade of the oar to take as large a figure as possible but restricting the movement of your hands to as small a figure as you can. To get the idea better, take a pencil and write a series of capital L in quick succession one under the other without stopping—try it. I have taught a dozen duck hunters the idea by this simple plan.

Decoy Duck Hunting—Try a small bore rifle for out of range birds, cripples, stragglers, etc.

If Ducks Alight—Out of range of your decoys, disperse them lest they attract others from your decoys—go after them.

Ducks Approaching Decoys—And flying with the wind invariably pass over the decoys, then swing around to alight.

Try Tolling—For canvas back or broad bills especially.

Best Time for Duck Shooting—Just before daylight or before dark.

A Slight Noise—Or whistle will often cause ducks to group or close together.

For Wild Geese—Use a 10 bore gun, 4½ drs. powder, 1¼ to 1½ ozs. No. 2 shot. Best time is in snow storm, as they are then bewildered and restless; Mallard also are similarly affected.

If at Forty Yards—A foot seems to far ahead, make it two, keep the gun moving and the bird falls dead.

American Wild Fowl---and Shooting.

Mallard Duck.

Teal Duck.

Duck Shooting on the Feeding Grounds with the
New Automatic Shot Gun.

Canvas Back Duck.

Canada Goose.

American Game Birds.
Sportsman's Favorites.

The Ployer.

The Woodcock.

Male and Female Mallards.

The Wood Duck.

The Grouse.

See Points for Shot Gun Shooters, etc., etc.,

Choosing a Shot Gun—Use a cylinder bore for brush shooting; a modified choke for field use; full choke for wild fowl, or a combination of the two of the three; let the barrels be 30 or 32 inch, with the gun weighing about 7 lbs. For duck shooting both barrels full choke is best.

Shot Falling.—A charge of shot will fall 8 inches in 40 to 50 yards.

Shooting at Close Range—The cylinder bored shot gun is preferable.

To Test the Fit of a Shot Gun—Bring it to the shoulder; if you do not have to crane or stretch the neck to sight along the barrels, it is a good fit.

Shooting Spherical Bullets—Use the cylinder bore so as the ball will pass through the barrel easily; it will carry accurately up to 50 yards with force.

To Scatter Shot—Place one wad on the powder, two or three between the shot, and use thin wads, over the whole put a thick wad.

Shell Extractors.—Always carry in a handy pocket a good shell extractor. It is well worth its cost and more.

Reloading Shells.—Good paper shells (not abused) can be reloaded six or more times, with safety.

In Shooting Flying Birds—The aim should be from a few inches to a few feet in advance of the bird, according to distance, speed, etc.; from 3 inches to even 3 feet or more at times.

Don't Shoot—At an incoming bird, wait until it passes you.

A Leather Coat—Should be used for fall or cold weather duck shooting; if too heavy, choose the yellow oilskin or waterproof canvas if wet weather especially.

"Tolling for Ducks."—Attract their attention by waving a red bandanna handkerchief on a stick keeping yourself out of sight; ducks are inquisitive and will often swim up to investigate, unless they are very wild.

315

Best Boat for Duck Hunting—Mullin's Duck boat. Scull oar rigged with cock pit covered with brush and hay, or rushes as a blind.

Duck Shooters—With a rubber blanket and air cushion can sit or lay on wet ground or marsh all day.

Best Shells to Reload—For shot guns Winchester, Yellow Rival, N. M. C., Nitro Club, New Victor, Peter's, etc.

Use a Cylinder Bore—If you desire to use *round ball or bullet* good for 50 to 75 yards, large game shooting, use a patched ball (to gauge the size of your gun) load 4 to 4½ drachms powder, F. F. G.; ⅜ felt pad on powder, ball seated *snugly* on top of wad, a little lubricant put around it and a wall of shell as in gallery ammunition.

Twist of Rifle Barrels—A proper twist is one that will spin a bullet fast enough to keep it *point on* to the limit of its range or flight, thus assuring accuracy. If the twist is too slow, the flight of bullets will be untrue and it will "tumble and keyhole," passing through the air longways instead of point on as it should. On the other hand, if the twist is too quick the bullet will *spin too rapidly* rending its flight unsteady, causing it to wobble, spin and hum like a top.

Incoming Birds.—Swing well ahead, keep your gun moving with the bird, pulling the twigger the instant the bird reaches the sight of your barrels.

Side Shots.—Aim and swing with the bird and well ahead, according to distance, wind, etc., hold well ahead, so as the shot will have time to reach him.

Birds Alighting—Or descending hold well under, always ahead of them, so as they will not fly with the shot.

Duck Hunting—In boats, leave the dog home, unless your clothes are waterproof and you don't mind his shaking the water off when he returns to boat. Make a blind decoy out of your boat is better, and use decoys.

Always Steer Clear of Fences—They scare any birds, ducks especially.

In Stormy Weather—Seek for ducks in heavy timbered woods or sheltered places.

316

Solid Comfort Seat Pad

Prevents you from getting wet and uncomfortable when it's necessary to sit down on a snowy log or in a leaky duckboat. Worn outside the trousers and instantly detachable. Made from the best materials and durably bound in yellow leather. Absolutely waterproof, and prevents chills, colds, rheumatism and rectal ailments.

Fastens to the trousers by two metallic hooks connected to the pad by adjustable bands of elastic webbing and a narrow leather strap about each leg midway between the hip and knee. In ordering state width across widest part below hips. Made in two sizes, 16 and 18 inches. Will literally last a lifetime, and is worth the price every day it's used.

The Shot Gun Sight

Is an invention that introduces a new and perfect system of sighting shot guns—so simple and effective that it makes wing shooting easy and certain. The two sights placed on or near the muzzle of gun clearly shows the killing circle.

When the bird is seen between the two sights and is not out of range, it can be bagged. A beginner will be surprised how soon he becomes a good  wing shot. As all double-barrel shot guns cross the center line at about thirty yards, after which the right barrel goes to the left and the left barrel goes to the right, this compensates for that difference, as you can sight directly down the barrel fired, and thus have aim directly in line of charge.

At cross going to the left, sight on left barrel and fire right barrel, and for right, *vice versa*. You will then give the bird the proper lead that will insure it being killed.

A little use of the sight will convince the most skeptical of its merit. It has been subjected to the most rigid test at trap and field, and will do all that is claimed for it.

They are made of the best spring steel, finely blued, are instantly attachable and detachable to any gun and does not mar the barrels.

The Patent Gun Sling

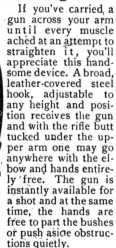

Gun Sling with Cartridge carrier

If you've carried a gun across your arm until every muscle ached at an attempt to straighten it, you'll appreciate this handsome device. A broad, leather-covered steel hook, adjustable to any height and position receives the gun and with the rifle butt tucked under the upper arm one may go anywhere with the elbow and hands entirely free. The gun is instantly available for a shot and at the same time, the hands are free to part the bushes or push aside obstructions quietly.

Handsomely made in natural leather and adjustable to persons of any size   Connected with the straps, and immediately above the hook, is a cartridge carrier. The cartridge carriers are readily detached to change from shot gun to rifle and vice versa. Mention size of cartridge to be used.

In Cleaning Guns—Nothing excels kerosene or benzine, afterward wiped and rubbed well with clean, dry rags (and elbow grease) then moistened with a little vaseline.

Secret of Becoming a Good Shoot—First, correctly judging distance. Second, speed of object (if moving) fired at. Third, holding the gun so as the object will meet the shot or bullet at the same time the bullet reaches it. Nine out of ten make the *serious mistake of shooting behind.* Fourth, making allowances for wind drift of shot correctly. Sixth, closely observing the faults of every shot and rectifying the errors.

For Duck Shooting—Use Nos. 5-6-7-8, chilled shot as some guns throw certain shot better than others. See which *your gun* is best suited for.

Use Waterproof Shells (Paper)—For Duck hunting, and never go on a trip without decoys, assorted ones. Don't select all one kind. Don't forget the Allen duck call, and to use the Ducks you shoot as additional decoys, the more the better.

Best Dog for Duck Hunting—A good Retriever, Water Spaniel or a cross between a Spaniel or Setter.

To Imitate a Duck Quack—Press the tip of your tongue at the upper roof of your mouth near the upper teeth and say "quack;" or say "me-amph" loud; Geese, "ah-hunk."

Use Dead Ducks—As decoys (all you have) stiffening their heads with a wooden skewer.

Best Time for Duck Hunting—November and December. Best gun full choke or right barrel modified choke; left, full choke, 10 gauge.

Shot for Birds—Prairie Chicken, Nos. 6-7; Quail, No. 8; Teal Duck, Nos. 7-8; Mallards, 5-6-7; Swan, Nos. 1-2; Geese, Nos. 1-2-3; Blue Bill, No. 6-7; Canvas Back, No. 4-5; Gray and Widgeon, Nos. 5-7; Red Heads, No. 6; Pintails, Nos. 5-6; Grouse, Nos. 6-7; Snipe, Nos. 8-9.

Duck Shooters Outfit—Clothes dead grass color, rubber coat dead grass color, long rubber boots, wristlets and gloves.

Table of Charges for 12-Gauge Gun.

Woodcock	3¼ drs.	1 oz.	No. 10	510
Snipe	3¼ drs.	1½ oz.	No 9	405
Quail and plover	3½ drs.	1½ oz.	No 9	395
Prairie chicken (Aug., Sept.)	3½ drs.	1½ oz.	No. 7	220
" " (Oct.. Nov., Dec)	4 drs.	1½ oz.	No. 6	158
Ruffed grouse	3½ drs.	1½ oz.	No. 8	300
Squirrels and rabbits	3½ drs.	1½ oz.	No. 6	160
Teals, pintails, etc	3¾ drs.	1½ oz.	No. 7	218
Mallards canvasbacks, etc	4 drs.	1½ oz.	No. 5	115
Geese and brant	4 drs.	1 oz.	No. 1	45
Turkeys	4 drs.	1½ oz.	No. 4	95
Deer (cylinder bore only)	4 drs.	3 layers of buckshot		

Speed of Birds' Flight.—The highest speed of flight per hour of birds in full plumage is estimated as follows: Crow 25 to 40 miles; mallard, black duck and shoveler, 40 to 50; pintail, 50 to 60; wood duck, 55 to 60; widgeon and gadwall, 60 to 70; redhead, 80 to 90; blue-winged and red-winged teal, 80 to 100; bluebill, 80 to 110; canvasback, 80 to 120; sparrow, 40 to 92; hawk, 40 to 150; wild geese, 80 to 90. The distance traveled by birds in ⅛ second is as follows: At rate of 5 miles per hour, .92 feet; rate of 10 miles per hour, 1.83 feet; rate of 12 miles, 2.2 feet; 20 miles, 3.66 feet; 30 miles, 5.5 feet; 40 miles, 7.33 feet; 60 miles, 11 feet; 80 miles, 14.66 feet; 90 miles, 16.05 feet; 100 miles, 18.33 feet; 120 miles, 22 feet; 150 miles, 27.5 feet.

In Estimating Distances—Underestimating is mostly common, it is rare that overestimating distance occurs.

Never Use—A cartridge or rifle of over 45-calibre or a bullet over 405 grains in weight

Always Follow—Powder makers' advice in loading cartridges. Don't experiment, this is for experts, not for you to do.

Best Powder for Shot Gun Cartridges—Hazards Electric, Duponts's Diamond Grain, Shultze, King's, etc.

A Leaded Rifle Barrel—Renders the arm useless for accuracy.

A Lubricator Receipt—Pure fresh beef tallow and vaseline to soften it is as good as the best.

Powder is Bought—By avoirdupois weight, but in weighing it for rifles the apothecaries weight is used. Avoirdupois weight is 16 drachms 1 ounce,

16 ounces 1 pound. Apothecaries, 20 grains 1 scruple, 3 scruples 1 drachm, 8 drachms 1 ounce, 12 ounces 1 pound.

Always Use—Soft pointed bullets for game hunting. They kill cleanly and quickly.

Choice of a Rifle—I am often asked the question what calibre and length of barrel do you recommend; a most difficult one to answer well unless I am informed exactly the purpose desired for. Generally speaking, I am in favor of a 303 calibre magazine rifle or 35 calibre. As to length of barrel the longer barrel will do more accurate shooting. But for hunting where shooting is seldom done at over 250 yards the difference is hardly appreciable, provided the barrel is sufficient length to permit a nearly complete combustion of the powder. (See about Rifles.)

Express Bullets—Are always superior to solid bullets for hunting purposes. They are sure killers for Deer, Elk, Moose and similar game. They mushroom on impact or spread tearing open a large wound and killing quickly, much more so than the regular pencil size and pointed hard bullet.

The All Round Shot Gun.—A 12-gauge gun, weight about 7 lbs., 30 inch barrels, right barrel cylinder or modified choke, left barrel full choke.

A Rubber Recoil Pad—Is an excellent device, if your gun kicks or affects your shooting.

Use a Glove Finger—On your twigger finger if it becomes sore or tender.

A Good Load for 12-Bore Gun.—3 to 3½ drs. of powder, 1⅛ oz. of No. 6 shot.

Never Use Cheap Ammunition.—Buy the very best from most reliable dealers.

Never Make Your Own Wads—If you want to be sure of satisfactory results in shooting.

What Gun Powder Is.—Saltpeter, 75 per cent; charcoal, 15 per cent; sulphur, 10 per cent.

The Ivory Bead Shot Gun Sight—Is an excellent one.

FIRST AID TO THE APPARENTLY DROWNED

This Shows One Method of Emptying the Patient's Lungs of Water Before Restoring Respiration

THE CAMP STOVE

How the Boy Scouts Arranged for the Convenient Cooking of Their Meals
at The Summer Camp

For Marsh Duck Shooting—Use grass color rubber or waterproof canvas hat and coat and rubber boots.

Large Game Charge—For 12-gauge guns 3½ drahms power; 1 oz. No. 1 or 2 shot, or mixed.

In Trailing Grouse—Approach them as if ignorant of their proximity, and shoot the instant you can, side shots are best; try and walk as though you did not see him, and he will not fly as quickly as though you come straight towards him.

Wild Ducks Flying—Travel over 100 feet in a second; if 50 yards away he will travel 15 feet in the time it takes for shot to reach him, hence the aim should be nearly 15 feet ahead; in windy weather they fly low.

Always Set Decoys—To windward of the blinds, and these had best be made *before the season*, ducks avoid any new or strange structures, are very wary of them.

A Good Blind.—A rubber blanket to lay on and yourself hidden by grass, rushes, etc., until near enough to rise and shoot quick, or cover yourself with grass color canvas.

Use Waterproof Paper Shells—For duck shooting; wet will not impair their fitting qualities.

Corduroy Clothing—Or canvas if drab color is all right for any kind of hunting, except "still hunting" its useless for that.

When Writing Us—The greatest favor you can do us is to send us the names of sportsmsn who hunt, shoot, camp, fish or trap game, clubs, etc., so as they may receive our books and matter pertaining thereto.

We Supply—Anything of *standard grade of quality* mentioned in our books, but do not handle any bargain sale goods—look out for them, a good article is worth a good price always. Write us concerning anything you desire.

To Secure Good Results—Get ammunition made expressly for the gun you use or make your own (see Ideal reloading tools.) Ammunition of other makes will do, but it is assuredly better to use ammunition made and intended for the very gun you use.

Use Warm Wristlets—Woolen ones for duck shooting in cold weather.

A Few Loads of Buckshot—May prove valuable in hunting with shot guns, (handy for big game) but not for a full choke gun unless loaded and shot well wadded by yourself. See too shoot buck shot elsewhere.

Killing Range of a 12 Bore Gun—Is from 50 to 60 yards, depending of course on the loads you carry.

To Shoot Solid Ball in Shot Guns—Use a lead bullet that will pass easily and freely into the muzzle when covered with *a cloth patch*. Place a heavy wad under the ball, a light one over it; the patch should hold the ball to the center of the shell.

In Using Buckshot—It is well to use a few small shot in the spaces between the buckshot, or use bone dust.

Woods Used in Gun Powder—Manufactured in the form of charcoal are black alder, poplar, willow and dog wood.

For a Quick Shooter—Modified choke is best, for a slow shot full choke.

Wild Geese—Are regular in going to and from their feeding grounds, so take advantage of the fact.

For Teal Duck—Use No. 7 or 8 shot, and aim well ahead always; if rising, hold above them; if drifting hold under.

To Moisten Dry Gun—Breathe occasionally through the barrels of it or, moisten the end of your cartridge.

In Flock Shooting—Select the leading or ahead bird, don't shoot at the center of the flock lest you hit only a straggler.

Good Shot Gun Target—A barrel head hung by heavy wire and swung hard from the branch of a high tree (swing quickly.)

Prairie Chickens—Frequent stubble fields in early morn or evening, near sloughs at mid-day.

325

Hunter's and Fisherman's Lunch.—Get two flat stones, and then gather sufficient wood. Into the fire the stones go, and the wood is heaped about them. Soon the intense glow of live wood embers indicates that the time has come. A Quail, Snipe or Trout (a sliver of bacon in each) are placed on one of the stones, first well dusted of its ashes, and the other stone is laid upon them. Now the hot embers are raked about and over the stones, and the lunch is spread on the big rock near the spring. O, ye epicures, who think nothing good unless served by a Delmonico or a Sherry, go ye into the mountains or trail, follow a brook for half a day, get wet, tired and hungry, sit down and eat these cooked on the spot, and learn of the choice morsels of the hunter's, trappers or fisherman's art.

Gun for Pigeon Shooting.—Select a 12-bore right barrel cylinder, and left full choke, chambered to stand heavy charges, or both barrels modified choke.

Never Loan Your Gun or Rifle—Lest you lose a friend.

Distance Covered by Game or Birds—In one eighth of a second:

12 miles an hour..........	2.2 feet.
20 miles an hour..........	3.6 feet.
30 miles an hour..........	5.5 feet.
40 miles an hour..........	7.3 feet.
60 miles an hour..........	11 feet.

Don't Fail to Sight Your Gun—On an "out of range bird;" its practice aiming even, if nothing else.

Don't Approach Game—from the windward side, get to the leeward of them.

Don't Forget to Aim—Under a bird that is alighting, or over them if arising, ahead of them if flying straight.

Don't Shoot at a Bird—Flying toward you; let it pass you first, then blaze away.

Don't Aim and Fire Carelessly—Or too quickly; rattled, excited, rapid shooting seldom counts; deliberation and carefulness is what brings accuracy and success.

Don't Overshoot.—The tendency of most sportsmen is to do this; better low than too high.

326

FIRE WITHOUT MATCHES

Getting the Spark and Producing a Flame to Start the Burning of
Dry Twigs and Sticks

Don't Fail—To cut the throats of dead game and draw the entrails, if you wish to have good meat.

Don't Blame the Gun.—They are seldom at fault; its the man behind.

Don't Forget—That extreme care and quietness are essential when hunting, "stalking" especially.

Don't Target Practice—On a hunting trip, wait until you break camp or are out of the haunts of game.

Don't Lug a Revolver—On a hunting trip, unless you are after encumbering yourself needlessly; a good hunting knife or a field telescope will serve far better.

Don't Sit—On the bare ground, better sit on your hat.

Don't Lose Your Bearings.—When in the woods one can easily get lost or turned around. Read the Campers Manual, for it tells you what to do in such an emergency. Send 10 cents to the author for a copy; you won't regret it. 100,000 have been sold to sportsmen, all over the world.

Don't Forget—To speak a good word for this book if it deserves it.

The Best Repeating Shot Gun—For field shooting, Winchester 12-gauge brush gun, 5 shot; 26 inch barrel; 7¼ lbs., model 1897, take down, or model 1901, cylinder or modified choke bored.

To Test a Shot Gun—So as to determine its accuracy or carrying abilities, chalk a target on a 30 inch circle 40 yards away, and note if the percentage of shot entering the circle is as follows: Cylinder bore, 40 per cent; modified choke, 50 per cent; full choke, 60 per cent; this is a good average. This is the gun maker's pattern test, with ordinary or standard loads. By now increasing or decreasing your charges or loads, your distance, size of target, etc. you can determine to a nicety, just how your gun shoots, enabling you to correct any existing faults before starting out on a trip.

Use Decoys—To leeward of your blinds, if in any way possible.

FIRST AID FOR A COMRADE

Hickory, The Boy Scouts' Dog, Is Carefully Treated After Meeting
With an Accident

In Wing Shooting—Always keep your gun moving with the bird, sighting well ahead, from a few inches to a few feet, according to the distance and speed of the bird, and direction it is traveling; and for better explanation I append a clipping herewith from a prominent sporting magazine (an authority on the subject) which will be found as a valuable aid in such matters. Gun used 12-gauge, 7¼ lbs., modified and full choke bored.

Flight of bird and lateral movement of muzzle, when pull of trigger is quick and when slow.

(Charge, 3 drams and 1⅛ ounces of No. 6; birds flying forty miles an hour.)

SLOW PULL OF TRIGGER (6 Seconds)			QUICK PULL OF TRIGGER (2 Seconds)		
Distance of Bird	Flight of bird during transit of shot	Lateral movement of gun muzzle by the shooter	Distance of bird	Flight of bird during transit of shot	Lateral movement of gun muzzle by the shooter
15 yds	6 ft. 6 in.	6.6 inches	15 yds	3 ft. 8 in.	3.7 inches
20 "	7 ft. 7 in.	5.7 "	20 "	4 ft. 8 in.	3.5 "
25 "	8 ft. 8 in.	5.2 "	25 "	5 ft. 8 in.	3.4 "
30 "	9 ft. 9 in.	4.9 "	30 "	6 ft. 11 in.	3.4 "
35 "	11 ft.	4.8 "	35 "	8 ft. 2 in.	3.5 "
40 "	12 ft. 6 in.	4.7 "	40 "	9 ft. 7 in.	3.6 "
45 "	13 ft. 10 in	4.7 "	45 "	11 ft.	3.7 "
50 "	15 ft. 9 in.	4.7 "	50 "	12 ft. 9 in.	3.8 "

NOTE—One second of time allowed for passage of shot through the barrels.

Best Time to Locate Ducks—October, November, moonlight nights; best time to shoot them is during heavy winds; best place to find them is in smooth or sheltered waters, or on the edges of sheltered woods. Best way to approach them at these times is against the wind, creeping up slowly, quietly and unobserved, lest they hear, see or scent you. Better spend more time looking for their favorite spots and flights, than in waiting for them to approach blinds or decoys, (except in flight shooting.

When Using Decoys—Always set them to the *leeward* of your blinds; arrange them so as their heads are anchored toward the wind. Do not group them close, but scatter them well.

I Do Not Recommend—The 30-30 caliber rifle (except for small game hunting.) It should not be used for large game. Choose instead the 303 always in preference to the 30-30, *for the reason that the bullet of the 303* fits the barrel more accurately, will show greater penetration and velocity, and is even more accurate than the 30-30. These are facts borne out by experience, honestly given. The 30-30 is a good rifle, *but not for large game.*

To Kill Mosquitoes—Either in a room or tent, camp or building, use "Mosquitoons," a small, specially prepared pyramid-like candle, which gives off fumes that are deadly to the mosquito, but not obnoxious to man or animal. *Try it once.* Its the latest 20th century idea, and is very efficient. *We carry a large stock of them.* They are made especially to kill mosquitoes; and when used in a tent, absolutely kills them.

Best Rifle for Squirrels.—22 caliber repeating rifle. Best place to find them is about beech or chestnut trees and high grounds. Best time, fall of year; hours, around sunrise and sunset; worst time, mid-day.

Wood Cock—Best time, toward evening or very early morning, (dawn). Best places, moist places near edges of low lands, swamps, etc., north side of hills, etc. (the moist sides.)

Best Time for Quail—Mid-day of sunshiny days, October and November. Best places, middle of fields, around small stubble or brush, or at edge of woods. Best way, with a good pointer dog.

Best Time for Ducks—October and November, early morn, (day break) or early dusk. Best place about feeding grounds, around edges of marshes, or in sheltered woods, along its borders.

Grouse or Partridge—Best time, early morning, stormy or cold weather. Best places, around berry bushes, etc; look for their regular roosts toward night.

331

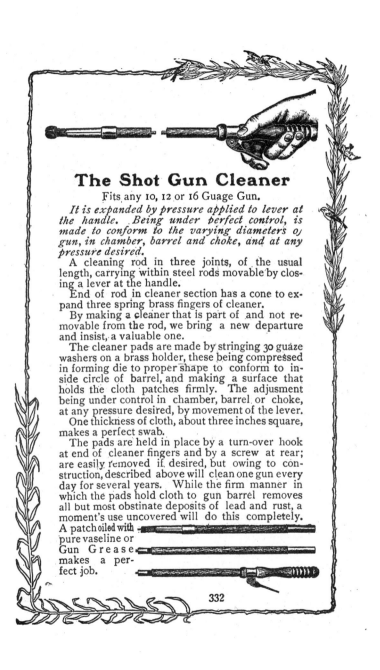

The Shot Gun Cleaner

Fits any 10, 12 or 16 Guage Gun.

It is expanded by pressure applied to lever at the handle. Being under perfect control, is made to conform to the varying diameters of gun, in chamber, barrel and choke, and at any pressure desired.

A cleaning rod in three joints, of the usual length, carrying within steel rods movable by closing a lever at the handle.

End of rod in cleaner section has a cone to expand three spring brass fingers of cleaner.

By making a cleaner that is part of and not removable from the rod, we bring a new departure and insist, a valuable one.

The cleaner pads are made by stringing 30 guaze washers on a brass holder, these being compressed in forming die to proper shape to conform to inside circle of barrel, and making a surface that holds the cloth patches firmly. The adjusment being under control in chamber, barrel or choke, at any pressure desired, by movement of the lever.

One thickness of cloth, about three inches square, makes a perfect swab.

The pads are held in place by a turn-over hook at end of cleaner fingers and by a screw at rear; are easily removed if desired, but owing to construction, described above will clean one gun every day for several years. While the firm manner in which the pads hold cloth to gun barrel removes all but most obstinate deposits of lead and rust, a moment's use uncovered will do this completely. A patch oiled with pure vaseline or Gun Grease makes a perfect job.

332

Marsh and Duck Shooting To-day.

Raft Building, Cruising and Fishing Tomorrow.

To Test Your Powder—Lay a small pinch on a sheet of white paper and apply a match. If it inflames instantly leaving the paper clean and unscorched, it is good, or rub a grain or two between the fingers, if they don't break or soil the fingers its quality is good.

How to Become a Crack Shot.—The whole secret is in discovering the faults of each shot and correcting them before firing another shot.

Always Practice—Both snap and deliberate shooting or aiming. Snap shooting is raising the gun quickly, aiming and firing as quick as the object is sighted, not waiting or wasting a second. Deliberate shooting is of course taking deliberate and careful aim.

Excellent Practice.—Lay the rifle on the ground loaded, throw tiny paper bags of flour weighted with a stone high into the air; quickly get your gun and hit them before they reach the ground. If you have this done for you turn your back to the thrower, and only turn around and shoot at the *signal* to do so. This is excellent practice for the eye, hand, distance, flight, quickness, etc.

Cheap Guns—Make poor shots and poor sportsmen.

Learning to Aim Well.—First, select an object to aim at. Second, throw up the gun with your eyes shut toward the object, when the gun touches your shoulder, open your eyes and see where your gun points; practice this getting your gun into line quickly. Third, fire at the object without a moment's hesitation, and note carefully the results, correcting any faults that exist.

Mercurial Ointment—Will cleanse leaded barrels.

Always Practice Shooting—With the same class of ammunition that you hunt with or the same loads exactly.

Hold the Butt Firmly—To the shoulder when firing, always when aiming and firing.

Too Much Powder.—To ascertain if your charges contain too much powder, lay sheets of paper (white) 10 to 15 feet from the muzzle of the gun and fire it, if the paper catches grains of unconsumed powder, you are using too much. Firing along the snow will give the same proof.

Buckshot in Cylinder Bores.—If it is desirable to shoot buckshot from a cylinder bore, such size should be selected as will chamber loosely in the bore—loading them in layers—three layers, with three shot in a layer. If it is desirable that they should scatter, place a card wad between each layer; if close shooting is desired, pour melted tallow over the shot after they are arranged in the shell.

Buckshot and Ball in Chokebores.—Bullets, buckshot and all shot larger than No. 1 should not be discharged from a chokebore. Ball *may* be shot from some chokebores a thousand times without injury; but there is *always* liability of jamming and no one can tell when it may occur. To use buckshot in a chokebore, when you are willing to risk conseqences, place a wad in the muzzle and press it down to the point where the choke is closest. Then by chambering the shot on the wad there determine the proper number to use in a layer in the shell.

Wire Cartridges.—They may be used in a cylinder bore for long range shots, but do not give good results when used in a chokebore.

Tight Wads.—A tight wad over the shot makes the shot scatter.

To make a Gun Scatter.—To make a shotgun scatter, divide the shot charge into three or four portions and place a card wad between each portion.

Killing Range of a Gun—Forty to fifty yards is the killing range of a 12-guage shot gun with ordinary loads.

In Shooting Flying or Running Game—Aim well in advance of the object so as to allow for the distance travelled by the game during the interval between pulling the trigger and the shot reaching its destination. A few inches or feet according to speed of movement. (note speed of birds flights.)

335

Tent Pole Accessories. Hangers, etc.,

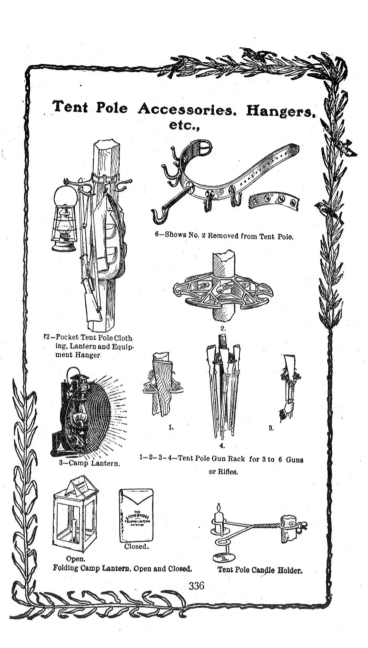

6—Shows No. 2 Removed from Tent Pole.

2—Pocket Tent Pole Clothing, Lantern and Equipment Hanger.

2.

3—Camp Lantern.

1, 3.

4.

1—2—3—4—Tent Pole Gun Rack for 3 to 6 Guns or Rifles.

Open. Closed.
Folding Camp Lantern, Open and Closed.

Tent Pole Candle Holder.

Rubber Specialties for Camp Uses

10—Rubber Bath Tub.

1—Sportsman's Rain Cape (Featherweight)

2—Cape Packed.

9—Rubber Wash Basin.

13—Poncho Rubber Blanket.

4—5—Rubber and Canoe Tumbler.

6—Rubber Toilet

12—Sportsman's Inflated Seat.

17—Rubber Toilet Case.

16—Canoe Seat.

3—Camp Bath Tub.

7—Rubber Bucket Closed.

14—Rubber Tobacco Pouch

8—Rubber Bucket Open.

15—Rubber Ration Bag.

337

PART THREE.

The Trapper's Guide--Hints for, etc

The Otter. (Fish Catching.)

Secrets of Trapping, Aids, etc.

338

The Midwinter Home of the Canadian Trappers. 339

The Trappers' Guide

Hoop Stretcher   Board Stretcher

It may seem peculiar that a book on hunting with the modern fire arms of today should devote a chapter to trapping and traps, but it is not the intention of the writer to identify this subject to the old time style of twitch-ups, dead falls, garottes, figure 4 or box traps, *but the modern trapping of today.*

Where I go into details of the old time plan, I might as well in my chapter on "Hunting," go back to the old flint lock or bow and arrow methods. But as we are now in the 20th century, I must necessarily dwell on the methods of the present time, and not of those that are obsolete.

If mere riddance of some obnoxious animal is desired we would not have to confine ourselves to either shot gun or rifle, for it could be done by using the "deadly strychnine,"a portion the size of a small liver pill mixed up in a piece of common fat, tallow, meat or fish would do the deed; even to the laying out of the monstrous Elephant (if right quantity be used) for after swallowing such a fatal poison, it would rarely live a few minutes after, so deadly and rapid is its effect.

So extremely virulent, however, is this drug that *it not only poisons the meat* but if left for any time renders *even the skin* useless, hence is never used by the trapper on this account, except in such cases as afore mentioned on some destructive beast.

Again, buyers of fur, refuse almost to buy skins that are full of shot holes; a rifle bullet even de-

340

creasing its value especially so should the ball plough a furrow in the hide. Hence the query of the experienced fur buyer or taxidermist to the sportsman, hunter or trapper *"Are your skins trapped or shot"* speaks for itself.

Furs or skins to be used as robes or clothing to satisfy the demands of fashion are assorted into grades *or primes* according to sizes and condition varying in value from 10c to $300. The small prime-skin of the Black Fox *being worth today that sum* and the fortunate sportsman or trapper who by a practice of the art during a single winter can clear in a day's time often a sum equivalent to that earned in a year, by some of his less fortunate brethren.

Among the valuable marketed skins today can be classed that of the following American animals that are to be found in almost every state:

Antelope	Foxes all kinds	Opposum
Bears all kinds	Lynx	Otter
Beaver	Marten	Raccoon
Badgers	Mink	Skunk
Cats all kinds	Muskrat	Squirrel
Deer	Moose	Wolverine
Dogs	Weasels	Wolves
Elk	Moles	Wild Cat
Fisher	Mountain Lions	

It obvious then, that some one must trap these animals. Hence to aid them is the purpose of this manual.

In the experience of the vast army of trappers at home and abroad, reaching to the heart of the Russian and Arctic fur bearing countries. No trap ever made has equalled the celebrated *American or Newhouse steel trap of today, for over 40 years the standard.* They are simple, (the secret of their success) efficient, cheap and adapted to and for the capture of any *animal* that walks, swims, crawls or creeps on earth or its streams at the present writing, not even excepting the Elephant.

It is unnecessary to enter into details as to the requirements of these traps or their construction, let it suffice to say that if the *"Newhouse Standard" is secured and used* you have the best and most reliable that money can buy.

341

In the capture of various animals the employment of several other contrivances are necessary but as these are best furnished from resources on hand in any locality where the trapper's art is practiced, they need not be included in one's outfit, but which will be amply described *and later can be improvised.*

Often, after the securing of divers animals it is necessary to *provide some means* rendering the freeing of themselves impossible as they are not adverse to even gnawing off their own legs to escape. Again, while caught thus their cries or efforts to escape often attract their enemies who partly devour them. Hence the employment of simple means to frustrate them as follows:

No. 1. By Use of the "Spring Pole"—Select a small tree near where your trap is to be set, trim it for use as a spring as it stands. If no small tree is available select a small, stout sapling (and setting it into the ground well and secure make it answer the purpose.) Bend down its flexible top, fasten the chain ring to it and secure it thus, while in its bent position *by a notch or hook* or a small stake driven in the ground. When the animal is caught *by his own struggle he dislodges the stake or hook* and the sapling springs into its normal position, carries or lifts him in the air, out of reach of prowlers and preventing his own escape by struggle or otherwise. About the only special requirement being that this *spring pole* be proportioned to the weight of the game it is expected to lift

No. 2. "The Slide"—*As all water animals* are mostly trapped in close proximity to their haunts or at the edges (even in their waters) and as they invariably plunge therein when caught the wily trapper avails himself and turns this into good account, against the animal, thus making doubly sure of his catch; *to hold and drown him there* no matter what his size. This is arranged by several means, the sliding pole or *chain* or a very *heavy wire* often answering the same purpose. This is secured to the bank and weighted with a "clog" or heavy stone in the water. *The chain ring of the trap* is then secured to this pole or chain which reaches to the bottom of the water.

The only essential being that the chain ring of the trap will travel down freely, to its base, being held by the clog or stone. When the animal is caught it leaps or drags the trap with it into the water and the ring sliding down the pole, chain or wire *prevents him from rising or returning* thus drowning him and preventing its flesh or hide being torn or discovered by his enemies or even frightening others. The other device is called

No. 3. "The Drag or Clog"—This is used mostly for land animals, either small ones or those of huge and tremendous strength, such as the Bear, etc. For these animals (*in fact for no animal) must the trap ever be staked fast*. Most people erroneously believe that traps (large ones especially) must be staked fast so as their *prey will be held there*. This is wrong. For if this is done they will either chew or pull their legs off or beat the trap to pieces. But, if on the other hand, they are only encumbered with the drag or clog *of say equal weight* (or even less) than their own, they will only drag it about or vent their spite on it, and its object is only to encumber the animal so as he *cannot run off; far* care should be taken not to fasten the chain at the center (of a log or heavy stick of wood) best *near of its ends*, lest it catch and thus permit him to tear himself out. The best way being to slip the chain around the heaviest, widest part of the clog and secure it there with a wedge; many cutting a recess for the chain so as to more securely hold it besides.

These are all the essentials for almost any trapping outfit and together with other items that I shall now describe complete all the necessaries for an extended trip.

The Trappers' Outfit

Like all other things, no man can excel in any art unless he makes a study of it. He must become familiar with the habits and haunts of animals, so as to locate them. Armed with such knowledge his outfit need not be *extensive*, and a dozen good traps in the hands of any careful trapper would equal a hundred with a shiftless one. As to what is needed is for the trapper himself to

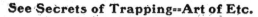

Sliding Ring and Chain used to drown trapped Water Animals.
(By permission of Northwestern Hide & Fur Co., Minneapolis, Minn.)

Traps for Water and Land Animals

"The Otter Slide" (at the foot trap is set)

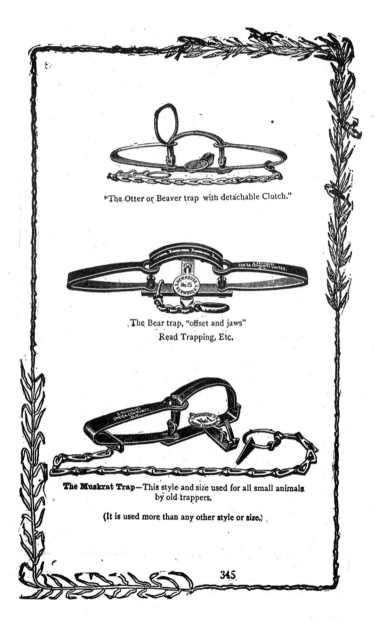

"The Otter or Beaver trap with detachable Clutch."

The Bear trap, "offset and jaws"
Read Trapping, Etc.

The Muskrat Trap—This style and size used for all small animals by old trappers.

(It is used more than any other style or size.)

determine; depend largely on the game he seeks, the country, its proximity to civilization or his method of living. Equipped with an outfit of traps, axe, spade, shot gun or rifle, warm clothing, food, a robust constitution and ever willing hands, *two men of intelligence can* today start out in the early fall and penetrate the heart of the woods and its streams, and by judicious management *erect even a comfortable winter hut* and by united labor and the thoughtful exercise of judgemnt live well, turning their skill to various good results, and by dilligence at the end of the winter, by turning their product over reap a snug sum, do they but select the right place and follow the instructions herein given to the letter. To those, however, not willing to be patient and labor to overcome successive failures patiently my advice is *first and last to leave trapping alone.*

No body of men are more honest, whole-souled, generous or contented than the intelligent class of American trappers living perhaps in the heart of the forests, on the borders of its marshes and frozen streams; his rough and genial face and his simple, honest greeting and fare renders the one who accepts of his hosiptality and frugal living (ever ready to be shared with you) equal to the entertaining hospitality that millionaire lackeys bestow on a generous guest, for there "dollars count" *here the man.* Often has the writer shared their frugal hospitality even to the borders of the *Hudson Bay trapping region* and I vowed if ever opportunity occurred I would strive in a measure to give to the world facts as they are concerning these men, honest faithful servants for all mankind, and as you, their more fortunate brethren, clasp around wives, sweethearts and children that you love, dainty or fashionable furs, console yourself with the knowledge that you have lent an aid to a worthy class, who perhaps now are facing winter storms and hardships that you may derive comfort and pleasure from the objects gained after many a ceaseless search, tramp and weary toil.

Secrets of Trapping

About every other writer on these subjects goes into *more or less. superfluous detail* describing each and every animal, color of their hair, weight, length and in tracing the specie back to the days it was first found; the purposes for which its fur was used *then*. The methods in existence at *that time* for their capture, together with varied (not instructive) experiences in capturing them.

All this, I admit, is interesting reading. But what the "Tyro" needs today *is information boiled down*. As to how to set traps and catch animals, the question of identification of species is an easy matter, after they are caught, for nowadays the trapper seldom finds in *his trap what it was set for*, I do not then propose in a volume of this size, to enter into such special details. And instead of giving information covering the many species, I shall confine my remarks to *general instructions applicable to all animals*. And instead of dwelling on individual kinds, shall simply classify them into with *two* species, viz:

Aquatic and Land Animals—For no matter what the kind, much the same are the methods used in their capture. About the only difference being the *size of the traps used*. The methods of setting and handling them varying very little.

The Secret of Trapping—Is in first *locating* the haunts of the animal. If it is an Aquatic or water animal, look for traces of them, closely inspecting every portion of such waterways, swamps, rivers, ponds or streams they inhabit. Search every spot that would leave the impression of their feet or body. Look about for "signs" *that is the first essential*, then try and observe the route of the animal so as to find their haunts. . Look for droppings, signs of recent meals, holes, and by careful examination at these places, you are apt to find a few hairs of the animal *which will indicate kind* that frequents there. Secret yourself at some point of vantage, watch and wait. True, it takes time and patience, plenty of it, but it's absolutely essential. Look for their runways, slides and routes. This done, set your traps in these

347

places, most carefully arranging them and leaving the place *just as you found it if you possibly can do so.* Destroy every trace of your presence there *and touch nothing with your bare hands.* If your traps are placed in the right spots you rarely need baits. These are mostly for attracting them. If, however, your traps (see traps) are to be set under water (as indeed most traps for water animals should be) you may handle them with bare hands with impunity.

If it is winter then you will find most such animals as Muskrats and Beavers living in their dome like structures, around sluggish streams, ponds, etc., the Muskrat especially, as Beavers do not always live in dams or huts (this is only done where water is unplentiful.) If water is there in plenty, *Beavers do not build dams* but make their nests under banks, with their entrances under water and their huts in front of them. If it is summer they swim or roam around and you are just as apt to find them one place as another about waters. The foods of aquatic animals are roots of flags, grasses, water plants and succulent plants that grow about the banks and shores of their homes. They are fond of berries, nuts, vegetables, wild oats, seeds, etc. The Muskrat especially being fond of flesh, apples, corn or vegetables of almost any kind. These are used for baits when necessary, and traps can be set in their play grounds, holes, or best where they enter and leave the waters, setting them a trifle under waters. If bait is used it should be stuck up on a pointed stick (fastened to it) and arranged in such a way *that the animal must step on the trap to secure it* (usually 8 to 10 inches high being ample) and the "slide" attached so as to drown the animal, that it may not alarm the others. If Beaver trapping, arrange traps at such points where the animal will pass or repass, always a few inches under water, drenching your tracks if any, to wash the scent away. If after Mink, set your traps either on land or water near their banks or holes (concealing them) with leaves, rotten wood, water grass, etc., using for bait fish, birds, flesh of the Muskrat, etc., (scented) and so arranged as he must step on the trap in order to reach it. Like

348

Animals That are Trapped.

The Badger.

The Skunk.

The Beaver.

The Muskrat.

Valuable for

Their Furs.

The Raccoon.

Read the

Trappers Guide

The Mink.

349   The Otter.

Enemies of the Hunter or Trapper.

The Wild Cat.

The Canada Lynx.

The Grizzly Bear—"Old Eph."

The Wolverine.

350 The Wolf.

other aquatic animals (although not amphibious) Mink had best be drowned. If after Otter, set traps at the top of their slides or better still where they land, which is usually where the waters are shallow (or in their paths leading to these places) and using the clutch or Otter trap (see traps.) These instructions are general and cover aquatic animals; so we will now go into detail about those of the more numerous specie, "*the land animal*"

In all cases where the use of traps are made baits are *necessary mostly only to attract* the animal, much more so than the feeding of them Natural foods abound in plenty. No animal depends on trap food or foods *put about by man for its existence*, that's why they are suspicious of it, no matter how hungry they may be, they regard all such dead food or bait with suspicion. *They choose or capture their own foods*, (and there are very few foolish animals.) Probably the Skunk and Bear are the only ones who are not suspicious. But this is not because of ignorance, but because nature has given them remarkable powers of defence, and they do not fear. That is why they are so easily captured, and called foolish.

Don't ever think because you have traps set and baited that this is all, for if you do, you will get nothing for your pains. The whole secret is in concealing your traps in such a way as *they cannot tell where the traps are*, and in passing or reaching over it, they will *step on the pan* and be caught. Don't ever put bait on the pan (like I have seen many do.) If you use bait, that is mostly for the purpose of decoying them, and as they step up to it to investigate or possibly reach it, if they are hungry, it must be so placed *that in doing so* they must set their feet on the pan without knowing it, and when you have mastered these details, you will know a little about traps and trapping, and one-half of the battle is won.

The Other Half—Consists in preparing your traps as the scent of most animals *can locate even the iron* of which they are made, especially so if it is rusty, requiring no little attention of the trapper to frustrate it. Again, traps should be washed and oiled, even smoked, and as said before, handled with gloves. This, however, is unnecessary where

351

traps are laid in waters (as indeed it is best to place them for all aquatic animals.) This should be done at points where previous search has revealed such places as they enter or leave the water, sometimes called slides. In all cases of trapping animals of any kind it is obvious that of the foods, those they like, are best suited for baits, be it *flesh*, *fish or vegetable*. If they are carnivorous animals, (flesh eating) flesh is undoubtedly preferable. If omnivorous (eating everything indiscriminately) almost any foods will suffice although preference should be shown to those kinds of which they are especially fond. If the animal is nocturnal, as indeed most animals are, night is the best time for their capture and *as land animals must come to the waters to drink,* their routes approaching such waters must be noted and traps laid in their paths at various points. In this, as indeed, all things, one has to tax his ingenuity so as to unconsciously lead the animal into the trap.

One of the most successful trappers I have known told me his success was due to setting his traps in such positions, as for instance, directly in the narrow path between two banks, well inside their holes, or in arranging logs almost V shape leaving the smaller part of the V open so as to permit an animal to pass through, and setting his trap *hid in the opening.* Again in naturally placing a twig or two in such a way as the animal would lift his feet over it and step on the pan (by his carefulness.) Again, in placing his bait well under logs and then arranging his trap in such a way, close to it, that the animal would *when he went to paw the bait out* touch the pan of the hidden trap. Again by leading a trail of tiny pieces of meat or blood to his trap and fastening his bait just over the trap. Another method which particularly struck my fancy was by cutting down a small tree and laying (as though 'twas killed by the falling of the tree) a bird or rabbit under it, leaving a certain portion exposed. This was carefully done and his traps deftly laid on either side of it. (*After those parts that were exposed had been found and eaten first.*) For the animal was pretty sure to return for the remaining portion

352

The New "Stop Thief" Wire Trap.

It is Set at the Holes of Animals; Dens, etc.,

This illustration shows the trap concealed. A coon is crossing the log—smells the decoy—His attention is arrested he turns back to investigate. (Continued on next page.)

The New "Stop Thief" Wire Trap

This illustration shows how the trap catches around the animal's neck and chokes it to death.

Above traps are especially designed for Gophers, Squirrels, Mink, Rabbits, Skunk, Raccoon, Badger, etc, etc.

Illustrations by Courtesy of North Western Hide and Fur Company.

(Specialists in Furs and Trappers Supplies)

Trap Set at Den of Skunks.

As these animals are unsuspecting no covering is needed over traps; as he enters he is caught and killed by trap choking and holding him.

under the log as a second meal. "Then," said he, "it worked like a charm." Still another was to bore with a two inch auger a hole in a log and to fill it with scented baits. The animal would use its paws to *dig it out* after it had licked out all it could (this was done first in many places.) Then when signs *appeared that some animal had been at it* his trap was laid and rarely without securing something. One of the best ideas is when a hollow log is found (or even a partly rotten one) is to scoop out a portion as though some animal had done it, baiting the interior and hiding a *trap or two* under the rotten wood that seems to have been scratched out. A trail was then lead to this log by several routes and a chance animal locating it would follow to the log and scenting the bait inside, would readily enter it, in the belief that a feast or a part of one was inside. The result was *one of the several traps hidden* secured him.

Such things as these are what count in the art of "trappers woodcraft," for it's mostly brains against cunning. The simpler the method, the easier the success. Trapping is a science, for it is devoid of sport. Probably none of my readers have ever heard before of the most simple yet effective small trap known *today* (unthought of years ago) is arranged by boring holes in billets of wild woods *and inserting around them sharp pointed horse shoe nails* leaving sufficient room for the head and shoulders of a small animal to pass through before it reaches bait concealed *behind its points.* As the animal cannot pass through after securing the bait, by its attempt to withdraw, it is pierced by the sharp points of the horse shoe nails and held there until the billet is split so as to remove it. And as these small animals serve as *bait,* leaving the larger traps free to be used for *valuable ones*, it is obvious that the plan is most excellent as a trapper's aid in securing fresh bait.

Oftimes old trappers preserve all droppings (manure) they find. Likewise remnants of feasts, feathers, etc., which they use with success to cover and hide their traps. Besides this they smear them with blood to prevent the scent of iron and causing the animal to paw in its vicinity as though some buried gante was there. Where baits are used all trappers make them doubly effective by using powerful scents some of them *truly "the king of stinks"* most offensive and nauseating to the user of them, yet so powerful are they that when used right they decoy animals for miles away. Of these there many among which is "fish oil" made by the simple plan of cutting up fish of any kind (rich or oily preferred) such as trout, eels, etc., into small bits, putting them into a bottle and exposing it to the sun. In a few weeks, according to the weather a rancid oil is formed, a few drops of which smeared over the bait or trap with a feather will draw most any animal to it that happens that way, while without it *it would have passed and repassed again.* Other powerful scents are obtained by the trappers from the animals themselves—from the Beaver (called castoreum) which is now a regular article of commerce. Others being secured from the Muskrat female or even from the Skunk, or a drug known as "assafoetida." Oftimes these are compounded or mixed together resulting in the *ne plus ultra* or quintessence of diabolical stenches, which despite their nastiness, irresistably lure many animals to their doom, and called "medicine." Again plants serve the same purpose, such as fennel, cummin, fenugreek, lavender, even the perfume of rhodium (oil of rose) costly as it is. No two trappers choosing hardly the same, "each swearing by his particular kind of stink" *yet all agree that without it,* oftimes all their efforts would be in vain, as by its use the chances of failure is reduced to a minimum. These can be purchased and should my readers desire to acquaint or test their virtues, samples can be had at an expenditure of 25 cents. By its use "trails" are made by dragging along the ground from distances away to the traps pieces of bloody meats, fish or entrails of fowl or animal which has been smeared in the preparation. At times the soles of boots are smeared with it, occasionally as the *trapper goes his rounds,* thus covering his entire line of traps (usually he visits or goes these rounds early in the morn) or especially at the approach of stormy weather. Nature has endowed all animals with the powers of knowledge necessary *as if to warn them to skirmish for their food* so as they can retire to their haunts until such time as the storm has passed, when they reappear as though by infinite command, even enabling certain species to hibernate, which is not by any means confined to the bear. When snow flies then *trapping is at its best*, for even the inexperienced can then follow the trail, while it also forms the easiest hiding places for the traps. Here a favorite method of old trappers is to bury bait, scent it and following its removal to place there his trap *with bait again below the trap*, for the animal is almost sure to return, pawing as usual to remove it, he places his foot in the trap and is caught. Another method of the artful trapper is to set his traps on the edges of shallow water, staked to the bank or "sliding pole" submerged just under the surface of the water, its distance from the edge of the bank being *about the reach of the foot of the animal.* He then cuts a sod of grass, just the size of the inside of the trap's jaws, and places *it over the pan* carefully. The bait is then placed beyond. When an animal goes to reach the bait he naturally places his foot on the sod of grass to support him, *when the trap is sprung* and he is caught fast; extreme care however, being taken that the trap and sod be placed naturally even with the surface and *seemingly a solid foundation*, and the bait, usually a dead bird or rabbit, placed about a foot or so away and secured by a cord and stone.

When however, the trapper is fortunate enough to secure an excess of meat, or to kill a larger animal such as Antelope, Deer, Moose, 'etc. by his skill with the gun or rifle, *away from his trapping district*, then he is in his element, especially if Wolves, Coyotes, etc. abound, for his success is assured. Skinning the animal and helping himself to its choicest portions for his sustenance and the hide; he disembowels the animal, applies his medicine and drags the entrails *towards the carcass from all directions* like the spokes of a wheel; he then sets his traps about the carcass, *a trifle away from it* and retires A day or night or two might pass without reward, but sooner or later success comes beyond his expectations, for such a feast cannot pass unobserved. Soon one appears, then more and more, until a veritable pack of savage

357

beasts are soon feasting. Should any touch his traps that lay a distance away, it is caught, then another and another, until his traps are full. If his *drags and clogs are right*, these howling with pain, retire to a distance, and their howls mingled with that of the beasts fighting for their share, fill the very air with trappers music. Morning comes and the trapper, rifle in hand, secures several more by his skillful aim. Fear he knows not, for seldom will the beasts (gorged as they are with foods) resent his appearance, especially as daylight approaches; seeking his traps and the animals therein, which are seldom afar, he dispatches his victims, and using their carcasses sets his traps **"ad finitum,"** and his winter's catch is assuredly successful. The writer himself had the pleasure of such an experience when employed in the service of the U S. Government, on the borders of Texas (1885 to 1893) and with seven rusty old Newhouse traps secured by the Indian scouts, none of them the regular Wolf trap (No. 4½,) captured no less than five Wolves and Coyotes, besides shooting down with our rifles before dispersing them, seven others, and as the Texas bounty alone (not counting value of hides) was then $25.00 each, I leave it to the reader whether it was good night's work; and were it not for the fact that we could not (being on travel orders) delay, there would have been no telling what our final aggregate could have been. In conclusion however, let me say that the carcass referred to, was in this case, several Deer shot by the Indians for food, and well staked down to the earth, to preclude any possibility of their being dragged away.

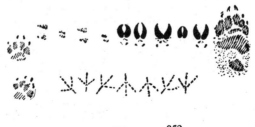

Trappers Aids

The Best Bear Bait—Is honey smeared on fresh fish, or burnt honey comb.

A Slendid Place for a Trap—Is between two logs where there is a passage way through which the animal must pass; by-paths as they are termed, natural channels, crevices or paths littered with hollow logs, etc. through which the animal must pass, or is apt to.

Never Handle Traps—With bare hands, use rags or buckskin gloves. Never spit about where traps are laid.

Use Scent Baits—Wherever possible. Barkstone, Fish Oil, Castorium, Musk, Assafoetida, Oil of Rhodium, Oil of Skunk, Amber, Anise, Sweet Fennel, Cummin, Fenugreek, Lavender or a compound of them all.

Read the Game Laws—Of the U. S. and Canada. Price 25 cents.

Soak a Piece of Meat—In the scent compound and drag it along on the ground between your run of traps, it is very effective as a trail to the trap, leading animals into them.

Clogs Used On Traps Should never be secured to a tree or stake, let it be a stone or log of size and weight equal to the game you desire to trap; fasten it so it cannot be jerked off.

No Sportsman—Hunter, trapper, angler or fisherman should fail to secure and read (post up) on the Game and Fish Laws of the U. S. and Canada, especially of the laws concerning the game where you propose to hunt them. Send for a copy, price 25 cents (coin or stamps) and avoid borrowing trouble.

Always Place Your Traps—Where you can inspect them with the least difficulty. Animals often visit traps a dozen times, smelling them suspiciously and leaving them by reason of that suspicion. If your traps are right never touch or change them. If a storm or blizzard comes, snow and cold in plenty, you will then get your reward, as the snow covers the suspicious part and the cold makes them hungry enough not to be too particular.

Trapper Packs—Including traps, have the limit of weight at about 60 to 75 lbs.

For Trapping Deer—Use the New House No. 4, for Skunk, No. 2.

In Baiting Traps—Always place the bait either on *stick above the trap* or in an enclosure, so arranged as the animal must step on or run over the trap, or better yet, jump up to get it; never place it on the pan.

Quantity of Traps to Take—Depends on the locality you trap in. If you travel by boat or team your supply need not be limited, but if you intend to make a business of trapping, the more the better. (See packing traps.)

Season of Trapping—November to April. Furs from May to September are useless. Winter furs only are in prime.

Always Set Traps—For aquatic animals where they can take to the water, and by weight of the traps and chains drown themselves.

To Make Fish Oil.—The scent used by many old trappers. Take Trout, Eels or fat fish of any kind, cut in small pieces and put them in bottles, and leave in hot sun, when an oil and putrid smell accumulates. Use this to scent your bait.

Bird or Fish Heads are Good Bait—In cold weather. Smoke your baits to give them a stronger smell, or smear your traps with blood, using a feather to smear it over them. Fried meats smeared with honey is good trap bait.

Use—No. 5 or 6 Newhouse traps for Bear, Moose, etc. No. 4½ for Wolf. No. 2½ for Otter.

To Capture Small Birds—Use bird lime made as follows: Take the inner bark of slippery elm which should be gathered in the early summer, scraped into a•pulp and simmer slowly in just enough water to cover it, stirring and mushing it so as to extract the substance; add to it linseed oil, and when thick enough like glue, it can be smeared over limbs or trees where birds frequent. The best bird lime is made from varnish or linseed oil alone, boiled down until a thick gummy mass.

If you can secure an *owl* fasten it to some spot frequented by birds, and a short distance away smear the limbs or twigs with bird lime. When the owl which is the most detested enemy of all birds is found, it will attract a veritable swarm of birds to that vicinity, when they will be caught by the quicklime that surrounds the captured owl.

An Indian Method in Winter—Of killing wild game, wolves, bears, etc. is to take a piece of flexible steel or whalebone, anything that has a bend to it, and bend it into as small a circle as possible, securing it with the sinews of the deer, this they insert in a ball of meat, flesh, fat and blood and allow the whole ball, (not a large one) to freeze. A number of these they throw out on the snow or ice, about the haunts of the animals; coming along they find them and being hungry, ravenously devour or swallow them, on account of their being hard and frozen. The heat of the stomach soon melts the frozen parts of flesh and sinews, when the spring coil straightens out piercing the stomach, causing agony, and death which in due time ensues, and by following the trail of the animal they invariably find them, perhaps locating others besides. In the Arctic regions where the writer spent over three years living constantly with various tribes of Esquimos, I have often assisted in the preparation of these killing balls, and witnessed their fearful results.

Don't Forget to Read—The Game Laws of the U. S. and Canada, before you start on a trip, (price 25 cents postpaid) ignorance of the laws excuses no one. Send for a copy and avoid trouble.

If You Like This Book—Send for its mates, The Complete Camper's Manual or How to Camp Out and What to Do; The Complete Fisherman and Angler's Manual or How to Catch Fish; each 140 pages, nearly 300 illustrations. Same price as this volume.

The three volumes all bound together in cloth, over 400 pages and 800 illustrations, prepaid to any address for $1.00. Splendid acceptable presents, any time.

For Cold Nights Sleeping—Use a pair of Arctic or loose sleeping socks. No fear of cold feet at night when sleeping. Price only 25 cents.

To Make Traps Rustproof—Dip them in a solution of melted beeswax and rosin.

Set Traps Whenever Possible—In the runways or paths of animals.

In Rutting Season—Use for Skunk bait, musk of skunk or rotten eggs with old meat.

In Baiting With Muskrat—Use for scent musk from the rat. In baiting with fish, use fish oil for scent.

A Practical Trap—Can be made by boring a series of two-inch or larger auger holes in a water logged stump or log, and driving in two or three horse shoe nails, so that any small headed animal who thrusts in his head to secure bait behind the nails cannot withdraw his head, because the nails catch and kill him.

Set Traps for Otter—At the foot of their slides a trifle under the water. Beaver also.

The Secret of Trapping Wild Animals.—My style of setting traps was most simple and very effective, although it required a good many traps to do the work. Knowing the habits of the animals I was trying to catch alive I adopted the following methods.

I set my traps only on the trails running through the thickest part of the woods. Here we would bury traps at intervals along the path by first digging a hole with a hatchet and removing the earth. Then we carefully laid a trap in place, laying a piece of canvas under the trap pan to keep the earth from interfering with the spring or clogging it. Next we carefully covered the trap with earth and smoothed the ground off, after securing the trap chain to limb of a bush or trunk of a tree. We were careful to place a few branches or stones on either side of the path ahead of each trap to guide the animal directly over the trap into it.

Then all was ready but one thing and that was the secret of our great success in trapping animals. We placed a small stick across the path right in front of the trap. This served to guide the animal's foot directly on to the pan of the trap, as an animal in walking on a trail will never tread on a stick, but always take a short step without touching it. A stick placed at the right distance in front of the trap will always have the desired effect. All animals while prowling through the woods will follow a trail when they encounter one for some distance before taking to the woods again. Consequently a line of traps set at intervals of a few rods along the paths through the woods is pretty sure to land any wandering animal.

Wolves Will Not—Touch dead game if it is partly covered with brush, leaves, etc., as they fear a trap.

Always Suspend Your Bait—A trifle over the trap so as the animal must step on the pan to secure it.

Shipping Skins, Etc.—We request Hunters or trappers who are shipping to us, when they kill extra fine specimens of Deer, Antelope, Mountain Sheep, Elk, Moose or Caribou, leave the feet, head and horns on. We want them for mounting purposes. They should be boxed and sent by freight and billed as green hides, than they will come at lowest freight rate. Also, when they kill well furred Bear, Wolf, Fox, Wolverine or Wild Cat, they should be skinned in good shape, head and feet perfect, leaving the claws on. Salt the skin of their feet and put some salt in their ears.

Don't Ship Skins—Unless caught in season and prime, and have them tanned right; for those however who are in the woods, away from shipping points, these receipts are mostly intended for.

In Skinning Hides—Keep the back of the knife close to the hide (always) and draw out the skin with the left hand, using a skinning knife to insure success.

To Salt Hides—Remove flesh or excess fat, put on plenty of salt thick, when the salt is absorbed put on more, roll up tight fur side out, cord it and is ready to ship.

To Catch Muskrat.—In the female muskrat, near the vagina, is a small bag which holds 30 to

40 drops. Now all the trapper has to do, is to procure a few female muskrats and squeeze the contents of the bag into a vial. Now, when in quest of muskrats, sprinkle a few drops of the liquid on the bushes over and around the trap. This will attract the male muskrats in large numbers, and if the traps are properly arranged, large numbers of them may be taken.

In Poisoning Wolves, Foxes, Etc.—Place the poison in center of meat balls.

Large Game or Whole Deer—Should never be skinned for shipment; draw the entrails, wash inside with cold water.

Game Birds—Should be shipped in natural state, undrawn, in cold weather; in hot weather draw as soon as killed, if to be shipped.

Never Dry Skins by a Fire—It ruins and spoils them.

Quantity of Traps to a Barrel.—Traps that are packed in barrels number as follows: Size No. 0, 30 to 50 traps to a barrel; No. 1, 25 to 35; No. 1½, 15 to 25; No. 2, 10 to 15; No. 2½, 8 to 12; No. 3, 6 to 10; No. 4, 5 to 8; No. 4½, 2 or 3.

Weight of Traps Per Dozen—(Newhouse) No. 0, 7 lbs.; No. 1, 10 lbs.; No. 1½, 13 lbs.; No. 2, 17 lbs.; No. 3, 28 lbs.; No. 4, 33 lbs.; No. 4½, 98 lbs.

Right Traps to Use.—No. 0, Rat or Gopher; No. 1, Muskrat; No. 1½, Mink; No. 2, Fox; No. 2½ and 3, Otter; No. 4, Beaver; No. 4½, Wolf; No. 5, Bear; No. 6 (for Grizzly Bear, Lions, Tigers, Cougars) it is the strongest trap made, weight 45 lbs.

Cost of Traps—Range from $4.25 per doz. with chains complete to $20.00 each, according to size. Price list as follows:

		Per doz.			Per doz.
No. 0	Rat	$ 4.25	No. 3½	Large Otter	$18.00
No. 1	Muskrat	5.00	No. 4	Beaver	16.50
No. 1½	Mink	7. 0	No. 4½	Wolf	40.00
No. 2	Fox	10.50	No. 5	Bear	75.00
No. 2½	Otter with teeth	14.00	No. 6	Large Bear	240.00
No. 3	Otter	16.50			

Traps above complete with all chains ready for use.

A Unique Trap.—Cut a small bush (spruce or pine is best) stick it up in deep snow or through the ice of a small river or stream; such a curious thing will attract animals to it, being new to them. Small pieces of meat, and several traps placed here and there about it, is pretty sure to land an animal or two after a few nights. Scent your main bait, which should hang so as the animal must put his foot on the pan of trap to reach it.

Another One.—Bore holes in the ground and fill them with bait scented, in a circle, your trap in the center, is mighty apt to catch something, especially if two natural logs V shape lay near it. It is sure death to Wolves if the bait is poisoned and frozen.

Burning Sulphur or Brimstone—Placed in the hole of any animal will smother them out or kill them.

Skunks in Their Holes—Will not throw their scent. *Old trappers* put their hands in and pull them out by the tail, hitting them with a club the moment their head appears. They will not bite at these times, so don't be afraid.

Trap Set for Skunk—Needs no covering, they are not suspicious but go right in.

All Water Animals—Are prime while ice is in the rivers or streams.

Clean and Smoke Your Traps—Using smoke from feathers of birds. Never handle them with bare hands. Wash them well and oil them first.

Wash Traps—With weak lye or soapsuds, then grease and smoke them over burnt feathers, and never touch them with the hands.

It is Not Safe—To send hides to market green except in winter or freezing cold weather.

Unseasonable Furs—Are graded 2, 3 or 4, last grades, and are only prime No. 1 in early winter.

Use McCall's Decoy—A powerful prepared scent to attract animals. Small can costs $1.00.

When Traps Are Set—Smear with a feather your *scent* baits over it, and you are almost sure of *success.*

365

Pure Strychnine—Costs $1.50 per oz. Sure death capsules for killing wolves, foxes, etc.

Use Buckskin or Moosehide Moccasins—When hunting or trapping; and do not stir up the ground when setting traps, be careful to leave the ground as near as you found it as possible to do.

Tanning Fur and Other Skins.—First: Remove the legs and other useless parts and soak the skin soft; then remove the flesh substances and soak in warm water for an hour; now:

Take for one large or two or three small skins, borax, saltpetre and glauber-salt, of each ½ oz. and dissolve or wet with soft water sufficiently to allow it to be spread on the flesh side of the skin.

Put it on with a brush, thickest in the center or thickest part of the skin, and double the skin together, flesh-side in, keeping it in a cool place for twenty-four hours, not allowing it to freeze, however.

Second: Wash the skin clean, and then: Take sal-soda, 1 oz.; borax, ½ oz.; refined soap, 2 oz.; (white hard soap;) melt them slowly together, being careful not to allow them to boil, and apply the mixture to the flesh-side as at first—roll up again and keep in a warm place for 24 hours.

Third: Wash the skin clean, as above, and have saleratus two ounces, dissolved in hot rain water sufficient to well saturate the skin, then:

Take alum, 4 ozs.; salt, 8 ozs.; and dissolve also in hot rain water; when sufficiently cool to allow the handling of it without scalding, put in the skin for 12 hours; then wring out the water and hang up for 12 hours more, to dry. Repeat this last soaking and drying from 2 to 4 times according to the desired softness of the skin when finished.

Lastly: Finish by pulling, working, etc. and finally by rubbing with piece of pumice-stone and fine sand-paper.

This works admirably on sheep skins as well as on fur-skins, dog, cat or wolf-skins also, making a durable leather well adapted to washing.

Above recipes are reliable if strictly followed; if skins are however, well cleaned of meats and part of the fat well salted, rolled up and tied, they had best be shipped us at once.

Newhouse Clamp.—A device for setting traps (large ones) $4.50 per dozen.

Trap Wrenches—For Wolf traps, etc. per doz. $1.50 delivered F. O. B. cars at factory, or Chicago, Ill.

A Novel and Effective Poison Trap—For Skunk, etc. Bore holes in logs, then fill with lard, tallow, etc., to which strychnine has been mixed. When it freezes they must lick it out, and it kills them before they can get far away. Scent the spot so as to attract them to it.

Another Good Way.—Bore holes in logs, driving horse shoe nails slanting in the holes, fill the recess behind the points of the nails with good scented baits; they will stick their heads and shoulders in to get it, but they can't get them out, for the points of the nails prevent it. For small animals this is excellent, even for rats.

Never Put the Bait—On the pan of the trap. Cover the pan with dry leaves or dirt or both, never use twigs on the pan, that is for the foot of the animal only.

Always Bed Your Traps—On bare, smooth ground then cover it with dry leaves taken from a distant spot, mixed with feathers.

Animal Poisons—Put up especially for killing Skunks, Weasels, Wolves, etc. in form of capsules ready for use. 40 cents per dozen. We have them. Larger doses for Bear, etc. 50 cents per doz. Pure strychnine cyrstals or powder as desired, drachm bottles, 35 cents each, postpaid. Tastelessly arranged ready for business.

The Best Book on Trapping—"Camp Life and Tricks of Trapping," 300 pages, 500 illustrations; postpaid $1.00. Write for one.

For a Complete Camp Cook Book—Send for a copy of the Complete Camper's Manual, or How to Camp Out and What to Do. 136 pages, over 200 illustrations.

Decoy Bait Scent—Is put up ready for trappers use, price 25 cents per oz. 1 pint can $2.50. We keep a supply on hand.

Trappers Tricks

Fasten Small Traps—To a cut branch of a tree about the weight of the animal you expect, using the same branch if needs be; to adjust your *bait over the trap, but rather choosing a natural bush or tree. Never set a trap until the last thing.*

For Signs of Animals—Dung, signs of a meal, feathers, bones, etc., shed hair, holes, dens. Set traps here

Preserve Leavings.—When you find feathers, etc. leavings of a meal, keep them to use in connection with coverings of the trap you set, or set a trap about it.

Skunk in Fall—Are often found in open fields, about small bushes, etc. In winter on higher ground.

A Good Dog—Is a trapper's valuable adjunct; always aiding you to locate trails dens, etc.

Good Baits—Are birds, fish, beef offals, rabbits, cheese, rotten eggs, entrails, etc.

Trapper's Patience—Study it; don't pull up a trap, try again and again; stick right to good places.

Opossums, Coons, Etc.—Are found in dense woods.

Always Keep Traps—Free from rust, well greased and cleaned.

In Setting Traps in Holes—Insert them well inside and scent them; don't place them outside, they can perceive the fraud. Cover with leaves.

Bait Gone.—When you find this, and trap still set, arrange your bait the other side of trap; leave the trap be.

Mink can be found—Near swamps, along streams and their waterways, especially where dead wood, logs, etc. are bunched. Look for their tracks in the mud, sand, etc.

HUNTING.

The Oil Reflector "Jack Light."
See article on Deer Hunting.

To Find Out—Positively if animals frequent a certain spot, place a small piece of bait there over night; if it is gone in the morning, set your trap right there carefully.

In Dead of Winter—Many animals hole up for several weeks or more.

Never Apply Heat—In drying skins; hang them in the shade is best.

Useless Tails.—Tails of opossum and muskrat are of no value, so cut them off.

Remove the Fat—Of all skins; fat left on heats and spoils the hide.

Best Month—For bears and badgers is March; water animals until the ice leaves.

To Locate Skunks—Look for their holes on rise of ground or hills near rocks, etc., examine all holes, and notice if black and white hairs are there, being lazy they choose holes already formed; look for droppings a little distance away; set traps close to holes.

To Trap Mink—Dig a hole in the bank near their haunts, place your bait inside your trap at its edge and cover it well; sprinkle water around so as to wash your traces away; before leaving it clog the trap of course, and use scent bait.

Never Set—Large traps without a trap wrench.

The Best Time—First stormy night, or before a storm the animals are then foraging for foods and seeking warm holes to den.

Skunks—Hole up in very cold weather in rabbit holes which they often kill and live on, until forced out by hunger or a warm spell.

How Animals Gnaw Loose.—The caught leg or foot becomes numb and some what painless, and the bone being broken, is easily detached.

Mark Your Traps—By filing your initial thereon, or by marks.

When You Succeed—In catching an animal, leave your trap and reset it; it often pays well, especially at dens.

Always Remove—Bones from tails of skinned animals; it rots therein otherwise.

369

Keep Skins—Loose and straight; don t roll them up; pack them straight is best.

Skunks are Easy—To trap. A rabbit often displays more intelligence as to traps than the skunk.

Bait for Mink—Any fresh meats, fish or fowl, muskrat meat, etc.

The Best Book for Trappers—Is unquestionably "Traps and Trap Making" by Hamilton Gibson; 300 full pages, price $1.00; over 200 illustrations; very complete and accurate.

To Attract Wolves—Place bones or large chunk of meat in fire and let it smolder. Use carcasses of other animals.

Smear Traps with Blood—Or dip in thin solution of melted beeswax or tallow.

Number of Traps to Use.—Six dozen traps are ample for any trapper to attend.

Always Sink Your Traps—To the exact level of the ground, leaving the surface as near as it was as possible.

Use Fresh Baits—Whenever possible; fasten them to a short stick and in the right position to lead feet into the trap.

Cut Up Old Baits—In small pieces and scatter them along the route of your traps.

How to Skin—Cat, Fisher, Fox, Lynx, Martin, Mink, Opossum, Wolverine, Otter, Skunk and Muskrat must be "cased," that is, not cut open. In skinning, cut at the rump and turn the skin inside out over the body of the animal, leaving the pelt side out.

After scraping, cleaning and drying, some dealers advise turning the skin back again, leaving the fur side out; but with the exception of Foxes, Red, Silver and Cross, the large dealers now prefer the skin left pelt side out, as the quality can be more easily determined by examining the rumps; and are better preserved and protected in the numerous handlings.

Badger, Bear, Beaver, Raccoon and Wolf must be "open," that is, cut up the belly from rump to head. After scraping, cleaning and drying, stretch to a uniformly oblong shape to the fullest extent of the skin, but not so much as to make the fur thin. When thoroughly dry, trim off any little pieces that spoil the appearance of the skin, but leave on heads, noses and claws.

No. 1 Skins—Must be large and full furred or prime; remember they grade down to 4.

Do Skinning, Stretching, Etc.—After you have tended all your traps. Skin and dry carefully if you market.

Jerked Meats.—If you have the fortune to kill a deer or moose in warm weather, and have an over-supply of meat that is likely to be tainted, you can preserve it by the following process: Cut all the flesh from the bones in thin strips, and place them for convenience, on the inside of the hide. Add three or four quarts of salt for a moose, and a pint and a half for deer, well worked in. Cover the whole with the sides and corners of the hide to keep out flies, and let it remain in this condition about two hours. Drive four forked stakes into the ground so as to form a square of about eight or ten feet, leaving the forks four feet high. Lay two poles across one way in these forks, and fill the whole space the other way with poles laid on the first two, about two inches apart. The strips of flesh should then be laid across the poles, and a small fire of clean hardwood should be started underneath, and kept up for twenty-four hours. This process will reduce the weight of the flesh more than half, bringing it to a condition like that of dried or smoked beef, in which it will keep any length of time. This is called jerked venison. It is good eating, and always commands a high price in market. An over-supply of fish can be treated in the same manner. They should be split open on the back, and the backbone taken out.

Never Set—Large traps without a trap clamp. Never place your hands about the jaws or pan, and don't handle a set trap.

Trapper's Best Friend—Is a good, well trained dog.

Don't Reset—Where sprung traps are found; try a new place thereabout. If bait is gone and trap unsprung, you are at fault, so reset in these instances.

371

Overhanging Trees—Or inclined ones, nail your bait to them. If your traps are set under right, are excellent places.

For Water Set Traps—(Traps set in water.) Use rubber boots and wade into the waters, avoiding the shores, or wash your tracks by throwing water on them.

Dry Set Traps—(Traps set on land.) Step always in your same tracks, using moccasins, not boots, or cover boots with skin tied on hair side out.

Wash Traps.—Oil and grease them well, smoke or cover with blood, beeswax, etc. and keep free from rust.

Use Dirt from Dens—Rotten wood, leaves, dung, small feathers, etc. for bedding down traps.

Always—Set your traps for the foot of the animal and arrange your bait so as he must set his foot on the pan to secure bait.

No Duty—On raw furs from Canada.

Skunk—Are the first animals to get prime in late fall and early winter. Water animals are last.

Bears and Badgers—Are only prime in midwinter and very early spring.

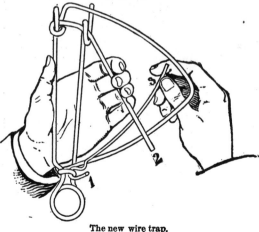

The new wire trap.

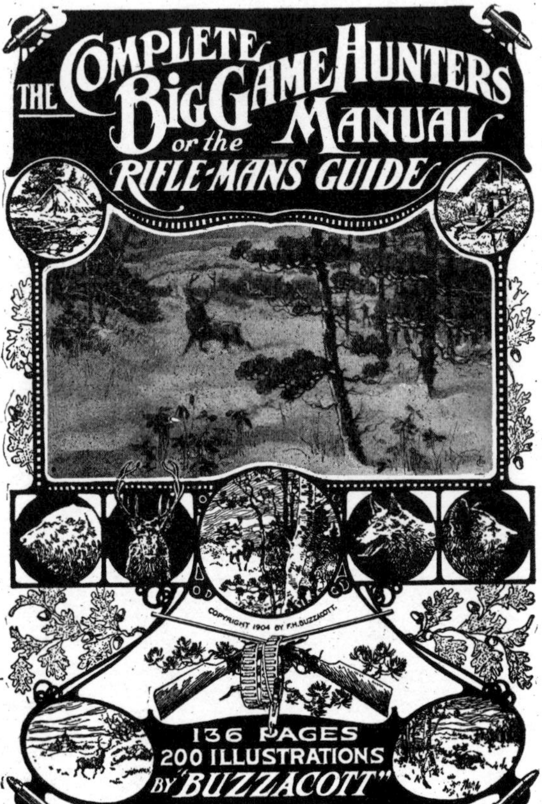

THE COMPLETE Big Game Hunters MANUAL
or the
RIFLE-MANS GUIDE

COPYRIGHT 1904 BY F.H.BUZZACOTT.

136 PAGES
200 ILLUSTRATIONS
BY "BUZZACOTT"

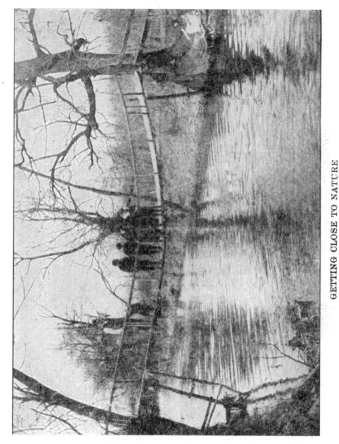

GETTING CLOSE TO NATURE

On a Country "Hike" Interesting Scenes Like This Are Found and Pleasant
Surprises Are Frequent

Getting a Move on Him.   374

The Hunter's Outfit

Equipped for a Five Days Trip.

MUCH has been written on what is best to take on a hunting trip, but a good deal remains to be said on *what not to take;* hence a few practical suggestions as to both may not be amiss. It is always best to travel right *but light*, including nothing cumbersome, yet all the essentials necessary to to provide for comfort and success. I advise for clothing in all seasons, medium weight and colored soft flannels or woolen garments, selecting only the very heavy woolens for mid-winter uses and always avoiding cotton clothing of any description. My article on clothing in the "Complete Camper's Manual"—or how to camp out and what to do—should be noted. About the most satisfactory dress is old worn, (but clean) even patched woolen clothing, supplemented by flannel shirts of either tan or blue flannel or wool, having turn down collars and breast pockets that button up. If mid-winter, those of double-breasted and reinforced shoulders and back are best, but for ordinary weather (summer or fall) single-breasted will suffice; light gray or tan colored flannel underclothing, over which should be worn a medium weight tan colored hunting sweater or knitted jacket with pockets woven therein. Woolen or buckskin leggings and three-quarter size Moosehide or Elkskin moccasins (for still hunting

375

Hunter's, Sportsman's, and Trapper's Hats, Caps and Gloves.

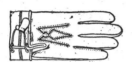

1—Buckskin Glove.　　　2—Storm Hood.　　　3—Woolen Glove.

4—Summer Hat.　　5—Double Bisor Hat.　　6—Soft Hunting Hat.

7—Campaign Hat.　　　　　　　　9—Summer Helmet.

8 –"Flap Cap" or Hood

10—Canvas Hat.　　　　　　　　　12—Corduroy Cap.
(Roll Down)

Folding Pocket Mosquito Hat—Open and Closed.

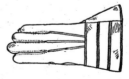

11—Corduroy
Cap and Flaps.

14—Buckskin Gauntlets.　　　376　　　15—Buckskin Gauntlets.

especially), never mind what other writers say about canvas or corduroy—my advice is to leave it out, unless it is very cold and dry weather, and you desire such garments for ordinary field or open shooting, and even then it should be made of the Army Khaki material, light and waterproof. The objections to either common duck, canvas, or corduroy clothing is that the first *makes too much noise in the woods*, the other too heavy, easily wet through and hard to dry; and on a run causes the wearer to perspire too freely, and do not absorb the heat or moisture; for wear or keeping out the wind either is good, but there are many other essentials—and many a sudden cold, chill, and other camp sickness can be traced to the free use of such clothing; unquestionably it is good to work in, but not to hunt in.

Such clothing is rarely used by the professional guide or old and experienced hunters, and never should be considered for *still hunting*, for it is not only too noisy, but entirely unsuitable for many other reasons. Use also heavy woolen socks if in the winter time, otherwise light merino socks with double heel and toe. Don't use heavy hunting boots unless you are used to them, (never rubber boots, they are useless except for fishing or wading.) Better select, if you desire boots, those of medium weight, three-quarter size. Heavy or high boots unless you are used to them, heat and weary the feet on a long distance trip, rendering the wearer tired and uncomfortable. I prefer a good shoe and canvas leggings, the outside of which has been covered with wool cloth or buckskin so as to render them noiseless almost *in the brush*. Let your boots or shoes be made of best waterproof material, soft and well fitting; the Putman oil tanned boots are excellent, and about as near waterproof as it is possible to construct.

For still hunting or winter use the moccasin three-quarter boot size, is the ideal footwear; although they will not keep out all the dampness, yet they will turn water readily, being made of oil tanned leather; they are softer than any other footwear, hence more noiseless. The lumberman's "Over" is also a popular favorite with guides and

Various Styles of Sportsman's and Hunting Sweaters, Jackets, etc.

Light, Medium or Heavy Weight.

1—Turn Down Collar,
Lace Front.

All Sizes,

All Grades

for

All Purposes.

2—Three Quarter
Jacket Style.

No. 10.
4—Fall Sweater
With Pockets.

3—Fall Jacket with Pockets.

5—Lace Front Sweater
With Pockets.

7—Sweater With
Full Pockets.

6—Sweater With Large Shell Pockets.

8—Tan or Blue
Hunting Shirt.

Gray, Tan, Brown or Scarlet Color.

sportsmen as they are low cut, and present very little surface for noisy movement which frightens the game; and with several pairs of woolen stockings it is practically impossible for cold and snow to bother or affect your feet. If the moccasin is too soft, better have it made for you double soled, which will add considerably to its waterproof qualities. All these things can be furnished at slight expense over the ordinary kinds, by specialists in such equipment.

Let your handkerchief be of extra large size, Bandanna style, 24 inches square, blue or red in color, for they can be worn as a neck scarf, used as a towel, bandage, sling, game decoy or signal, even as a pack sack; while its color will not soil easily. For the hat choose a soft felt one, with medium wide brim to shade the eyes or shed water. Color brown or drab is right; let it have a high crown, style about like the U. S. Army officers campaign hat, *which will hold and carry water like a bucket*, (handy at times) a leather hat band tightens the fit in windy or stormy weather, and if a string is tied to it and fastened to the back collar of your shirt, you will never have to go back after, or suffer the loss of it, on a run. Never take an overcoat, no matter if it is winter, "old backwoodsmen don't." A chamios shirt or an extra shirt will do the trick. Two changes of clothing is ample for a month's trip, and with a pair of extra overalls for knocking about camp and a sweater or jacket, you have a third change, and can thus even dispense with that useless article on a hunting trip, the coat; never forget the sweater, for of all things on a trip its the one thing; if its made right and for the purpose. They are cool in the warm, warm in the cool, free and easy fitting; and I know of no single garment better suited for hunting purposes. In color it should be khaki or tan, although many deer hunters choose red or scarlet. Don't take fur cap or gloves, unless its an Arctic trip; better good woolen gloves supplemented by oil tanned buckskin ones. If a cap is desired let it be a good woolen one, either a hunter's Toque cap, or the regular cap with ear flaps that can be pulled down over the ears if required. Don't use mittens if you

379

Standard Type of Hunter's and Sportsmen's Jackets, etc.

Canvas, Wool, Corduroy or Leather

1—Hunter's Winter Jacket.

2—Hunter's Game Coat.

3—Hunter's Vest.

←—Genuine Astrakhan Coat.

5—Reversible Sportsman's Coat.

6—Corduroy Hunting Coat.

7—Winter or Arctic Hood Coat.

want to be ready for quick action. For winter hunting in the woods or mountains, snow shoes should be provided. Sewing or repair kit, needles, thread, soap, bachelor buttons, salve, bandages, court plaster, should be carried in a "camper's ditty bag." Leave out razor, strops, etc. (if you wish) as often a week's growth of beard in the woods comes in handy, especially if insects, or frosty winds prevail; its nature's protection to the face, besides gives you a chance to see how you look, and shows the folks that you really have been hunting.

A dry, warm, soft bed is about the most important item of all, in your camp outfit; nothing is worse than a hard, cold bed—your health, comfort, rest, everything depends on the satisfactory qualities of your sleeping outfit. For cold weather (fall or winter uses) nothing can equal the the Ideal Sleeping Bag, which is absolutely *wind*, *weather water* and *cold proof;* for milder or summer uses the Camp Combination fills the bill exactly (see illustrations.) If you have neither, never venture into camp without at least providing yourself with a long, wide strip of canvas, or heavy duck (waterproof khaki if possible) of sufficient size to allow one-half to be placed under your bedding on the ground (or preferably over a bed of dry leaves, twigs, brush or browse) the other half to cover your blankets and tuck under you, so as to keep the warmth in and the cold and dampness out. Don't lug a pillow along; take a pillow case and into it lay neatly folded your clean, dry clothing, (not bunched up) and it will form a capital pillow. If you dislike to sleep in the underclothes you have worn during the day, provide yourself with a suit of tan colored, military pajamas; and if you are of the *cold feet tribe*, a pair of sleeping socks will fill the bill. Don't permit yourself to be coaxed into buying an Air Mattress and Pillow, better put the price $15.00, and the weight 15 lbs. into good soft, warm blankets, sleeping bag, or combination mentioned before, and you won't regret it. Never sit or lay on the bare ground; a bed of leaves, grass or small twigs under your canvas or bedding roll will answer the purpose. If its raining, your can-

381

Sportsman's and Hunter's Foot Wear.

For All Purposes.

1—The "Shoe Pac"

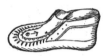

Moccasin Slipper.

We Handle All Reliable Grades.

7—Army Boot.

9—The Army Shoe.

2—Canvas Leggins.

Puttee Leggins.

11—Snow Shoes.

14—Moose Hide Moccasin.

10 -Sleeping Socks.

18—Skie.

382

5—Sportsman's Boot.

8 - ¾ Hunting Shoe.

6—Hunters Boot.

vas or bag and your extra blankets are better than the "nothing so rare as resting on air plan. If sitting down, sit on your hat, anything, only keep off the bare ground; squat as the Indian does is better.

For shelter the "wall tent" is about the best, and in hot weather should be provided with a double fly. But if portability is necessary choose that of the "Miner Wall Tent" with a jointed single pole; some prefer the A or wedge tent, but the "Miner Wall" gives more available room, while the single pole necessary, can be taken along if jointed right, or if cut from good size tree or branch enroute it will answer the purpose admirably. If its cold nights, don't forget the small conical tent heaters, called the Sibley stove, as adopted by the U. S. Government. It is not pretty, but the heat it will distribute in a tent and the simple way it does it, creates an admiration for its inventor, whoever he was. If your tent is for cold weather uses, let it be of 10 or 12 ounce Army Duck, white or khaki (tan) color; but if for a summer trip or you pack light, let it be of "balloon silk." For tent pins choose malleable iron ones; they won't break, and a dozen can be carried in the space of half a dozen wooden ones. As to weight there is no difference, small ones being 2 ounces each and large ones 3 ounces. Cut out everything of unwieldy size, bulk or weight. Let the camp axe be of the safety pocket size, for its a little wonder; small enough to sharpen a pencil, or fell a good size tree; and with a reliable hunting knife, that of the Marble Ideal Pattern, you are equipped with cutting and chopping apparatus to serve a lifetime.

If your rifle be of the standard make and grade, Winchester, Remington, Savage, or equal pattern, 40 to 45 caliber, I cannot advise you, on better; if however you are about deciding the purchase of one, let me suggest 303, caliber; never over 35 caliber in this 20th century should be used, *for even big game hunting;* and if you use soft nosed or express bullets in your cartridges you are equipped simply splendidly. The 303, or 35 caliber rifle is the ideal weapon of to-day, it is all right for the largest kind of game, Moose, Elk, Bear, etc. Never use "the hit to-day—kill tomorrow" ammunition if you are using a rifle. What you want unless you

383

The Sportsman's Ideal Sleeping Bag Outfit Complete.

Wind, Weather, Water, Cold and Snow Proof.

Used as a Mild Weather Outfit.   Dry Enough for Rainy Weather.

No Tent Needed Even in Mid-Winter.   Warm Enough for Winter Use.

Ready to Roll Up.   384   Rolled Up.

are an expert sharpshooter, is the crushing, stopping, dropping power of the soft nose or express bullet; finer or steel tipped and hard bullets of the military type, go clear through flesh and bone, and do not kill until many miles are between you and the game, (unless hit in a vital spot) lost game resulting. What you want is the tearing, crushing, killing power of the express bullet which mushrooms on impact, and which inflicts a deadly wound.

If your weapon is a shot gun, let it be of 12 gauge, hammerless ejector, if you can afford it, anyhow let it be 12 gauge, which is pre-eminently the best gun for all round uses; let the barrels be 30 inch; right barrel, cylinder or modified choke and the left, full choke bored; weighing about 7¼ pounds.

Let your cartridge belt be of woven material (not leather or canvas) and provide it with shoulder straps like suspenders to keep the weight from your hips. If using a rifle, chamber every cartridge you put in it, so as to avoid misfits or a stuck shell at the critical moment, owing to any fault of your own; and carry looped to the belt *or somewhere, the Ideal Shell Extractor.* In your belt 20 to 30 rounds of ammunition is enough for any single day's jaunt, unless you are a mighty poor shot, or a butcher, or game hog by profession, in which case change your methods and practice sportsmanship.

I have mighty little respect for the hunter who kills for the mere gratification of a slaughtering mania, everything he sees: while no man can help but admire the true sportsman, who quits after a fairly successful day's sport and skill. Game is none too plentiful, and it is owing to such wanton destruction that our Maine and other woods, (despite railroad advertisements and alluring literature to the contrary) is depleted or almost so; fortunately laws are made dealing with these things, but at times even laws are useless, and it is only by direct appeal to the manhood of men, and by proving the necessity of their observance, that the indiscriminate

385

slaughter and extinction of our game can be stopped; and as a member of the American Sportsman's Association, I appeal to all brother sportsmen to discourage the wasteful and useless slaughter of game; man has by such methods already rendered many species extinct, and others nearly so. The domain of the wild animals or game is already on the wane; for rapidly enough are we pre-empting heretofore uninhabited territory.

Some day man will utilize all the earth for some purpose or other, then the day of wild game or animal will have passed, except perhaps such as may be housed in menageries, and the species allowed to propagate for the benefit of those interested in zoology. Hence I say be reasonable, and quit after a fair day's sport, and do not keep killing just because you can.

As to the revolver for a hunting trip, leave it out, it is rarely useful or needed. Choose instead (the same weight) either the U. S. Government (adopted) Binocular Telescope or a pair of good field glasses, straps and case, which you will find invaluable for sighting and making sure of game; across distant waters or midst hills, by its aid, what often appears to be a stump or rock, shows to be game or wild animals; saving an immense amount of tramping around, and enabling a search with the eye, from a point of vantage many miles in extent, revealing to you the presence of game that otherwise you would have never discovered. Such things can be carried by your guide or companion.

If on distant trips a sportsman's haversack should be carried, and to equalize and distribute its small weight, a canteen filled with pure water or tea; in this haversack should be carried if desired, extra ammunition, safety compass and waterproof safety match box, thus insuring the hunter several days supply of warm fires and smokes, in case of a wetting or an aggravating fall in crossing a river or creek; for when hunting there is no telling when some accident will happen; you might for instance, after a long chase in distant timber be unable to find your way back to camp. Then a dry match, a smoke, fire, shelter and a hot cup or canteen of tea will not come amiss.

All of these things are essentials, not luxuries by any means, and can easily be carried in a spare pocket or a corner of the haversack. To its strap or buckle ought to be fastened the tin cup and in the other pocket of it (a good haversack has several pockets) some salt and pepper or a light lunch of some kind; a bacon and flap-jack sandwich is right; never carry fresh bread or even crackers in a haversack, the motion of the body or jolting it gets results in only crumbs or cracker dust, when you are about famished and ready to eat; and right here let me suggest that before you start on the return trip *or a renewed jaunt,* take time to stop and rest a while; build a fire, warm up a cup of tea, broil a steak if have killed game, eat a snack, which your salt and pepper renders a dainty morsel; light your pipe, and the rest and good it will do you is not to be overlooked or measured by words. Don't think these things are cumbersome, why they don't add two pounds to your outfit, and the guide or companion, if he is a good one, should never go into the woods without them, even though yourself should deem them not necessary.

If its in the rainy season, a featherweight sportsman's rain cape (pocket size) is a convenience, as it folds up in small compass and weighs only 18 ounces, while it covers and keeps you dry, when the rain suddenly comes down in a flood, reaching as it does below the knee or legging tops; if winter time of course this can be dispensed with.

If your trip to the woods occupies a week or more, I suggest also a Pocket Medicine Case and contents (sportman's size) together with the U S. Government's (adopted) First Aid Packet for wounds; the last mentioned weighing only 1 oz., and which can be tied to your cartridge belt when on a trip. These both would fill the bill for emergency medical supplies for many a different short trip or for quite a large party, at very small expense, either as to bulk, weight or cost. The medicines put up therein being of tablet form, in screw top phials, printed instructions with them, and which serve every purpose for the home or sports-

Sportsman's and Hunter's Specialties.

1—Binocular
Field Glass.

2—First Aid Packet
for Wounds.

3—Pocket Stove.

4—Folding Compass.

6—Water Proof Safety
Match Box.

5—Sportsman's Haversack.

7—Pedometer.

9—Camp Scales.

8—Medicine Case Pocket Size.

10—Watch Case
Compass.

11—Field or Marine Telescope.

388

12—Safety
Compass.

Portable Water Cooling Canteens, Flasks and Filters.

1—Pocket Flask, Glass Top (Screw Top.)

6—Camp Filter. 1 Quart a Minute.

11—Water Filter.

2—All Aluminum, Screw Top.

7—Rubber Covered Flask.

12—Wicker Flask.

3—Vest Pocket (long) Flask, Screw Top.

8—Leather Covered Flask

13—Wicker Flask.

4—Screw Top Pocket Flask

9—The Celebrated Water Cooling Canteen. U. S. Army Pattern.

5—Oil Flask (Tin) Screw Top.

10—Same as No. 9.

14—Protected Flask and Drinking Cup.

man's camp; in fact in my own home I have a case and seldom have any occasion for other medical service; and as a "life a-woods" usually by the change brings on petty disorders, it is nowadays a most valuable adjunct to the outfit, necessary for smoothing it. (See illustrations.)

Last but not least, a few words as to carrying or transporting the outfit either to the woods or enroute home; for this nothing can equal the "canvas carry-all or roll up," (the long, wide canvas recommended for sleeping or bedding purposes); which is laid flat on the ground and the dozen or more articles of clothing and equipment, anything you desire to be carried or transported, laid across and on top of your bedding; the sides of the canvas are then turned toward the center (see cut) and the whole rolled and strapped into a suitable bundle as illustrated. It beats anything ever devised for carrying an outfit, and if packed right nothing can ever be lost from it or smashed. It simply defies breakage, and is proof against rain or wet, or the throwing about of heartless baggage smashers. If tent, cooking outfit, stove and other "duffle" is to be carried, the whole can be stored in a folding or *sectional trunk boat* or sportsman's outfit trunk, even to the jointed tent poles being packed therein, thus permitting of an entire outfit for a party of three or more persons to be packed and shipped as baggage, without extra expense, beyond that borne by the party for travel alone.

The Four Person Complete Outfit Packed.

About the Rifle (For Big Game Hunting)

In these days the selection of a good rifle for the use of either Tyro or Sportsman is an easy matter, the most important desideratum being the selection of the most fitting caliber, and the cartridge best suited for its purpose on the game you seek. I have probably received in my time many bushels of letters requesting information as to the *best all round rifle*, as well as for facts concerning it, hence the following suggestions for the guidance of my readers may not come amiss.

Such a thing as an all round rifle cannot in the nature of things be made. We have not yet produced a rifle that will kill anything from a *humming bird to an elephant*, but taking the meaning in an intelligent sense, as applying to the rifles to-day, we can pretty near approach it.

If the reader is about to purchase or select a rifle, in these days of high explosive Nitro (smokeless) powders, etc., let him pin his faith to those of *less caliber and weight* than was necessary a few years ago. But if he be equipped with any of those I mention in the course of my remarks, don't change—stick to it, for you have one that you can *honestly swear by* for a long time to come. Perhaps the most effective weapon of to-day for large game hunting I believe (and this belief is based on experience and observation covering many years of hunting, using many different kinds and grades of rifles) is that the Winchester 35 caliber 5 shot repeating rifle, model 1895, using the 35 Winchester cartridge and soft point bullet is the most powerful game-killer in existence *to-day*.

Some idea of its tremendous stopping power (the all important in large game hunting) can best be realized when it is known that the striking energy of its bullet (see illustration) at 200 yards, is greater than the muzzle energy of that well known and universally respected Winchester 45, 70, 405, of which mention here is superfluous.

The cartridge for this rifle is fitted with 250 grain *"soft pointed metal patched bullet"* (the ideal bullet for large game hunting) loaded with a special smokeless powder, which imparts to it a muzzle velocity of 2,200 ft. seconds, thereby developing a

391

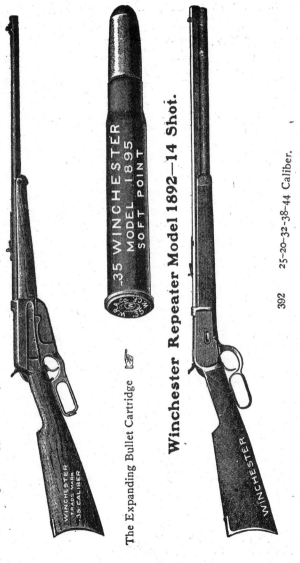

The Winchester Repeating Rifle—Model 1895.

Box Magazine—35 Caliber—5 Shot.   This Model also for 30; U. S. Army 303; British 38-72 and 40-72.

The Expanding Bullet Cartridge ☞

.35 WINCHESTER
MODEL 1895
SOFT POINT

Winchester Repeater Model 1892—14 Shot.

25-20-32-38-44 Caliber.

392

See Article on This Rifle.

muzzle energy of 2,685 lbs. and having a remaining energy of over 1,500 lbs. at 200 yards range, a trajectory of *less than* 5 inches, while its penetration (by test) 15 feet from the muzzle is 15⅞ inches pine boards. The rifle is furnished with a 24 inch round barrel (nickel steel,) plain walnut stock, weighing in all about 8½ lbs. and is unquestionably an ideal weapon for the hunting of the largest game known to-day. (See illustrations.)

Other efficient weapons for the sportsman (well known) are the Winchester models of 1873, '83, '86, '95 40, 44 and 45 caliber, these of course applying to rifles used for large game hunting, both extensively known and used.

Another remarkable weapon which approaches nearer the "all round rifle" idea is the Savage Repeater 303, 6-shot, which for all game up to and including Deer, Moose, etc. is a splendid rifle, and the sportsman who is blessed with such an arm, has one of the best big game guns on the market. With all due respect to other good weapons and makers of them, I certainly consider *this one* as a most up-to-date twentieth century rifle. Fitted with a *Lyman* combination rear sight and the "ivory jack" front sight it is simply perfection, and will group its shots with force and precision in as small a circle if held right (as any rifle should be) with the best of them. Select a 26 inch round barrel, and you have a rifle weighing 7½ lbs, that will hold its own with any and the *best of them.*

Another rifle which is receiving much attention at present from those desiring a small yet powerful calibre rifle, is the 30-30; yet my experience has been that for large game hunting, a trifle heavier calibre makes a better gun. What the sportsman wants is *stopping, smashing power,* which can only be obtained from a heavier bullet. Hence my recommendation of the soft point or express style, as their mushrooming or upsetting qualities on impact, are both terrific and deadly. High velocity, thin or hard pointed bullets are no doubt fine for military or long distance shooting, possessing greater initial velocity (rapidity) and much flatter trajectory (straighter flight) but their penetration is so great that they *go clear through bones and all,* neither breaking the bones or wasting,

Cartridge Holders, Cartridge Belts, etc.,

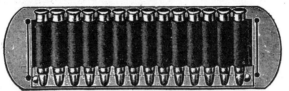

1—The Belt Attachment Fastens to Any Common Belt.

Pistol Holder.

5—The Shell Box.

6—Bedell Game Shirt and Cartridge Holder.

2—The Woven Belt Without Supporting Straps.

(with straps)

7—Money and Bill Belt.

Money and Pistol Cartridge Belt.

8—The Miners Gold Dust Belt.

3—The Thimble Belt (Shot Gun Cartridges.)

394

4—The Army Pattern.

Sportsman's and Hunter's Favorite Patterns,

blood, and a strong animal hit thus is seldom stopped, unless a vital spot is reached, and invariably large game struck by them continue to run, oftimes resulting in their crawling off to die elsewhere—or lost meat. No hunter cares for the necessity of a repetition of a lot of shots, or prolonging the sufferings of a wounded beast. Again wounds caused by them *do not bleed externally*, rendering it difficult to locate them, and ever making the tracking of wounded game more difficult. What the big game hunter needs is stopping, crushing power that will lay an animal low; and as most game is shot at fairly close range, say 300 yards, where is the necessity of long range, thin, metal jacketed, or small hard bullets. If there are a few cartridges for the purpose, carried in the rear of the sportsman's belt answers both occasions.

Another popular weapon for small game up to and including Deer, is the 38 caliber,. using the 38-56 cartridge; while others prefer the 40-60 or 65, yet by many is considered too heavy, its weight being 9¼ lbs.

Still another good weapon is the Marlin, 1893 model, 38-55, 10 or 11 shot, 7¾ lbs.; using the 38-55 smokeless cartridge and mushroom bullet. Indeed it is an easy matter to select a really excellent weapon without patronizing those of the *imported kind*, as for instance the Manlicher-Bolt rifle, for which *double price is asked*, as against the equally efficient and thoroughly reliable American weapon.

About Rifle Cartridges

In this the sportsman or tyro should provide a sufficient supply to ever prevent any possibilty of running short; fifty rounds being ample for any ordinary trip of several weeks or more duration. For this he should select that known as fresh "fixed" or ready made, avoiding that which has stood on the shelves of small dealers until it has aged, as this has deteriorated in quality. If he be wise, he will before starting out on a trip *"chamber every cartridge"* he places in his belt, so as to avoid misfits and a possible jam at the critical moment. I have myself often found in the best of makes, a shell or two of larger caliber than the others, yet so much alike in appeararce that it would readily pass muster, until a hurried insertion of it in the chamber, rendered the arm out of business until it could be removed (at times no easy matter.) Carry in a handy pocket a shell extractor, for with such as this (barring a break in the action, which seldom occurs in a well kept rifle) your "shooting irons" are Q. K. for a trip anywhere. (See illustration.)

Care of Rifles (See also Hits Around the Bull's Eye)

And now a word as to the care and use of a good rifle. Let me urge the reader to keep it good, just as you got it from the makers if you can. Don't experiment—leave that for experts to do, or at least wait until you are qualified to do "monkey business" with your gun. This is an age of dickering and tampering with sights, filing off a bit here and there, and I may say, practically ruining fine weapons; and if the reader could only see the condition of some most excellent rifles (hundreds of them that *have been shipped in to be fixed,* he would be amazed at the absolute absurdity of some of these changes. Nine times out of ten when a rifle leaves a responsible maker or factory, it has been tested and found not wanting; occasionally one might slip through unobserved, but if so, its fault will be rectified without question, if you will but make it known. Many a good, reliable weapon has been nearly ruined by the "doctoring" prescribed for it by the other fellow who knows it all. Nine times out of ten the rifle will do the work, unless the *man behind is at fault.* By all means avoid the suggested changes recommended by the "rifle cranks." Honestly there are some men who think they can make a rifle shoot around a corner by their own method of adjusting and changing its sights, etc.; and frankly if you could but see some of those sent in, you would think that they had mighty nearly succeeded, and a little more of such experimenting would have caused it to even shoot so as it would hit themselves. One-half of the guns sent in are the results of such work. Not one man in ten knows how to even take a sight off correctly, for simple as that appears, there is a right and a wrong way to do it. Show me the man who has confidence that his gun is right and *that he is at fault*, and I will show you the making of a first-class shot.

Better study by careful practice with a few observed shots at a target to *know your Gun*. Taking it apart occasionally so as to learn and familiarize yourself with its action, is commendable, but to attempt to make it better, unless you are competent to do so, is a fallacy that savors of gun repair shops, express charges and a diminishing size of your pocketbook. Better put the time and money in a little careful target practice, and learn something about shooting, estimating distances, gauging your sights; windage, e c. Don't wait until you start on a hunting trip to do it; one of the very reasons game to-day is so hard and difficult to approach is because of it. Take my advice, find a *large hill*, hit it a few times, then bring your shooting down so as you can bunch a few bullets at various ranges in a circle two feet in diameter; then you are ready to pack up, go to the woods and stand a fair chance of bringing home meat, after once locating it.

About Rifle Practice

Good shots are made, not born. A man may be pre-eminently fitted to be a first class shot, but unless he graduates at practice, somehow he is liable to "hit the wrong target and thus score a miss." Practice only, can render a man proficient, especially so, be it backed up by close and studious observation of every shot he fires; without that an ammunition wagon would be necessary, and even then final results would be doubtful. Don't think either that you can obtain such practice in a shooting gallery, for its the rifle you intend to use on a trip and its very cartridges that you need practice on. A few hours of such as this, is time and money profitably, aye pleasantly spent. (See Hits Around the Bull's Eye, Target Practice, etc.) as there are many points which the rifle man will do well to consider as well as the following·

397

Suggestions for Practice

Go out occasionally in the woods and select a high hill, or bank of earth sufficiently large and steep to avoid any bullets from going over or to either side of it, lest they hit some inoffensive animal or human being. Cut down a little of the bank, (say 5 to 10 feet from its base) and arrange in as near an upright position as possible, a white cloth or paper; after marking with charcoal or paint, a number of rings around a black center, skewer the cloth with pointed twigs to the earth, bottom, top and well around its edges, and you have a most excellent target and butt, or *back-stop for your bullets.*

Take your rifle and the cartridges you use on your hunting trip, together with a few cut stakes or branch cuttings so as to set them up when you mark a range, after locating and measuring it. Now measure the size of your ordinary step or pace (which we will say for example is 24 inches,) walk straight away from your target, and when you have paced off 100 yards stick up your stake as a *marker* for that range, then pace off various ranges up to 300 yards (more if you desire it) You now have a practical *known distance range,* and are ready for excellent target practice. Commence at your nearest range and put in a few shots, doing your level best to get them in; notice your hits and correct any existing evils as to your shooting, before you proceed to try other ranges more distant —take your time here, and when you can bunch your shots in well, go on to the next range that you paced off and staked. When you are fairly proficient at these *known distance ranges,* pull up the marks indicating them, and you are ready for the finest kind of practice that an embyro marksman can indulge in. For this a fresh cloth or paper target should be arranged over the old *one*. If you desire to mark your shots, the charcoal will serve to do this, by marking the shots at each range differently. Start out on a *run* away from the target, just as you would if running after game, so as to test your shooting, (while you are partly winded) pay no attention to your paces or the distance of ground covered by you, and when you think

398

you have gone far enough (say 250 to 300 yards) turn and face the target, load, adjust your sights, windage, etc. if required, and put in a few shots in various positions, kneeling, sitting or laying flat on your stomach (prone.) Such practice as this, unknown distance rapid firing, calls for quick action estimating distances, etc., that is of great value to the hunter especially. Try and learn always, "binocular shooting," keeping both eyes open—for mark you, the closing of one eye should have ended when flint locks and powder flashes went out of date, but somehow its fashionable still; and strange to say most shooters have been doing it ever since; not altogether useless I will admit, as it is well to use one eye in learning to aim, should the use of both both prove confusing; but it is always best that one should master the art of keeping both open whenever possible, and by sighting with either eye, the marksman will soon accustom himself so as to keep *both open*, which is by far the better way. It is the style practiced by most of the expert shots of the world, and it has been proven beyond dispute, that there is no more necessity for closing one eye in shooting, than in archery, base ball, billiards or bowling; to test it close one eye as you read this, and see if your eyesight is improved. Even the military is now trained to this. Try it some time on such practice as I have recommended, and let results speak for themselves. If you have already acquired the habit of keeping one eye closed, it may be a trifle confusing at first, but results sooner or later will show you that I am right, and your shooting will be more accurate when you have mastered the art of binocular aiming and shooting.

As for the method of target practice I have described, it is on the lines used by the most expert marksmen of the day, especially with our foremost military (American) crack shots; and as they have at divers occasions wrested the highest honors from the flower of the world's armies, I leave you to judge whether or not it is worthy of at least more than passing attention from you. Follow these rules, pay close attention to every shot you fire, remedy existing faults, and when you can at various unknown ranges, adjust your sights quick-

399

ly and group a few shots in a 24 inch space, hitting the mark 3 out of 5 shots, congratulate yourself as being ready and capable of going on a trip, and holding your own with the best of them.

In conclusion, I advise the use of the *following sights* fitted to your rifle, provided it is to be of either the grades I mention, viz:

For big game hunting with the *Winchester '95 Model*, 35 caliber the Lyman Sights No. 21, No. 6, and either No. 4, 28 or 20. For the same work with the *Savage 303 Rifle* No. 1 or No. 21, No. 6 and either No. 4, No. 28 or No. 20.

(See Lyman Rifle Sights elsewhere.)

This sight is NOT like any other, except in optical principle. The price is only $3.00.

Marble Automatic Flexible Joint Rear Sight

These sights combine all the desirable features or other makes with several radical and important features that make them the final and matchless standard of sight construction. The improvements over other sights are;

1st. STRONG COILED SPRING IN THE HINGE JOINT. This automatically and instantly brings the sight to position for shooting, no matter how much it is knocked about in the brush or by a firing bolt. This feature alone more than doubles the value of the sight—for many valuable shots have been lost on account of other makes of sights not being in position when most needed.

2d. ADVANTAGE OVER RECEIVER SIGHTS. The automatic joint permits the use of the Marble sight on rifles with long firing bolts. Receiver sights are of little value in running shots where quick aim is absolutely essential to success, on account of being too far from the eye for one to derive the benefit of the optical principle of the small disc.

About the Savage Rifle

One of the most reliable and accurate rifles today, deservedly popular with many of the most noted hunters of large and dangerous game, is the Savage Hammerless Repeating 6-Shot Rifle, caliber 303 (as is illustrated elsewhere) using all standard size of game cartridges. The most effective being the 303 *smokeless powder cartridge and expanding bullet.* It is an ideal weapon weighing about 7½ to 8 lbs., and *one which by the way* has completely upset the theories of many old and experienced old-time hunters, who had considered a larger caliber and bullet necessary for effective results on big game. They derided the small caliber rifle and bullet *before they had used them.* because their experience had been only with black powder, and under such conditions as this, *their deductions were correct.*

All this however has been changed, and today modern smokeless powder is responsible for it. That is the secret of the enormous smashing power of the smaller 303 caliber rifle. For with immensely increased velocity, the soft nose of an expanding bullet *trebles its size* on impact with even the softest of animal tissues or flesh. Splitting its jacketed portion and deforming the whole bullet to such an extent that the wound made by it, actually covers a larger area than ever before seen. And so rapidly is knowledge of these facts spreading *that to-day* many of our best sportsmen are discarding the large caliber rifles and re-arming themselves with the more modern (smaller) yet equally effective weapon the 303, so much so that soon it will be unnecessary to take up space in disseminating such information.

Couple these facts then, together with the knowledge that a metal jacketed, hard bullet or miniature cartridge and bullet can be used (on the smallest of game) with a lighter load behind it, and you have my ideas of an all round rifle.

(See "Savage Rifle" caliber 303. and *Expanding Bullet Illustrations.*)

401

THE EFFECTIVE "SAVAGE" 303. REPEATING RIFLE. (HAMMERLESS)

(See Article on this Rifle.)

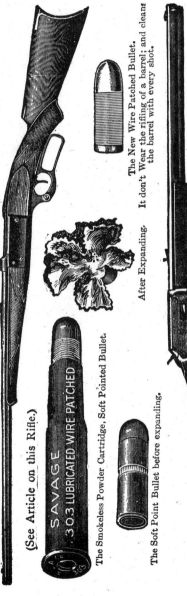

The Smokeless Powder Cartridge, Soft Pointed Bullet.

The Soft Point Bullet before expanding.

After Expanding.

The New Wire Patched Bullet.
It don't Wear the rifling of a barrel; and cleans
the barrel with every shot.

An Excellent Weapon for the Big Game Hunter.

Also used with Miniature Bullet for Small Game.

The Celebrated "MARLIN" RIFLE (for Big Game Hunting) Safety Repeating Model 1892.

402

About Rifle Sights, Etc.

**No. 1 Lyman Rear Sight
(Raised)**

For practical service, accuracy, etc. the best of rifles **can be made better** by the use of correct sights. No matter how good your rifle may be, how great its range, velocity, penetration, etc., unless it carries true to the object aimed at through its sights, the arm is valueless.

In hunting where game is hard to approach, and quick shooting essential, the accuracy of sights— **ease and rapidity** in aiming is essential, and has received particular attention by specialists in these lines—so much so that even the most noted rifle manufacturers admit the superiority of those of the **"Lyman Standard"** of which I write now

The optical principle involved in Lyman rear sights is quite novel in its application and is clearly illustrated here. When aiming, the Lyman rear sight has the appearance of a ring or hoop, which shows the front sight and the object aimed at, **intercepting no part of the view.**

How the Small Hole Appears when Aiming.

403

"Now, Sir," said the Guide. " Is your best Chance."

Thus it gives an approximate idea of the sight when aiming. It will be noticed that the top of, rifle barrel, from front sight and game, are seen as distinctly as though no rear sight were used.

This cut illustrates the obstacles which meet the vision of the shooter **when using open sights usually furnished with rifles.** When aiming, the most important part of the view is shut out, aside from the great diffiulty of quickly getting the front sight in the notch of the rear sight. It is thus evident almost at a glance that the aperture of this sight being near the eyes, is greatly magnified as compared with the notch in the common open sight as shown above. Hence my advice to the tyro or sportsman is to have his rifle fitted with Lyman sights, whose superiority over ordinary grades is not to be questioned.

To obtain the most perfect results with these sights, it is very important that the owner of a rifle when purchasing a set of sights, secures only those which are made for the **make, model** and **caliber** of rifle, for which sights are intended.

The Lyman Receiver Rear Sight for Rifles I Mention. No. 21

404

With either of these sights almost instantaneous aim can be taken, for the object is sighted as quickly as if only the front sight were used.

This sight cannot shut out the view of the front sight, nor the object to be aimed at; while with any other rear sight the chief difficulty in aiming is to bring the sights and object quickly into line without interfering with the view of the front sight or the object. This sight can be used when the light becomes too dim to use any other rear sight, hence its great value in the woods or late in the day. Old eyes that can no longer use the crotch sight, can use Lyman sights and shoot better than they ever could with the common sight.

They are **indispensable** for a hunting rifle, and makes it possible to bring to bag much game that is on the wing, with your rifle. By their use it is a hundredfold easier to shoot **moving objects, running or flying, and both the eyes can be used as well as one eye;** it is also **far more accurate** than any ordinary open sight, and in most respects is better for target shooting than the ordinary peep sight. Any kind of front sight can be used with the Lyman rear sight, although I advise a Lyman front sight in cases for best results. They are so simple and strong that there is no danger of their being injured.

So vastly different are these form of sights in use, that a first "squint" through a Lyman sight invariably brings forth the exclamation, "Why, I can see everything in a 40-acre field!" so clear and distinct are objects aimed at through them. Even still better results can be obtained by using in connection with either of the **rear sights** mentioned either of the **front bead sights** I illustrate; for they have all won the praise of celebrated hunters and marksmen the world over.

IVORY BEAD FRONT SIGHTS.

No. 3.

This sight gives the sportsman a clear white bead, which can be seen distinctly against any object, in the woods or in the bright sunlight. The contrasting black neck of the sight makes the bead all the more prominent.

This sight is better than the No. 3 sight for a hunting rifle. The ivory is so well protected by the surrounding metal that there is no danger of its being injured. It is also a very accurate

No. 4.

sight, and many prefer it to any other sight for "all around" use.

No. 20—The Ivory Jack

A good sight for quick shooting, also in poor light or with the Jack at night. It will surprise many to find that this large sight is very accurate and that fine target shooting can be done if used with the Lyman rear sights.

This sight has lately been put on the market to meet the demands of a number of sportsmen who desired a sight with an ivory bead smaller than that of the "Jack" Sight, and still larger than that of the No. 3 Front Sight.

No. 28—The Semi Jack.

THE LYMAN LEAF SIGHT.

No. 6.

Both leaves folded down.

Using the straight bar.

Using the crotch.

One leaf is a bar with a triangular ivory center, the other is a wide open V crotch. Many sportsmen who use these sights do so with the ordinary crotch sight on the barrel. The crotch sight is much in the way and the shooting is done at a great disadvantage. Lyman's No. 6 Leaf Sight can be put in place of it. It folds down close to the barrel, allowing the shooter to use the Lyman Rear Sight in an unobstructed manner, and the result is that the shooting is much better than when the ordinary crotch sight is on the barrel. Although the shooter should in any case use the Lyman Rear Sights for nearly all shooting, he has the sat-

406

isfaction of knowing that if he wishes to use this leaf sight, that it's the best form of crotch and bar sight in use. **The bar leaf is excellent as a twilight sight or when used at night with a jack.** The right hand screw, indicated by arrow, adjusts the leaves to fold as tightly as desired.

Ivory Bead   **Front Sights**

No. 26

No. 24—Jack.   No. 32—Semi Jack.

The above cuts show Lyman's Ivory Bead Sight No. 26, "Jack" Sight No. 24 and No. 32 "Semi-Jack" Sight, made for the following rifles only: Winchester Model, 1895, Rifle, .30 U. S. A. and .303 British calibers; Winchester Carbines; Lee Straight Pull Rifle; Remington-Lee Sporting Rifles.

SIGHTS FOR REVOLVERS.

No. 16—Smith & Wesson   **Colt.**

Revolver
Rear Sights

No. 19—Smith & Wesson   Colt.

When ordering, give make, model and caliber of revolvers. There should be no other sight or obstruction between the Lyman Front and Rear Sights.

IVORY SHOT GUN SIGHTS.
The New System of Sighting Shot Guns.

There has always existed a serious difficulty in aiming shot guns, and this has increased with our modern choke-bored guns. One of the difficulties of shooting is that the gun is not often used twice from the same position; the shooter often having

to take a sharp right or left position, which makes
it more difficult to align the gun the same. By using a small and short ivory sight placed well forward on the rib, wonderfully good results are obtained. Not only is the vertical alignment readily
obtained, but as the two sights are seen quite distinct and away from each other, the lateral alignment is made at the same time. This is a most
important point, for one of the common mistakes
is aiming too close to the gun rib, which results in
under shooting. This system is sufficiently accurate for rifle shooting at short distances. It is on
the same principle as sighting over the surveyor's
stakes. These sights are becoming more popular
every day, both at the trap and in the field,

The engrav-
ing herewith
gives the ap-
pearance of
the sights
when aiming
at a straight-
away bird. It
will be notic-
ed that the
muzzle sight

The Sights on a Gun.

is the most prominent, and when the aim is taken,
should be seen above the rear sight and in line
with it. In this cut the elevation of the gun is
right, but the rear sight shows that the gun is out
of line, which would not be discovered if these
sights were not used.

No 10—Front.

No. 11—Rear.

Unlike the ordinary metallic sight it does not
glimmer in the sunlight and it can be seen in a dim

light. Another improvement in this sight is its large size. Almost every sportsman knows how little is the value of the ordinary sights; in fact they are generally made so small and of such material as to be hardly seen at any time.

In concluding this article on sights, I confidently recommend them; and the hunter using either a rifle or shot gun, will add considerable to his rapidity and accuracy (the all important in hunting) by the use of them. Nothing is more important than to provide sights that enables you **at a glance** to sight correctly and determine whether or not you are holding the gun right, thus contributing largely to your skill and success as a marksman.

Again, use only such rifles as are, to your mind, fairly accurate, for few shooters can hold a rifle well if they have no confidence in it. The position should be the same as in shooting a shot gun. Keep your attention on the object you wish to hit, and while bringing up your rifle decide where you wish the front sight to be in relation to it and shoot quickly. If the object is stationary at ordinary distances, the sight should be on it. If at a long distance, the sight should be held over it. If the object is moving, the sight should be ahead of it. When shooting, never flinch, for this is fatal to good work. Do not take your eyes off the object until the shot is fired. Pull the trigger so that the rifle is fired *when the sight first reaches the object*, for it will never do to hesitate and try for a second aim. Another fault in most shooters is the habit of flinching, principally from the fear of the report and recoil. When the rifle is held properly, the recoil is felt very little, even with heavy charges; and if one is to be a successful shot at any kind of shooting, he must have the courage not to consider the noise and kick of the gun, for any danger to the shooter is simply imaginary. Give your whole attention to pulling the trigger when the front sight is on the object.

A Bit About Bullets

The New Lubricated Wire Patched Bullet

In this the 20th century, days of modern nitro-smokeless, high velocity powders; quick, twist, high pressure rifles; hard metal bullets, etc., one is apt to consider that we have reached the limit of perfection. But we must not pass over so easily, certain defects which American ingenuity leads the world in discovering and remedying.

What is perfection in a rifle, its powders, etc., without **perfection in the bullet besides.** Have you ever given this a thought. If you answer no, then we had better come together, for a while at least, on the seemingly insignificant subject, though really the most important of all—**A Bit About Bullets**, on which so much depends.

In my various articles on rifles, etc., I have rererred to trajectory, velocity, accuracy, soft point bullets, etc. I will now here in its proper place, devote a chapter to the **best bullet**, directing the attention of my readers to the page of illustrations accompanying this chapter for explanation thereto.

While we are drawing nearer and nearer to perfection in all things, we have not yet produced an **absolutely perfect bullet.** By this I mean one having perfectly straight flight, true flat trajectory (see illustration); nor have we one that will not wear out the rifling of a barrel; yet we have **pretty nearly succeeded,** as this chapter will show. So far, thousands of bullets have been produced, all of which, while they possess certain advantages over others, **still have disadvantages** Yet there is one bullet that is an exception, for it **possesses features of merit** that are not to be found in any other bullet of today. In this I refer to the **Lubricated Wire Patched Bullet,** now put up by the National Projectile Works, illustrations of which accompany this chapter.

As to patched bullets and explanation thereof, nearly every hunter knows that no gun ever shot so well, **and still shoots so well,** as the old muzzle loader, with its common greased cloth cover or patch, which was common in those days. But the

Famous Bullets for
Big Game Hunters.

A BIT ABOUT BULLETS.

Read Article,
"A Bit About Bullets."

MID-RANGE HEIGHT OF TRAJECTORY.

LINE OF SIGHT

RANGE

TARGET

Illustration showing course of a rifle bullet's flight.

The new Wire Patched Bullet Reduces this Trajectory.

The Mushroom Bullet
30-30-170 Marlin.
Before.

.303 SAVAGE
LUBRICATED WIRE PATCH
SOFT POINT

The Latest Bullet

No. 3

The Paper Patched
Bullet.

After.

GOULD'S
45-330
EXP.

The Gould
Express Bullet.

D

411

After Expanding.

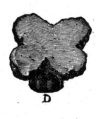

The Keene Split Bul-
et before expanding.

patch which then **lubricated** the path of the bullet as it passed through the rifle, **and wiped all residue behind it,** had a bad fault, when a new charge was rammed home, because it carried down to the base of the rifle with it all the **residue of former shots,** and the gun because of this, became sooner or later what hunters called "breech burnt."

The breech loader did away with all this, true; but even this had disadvantages peculiar to itself. The dry bullet leaded the gun more or less, or because of **no patching**, or improper patching failed in accuracy or proper strength of carriage.

To obviate this then, a paper patch was used, but the shell could not be crimped upon it, and it contained no lubricant. It was useless in a magazine gun, for the recoil of discharging the arm loosened the bullets; hence they could be used for single fire **only with credit.**

With the advent of high pressure or power rifles, to withstand increased velocity, etc., a harder bullet became necessary, and the metal cased one was produced to fill the bill, but it was found to injure or affect the life or the rifling in the rifle barrel; rendering the arm useless as far as accuracy was concerned, before 1,000 rounds was fired; it having been proven that after 1,000 rounds, bullets (key holed) (turned lengthways) before they had traveled two hundred yards, by reason of the injury to the rifling, despite the fact that a lubricant was used with it

Thus the ordinary lead bullet possessed advantages over those of the hard metal pattern, but they possessed **less penetration,** stripped on the rifling, and leaded the barrel; oftimes besides were apt to expand laterally, thus impairing accuracy.

To obviate and remedy the objections to both the soft and hard bullets, and to retain all the good points of both, has come the **Lubricated Wire Patched Leaden or Soft Metal Bullet,** which has been found to possess these distinguishing features. 1st.—It will not injure the gun or its rifling; at the same time it completely fills all the grooves of the rifling, thus forming a perfect "gas check." 2nd.—With less friction, velocity is increased, while the trajectory (straighter flight) is flatter than with any other bullet ever made: 3rd.—**It cleans and lubricates the barrel** with every shot making swabbing entirely unnecessary while firing; **no matter how short or long its duration;** besides being adapted to any style of gun, slow or or rapid twist, black or smokeless powder power, and maintaining a uniform accuracy in shooting, superior to any other form of missile known or used today.

This is arranged by winding a **lubricated cotton covered annealed iron wire** tightly and closely around a soft metal projectile, so that it can not be loosened; thus forming a greased jacket or patch for the bullet, which not only prevents heating or fouling the barrel, but serves to prevent effectively any lateral expansion to the soft metal; imparting to it the advantageous characteristics of a hard metal bullet, without any of its disagreeable affects; while the patch effectually cleans and relubricates the rifle barrel with every shot.

When these points are better known, I predict a general adoption of this bullet, for the reason that they will do more damage on large game, than any other bullet made with **less damage to the rifle itself,** and as a well known writer in a recent issue of **"SPORTS AFIELD"** who has tried them, says: "My advice is that when you put a hundred miles of howling wilderness between yourself and your base of supplies, include some of them in your cartridge belt, for you can rest assured of results, with a cheerful mind that the Lubricated Wire Patched Bullet is the best bullet today."

In conclusion let me state that these bullets are also made in the **45, 70, 300 Gould Express** bullet. See illustration made to take in the **hollow point** a No. 1 primer and 5 grains **Riflite** powder, thus rendering a **deadly explosive bullet** for large game, short range shooting, **and in still other well known calibers.**

.40 CAL. EXPRESS BULLETS.

413

Reloading Rifles, Pistols, Etc.

To reload one's own rifle or pistol shells is as interesting and pleasant a pastime as is the shooting. There is also great economy in it. To learn about the various powders, the proper quantity required to produce certain results in the different arms, is of the utmost interest to the lover of firearms. *The real sportsman must not only become acquainted with all of the peculiarities of his rifle, but also with the ammunition he uses in it.* He can do this only by long and careful experimenting. To such shooters are we indebted for the great majority of the improvements in arms and ammunition. The manufacturers are continually telling the shooters that they cannot do this or that, they can not reload their shells, understand about powders or bullets, that the only way is to take the factory products and buy new a cartridge every time the arm is shot. On the other hand the intelligent shooters are continually reloading successfully and improving on the factory ammunition, which improvements are finally adopted and brought out by the factories as results of their own great experience. Some of the highest scores by military matches and civilian sharp shooters are invariably made with reloaded ammunition

To reload shells, the operator must go at it in a careful and intelligent manner, and proper implements must be selected for the work that is desired. The reloading tools made by the Ideal Mfg. Co., New Haven, Conn. are very popular and well known by all shooters of rifles, pistols and shot guns. We therefore select a few cuts of various implements, and are indebted to the Ideal Mfg Co. for the use of the electrotypes. The first secret in the success of reloading shells is the preservation and care taken of them after discharge. Whatever powder may have been used, the old spent primer should be removed and the shells properly cleaned as soon after firing as possible. They should be cleaned in strong boiling soapsuds or soda water, and thoroughly dried by rinsing well in clean hot water, so that they will dry by their own heat when taken out. Be sure they are perfectly dry in the primer pocket before putting them away, or they may corrode. *It is best to de-*

cap on the ground immediately after firing, while the residue in the pocket of the shell and about the old primer is soft and wet, for while dry ing corrosion commences.

Cut "A" shows a handy pocket imple- ment for this purpose, weight only six or seven ounces.

IDEAL
RE & DE-CAPPER.
FOR RIFLE & PISTOL.

Cut "A"

The general style of reloading tools is the same, differing only in weight, size and strength for the different cartridges. In the various cata- logues, each tool is designated by name or num-

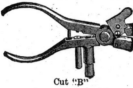

Cut "B"

ber, telling for what particular cartridge it is made. Cut "B" rep- resents a loading tool combined with bullet mould. This style of tool is very popu- lar on account of its being complete and compact, with no extra pieces to carry or get lost.

Relative to powder we would caution all to be very careful when using the different brands of smokeless powders. If you are not familiar and do not know *well* the particular brand of powder that you are about to use, find out from the manu- facturer of it whether it is the correct kind for the arm you are using, and what the proper charge for it should be. The general term "Smokeless Pow- der" does not make known what the possibilities or probabilities are, *for under the name of smoke- less powder, there is great variety*, some of which require but a very small amount for the proper charge, while with others six or eight times as much will be required for the cartridge. When writing or speaking of smokeless powders, always be sure and designate what particular brand you are talking about. If it is Schultze, Hazard's, Du- Pont's or Laflin & Rand smokeless powders, state whether it is Du Pont's shot gun smokeless, or Du Pont's 30 cal. Annular, or Du Pont's No. 1 or No. 2 smokeless. When referring to Laflin & Rand's smokeless you must specify what particular brand

415

"Infallible," "W. A. 30 cal." "Lightning," Bulls-Eye," etc All of these various powders have their own peculiar value, and are *perfectly safe* when used intelligently for the purpose for which they were made. *In no case, however, must these powders be used as a substitute for black powder without ascertaining whether they can be used, and if so, what quantity is required for a charge in the particular arm in question.* Such information may be secured at any time by dropping a postal card to the makers of the powders or to the Ideal Mfg. Co. The different powders vary in bulk and specific gravity so that a charge cup that will hold a given quantity ing rains weight of one kind of powder. will not be correct for other powders. The only implements that we know of on the market that will measure in grains weight, all of the various powders, are the Ideal Universal Powder Measures. These have the approval of all manufacturers of powders and are well recommended. When these measures are set in accordance with the tables of comparison that accompany each implement, any and all charges of any of the various powders required for pistol, rifle or shot gun, may be secured.

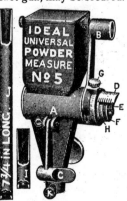

Cut "C"

The very latest improved implements produced, are here illustrated. (See cut "C") No. 5 Universal Powder Measure, is really four measures combined in one. The first measuring from 1 to 15 grains graduations being for 1 grain each graduation. The second measuring from 10 to 50 grains each graduation. The third from 40 to 140 grains, five grains each graduation. The graduations on the fourth are in ¼ drachms, from ½ drachm up to 5 drachms, the old shot gun measurements. In Measure No. 6,)See cut "D,") the portion on the right side is

same as No. 5 with an additional measure on the left side for small priming charges of different powders, the graduations being from 1 grain up to 10 grains, one grain each graduation. The value of this is fully appreciated by target shooters who use the 32-40 and 38-55 single shot rifles. Tak-

Cut "D"

the 32-40 as an example, they generally use the same shells over and over, some of which have been shot hundreds of times. They use the long drop tube which settles the powder snugly in the shell. A priming of DuPont's No 1 smokeless powder from 3 to 5 grains is dropped into the base of the shell from the left side of the measure, the balance of the space in the shell being filled with F, G. semi-smokeless powder dropped from the other side of the measure, and on this is seated a wad of blotting paper. The bullet is seated in the breech of the barrel with a bullet seater. (See cut

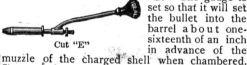

Cut "E"

"E." The gauge is set so that it will set the bullet into the barrel about one-sixteenth of an inch in advance of the muzzle of the charged shell when chambered. Some of the very highest scores at target shooting have been made with rifles loaded

No. 2

417

in this manner. Many shooters prefer paper patched bullets. (See cut No. 2.) These however, require more care and time to prepare than grooved bullets. An outfit for target shooters for such loading, consists of the No. 6 Universal Powder Measure, two or three empty shells, Re and De Capper and a Bullet Seater. Each measure has a close fitting cover that fastens with screws, so that when filled with powder and the slides closed, no powder can escape however it may be carried. They carry nicely in the sportsman's grip, and may be readily fastened to a bench, table, or cleat on the wall at the range house.

Cartridge shells expand more when using high pressure smokeless powders than when using low pressure smokeless or black powders. When

Cut "F"

shells do expand and are so large as not to enter the chamber of the arm freely, they should be resized or reformed the whole length to their original shape and size, so as not to stick and clog the action of the arm. A suitable implement for this is here illustrated. (See cut "F.") Full instructions how to use, accompany each tool. All shells, however, do not expand so as to require resizing the whole length. The muzzle may be increased in size so a bullet of the proper diameter will fit loose, yet the shell enters the chamber of the rifle easily. In such a case the muzzle of the shell only may require resizing. The reloading tool shown in cut "G" is a very popular implement; especially is it appreciated by those who use the high power rifles, such as 30-40, 30-30, 303 Savage, 303 British and all arms using metal jacketed bullets.

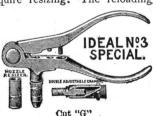

IDEAL No3 SPECIAL.

Cut "G"

All metal covered bullets *must* fit the shell snugly. A shell that is expanded at the muzzle and is large for the bullet *must be* resized. The No. 3

tool here illustrated,. has a muzzle sizer with which muzzle of shell can be readily resized.. This operation must be done while the shell is empty. A shell cannot be properly resized while the bullet is in it. Single and double adjustable chambers which are a part of this tool, when ordered to go with it, enable the user to seat the bullets various depths in the shell, also to crimp or not to crimp as desired.

Owing to the grooves in the metal covered bullets being located differently, when made by the different manufacturers, great trouble is experienced when bullet is seated in the shell, by the groove not coming perfectly even with the muzzle of the shell. This prevents crimping the end of the shell into the groove. With the double adjustable chamber, the bullet can be seated to any depth desired, and the chamber adjusted to crimp the shell on the bullet at the proper place, thus all variations that may take place in the length of the shells, or the location of the groove in the bullets are overcome.

For the benefit of those readers who may be using arms requiring headless or rimless shells such as 7m-m or 7.65m m Mauser or 30-45 U. S. Springfield rifles, or 32, 38 Colt's Automatic or 30 Luger Automatic pistols, we would say that the Ideal Mfg. Co. make a tool similiar to No. 3 here illustrated, with an additional contrivance made especially for headless shells. This tool is designated as Ideal No. 10.

All who use a modern high pressure quick twist rifle for sporting purposes, soon recognize the fact that it is very expensive to buy a new cartridge every time they shoot.

Trouble has been experienced by some when attempting to economize by reloading their shells and using cast bullets. Most of the trouble however, has been through the lack of knowledge of an essential point or two. A cast bullet for the quick twist rifle must always be harder than for the slow twist, about one part tin or antimony to ten parts of lead. A good mixture also used is one-half type metal to one-half lead, also one-half chilled shot to one-half lead. Such cast bullets must never be used with the regular full charge of

419

high pressure powder; if high pressure powder is used, the charge must be decreased, or other low pressure smokeless powders used. As the pressure is reduced the cast bullet must be shortened and the bearing lengthened, thus making a very different shaped bullet than the regular metal covered one, that is used with full charge of the high pressure powder.

The cast bullet must also be *larger in diameter* than the metal covered, so as to positively prevent the escapement of gas as there is little or no upsettage of the lead bullet, when low pressure smokeless powders are used. There is no doubt, however, that with the proper cast bullet and the proper kind and charge of smokeless powder, the 30 calibre and other quick twist rifles will shoot more accurately at ranges of 400 yards and under, than they do with the regular high pressure ammunition. The three bullets here illustrated are record makers, and are well known by many users of 30 calibre rifles. No. 308206 was designed by Horace Kephart of St. Louis; No. 308223 by Dr. W. G. Hudson, of New York City, who is recognized not only as one of the best rifle shots, but

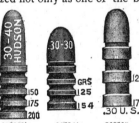

308223   308241   308206

but one of the foremost theoretical and practical men on small arm ballistics in the country. No. 308 241 was designed by Mr. Barlow of the Ideal Mfg. Co. With this bullet Lieut. W. C. Gannon of Co. C., 4th Reg't Infantry, New Jersey National Guard in October, 1902, made ten consecutive bulls-eyes, 200 yards, Creedmoor target at Marion, N. J., off hand, with regular military open sights, and on October 10th on the indoor 80 yard range at their armory, standing off hand, he made five successive bulls-eyes, the other one being a four, scoring ninety-nine out of a possible one hundred, which is believed to be the highest indoor score ever made with a military rifle (30-40 Krag.) There

was no cleaning after shots, and when finished
there was no leading. Lieut. Gannon is always
ready to assist those who are interested in shooting. His address is 341 Montgomery St., Jersey
City, N. J.

The information relative to this shooting, he
gives as follows: For the 200 yard range, sight
elevation was 600 yards; for the 80 yards the elevation was 415 yards. In the indoor shooting he
used a peep sight. The shells were made by The
Union Metallic Cartridge Co., primers U. M. C.
No. 8½. For 200 yards the charge of powder was
9 grains of Laflin & Rand's "Sharp Shooter" and
for the 80 yards, 8
grains of the same
powder. Bullet
lubricated and siz-
ed to 312" diam-
eter, with the im-
plement here illus-
trated. (See cut
"H." (Standard
diameter of 30-40
is 308.) Bullet was
seated in shell with
No. 3 tool, forward
band out, no crimp,
shells indented
with implement as
per cut "I." The
indentations are
preferred by many
shooters rather

TWO in ONE.

It GREASES
and SIZES 500
to 2500 bul-
lets, with ONE
stick of lubri-
cant, without
soiling the
hands.

Price, $5.00.

Cut "H"

than the groove in the muzzle of the shell to prevent the bullet from receding. The groove when
fired stretches out, leaving the shell long, and in
many cases, they break off at the neck where the
groove was, leaving that piece of the shell in
the chamber of the rifle, which is a very
serious matter, unless one happens to have a
Broken Shell Extractor (See cut "J") with him. No
rifleman should be without one of these essential
little jokers in his pocket, for he is liable to require one at any time when shooting.

To cast bullets properly, requires a little experience. The mould and metal should be very hot.
When conditions are right there should be no
checks or wrinkles on the bullet. A good casting
outfit is here illustrated. Pot holds about eight
pounds of metal; cover will fit any stove. The
metal is not poured in the mould, but the dipper
is connected with the mould and the weight of the
metal in the dipper forces out all air, and presses
the metal solidly into the corners of the grooves,
leaving them sharp and the bullet smooth and full
in size.

If our readers are further interested in this line,
we would advise them to enclose three stamps
with their name and address, to the Ideal Mfg. Co.,
No. 42 U St., New Haven, Conn., asking for the
"Ideal Hand Book of Useful Information to
Shooters." Every one who shoots should possess
a copy of this interesting book.

Hints to Reloaders of Rifle Ammunition

Be sure to keep shells clean or clean them. Remove old primers as soon as possible. (Wash and dry the shell if necessary.) *Use Ideal reloading tools*, open the mouth of the shells well, so as bullet will enter without scraping or cutting it.

Use correct primers as per instructions on box of shells originally purchased; *be sure to seat your primers* at the bottom of pocket of shell, lest it cause premature explosion by ordinary contact with others. *It is now ready for the powder* and the following relates to black powder only:

For powder to be used in rifle cartridges, containing fifty to one hundred and twenty grains, we recommend the following brands and sizes of grains as giving the best results:

American Powder Company's "Rifle Cartridge, F. G.," Hazard Powder Company's "Sea Shooting, F. G.," E. I. DuPont & Company's "Du Pont Rifle, F. F. G.," Laflin & Rand Powder Company's "Orange Rifle, F. G.," King's "Semi-Smokeless, F. G. or C. G."

In rifle cartridges containing from twenty-five to fifty grains, use one size smaller of the same brands.

In pistol cartridges, two sizes smaller of the above brands will give the best results.

Where powder is to be compressed in a shell we earnestly recommend the American Powder Mills' Rifle Cartridge Powder, and Du Pont Rifle, F. F. G., as being United States Government standard. King's Semi-Smokeless, F. G , is also good.

F. G. is the size suitable for use in the 50-95 Express, 45-70 Government, 45-60 and 40-60 cartridges and others of similar calibre.

F. F. G. is suitable for .44, .38 and .32 Calibre, Winchester, Savage, etc.

In such cartridges none of the high grades of powder should be used; we refer to such brands as Hazard's Electric, DuPont's Diamond Grain, etc. These powders (most excellent for use in shot guns) owe their quick burning properties to

423

their peculiar manufacture; they are not hard pressed powders, and, when compressed in a cartridge shell, they cake behind the bullet more than the harder pressed brands, and give high initial pressure and very irregular shooting without greatly increased velocity.

In charging the shells with powder, dip the scoop full, scrape the top off even and pour into the shell, then enter the bullet into the mouth of the shell with fingers as securely as possible, then place the cartridge in the loading chamber and press it in *until it reaches the head*. A good firm pressure should be all that is required to do this, and, if by so doing the cartridge cannot be forced to the head, there is too much powder in the shell. (Use Ideal powder measure.) Now seat the bullet in the charged shells, the mouth of which is crimped or bent over inward on the bullet, contracting the muzzle of the shell .02 or .03 of an inch smaller than the diameter of the bullet, through which it must tear at discharge, thus destroying its accurate size and shape before it strikes the rifling of the barrel. That it does this is easily demonstrated by an examination of the shell after discharge, for a new bullet cannot be entered into the shell again until the mouth has been opened, yet, through it, a bullet has already been passed, raking it the whole length. Further comment is unnecessary.

Crimping the shell, however, is required to prevent the possibility of bullets working loose and getting out while passing through the mechanism of some repeating rifles; then again the crimp is necessary in other cases to prevent the bullet from being forced down into the shell which would interfere with the action of some arms. Revolvers require the bullets to be firmly crimped in, for if they jump forward in the unused chambers at the time of the discharge, on account of the recoil, it will lock the cylinder so it cannot be operated; so also will it lock the mechanism of some repeating rifles. *For these various reasons shells are crimped.*

Reloading Smokeless Powder Cartridges— Low pressure smokeless powder cartridges may be reloaded as easily and as frequently as black powder cartridges, but the reloading of reduced bores, such as .10-30 and .25-36, with high pressure powder is attended with more difficulty and less satisfaction. It will be found necessary to resize the muzzles of the shells after each round and the entire shell after each two or three rounds, and the shells split and break in all manner of ways. A small percentage of the shells may be loaded 20 to 25 times, but the majority will break in the first 10 shots, and some will split the second round. Why this is so has not been positively decided. Some authorities hold that a chemical action takes place in the brass, induced by some ingredient of the powder or of the strong priming, while others think that the action is simply a physical one to be expected from the heavy pressure sustained.

Smokeless Powders—Smokeless powder is undoubtedly the powder of the future, but it must be used exactly as directed unless you are in search of an early grave. Within the past few years there has been considerable activity on the part of the powder manufacturers to develop smokeless powders suitable for the various rifles in use, with the result that today there are many smokeless rifle powders which can be used with perfect safety and which, further, give excellent results as regards power, accuracy and keeping qualities. At the same time we must urge upon all riflemen who desire to reload ammunition with smokeless powder to use utmost caution. Follow carefully the directions of the powder manufacturers, even to the most minute detail; do not experiment rashly; let others do the experimenting.

Smokeless powders are of an entirely different nature than black powders. With black powder, for instance, you always use a certain degree of compression, or at least pack the powder firmly. This is not to be advised with the majority of smokeless powders. A charge of black powder may be materially increased, with or without compression; with smokeless powders, the compression may develop a tremendous pressure, while even the increase of load may bring too high a pressure, or at any rate produce unsatisfactory results and possibly serious accidents. Never use high pressure powder in low pressure shells. *Never compress nitro powders.*

425

Adopted by the U. S. Government.

For the extraction of broken shells from rifles above shell extractors for the following rifles;—

.25-20 Single Shot.	.30-30 Savage.	.32 M. H. P.
.25-20 Repeater.	.30 40 U. S Gov't.	.38-55.
.25 35 Winchester.	.32 M. H. P.	7 mm.
.25-36 Marlin.	.32-20.	7.65 mm.
.32-40 M H. P.	.303 Savage.	8 mm.
.30-30 Marlin.	.303 British.	.45-70.
.30-30 Winchester.	.32-40.	

The Bergersen Shell Extractor

Extractor with section of broken shell

Extractor ready for use

Many a gun has been ruined through the misdirected efforts to remove a broken shell from a rifle. When a cartridge head pulls off it leaves nothing for the extractor and ejector to grasp and the gun is out of commission instantly. This is always annoying - sometimes it's mighty serious.

The Bergersen broken shell extractor slips inside the broken shell, grabs it by the nose and one motion of the lever throws out extractor and the broken section. The cut shows how, fully.

For safety's sake carry one of these broken shell extractors with you.

How and Where to Locate the Hunting Camp.

Taking it Easy in Camp.

Alike other things there are a few pointers to consider in the selection or establishing of a suitable camp, *and a few things that should not be done* in this as in anything else. These are times when railroads are very liberal in transporting camp outfits; and the up-to-date sportsman or hunter should provide himself with a well made, *canvas lined* packing box of such form and size as to hold his entire outfit, or that of his party. These are put up especially for the purpose by specialists in camp outfitting; while they are plain in appearance, durable and roomy, they save all expense of transportation, by reason of their being checked as ordinary baggage. The object of lining with canvas is to keep dampness out and when unpacked they can be used as the "grub box" or table; and if care is exercised in packing and the selection of the outfit, even tent, poles, pins, camp furniture can be packed therein. If desired for the rations, I advise a separate chest for reasons that are obvious. On arrival at the terminus of railroad transportation, the camp outfit should be transported to some convenient and distant spot, and a headquarter camp arranged, as comfortable and complete as possible and maintained as a *"base of supplies."* From here the party starts out light, and if care is exercised in judicious out-

427

fitting, it is an easy matter to travel from place to place *lightly equipped.* Camping on your trail when the day's bag has been sufficient, hanging up your game, marking the spot by taking bearing of it, *and pursuing your journey on* until such time as is necessary to receive new supplies, when the retreat to headquarters is made. By this means the sportsman or hunter can scout or cover hitherto unexplored or unfrequented territory, whereas on the other hand (especially in these days) if he depends on the vicinity of a few miles of his camp to furnish him sufficient hunting, he is mighty apt to get left; these remarks of course, applying mostly to large game hunting.

To the sportsman in search of small game, in brush, hills, or about the shores of marshes, no camp whatever is needed, as in most cases some civilization is near to his favorite shooting grounds, while his stay is limited to a range of a few miles. Yet even these are beginning to realize that a few days of "*Camp Life*" adds greatly to the charm, ease and benefit of a trip. No sportsman after a hard and successful day's bag or jaunt, enjoys the weary tramp and necessary lugging of his game a great distance, for often such a day's sport entirely unfits him for another. Sportsmen too are now beginning to realize that the cost of a suitable small camp, and the novelty of it, really in the end costs less than their accommodations elsewhere; especially so if two or three number the party, or their stay is for several days or more, and hunters and sportsmen's camps are springing up, dotting the places here and there amazingly; no need of elaborating, the simpler the outfit *provided it does not lack essentials*, the greater ease and comfort you enjoy therefrom.

It is obvious to the intelligent that the plan of putting up at regular hunting camps, that have been established for several seasons or more, is poor policy. I care not how close they are to the *game regions*, they might *tap the best inhabited territory* for wild game in existence, but the very fact that game has been *hunted* from there, is conclusive evidence that the *game* has gone to *other regions*. no man can dispute that fact, and there is nothing left to be done but to choose the alterna-

The Most Compact Sportsman's or Hunter's Outfit Known.

1—Camp Cot and Mosquito Netting

2—Camp Table and Shelf.

3—Camp Easy Chair.

4—Camp Stool.

5 - Camp Stool.

6—The Tent for Two Persons.

8—Camp Cooking Outfit and Dishes.

10—Camp Bed.

7—Camp Chair.

9—Bedding Roll Up.

11—Box for Entire Outfit.

tive of a long trip (perhaps a tedious and costly one) to locate *the game.* Hence I say, the sportsman who starts out prepared *to camp on the trail of game* in the midst or borders of their territory, savors in itself of both novelty, sight-seeing and success. One of the very reasons that it is useless to start out hunting without a guide (and an experienced one) is because of this fact. It would be far more sensible to take this guide, with an outfit and start out, and place as much space and distance between these so called hunting camps as possible; for the chief novelty in them or (claim to patronage) consists of the charm of surrounding country, simple furnishings, and the stories told of great hunting *that has been done from there.* Couple all this to the cost of your board bill, guide and *extras* that creep in, and you have *spent* about what an outfit would cost you, and which would serve *your purpose again for many a trip to come.*

With a good guide or packer, the sportsman can by traveling thus, locate his own game almost, and enjoy himself to his heart's content; many a sportsman has already gone into the game fields and come out as he went in (except for a hole in his pocket book) by trusting to the alluring literature that has been circulated by enterprising railroads, hotel and boarding camps, as to the enormous quantities of game being found thereabout. Hence my advice is to fight shy of these things, cut loose from them and with a competent, trustful guide, go out into the woods yourself, *as far as you possibly can toward* the haunts of the game you seek; travel as *light as possible,* consistent with simple comfort, and you will reap benefits such as you never dreamed of. There is *plenty of game, any amount of it,* but they are not waiting around hunting camps or mountain hotels. The simpler the outfit the better; a sharp knife and a pocket axe, and you cut shelter if needs be that a half hour's work will render as warm and waterproof almost as a good tent. Dry wood is there in plenty for your fires or warmth; leaves or dry grass or even "browse" (twig tops) for your bed; a coffee pot, a fry pan and stew kettle (nested) and you can prepare anything from a broiled snipe to a Moose

Tricks of Woodcraft.

Things That Can Be Made In Camp.

1—Blanket Tent.

17—Brush Tent.

2—Spoon   3—Knife   4—Fork

5—Camp Shovel

8—Bark Plate.

11—A "Game Spit"

6—Pot Hook and Poker

13—Camp Sun Clock Dial

16—Bark Shanty

7—Tomato Can Cup.

10—Camp Broom.

9—Camp Fire Tongs.

12—Tomato Can Candestick

14—Brush Lean to Teepee.

15—Camp Fire Place.

steak or a hot biscuit. No need of salt pork or canned Boston fruit (baked beans) leave 'em out. A small bag of salt and pepper, a little self-rising flour, coffee and sugar, a piece of select ham or bacon and with what your rifle can and will *furnish* (you could live a month.) Ten pounds of raw, good nutritious food will last any man for any 5 day trip (and if you want more) send back your guide to the "headquarter camp" for it, that's what you got him for, while you stay around and enjoy or fix up camp. All this is pleasure and far above the kind found on front porches of hotels or hunting camps. When night comes any man possessed of ordinay intelligence and the facts laid down in my book on camping can render such a trip a charm. Try it once if you are after *meat or sport* and see if your success is not double what it used to be. Go after the game if you want it. That's the whole secret of the successful "big game hunters," all of which invariably adopt such methods of which I write, none of whom are to be found patronizing such places.

As to the proper methods to be used and the details of such trips; as my other book, *The Complete Campers Manual or How to Camp Out and What to Do*, covers this, it will be needless for me to repeat here what I have already written, for there is much to be said of other things.

The Camp on the Trail.

Kinks About Camp Fires and Cooking.

The Camp Fire Crane.

The Game Spit.

The Green Log Fire Place.

Oven from Two Bake Pans.

Oven from Two Tin Pie Plates.

Frying Pan and Plate Oven.

The Green Bark Oven.

Wind Guard or Radiator for Cooking.   `433

The Ground Trench Fire Place.

Going Hunting

A Type of Hunter's Camp.

I have probably dwelt sufficiently as to the details of preparation outfits, methods of hunting, tracking, etc., so perhaps a change of tactics as to the art of finding game and securing it, will be timely and not altogether lost, especially to the new beginner, for whom this volume has been mostly written. *To those that have been there* it will probably savor of old times, and still even they might get a pointer or two, for none of us know it all. Today the greatest difficulty is to locate and approach game, so when you start out among the game fields where *lies hidden somewhere* in its depths or borders, the game you seek, change *your* tactics, aye here s the rub—the moment you cut loose from camp or cabin, go cautiously, slowly, *straight in the face of the wind or quartering against it*, bearing in mind that every animal is endowed by nature with remarkable powers such as you never possessed. The whole secret of successful hunting for game is to meet and match their shrewdness and cunning with yours. Their very existence depends on their watchfulness, for they have many enemies besides man. This has quickened their wits until the animal intelligence is equal, or in many respects superior to that of human, and their way of using their smelling powers, scenting their friends or enemies is marvelous; *a hundred times more keen and acute than that possessed by man*, so much so that the secret of old trappers success lies mostly in taking advantage of that fact. Every animal is endowed

434

by nature with powerful sense of smell, sharp ears able to catch the slightest unusual noise or sound, eyes that can quickly detect strange or unfamiliar movements. They know where and how to hide, even to throwing you off their trail, and *if you go lumbering along* thinking of great hunting in yonder woods a mile away, perhaps a dozen chances you will miss, right about or close to you. Many an unlikely spot or place that might seem to you barren of life, could afford you royal sport; and as you tramp noiselessly (you think) through the woods or over hills, you would be astonished did you but know, that the very game you seek has perhaps avoided you time again. The keen eyed, eared, nosed rascals are seldom caught napping, and are ever alert to the slightest unusual sound or noise, a slight cough, or sneeze, the blowing of the nose or the snap of a twig in your path, oftimes being fatal to sport. Go slowly, cautiously, seeking the cover of every natural rise in the ground, knoll, bush, bank or tree, carefully peering over them, before starting anew into spaces beyond, *as does the Indian, master of the art that he is,*

If you are wise, select a good place where you can be partly hid, in such likely spots where game abounds, near woods, thickets, waters, or heavy brush, at a point where your observations cover as large a vicinity as possible; select a comfortable seat or log and *sit still, watch, listen and wait,* you'll find the plan equally as well as tearing through the brush. If your up-to-date use your Binocular Telescope (a wonderful glass if you have the right kind) and search far and near for signs of life. By its use, a white object in the distance which you could have sworn just moved, turns into a shiny rock, over there a black one turns into a tree stump, and you have saved two miles of tramp. Bringing its focus to bear across distant waters and the *value of that glass has paid for itself,* for there perhaps where no human eye unaided could reach, is the game you seek. Reader have you ever been there—where the first thing you do is to jam your hat down, grip yout rifle and wake up to a life of action, with the blood coursing through your veins and your twigger finger itching like blazes. Even as I write a feeling of the *"I'll tell you about*

On the Trail of the Game. See pages

"Lively Now—

Lively."

"Im in a Hurry Too."

"Where are They Now?"

Another in Sight
"Say—Aint that
Glass a Peach"

"At Last,"

it—kind." permeates my frame; but I must forbear, lest I disregard my promise to leave stories out. Never mind the distance, what true sportsman cares for that. Game is there—no, yes, yes, there it is, one, two—that's enough and you are off, but how—*stop a moment*, how is the wind, natural cover, the best way. These are the essential points to consider for the longest way round is *often the shortest road to success* "Say aint that glass a peach"—taking a generous chew of tobacco, you start out, and wend your way making a long detour, so as to keep the wind quartering or directly against you; here a dense growth of underbrush affords a generous shutting off of the game from your view; *just the thing for here*, stooping down and running low, a few hundred yards is gained, now crawl to the edge of that knoll; use your glass again, yes, there they are, two beauties, *its a Buck and Doe*, see his horns; they are slowly feeding on the ridge, there, he moves away a trifle and up goes his head, as though he had scented you, no the wind is right for down goes his head, and its safe. *Stow away your glass;* now is your chance go straight toward them, *crawling on your hands and knees for a close range*, take off your hat until you pass that level at least, (brush it off) the string tied to it at the back of your shirt collar, secures it over your shoulders back out of the way; there you are now as far as you can go safely for they are moving about again. Your rifle magazine is full, long ago you had a good cartridge ready in your chamber; now the distance say 250 yards, "*windage half point left*," aim where, at the Buck of course, *unless you want both*; if so, shoot the Doe first, aiming at either, always just behind the right shoulder a trifle low; now I will leave you for I have other duties to perform Concerning many things of interest to *some one else* and if you fail to secure meat, surely it is not my fault, for *I have led you to it*, and can do no more.

Pocket "Binocular Field Glass."
　Small as an opera glass.
*More powerful than the largest
　Field Glass.*

Illustrations of "GOING HUNTING" Chapter.

"Yes—there they are."

"Stooping **down** and running low."

"Aim where."

"Just below and behind the shouler, a trifle low."

"Luring"—See Chapter on Deer Hunting, Page —.　439

Deer Hunting (Read the Game Laws We have them.)

In this as in anything else, the hunter will do well to study the habits and peculiarities of the species. It is poorest in spring or summer, hide and meat both; is sluggish, indifferent and easily approached. Later in the fall they are at the best; he puts on more flesh, eye and mind become active; his scent becomes exceedingly acute, and as his horns grow hard, losing their velvety covering, sight and ability to run increases and he is fitting for a worthy hunter's skill.

November and December are the best months; at this time doe, buck and fawn travel together and much care is necessary to locate and approach them, and the hunter should search for them cautiously, proceeding *in face of or against the wind*. Failure to do this is time and tramping thrown away. The best method is by "stalking". The clothing worn should be of neutral color (tan color) is best; while the footwear should be of soft, noiseless material, either the rubber "shoe pac," or *better still* the double soled Moose hide moccasin, three-quarter length. The ideal time is after a light fall of snow, when they can be easily trailed, and the poorest time is during heavy winds, or when the leaves are unusually dry *making a noise under the feet*. When the ground and leaves are wet is a good time, especially if the wind is very light; they are then well in the woods or thickets away from water, as the moisture on the "browse" suffices to quench their thirst. If snow is on the ground and is of a thin crusty surface, it is bad, for they will hear the crunching sound of your footsteps as you go along; but if

soft and fresh, it is at its best. The principal difficulty in regions where they have been hunted
much, is to locate them, and for this purpose no
hunter should fail to provide himself with a powerful, yet light *Binocular Field Telescope*, (not the
ordinary field glasses) as these are too large and
have only half the power. If you choose the right
kind, as is now *adopted* by the U. S. Government
it can easily be carried and used by the guide or
companion (in a pocket) and is far more useful
than the second rifle, saving perhaps many a long
useless tramp, and locating game of all kinds that
would otherwise be lost to the hunter; indeed the
importance of this should not be underestimated,
as nowadays the hard work is to *find game*, the
rest is comparatively easy, and it is pretty safe to
say, that for every deer that the ordinary hunter
finds, two have seen and avoided him.

The early morning or toward evening is the best
time for all hunting, especially toward the last
quarter of the moon, or during cold, cloudy weather when the sun is partly hid. If snow is on the
ground keep a sharp lookout for their trail, as this
will aid you in tracking them; when these are observed the hunter should endeavor to ascertain if
the animal who made them, be walking, feeding or
running, and the careful, observing eye will detect
whether or not the animal has browsed, roamed
along, by the unevenness or the straight line of its
tracks, and the distance between them. If running,
save your steps as he is not to be found in your
locality; better strike off diagonally from the course
you have been following, in the hopes of heading
him off or locating more. If feeding, now is your
chance to *use your glasses*, so go cautiously to any
high point of ground, partly conceal yourself and
cover a large field of distance with them. If you
find their droppings, examine it to see it it is fresh,
or a day or so old; this is woodcraft. and an intelligent, observing eye need not be experienced to
detect many such things that are of vast aid. If
after the early hours of the morn or mid-day they
will be found on or toward side hills, or in the
thickets, usually however, on the former, where
they are feeding or resting. If early morn or toward evening, look for them toward or near the

"What is it?"   (Illustrating where a powerful Field Glass comes in most handy.   442

water, especially so if the weather is somewhat mild and warm; about the edges of swamps, ridges of hills etc., where they feed on the browse of hemlock, cedar, nibbling the twigs, shrubs, etc. or rubbing its horns against the bark of trees and small bushes. If the snow is deep look for them where the timber is the thickest and where fallen trees furnish twigs and high branches on which they feed, hemlock, cedar, etc.; in fact some old hunters cut them down for that purpose, sometime previously so they will find them.

If following a trail or fresh tracks, go slowly and cautiously, as they are ever watchful of *their back track or trail.* When you locate them don't fail if necessary, to make a detour around so as to get to leeward of them, don't forget that; always hunt any game against the wind, it is simply useless to hunt with the wind behind you or at your back, for if you hunt and proceed toward them *against the wind* they cannot scent you, unless they cross your back track behind you; let the wind get between you and the game, then they can't scent you. Don't approach any game with the wind at your back, as this carries your scent to them and they will off like a flash; get to leeward of them at any cost, then you are practically sure of a good shot, if you are careful and don't get too hurried or excited, for they are ever alert to the slightest unusual sound or noise about them, the doe especially. In October she goes into the thicket to hide from the buck who is watching for her. In November its different, the doe comes out to the buck, and the fawn usually accompanies her. If you are cool and a good shot, you can select from the three, so look about for them. Indians shoot the doe first, then the buck, last the fawn, which will hang around and can be often run down and caught by hand. Sportsmen however should hesitate to wipe out a family thus; content yourself with shooting the buck. If the animal takes alarm often a sharp whistle or noise of any kind brings it to a dead halt, then do your level best to drop him with a well planted bullet behind and below the shoulder, for if you fail it means no meat. If tney catch sight of you remain rigid, don't move

443

'a muscle, as they will very quickly take fright and detect anything of life or movement, so keep still.

When shooting at deer (or anything else) the careful hunter should always take eye note of the place where the game stands before he fires, especially so if deep grass, or brush abounds, lest his shot fails to be deadly; this of course is unnecessary if the ground is open and level, but if otherwise he can better locate the spot, so as to search for some signs such as blood, which reveals the fact that the animal has been wounded, for often an error of 10 feet in a bushy locality causes the loss of a fallen or shot animal, especially by an excited hunter, who regards its sudden disappearance as an indication that he has not hit it; often too when well hit, they will run swiftly a short distance and drop, crawling to some unseen hidden spot to die. Rarely will a wounded animal run far if hit, unless *hotly pursued and forced to*, as they lay down to ease the pain or from weakness from the loss of blood. Again, hard bullets (which I advise against) especially those of small caliber, make such a small wound that but little blood flows externally, and unless there is snow so as to make their track plain, there is nothing to indicate where they went or what; so it behooves the hunter to not only know the spot, but to search well and thoroughly about it. In shooting at deer (when running especially) two out of three hunters err and *overshoot* their game, this is because he aims at what he sees, usually only the upper portion of its body, or by reason of faulty sighting. My advice is to always aim below what you see, especially so if the animal is on the jump, then never shoot except to hit it *when it reaches the ground*, and then fairly low, a shot at the foreshoulder stands the best chance; if running aim ahead of it, then the chances are that the bullet will find some part of his anatomy. If head on, aim at the center of its chest, no matter what the position, aim at the biggest part of him and low. Don't forget if he is on the run that the sharp whistle mentioned before will often cause him to stop a second; that means your best and last chance. Remember also to aim low as the depth of grass, brush, etc. deceives the eye, and the hunter who follows this advice will hit

444

two out of three times, as against aiming at the center of the body or higher. Such however has been my experience and observations while hunting in company with other sportsmen, and my lessons have been taught me by past masters of the art—the Indian, who slowly and silently approaching his game, seldom fires a wasteful or useless shot, and who rarely returns empty handed, as a result of his studied woodcraft and skill, all of which, his white brothers have more or less tried to imitate.

Again in approaching wounded or fallen game (no matter what the kind) always do it with a fresh cartridge chambered ready for immediate use; many a careless hunter has lost the game he has downed, by approaching a hit animal who was only laid out by shock, more than a deadly wound, and who although hit, staggered to its feet and by a few bounds in the brush was lost, before the hunter could bring a fresh cartridge to his weapon, in his surprise.

Again, if the game you seek to approach is on distant and open ground, do not fire at them at long range, unless you are a crack shot and especially good in measuring or estimating distances, familiar with the adjustment of rifle sight, so as to allow for the bullet's drift (windage) take time to correctly gauge your sight; better crawl within closer range seeking the cover below any little rise in the ground, hummock, rock or bush, that will serve to hide you from them, working up slowly toward them, moving cautiously against the wind. If the wind is light, old hunters, woodsmen, etc. place their finger in their mouth, moistening and warming it thus for an instant then holding it up in the air, and by the coolest side, determining its correct direction, as often as occasion requires. When you get within fair range select a little knoll or rise in the ground, and *laying prone behind it* arrange a rest for your rifle. If the game has not yet sighted you there is no need of undue haste whatsoever; take careful mental note of the distance and deliberate aim, never (unless you are an expert marksman) at his head, choose a spot just behind his shoulders every time; often they can be lured within rifle shot by the sportsman hidden

445

where he cannot be seen, displaying and moving a handkerchief tied to a twig or ramrod (see illustration). All these peculiar traits are to be taken advantage of by the hunter, the effect of which add considerably to his sport and knowledge. They are ever alert to the slighest noise (the snapping of a twig even) and when frightened they invariably put a mile or so of distance between the object of their fright and themselves before stopping again; resting on hills and constantly wary of the direction from which they came; hence if you desire to approach them again, it is best to work your way around them anew, and not to follow in their trail.

In the early season Deer are very fond of frequenting the waters of certain lakes and streams, and often when pursued will take to the waters, always swimming away with the current if any exist, never against it, and ordinarily visiting these waters at certain intervals, by the same route. They are extremely fond of lily pads, rushes, etc. especially the roots, and are often found immersed to their necks in the water, for the purpose of ridding themselves of annoying insects and flies that abound; returning periodically to the same spot for their accustomed immersion or feed, by the same route, these are called runways, and when located, a watchful wait in the early morn or eve, is mighty apt to bring success to the sportsman. At times salt is placed in these runways, of which they are very fond, or a natural salt lick is found in which case Deer are almost sure to frequent that spot.

Another method of hunting Deer is by what is termed "jacking". On dark nights the hunter provides a boat and a bright light, having a reflector thereon. The light is fastened to the head of the hunter, or in the bow of the boat, and the l ght brought to bear along the shores, sweeping by its reflected rays as large a distance as possible, propelling the boat noiselessly in deeper waters. At these times an animal along its banks, attracted by the light, raise their heads to perceive it, the occupants of the boat then perceive two glaring small balls of fire, which is nothing more than the reflection of the deer's eyes toward the jacklight, and if the sportsman has never seen such before, the effect will cause him no little surprise, so much so that it has been known to render them incapable of taking aim, causing much merriment for the older sportsman or guide. This is termed the "*Buck Fever*" and there are few that do not experience some such sensation. Usually these lanterns are made with a hinged cap (see illustration) covering the reflector, for the purpose of shutting out the light, for a trip further down or up stream, as occasion desires, and enabling the occupant of the boat to suddenly sweep any portion of the shores they deem most likely. At other times fires are built, but it is rarely productive of good results. At times these lamps are fastened near the breech of the rifle, elevated over the barrels so as not to interfere with the sights, and so greater accuracy can be had when aiming. I have often hunted thus, years ago, when game was more plentiful, and must admit that there is a fascination about "jacking" or fire-hunting that is intensely interesting, and the strange wierd sight of the glaring eyes with the unusual incident of the surroundings, and quiet, amply repays for the watch and wait. Good marksmanship here is of course essential, unless a shotgun loaded with buckshot is used, but as this is most unsportsmanlike, it should not even be considered.

Many hunters also resort to a similar plan for "night hunting" usually at a natural salt lick if found, or at some point where the Deer frequent; at times salt is strewn about, a few days previously so as to attract them to that vicinity. A light is then fastened to the head of the hunter (or manipulated by a guide or companion.) When a Deer is located by the "shining light of their eyes" the rifle is brought into play with deadly effect. Many hunters using simply a candle and cylinder of birch bark, fastened to the hat. All these methods however, are mentioned here simply to show the various plans of different hunters, and not recommended to the reader. Laws are against their employment and wisely so, for either still hunting-stalking, jumping or tracking are far more sportsmanlike and equally successful, and lest my readers do not understand these better methods, I will briefly describe them.

Still Hunting means taking a stand or location about various runways or haunts of wild animals and waiting for them to appear within rifle shot. In "jumping" Deer, the hunter moves carefully from point to point, shooting at the animal as he jumps from his hiding place and runs away. "Stalking" means to approach (carefully) game sighted at a distance, taking advantage of wind cover, etc., so as to approach within good rifle range; while "tracking" means to follow their signs or trail carefully until located, and so rewarded by a successful shot at them.

Another method of hunting Deer is by *"Hounding"* or locating the trail of Deer by starting dogs after them. I have had considerable experience in this method with the Indians, but more especially during my Arctic voyages in Polar Bear hunting (of which I will speak of later on) if dogs are plenty, sportsmen start at different sections, covering as large a space as possible; certain signals or code of them being arranged before hand, when a trail is found, the yelping of the dogs indicate its proximity.

In order that too many dogs do not follow the same trail they are held in "leash," and which is oftimes a most serious and hard duty to perform. When a Deer is pursued by hounds it invariably takes to the water, if near it, in the endeavor to throw the hounds off the trail and unless a boat or canoe is at hand, usually gets away, from the sportsman at least. To overcome this the hunter takes station near the points where these runways exist and act to intercept their flight as indicated by the hounds in order to secure the chances of a successful shot or more. At such times as these it has been known for Deer to run into the very heart of a sportsman camp; even toward the hunter as if for protection. It is certainly an unsportsmanlike method of hunting, and is only mentioned here in order that my readers may become familiar with the methods employed. Besides this hounding is unpopular and well, so, owing to the fact that it renders the meat inferior by overheating, although it is pardonable at times, and under certain circumstances. Like the following which came under my personal observation, of a crippled old Indian who used to start out with a dog tied to his body to aid him in locating a trail and in following it. When, however, the dog located the nearness of the game by its actions, it was promptly and *by the leash* securely fastened or staked to the ground, while the old, but crafty cripple changed his tactics to stalking evidently for the true, sure sport there was in it, and he got his meat every time.

In concluding this article on Deer hunting let me give this last word of advice to the hunter: Never shoot at a Deer or Moose when swimming in the water. Wait until he comes to shore. If you follow him unobserved he won't go far before he will steer in (usually below some distant point) and take to the woods again; and should perchance he strike out for the opposite shore and you cannot follow by boat or canoe let him have his life for his display of intelligence, for he has fairly won the fight and outclassed you in the art of sportsmanship.

Last but not least, the sportsman should adhere to this rule, never in Deer hunting permit yourself to shoot at anything *smaller than Deer.* A shot at a bird or small animal might spoil your chances for big game that day. Again post up on the game laws, unless you travel with a competent guide, and if this is the case follow his instructions, treat him with respect, kindness yet firmness. It is his duty to work, carry the burden of the pack and render your trip comfortable and successful. Satisfy yourself thoroughly as to his worth before hiring his services. Go slow about it. Don't get a cheap man. There are plenty of good ones (usually registered guides and well known) and if you use him right he'll wear himself out in a faithfull way trying hard to get you all you went after and more. A cheerful, encouraging word, instead of an unkind remark, willl stimulate him to renewed efforts and perhaps at the moment you think a trip useless, lead you to success that will live long in your memory of his capability, faithfulness and value.

449

Moose Hunting

(For where to find Game, read the Game Laws.)

"Taking it Easy in Camp."

To those who desire the ideal sport of hunting for this King of the forest, *I particnlarly invite attention to my chapter on Deer hunting*, as much the same methods are to be employed, by reason of its being a specie of the same family. It is a monstrous animal, often larger than a horse in height, towering up 6 to even 8 feet at the shoulders, and weighing from 800 to 1,200 lbs.; the broad and spreading antlers of the Bull Moose, measuring from 3 to 5 feet between tips. Their hair is of a coarse brown, dwindling down to a yellowish gray at the lower extremities of the body. At the approach of winter, especially on the neck of the animal this hair grows unusually thick and dark, terminating in an immense tuft, not unlike a horse mane. Its habits are alike to the Deer, and when pursued it will not hesitate to attack the hunter. As the laws of most States forbid the hunting of these animals until the fall of the year, it is hardly necessary to enter into details concerning them in the earlier season; but as it is well for the sportsman to thoroughly acquaint himself as to their life and habits, a few facts covering this might not come amiss.

Late in the spring months (about June) the Cow Moose seeks the exclusion of the forest and thicket bordering distant waters, and brings forth her

"Calling."

young, usually one to three, according to the age
of the mother, who hides her young amidst the
dense growths of underbrush, while it feeds on the
nourishing foods of aquatic plants which borders
the waters, (stems of rushes and the succulent roots
of the water lily,) and moist grass that overhang the
water banks. It is an ugly animal with a long peculiar shaped nose, ears, and small eyes. At
these times they can be easily approached by the
cautious hunter, but as the laws of most States forbid their shooting at this time, it can only be to observe and study them. It is at these times also,
that the Bulls frequent the waterways and march-
es in search of such foods also, their favorite being
the lily pads, wading out into the waters to reach
them, burying their noses and often submerging
their bodies, uttering seemingly, snorts of delight.
Later in the season, toward October, the Bulls
roam far and wide, seeking for the female, whose
wierd, nerve-trying, plaintive wail is often closely
imitated by the experienced guide or hunter in
search of them, and termed "Moose calling." To
do this he selects and forms a cone from a piece of
thin birch bark, and taking position towards evening near the waters where they come to drink,
sends forth in imitation the long plaintive wail of
the female, and should perchance this sound, in
the stillness of the forest woods, and which starts
with low grunts and groans, ending in a long drawn
wail or roar, reach the ears of the searching or lis-

"They Aimed Below and Behind the Shoulder."

452

tening bull, he will promptly be heard forcing and crashing his way towards its source, sniffing the air in his endeavor to locate the expectant female, and emitting grunts of satisfaction at the chance of finding a worthy mate; should perchance two bulls meet thus, they often fight with each other, and such a scene as this will repay the hunter alone for the expenses of any trip. Another noise made by the Bull Moose is termed "chopping" resembling somewhat the sound of chopping wood in the distance, and which is caused by a forcible opening and closing or clapping of their jaws. This sound is often reproduced by old guides or hunters rapping with the broad part of an axe, the bark of a partly hollow tree; these things however are only of service in the early part of the season.

Unquestionably the best time for Moose hunting is after a fall of snow (October or November) when the route chosen should be along the hard wood ridges where they frequent, bogs, swamps and certain runways, among the wilderness. In hunting them (as it is done mostly by trailing) the services of an experienced guide is essential, unless the hunter himself is familiar with such methods. For equipment choose that mentioned in the chapter on Hunting Outfits, not omitting the field or Binocular Telescope (as this of all things is desirable.) If the snow is deep or not, do not venture afar without a pair serviceable snow shoes, warm clothing, provisions and material for fire and warmth. At these times Moose, when winter snows and cold exist, work gradually into the depths of the forests, seeking the natural shelter from exterior storms, browsing on the branches of trees, twigs of the ash, poplar, birch, maple, willow and other trees, small bushes or sprouts, such as have not been covered by the blanket of snow. If the snow is unusually deep, like the Deer, they form what is known as "yards" by tramping down the snow, thereby forming numerous paths around and about where they feed, enclosing in these yards the various trees which furnish them with food, often embracing a newly fallen tree which has been perhaps *cut down by a shrewd hunter or guide* to serve a sportive purpose, the boughs and branches of which with its tender buds and twigs, they are very fond of as food, and the fortunate hunter who locates one of these yards, is apt to find three or more Moose, that will furnish sport enough to satisfy his every desire for that trip at least.

The Moose is also trapped by old trappers in distant and northern woods, the Newhouse trap No. 6 being especially adapted for the purpose; no bait is used, it is simply placed under a light cover of snow in these yards, where the Moose frequent; or in runways, usually directly under the tall branches on which it likes to feed. Reaching up to browse as usual, it places its feet on the pan of the trap, which is chained to a clog and hidden a short distance away; care must be taken that this clog is not too heavy, sufficient only to act as an impediment, which serves to hold them in the vicinity until the trapper makes his regular rounds. The animal is then dispatched, and its fine flesh forms a winter's supply of food that cheers the heart and warms the stomach of the trapper, during the long and lonely winter months. As the methods of trailing and still hunting them do not differ from that of Deer hunting materially, it is only necessary for the reader to study that article, which by many experienced hunters is considered most thorough and complete.

"One Hit with a "Savage Rifle "303;"

Hunting Bears (Game Laws tell where they are.)

Much the same tactics should be employed in the hunting of these animals, no matter what the specie. Armed with the modern weapon or rifle of today, the hunter with a fair amount of coolness and courage *has every possible advantage* Even if alone, no one should hesitate to attack one, unless he is a mighty poor shot, or his arm inadequate. Years ago, even today the savage hesitates not to attack them with bow and arrow, or rudely fashioned spear. Our forefathers armed with the muzzle loader "flint lock" gloried in the sport, why then should the sportsman of today, armed. with the deadly magazine rifle, high explosive, and modern bullet, even think twice about it, unless he is an arrant coward or a mighty poor shot; for surely are the odds much against the bear in every way

Rarely has it been known for a bear to attack a man unless forced to; indeed quite the contrary. Nothing living has a greater desire to avoid man than the bear—despite the numerous yarns to the contrary (much as you like to believe them.) They will turn tail and run every possible time they get a ghost of a chance; rarely will they venture to attack any man, even if hungry, unless forced to, -provoked or wounded.——

Unquestionably the easiest and best way to hunt Bears are with hounds—or without them, with a companion. Either way you have the bear at every disadvantage. One of the chief reasons of fearing them is that such terrible exaggerated stories have been written concerning them, that most hunters hesitate on this account; yet those who once have pluck enough to attack them, *welcome the second opportunity,* and this can be well applied to any savage animal. There are plenty of hunters who positively refuse to risk a shot at anything, where there is the least element of danger from the animal defending itself, however slightly, and I leave the question open, are these *men, sportsmen, hunters or what.* Hence I say never let the opportunity pass, even if you must seek companions to help you; never give up until (if fortunate enough to get the chance) you have that Bear's hide and head to grace your parlor or den—get him somehow, if you have to climb a tree and shoot down at him, for no bear could ever possibly get a man of common ordinary grit, who perched up astride a limb, rifle in hand, got in the first licks.

There are plenty of men who would pay largely for the chance you might be only too willing to throw away, for are you fitted in any way up-to-date, possessed of ordinary skill and courage only, the danger is comparatively small; any old hunter or trapper will tell you that. Bear in mind however; I do not mean to infer that some knowledge is unnecessary, far from it. To kill a baby fawn, one must know how. Remember I am speaking of the hunter who has already mastered the art of handling a rifle or gun fairly well; if he can do this and is not short of ammunition, that same man can kill a bear, does he use ordinary judgment and hunters sense to that end.

Bears are mostly omnivorous in their existence, living mostly on vegetable foods, nuts, berries or animal flesh, being especially fond of sweets or honey of the bee, and will eagerly risk *his life to obtain a feed of the latter*; this is taken advantage of by old trappers who use it in many ways to effect their capture; no animal being more easily trapped than the Bear (which does not auger well for his remarkable cunning which we so often hear lauded.) Probably the best time for Bear hunting is before winter sets in, as in the spring they are not at their best, while the depth of the winter finds them hibernating in their winter retreat. October or November is best after the first fall of snow, when their track or trail can be followed, and if the hunter can only secure a few good dogs, even if alone, the question of danger *to him* is indeed small, while the possession of a Bear skin is a trophy that will remain a source of congratulation to your prowess and skill, sufficient to make you eager to go again, should ever opportunity occur.

In Bear hunting there are a few simple rules to follow that invariably promises and secures absolute safety and success. 1st.—Commence firing at them at long range, taking careful and deliberate aim and *being sure* of lowering your sights should

"READ" CHAPTER ON BEAR HUNTING

457

he come towards you. 2nd.—Never turn your back or run from him, dodge him you may; stand your ground you must, but run—never. 3rd.—If you have a companion let both of you take position at some distance apart, so as to detract the attention of the Bear alternately 4th.—Preserve that position—and say, Bear hunting is shorn of its danger, and is real genuine sport, *even if neither of you are crack shots* so long as you are game.

In shooting at Bears, unless you are good shots, don't aim at their heads, aim to break both shoulders and a trifle low; pump in quartering shots through a front shoulder and out through the heart and lungs, *if you want to reach a killing spot;* a ball aimed at his head is seldom effective, unless put behind the ear; aim to cripple him firing and reloading alternately, shots through the ribs or stomach does not lay him out by any means, and only makes him intensely savage with pain, and a Bear thus wounded is certainly all every writer ever claimed, and a little more besides, often requiring 10 or 12 hits to finish them, unless a ball be planted in a vital spot. Don't overlook the maintaining of that distance apart or the alternate shooting, and you are a match for any single one at a time, Bear or Bears that you can locate; and now I will conclude with a word of good advice. Never tackle a male and female Bear with cubs, walk all day or a week to avoid them; they won't molest you unless you do them, and don't ever hurt the cubs, whatever you do, *don't do that.* If you meet the female and cubs alone, center your efforts on the mamma, but leave the cubs be, and if she chases you, *deserting her cubs to do it,* hit the cub if you can, and a cry from it of pain will cause mamma to go back to her cub quick as a flash. These are the points of Bear hunting, and if you can only *bear* them in mind you will be a most confirmed Bear hunter all your life. These are facts and are the methods employed by most noted and experienced Indians and hunters alike, and having passed the greater portion of my hunting life with the former, both the American (Simon pure) Indian, serving with them in the service of the U. S. Government, on duty with them in their own Indian country for five consecutive years, mostly on scout duty, and again with the (Annuit) or Esquimaux Indians of the Arctic ocean for three consecutive years in the frozen regions of the north (see introductory page) living as one of them, during the Arctic voyages of which the writer was a member, will I trust assure you of my personal experiences on the subject of what I write now.

By these methods even the "Silver tip" Grizzly or the most fierce of all the Polar, are easily mastered without dogs, although the employment of them renders such hunting easier still, (except for the dogs) as one stroke of his paw is often sufficient to send them *disemboweled* a distance of five or ten feet. These animals simply prevent him from pursuing the hunter, at least until he has dispatched or routed them. As stated before Black, Grizzly, or Polar Bears hibernate in winter, bringing forth their young (usually two or three), living on their fat gained before retiring to their haunts, drawing sustenance (so the Indian claims) from its body by continually licking its huge paws and the porous soles of its feet, and where owing to inaction it requires no other food. Any of these animals can be caught by using No. 5 or 6 Newhouse traps, baited with fish or pork, and scented with honey or burnt honey comb; entering freely any kind of trap or dead-fall arranged for them. (See Hints on Trapping.)

"Bear Tracks"

"Other Tracks"

459

Pack Mules, Packing, and Outfits

"Loading Up."
(Animal Blinded.)

A pack mule or burro (that has been used for this purpose) should be secured if any way possible. It not, select any good stout pony, broncho, burro or horse, **preferably one that has been well broken into the saddle,** quiet and used to hard work. It should be a rather low animal, **strong, stout and chunky built;** always avoiding any that have wild or vicious habits, or those not used to rough country roads or fields. It should be gentle, sound and sure-footed, and the broader the back the better. Steer clear of the idea **"that any old plug"** will do, lest he give out when too late to remedy the evil, and leave you in the **howling wilderness** with a pack saddle and pack on your hands. In a shift the any old plug is better than nothing—true; but you are taking big chances. Examine carefully the feet, legs and back—**especially the latter** if you pack "hard.

Avoid those having sores, foot or leg diseases, unless you want to borrow trouble.

For the outfit you need a common stout halter and **"lead rope"** (15 feet long) next a good **"Saw Buck"** pack saddle or **Aparejo** if you pack heavy. This is a fav-

An old Army Packer at Work.

orite with many western and Army Packers of experience; where heavy loads and long trips are essential. Either can be procured of specialists in outfitting. Have them rigged complete with **"double cinches"** and breech straps as shown. Next a good 1½ inch **Lash or Hitch Rope,** the longer the better (if in reason.) I am aware that many writers give the size

PACK SADDLE

right down to a foot, but my advice is to choose about 10 to 20 feet more every time (take 50 ft. of it) let it be raw hide if you can, if not a good manilla 1½ inch hemp rope will do. The **Hook to the Cinch** (shown in illustration) should be of good stout brass, riveted to the cinch and bound in with good strong leather; while the cinch itself had best be of twisted flat strands of horse hair about six inches wide. Next comes the **Sweat Cloth**—(for this a piece of clean worn gunny

Pack or Lash Rope, Cinch and Hook

sack is excellent.) Next, two or three good saddle blankets, which can be your bedding at night (if needs be;) fold these as you would any saddle blanket, into six thicknesses each so as the whole will form a **soft pad** (and thus prevent the back of your animal from getting sore;) last of all cover this with a very heavy piece of 12 oz. Army canvas, or a square of carpet will do, so as to keep the pack from chafing or soiling the blankets. Over all this (taking great care that no wrinkles are in any of the folds) place your pack saddle, seating it correctly and securely, adjust your breech, cinch and breast straps, and you are ready for your "pack load."

If your animal is not used to packing, I advise that he be blinded by a handkerchief (the large bandanna) so as to keep him quiet, yet if you can dispense with this, do so. Now pass your lash rope and cinch under the animal and adjust your load,

461

Tightening Up a Bit.

taking care that both sides are as evenly balanced as possible. **It is important that an equal distribution of weights be made;** let the heavy soft or bulky articles go on first, so as to form a resting support for other and smaller ones. An experienced packer can adjust and secure a pack load alone, yet ordinarily two persons will be necessary one on each side (nigh and off side packers;) the nigh packer passes the hitch rope **over the load well to rear** of the animal, the off side packer now does his trick, which consists of pulling it toward him, until he has sufficient rope to form **a slack loop,** which he returns to his partner, who stands with the hook of the cinch in his hand ready to **engage the loop,** cinching it to the animal's body or belly, returning back and passing it under the

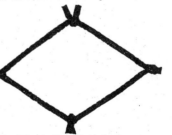

The "Diamond" without the Loops.

standing rope, looping it as usual; tightening up **every inch of slack** already about the pack, passing the **loops well to the front and rear,** engaging them with the ends and hauling as tight as possible (don't be afraid of getting it too tight) indeed old army packers punch the animals' ribs, for they have learned the trick of filling their stomachs with wind so as to avoid a tight pack; by this means often a foot of slack can be gained, and it **means a good deal.** By quartering the pack rope each time it is passed from front to rear, rear to front, and securing these loops. The diamond

How will I get it all on.

is formed as shown in illustration, except that this one shows also a bird's eye view of the "Diamond Hitch" (in center) **which secures the whole** so as it cannot work loose or slip. As sizes and kinds of packs vary so, it is a difficult matter to give detailed instructions to fit all cases; hence **experience— and that only** can aid one to master the art.

Before con- concluding this chapter I deem it wise to mention and

Alforja Saddle Bag Pack.

Diamond Hitch

illustrate another excellent device used in connection with pack saddle, referring the reader to the illustration of the "Alforja" Saddle Bag (Side Packs) which for a **hunter's outfit** are undoubtedly superior, inasmuch. as **two of these** can be be used one either side of an animal; while the form is such that they **can be extended** and loaded down

463

with an infinite variety of almost everything (small
or large) without danger of losing any of the contents. As shown these hang to the **horns of the
pack saddle,** and are made of extremely heavy
canvas, **leather bound;** size 24x18x12 inches, capable of carrying from 75 to 100 lbs. each, and are
provided with canvas flap covers which keep out
the dirt and dust, as well as permitting easy ac-
cess to articles stored or packed inside. By using
two of these and securely lashing over their top,
any other bulky articles such as provisions, bedding, utensils, etc., a pack outfit can be carried
with ease, convenience and safety, to accommodate
any ordinary sized hunting party, enabling them
to take a trip to otherwise inaccessible regions.

Still another method of using a pack animal, one
especially popular with the natives of Cuba, Porto
Rica, etc., where the writer served with our troops
during the Spanish-American war, is accomplished
by using two immense canvas or leather bags
made in one piece; the openings to the bags being
like immense flap pockets on the top of pack.
This bag was simply lifted on the back of the animal and strapped there, with breast, breech and
belly straps. It was then loaded up until its contents fairly hid the small "burro" carrying it; besides this the driver usually perched on top of it
himself. It was a simple method of packing, and
the way the animals traveled over rocks and steep
mountains, showed its simple efficiency for the purpose; for equipped thus, a party of three sportsmen could travel from continent to
continent, equipped most complete
in every detail.

The Pack Train in the U. S. Army.

Hints and Pointers for Hunters, Sportsmen, Etc.

A series of suggestions invaluable to those who possess
either rifle or shot gun

Toting the Game to Camp.
(How to do it.)

Read also
Hints and Pointers in the
Camper's Manual.

Do you
possess a
a copy
of the
Fisherman's
Manual.

The Camp in the Woods. (Cut Poles for Tent Poles.)

465

Hits Around the Bull's Eye.

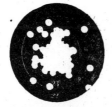

You Can Obtain—A supplementary chamber which can be placed in the chamber of your hunting rifle, so as to shoot therefrom pistol cartridges for practice or small game (called rifle cartridge bushings) chambered for 32 caliber Smith & Wesson or Colt's new police center fire cartridges, which admits of the regular short or long being used in 303. caliber rifles, all .30 caliber or Winchester .32 special for short range work or killing small game. Or you can obtain miniature cartridges for small game shooting.

Best Treatment for Snake Bites.—Tie a cord or handkerchief above the wound and twist tight; cut around the wound and suck the blood therefrom; perfectly safe if no sores about the mouth. (Don't use whiskey.) Cauterize the wound by burning it is good. An old saying and a true one is, whiskey for a snake bite is about as good as carbolic acid for sun burn.

The Ideal Combined Holster—And carbine stock attached to a modern pistol, (see Luger or Colts Automatic Pistol) converts it into a rifle. An absolutely unique article for sportsmen, travelers, prospectors, cattlemen, officers and all who use large caliber weapons. Transforms a revolver or pistol into a rifle instantaneously. Makes every person a good revolver shot, insuring absolute accuracy of aim. Attaches by removing plates from grip and substituting special plates furnished. No mutilation of weapon. Holster feature absolutely original—weapon can not be shaken out or dropped out. Holsters now ready for Smith & Wesson .38 Military; Colt's New Army and New Navy and Luger Automatic Pistol.

Don't Shoot—Until you are sure its not a human being; hunters sometimes crawl on all fours too.

Don't Start—On a trip without a lunch in your pocket or haversack.

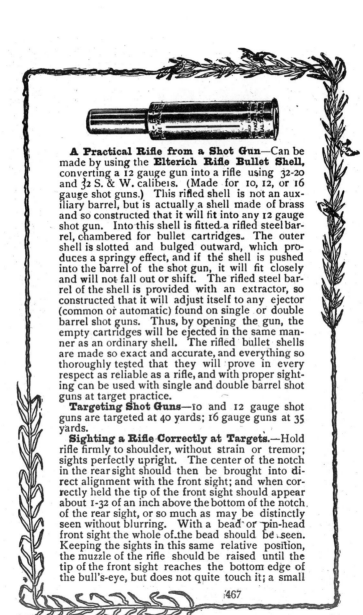

A Practical Rifle from a Shot Gun—Can be made by using the **Elterich Rifle Bullet Shell,** converting a 12 gauge gun into a rifle using 32-20 and 32 S. & W. calibers. (Made for 10, 12, or 16 gauge shot guns.) This rifled shell is not an auxiliary barrel, but is actually a shell made of brass and so constructed that it will fit into any 12 gauge shot gun. Into this shell is fitted a rifled steel barrel, chambered for bullet cartridges. The outer shell is slotted and bulged outward, which produces a springy effect, and if the shell is pushed into the barrel of the shot gun, it will fit closely and will not fall out or shift. The rifled steel barrel of the shell is provided with an extractor, so constructed that it will adjust itself to any ejector (common or automatic) found on single or double barrel shot guns. Thus, by opening the gun, the empty cartridges will be ejected in the same manner as an ordinary shell. The rifled bullet shells are made so exact and accurate, and everything so thoroughly tested that they will prove in every respect as reliable as a rifle, and with proper sighting can be used with single and double barrel shot guns at target practice.

Targeting Shot Guns—10 and 12 gauge shot guns are targeted at 40 yards; 16 gauge guns at 35 yards.

Sighting a Rifle Correctly at Targets.—Hold rifle firmly to shoulder, without strain or tremor; sights perfectly upright. The center of the notch in the rear sight should then be brought into direct alignment with the front sight; and when correctly held the tip of the front sight should appear about 1-32 of an inch above the bottom of the notch of the rear sight, or so much as may be distinctly seen without blurring. With a bead or pin-head front sight the whole of the bead should be seen. Keeping the sights in this same relative position, the muzzle of the rifle should be raised until the tip of the front sight reaches the bottom edge of the bull's-eye, but does not quite touch it; a small space intervening just perceptible to the eye without straining. With aperture front sights, the aperture in the bead should "ring" the bull's-eye, allowing a thin white ring to show equally around the bull's-eye.

Variation in grouping shots is due to difference of holding the sights, firing with varied pulls of the trigger, etc., and defective eyesight, far-sightedness, near-sightedness, etc.; in which case the sights should be altered to the shooter's method of sighting. If this is done, it should be remembered as a general rule, that however the adjustment of the rear sight may be changed, the effect will cause the rifle to shoot in the direction toward which the rear sight has been moved, *while any alteration of the front sight produces an opposite effect;* as an example, if the rear sight moved toward the right, the rifle will shoot further to the right on the target; while if the *front sight is moved to the right, it will shoot to the left;* if the front sight is filed off or made lower, it will shoot higher, and so on.

Trajectory or Flight of Rifle Bullets.—The path which a bullet follows, called its trajectory, from the instant of leaving the muzzle of a rifle until it strikes the target, is a continuous curve, no portion of which is a straight line. This curved path is due to the force of gravity acting in a downward direction upon the bullet, which deflects it more and more, as the range increases, from the straight line in which it was projected upon leaving the rifle. The bullet is deflected still further by the resistance of the air, which tends to increase the curvature of its trajectory by retarding its velocity. This effect is most noticeable when firing at long ranges. In order to determine the killing zone of any bullet, it is customary to give the mid-range height of its trajectory, which is the height of the bullet above the straight line from muzzle of the rifle to the point where bullet strikes the target.

Fire Promptly—Long drawn or long aimed shots make unsteady, inaccurate shooting; uncertainty is responsible for many misses and errors.

Don't Experiment—With ammunition, leave that for experts to do.

Brayton's Auxiliary Cartridge.

This is the latest and only successful device by which the difficulties pertaining to target practice or small game shooting with a large caliber rifle can be eliminated   This device does away with all the expenses and paraphernalia necessary to reloading shells with reduced charge; completely overcomes the lack of uniformity is very accurate, easy to manipulate and economical.   When the auxilary is handled with care it is practically indestructible, some having been used to fire more than three thousand rounds each.

Brayton's Tubeless Telescopic Rifle Sight.

The problem solved. A cheap and accurate substitute for the expensive and cumbersome telescopic tube. This device will increase the chances of securing game and reduce the danger of mistakes and accidents.

The magnification is four diameters which is about the power of average field glass. They comprise a 1/16 inch ivory bead front sight, bar middle sight and the cells and lenses complete. They can be used with or without the rear peep sight.

In aiming, first look below the edge of the rear lens through the sight opening and find the top of the front sight. Don't attempt to sight through the rear lens but below it.

These sights are adapted to any form of rifle which has removable front and middle sights. In ordering give the make, form, size and length of rifle barrel, and the distance from the rear or front sight to rear of middle sight

Made now for Savage rifle only.

Models 1899 and 1903 all calibers.

469

Hunters Don'ts

Don't Leave—Loaded fire arms around camp or anywhere else.

Don't Pass—A loaded gun to a brother hunter or anyone.

Don't Climb—A fence with a loaded gun in your hands.

Don't Let—Your hammers rest on the plungers.

Don't Go—Hunting without a good reliable broken shell extrator, or without fitting your cartridges into the chamber, proving them.

Don't Shoot—With one eye closed; learn to keep them both open.

Don't Let—Your gun remain dirty over night; never polish it so as it shines.

Don't Use—Too much oil in the action of a gun or it will gum and stick.

Don't Let Rust—Stay in the barrels, it will eat a hole in them.

Don't Vary—From powder manufacturers directions, if reloading cartridges yourself.

Don't Put—A poor shell in your cartridge belt, better throw it away.

Don't Use—Shot gun powder for rifle cartridges or *high pressure* powder in *low pressure* cartridges.

Don't Fail—To smoke your sights if they are worn or shiny.

Don't Wear Boots—When "stalking," use good Moosehide or Elkskin moccasins, three-quarter boot size.

Don't Start—On a long trip without a safety match box (filled) and a reliable pocket compass and a hunting knife.

Don't Approach—Any wounded game, without a cartridge in the chamber of your rifle, ready for any surprise.

Don't Carry a Loaded Gun—With hammers down, its dangerous.

Don't Try to Do—Accurate shooting with a dirty gun—you can't.

Ball Bearing Steel Cleaning Rod.

This is far the best cleaning rod on the market, because by its scientific construction it allows the swab to reach into the rifling of a gun and follow it through all its turns—thus cleaning it perfectly—where a one-piece rod merely gathers the dirt into the rifling and leaves it there. Made from spring steel, carefully tempered, and with a heavy coating of nickel over a plating of copper The handle is made of turned brass, and contains a grease cup closed with a screw cap at the butt. The handle and rod are fitted with a double set of ball bearings to receive the thrust and pull of cleaning. A thorough cleaning saves guns—imperfect cleaning means poor shooting.

The rod is finished with a jagged or slotted end as preferred. *Mention caliber when ordering.*

The Improved Front Gun Sight.—A glance at the illustration tells the story. It is the only sight which allows you to see under as well as over. On long ranges where you cannot wait to adjust the rear sight, accuracy is insured by the fact that you can see the object aimed at under the sight

Improved Front Gun Sight. It eliminates guess work in this kind of shooting to a very large extent.

Used in connection with our improved rear sight you can shoot quicker and more surely and see the object much more clearly than with any other sights.

It's adaptable for any gun of any caliber, and is just as valuable on the big bores as the little ones.

Made $\frac{1}{8}$, $\frac{3}{32}$ or $\frac{1}{8}$-inch beads, as preferred, with choice of ivory, German silver, gold, alloy or aluminum.

Point Blank—Distance which rifle will shoot over level sight without allowing for drop or rise of bullet. Natural point blank corresponds to natural line of sight.

A Suggestion as to How to Build a Boat.—If such wood is unavailable, construct a raft and push pole from cut wood, lashed with the pack ropes, secured by cross pieces.

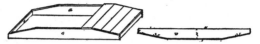

A sharp axe and knife, green vines will serve as ropes, or thongs cut from a green skin, are all the tools necessary. In a few hours a most serviceable raft can be thus improvised for a a party of several sportsmen, and propelled by long slim push poles.

If You Ever go a Fishing—Don't forget to secure a copy of the Complete Fisherman's Manual or How to Catch Fish. 150 pages and nearly 300 illustrations. Send for one now.

If You Ever Go Camping.—The Camper's Manual is the one you want. *Splendid presents* are the *three* books. Over 400 pages, nearly 1,000 illustrations in all. You miss a treat if you have not got them.

Our Manufacturing Plant—Covers a space of over 50 acres, exclusively devoted to the manufacturing and producing of camp equipment, hunting and fishing products, of every conceivable and reliable description. We can make anything special to order that can be made of wood, metal or canvas, that's in our line; and have supplied to the military forces of the U. S. alone, 20,000 to 25,000 Army Field Ranges and Cooking Outfits for the use of volunteer and regular troops in camps or field. Manufacturing eight distinct styles of camp stoves alone, sizes from 100 men each to 2 persons each.

To Corn or Salt Meats—For keeping 2; gallons of water, 4 pounds salt, 1½ pounds brown sugar, 2 ounces saltpetere, ½ ounce saleratus; cut meat to chunks about 6 pounds, immerse 8 to 10 days and its corned ready for use or keeping.

Hits Around the Bull's Eye

To Carry a Gun.—The safest way is on either shoulder, muzzle up. When hunting and when game is apt to be "flushed" any time, in the hollow of the left arm; never carry it muzzle toward a companion or dog; better under the arm so as the muzzle will point to the ground a few feet ahead of you, so as to rest your hands.

Learning to Aim.—Tie a sheet of paper to a long string and secure it where a strong wind will swish it in motion, and practice sighting at the moving paper; its better than aiming at a still object. Don't snap the hammer uselessly.

To Clean a Foul Gun or Leaded Barrels—Pour in a little quicksilver, shaking it about; the quicksilver and lead will form an "amalagam" and clean the barrels thoroughly. Never clean leaded barrels with emery cloth.

Use Fresh Beef Tallow—As a rust preventative. If through with your gun for the season, insert in the barrels a "nick plug" or fill barrels with pure tallow or fresh beef fat.

To Learn Distances—Practice estimating distances as you go along from one object to another, counting your steps or paces; if your regular step for instance is 24 inches, 100 steps is 200 feet; practice this, estimating as you walk along, selecting objects say 200 to 300 yards distant; when the time comes for you to estimate distance quickly, such practice as this will enable you to come pretty close to being right. This is the military method of practice in estimating distances. Measure your regular pace and use same as a guide.

Tight Wads—Over shot or dividing the shot with several wads, makes a load scatter.

Oil for Guns, Rifles, Etc.—Sperm oil or fat of Grouse is excellent.

Pointers to Shooters Who Use Nitro Powders.

Regular Loads of Standard Nitro Powders—do not produce a greater strain than similar loads of good black powder, and while they will give a

472

greater force than cheap black powders, they have less bursting strain than the fine grain high grades of black powder. By observing the following rules you will have no trouble or accidents.

Don't Vary—From the directions and loads on the powder can when loading Nitro powder. Don't accidentally put two loads in the same shell. Do not use rags or tow for wadding. Don't put more than one cardboard wad over the powder, but fill up with Black Edge or other felt wads. Use one thin wad over the shot. Don't crimp the shell more than a quarter of an inch. If your shell is not full add soft wads over the powder. Don't ram the powder hard. Always look through the barrels before loading to see that there is nothing in them. Don't ram the wad edgeways into the powder. Don't load shotgun powder in rifle cartridges. Don't put the muzzle in water, especially in very cold weather, when a coating of ice may form inside the barrel. Don't shoot buckshot in a choke bored gun. Don't rest the muzzle in snow, mud or ground. Don't carry your shells in the same pocket with small coins.

Follow These Instructions—And you will never have a bursted gun barrel, When loading shells try to get into the habit of putting a wad over the shell after you put in the powder. This will remind you which shell already has powder, and you will not accidentally get two charges in the same shell.

A Loose Wad—Over the shot has been known to bulge a barrel. All guns as a rule are tested by the makers. Gun barrels usually burst at the breech or chamber when caused by an overload of Nitro powder, and at or near the muzzle when caused by some obstruction inside the barrel. We have never heard of a gun barrel bursting from black powder unless there was some obstruction inside the barrel, such as mud, snow, sand, leaves, a wad, a cleaning rag or the muzzle being held in water. We advise every shooter to always look through the barrels before loading. If you burst a gun barrel don't blame the maker of the gun, but stop and trace the cause, and you will probably find you can trace it to one of the foregoing rules.

Leading inside of the barrel is sometimes caused by using chilled shot with black powder or soft or chilled shot. To shooters who have guns bored for black powder and wish to use Nitro powder in them, we advise using a wad one size larger than they use for black powder.

Always Use Soft Shot—With black powder, chilled shot with Nitro powder; in any gun chilled shot with black powder will lead a barrel quicker than soft shot.

Soft Shot With Nitro Powder—Has a greater tendency to bunch in and lead the barrel than chilled shot.

To Restore Color to Sights, Etc.—Even small parts of a gun or rifle can be colored by holding in a gas flame until the color appears, then dipped in cold water.

Stain or Coloring for Barrels, Etc.—1 oz. muriate tincture of steel, 1 oz. spirits of wine, ¼ oz. muriate of mercury, ¼ oz nitric acid, ⅛ oz. blue stone, 1 quart water; allow to stand for several weeks or more to amalgamate. . Clean well and remove grease, oil, etc. with lime and water. Lay on the liquid with a sponge every few hours, until a sort of rust appears then rub it off with a wire scratch brush; continue the treatment until the color suits you, then wash well in boiling water and rub the barrels well until nearly cool, (an excellent brown color.)

Use to Polish the Stocks—Of rifles or guns, simply raw linseed oil (not boiled) rubbed well in, then polished.

The Life of a Rifle Barrel.—The rifling in a barrel lasts for about 2,000 to 3,000 rounds.

Saving Shells for Reloading.—Keep them clean and dry, wash well in hot soapsuds and water, wrinse in very hot water, and be sure to drain and dry well; the heat of the hot water will dry them if drained well. Never reload a shell that has corroded parts.

Don't Use—Reloaded rifle ammunition for hunting; its often unreliable. Select the very newest and best, unless you reload *yourself*.

474

Never Start Out on a Hunting Trip—Without chambering your cartridges that go in your belt, thus avoiding misfits. Use poor shells for killing wounded game.

Use the Cartridges—From the rear of your cartridge belt, keeping the nearest ones handy for an emergency.

In a Tight Place—Keep a cartridge or two in your left hand, ready for quick action, and keep your magazine full.

Smokeless Powders—Are divided in two classes low and high pressure. The first named being mostly used in old black powder cartridges, the latter for cartridges of the military type.

The 30-40 U. S. A. Cartridge has a breech pressure of 40,000 lbs. to the square inch, the 236 Navy nearly 50,000 lbs.

In Using Smokeless Powder—Use very clean shells, always prime with Nitro primers; never compress Nitro powders.

Never Use Shot Gun Powder—In rifle cartridges, or high pressure powder in low pressure cartridges.

For Shooting Buckshot—Have your barrel cylinder bore.

In Using Hollow Point Bullets—Fill the hole or hollow with wax, tallow or soap.

For Long Distance Shooting—Don't use express or hollow point bullets.

For Fine Target Shooting—Use patched bullets.

A U. S. Army—Military screw driver is the ideal field pocket or belt screw driver, price 25c.

How to Find Out the Twist of Rifling.—Lubricate the inside of the barrel well. Take a bullet that is large enough to fit snugly so as to get a full impression of the rifling. Force is through the barrel carefully. Get a piece of straight wire smaller than the bore of the rifle; drill a hole in the bullet and fasten one end of the wire to it; shove the bullet with the wire fastened to it from the muzzle to the commencement of the rifling at the chamber.

Fasten the barrel in a vice or otherwise; make a chalk mark on the breech and muzzle of the barrel, also one on the wire in alignment with those on the barrel. Make a mark on the wire even with the muzzle, and force the bullet toward the muzzle, and when the chalk mark on the wire has turned completely around, and is again in a line with those on the barrel, measure the number of inches the mark on the wire has traveled from the muzzle of the barrel, and you will find what you are looking for. The rifling of a barrel is from two to five-thousandths of an inch deep.

For Game Shooting.—Always use soft point bullets.

In Cold or Winter Weather.—Guns or rifles should be wiped dry of oil and not brought or put in a warm place; but left until through using out-of-doors or somewhere in a cold and safe convenient place.

Never Reload—Smokeless powder catridges, never compress smokeless powder; it's dangerous.

Never Jerk—The trigger of a rifle or gun when firing; a steady pull with the gun held firmly to the shoulder is correct. Study and observe the faults and points of each shot.

Killing Range of Revolvers.—A good revolver will kill at 50 to 100 yards.

Crook of Stock.—Generally a tall person or one with long arms needs a gun with a long and crooked stock, and *vice versa.* A too straight stock makes a gun shoot high; a too crooked stock makes it shoot low.

Length of Barrels.—The shorter the barrel the greater the range of divergence of the charge. Long barrels shoot closer than short, and will kill game at greater distance. For quick shooting, and cover shooting, 28 to 30 inches is about right in a 12-bore. Short barrels should be charged with a finer grade of powder than longer ones.

Best Powder for Rifle Cartridges—Use American Powder Co.'s Rifle Cartridge, F. G. Dupont's Rifle F. F. G. Laflin & Rand's F. G., King's Semi-Smokeless F. G or C. G.

476

We Mount Animal Heads, Birds, Etc.—Tan or make into rugs all animal skins; first class service. Send us your hides and instructions by express prepaid; see our Trapper's Guide. (Market prices allowed for furs.)

If Cornered by a Savage Beast—And have the misfortune of having your gun or rifle rendered useless, making a hand to —— fight necessary, try and wrap a garment, coat (anything) around your left hand or arm or take a stick or club in that hand, leaving your right hand free for your knife, club or revolver, and thrust the stick or club that is in the left hand into the mouth of the beast. All wild animals vent their spite on the objects nearest them; hence tamers of wild animals allow them to vent their spite on a staff or rod thrust into their face or teeth, causing the animal to vent its spite on the object nearest them, and which they think is part of yourself *because it moves;* even a cat or dog will do this, as its animal nature. So use the left hand to detract the animal's attention or rage, keeping the right free for the *attack.*

At Short Range.—Always aim low, the tendency is to overshoot; aim at below and behind the shoulder, a vital spot.

To Avoid Spots.—To keep the barrels of your guns from spotting, you should clean them thoroughly after each day's shooting; so clean that you can run a tightly fitting white cloth through without soiling it. Then grease the barrel thoroughly with vaseline, applied by a cloth fitted loosely on a cleaning rod. The muzzles of the barrels should then be corked, so as the air can not get in. When putting your gun away for the winter, or for any considerable time, it is a good plan to fill the barrels with beef or mutton tallow. When you want to use the gun it is only necessary to warm the barrels and the tallow will drop out. Another absolute preventive of rust is the wick plug.

If Pursued by Game—Or wild animals aim to dodge instead of running from it. Don't turn your back to it, face and dodge the danger or you are a goner sure. All animals are more or less afraid of man and even a bear will run from a man unless forced to stand his ground. They will rarely provoke a fight and will run from even a barking dog; when wounded or forced to fight, *only a most fatal wound* is effective. The writer has personally seen on my Arctic voyages a Polar Bear shot with 45-calibre bullets in eleven different parts of his body and still keep on fighting desperately and I am informed by the best of authorities that it is by no means an unfrequent affair. Tenacity of life is surprisingly evident in all large and savage animals, so act accordingly. Don't think because they fall that you are sure of them. The shock stuns them, but they soon recover, so never approach them except with extreme cautiousness fully prepared for a sudden and most furious attack. Don't be over confident.

How Does Your Gun Shoot Sighting.—Don't forget that rifles often need sighting, especially new ones. Rifles correctly sighted by or for one person (even an expert at the factory) may need resighting for its owner or other person, for there is a vast diffence due not only to the eye but to the manner of taking sight, whether fine or coarse, hence the owner of a rifle *must sight it to his own eyes,* don't ask anyone else to do this for you, unless he is going *to do the shooting for you* It is generally advisable to sight a rifle at the shortest range for which it may be used, for it is then an easy matter to adjust it for longer ranges by simply elevating the rear sight. To test or sight a rifle properly, never fasten it, but rest it on a bag of sand or earth, or similar cushion support. Never fasten it in a vise or anything of the kind, securing a steady rest for the gun and body both. Pressing the butt firmly to the body and *always* using the exact cartridge you intend to use regularly for hunting purposes, ascertaining exactly how each bullet hits the object aimed at. If it shoots *too high*, lower the slide in the rear sight, if too low, raising it. A higher front sight causes a rifle to shoot lower or vice versa. In other words the elevation of the rear sight, the lowering of the front sight, or the substitution of a lower front sight *increases the range.* The lowering of the rear sight, the raising of the front sight or the substitution of

478

a higher front sight *reduces the range.* If the rifle shoots to the right move the rear barrel sight to the left, or vice versa. If your barrel sight needs changing, or by accident gets battered, or you desire to substitute another kind, drive out the sight from left to right and in putting in a sight drive it from right to left in.

A Good Investment—For the Hunter, Trapper, Sportsman, Angler or Fisherman, is a copy of the Game Laws of U. S. A. and Canada. especially of the State where you go hunting or fishing. Price 25 cents. Have you a copy.

If Your Mouth is Parched or Dry—And water not at hand, place a small pebble or button in your mouth and keep it there until it draws saliva and relieves in a measure your thirst. A thousand such receipts are in our Camper's Manual.

How to Make a Clam Bake.—Get a pile stones a hundred or more about one-half cobble size *flat* as possible (any stones will do if flat ones are scarce) the rougher the plant the more the fun; gather a bountiful supply of good hard wood firewood, start a rousing bonfire, from this secure a deep, live bed of embers and coals (red hot) throwing your stones into the fire when the embers begin to form and let them get piping hot, when this is done right you are ready for the bake. Next take a pile of wet seaweed, sea grass, rushes, even wet green grass will do (but sea weed or sea grass is best) and over a layer of hot stones spread a layer of the sea weed, two or three inches deep, so as to make a steaming bed, then strew over it clams, sweet potatoes, green corn, etc. (if you wish or clams only) if corn is used leave on a single husk, cover it all with sea weed and more stones, and let the mass steam and cook for 45 minutes to one hour, or until the larger articles are well done. Watch it so as it won't burn, if too hot or dry souse it with water. With *green bark* plates, twigs forked branches, etc. (never use plates, knives, etc. or you lose half the fun) go at it and help yourself, the more the merrier. Pepper, salt, vinegar, lemons, constitute the finishing ingredients for a feast worthy of the goods—try it.

Anti-Rust Ropes (Wick Plugs.)

For shot guns, rifles and revolvers, will positively prevent rust and pits. These ropes are of a special weave to insure fitting the barrels perfectly. Once the ropes are saturated with oil, it will be years before they need it again. They are easy to put in and take out. *All air and moisture is perfectly ex-*  *cluded* from the barrels, and it is *impossible for them to rust* if the *Bradley anti-rust ropes* are used.

Fine guns and revolvers need constant attention to keep them in good condition. By using these *anti-rust ropes* your fire arms can be laid aside for a whole season with the assurance of their being as bright as the day they came from the maker.

Testing Rifles and Guns—Rifles are tested *up* to 200 yards. Shot guns, 35 to 40 yards.

Latest Models—Guns of later model *does not imply* that they are any better or that it has superseded earlier models. It simply means that later models are designed to meet the requirements of different kinds of shooting, *diversity of tastes, etc.* For instance, model 1873, there is no better rifle made.

Cartridges of Like Calibre—Often contain different weights of powder and lead so they might require a different twist. (See twist of rifle barrels)

In Testing Rifles—Mostly the British Government test is used, proof as follows: The barrel is locked to a firing table loaded with a charge of powder and lead *twice as great as is intended* to put in the shell it is chambered for. This is after first or rough boring. If O. K. it is given the second, finishing boring and then subjected to the lead test, which discloses any irregularity in the barrel. This test is repeated after the final rifling.

Weevils in Flour or Hard Bread—Can be killed by placing same in a very hot oven for a few minutes.

For Snow Blindness—Charcoal rubbed about the cheeks and eyes relieves and prevents, or use smoked or blue or green glasses.

To Remove Candle Grease—From clothing in camp take a hot spoon or iron of any kind, lay a piece of absorbent wrapping or blotting paper on the grease, press the hot iron over it and it will clean the candle grease, removing it as slick as a whistle.

Never Use Bullets—Over 405 grains for large game hunting.

For a Hunting Rifle—A low trajectory is of course desirable, but at the same time it is not desirable at the complete sacrifice of accuracy. An arm which is very accurate and with which the shooter can place his shoots for perfect scores at the various ranges may not be suitable for the same person to use hunting, because if the shooter should err in estimating distance it would probably result in missing the game, although were the exact range known he could undoubtedly strike just the spot he wished.

A Flat Trajectory—Is valuable in a hunting rifle, as it lessens the errors caused by the variations in distances incorrectly judged, and also obviates the necessity of frequent changes of sights and of calculations by holding over and under at various ranges, especially in the case of running game. Consequently, in selecting an arm for purely hunting purposes, it is desirable to obtain one with a reasonably low flight of bullet. Such a rifle will give good hunting results, although the same amount of accuracy can not be obtained at the longer ranges or in shooting at known distances as with the rifle with higher trajectory. This is particularly true of the old style ammunition, where the bullet has a tendency to fall off badly at longer ranges.

Our Check Book—Is behind our guarantee, "Goods as represented or money refunded."

Why Lost Hunters Travel in a Circle.—There has been many attempted explanations why lost people in the woods travel in a circle. The solution is, the lost one has his mind fixed that he must travel to the left or right (as the case may be) that fact being uppermost in his mind he continually inclines that way, resulting in his traveling in a circle. This can be avoided by selecting some distant object to guide himself by, and not losing sight of the same object. If at night select a bright star, as the sailor does. See article on lost in camp in the Complete Camper's Manual.

To Make "Pemmican"—That will keep. Take jerked or dried beef strips and pound them to a powder or pulp, mix with fat (warm) beef tallow, sugar and raisins. Put in bladders or skins and tie up air tight, (Used extensively by Arctic and other explorers and if kept air tight will last for years.

A High Velocity—Is valuable because this is of great assistance in shooting at moving game. It is apparent that using a rifle, shooting a cartridge with high velocity, the necessity of making calculations for the distance the game will run. is to a degree reduced, and this enables the hunter to aim more directly on the game instead of far ahead.

Penetration is Necessary—In order to give killing power to the bullet, enabling it to penetrate until it reaches a vital spot or strikes resistance when it can do damage. Generally speaking, a light charge of powder, with a comparatively heavy bullet, gives greater accuracy, while a heavy charge of powder with a comparatively light bullet, gives higher velocity and flatter trajectory. A heavy bullet will give great penetration, while a bullet of lighter weight with a heavy powder charge is more apt to spread. In seeking after flat trajectory and high velocity with the old black powder cartridges, some combinations were devised which secured these two objects, but accuracy was sadly wanting, as some of these cartridges could not make a group of ten successive shots at 200 yards in a circle of much less than 20 inches diameter. This was carrying the search to extremes. A rifle can hardly be considered very valuable for huntmg purposes, except for some special styles of hunting, unless it can group its shots under reasonably favorable conditions in at least a 12-inch circle at 200 yards. For a hunting rifle, what we need is the *power*, so as to give the velocity, and consequently energy. Then we must seek a bullet to utilize this energy. There are two types of these bullets. One used to some extent by foreign sportsmen has a full metal-case, with the jacket split on the side so that it collapses on impact. The one most in vogue now is a metal-patched bullet, with soft lead point, which mushrooms on impact, and in this way has exactly the same effect on animal tissue as the large calibre bullets, together wtth the advantage of a higher velocity.

One Pound of Powder Will Load

1166	Cartridges with	6 Grains	100	Cartridges with	70 Grains
538	"	" 13 "	93	"	" 75 "
350	"	" 20 "	85	"	" 82 "
233	"	" 30 "	82	"	" 85 "
175	"	" 40 "	77	"	" 90 "
140	"	" 50 "	78	"	" 99 "
107	"	" 65 "	80	"	" 200 "

Still Hunting for Deer.—The best time for still-hunting is in running time, in the months of October and November, after the does are with fawn and are running and hiding from the bucks. When you see a doe running through the woods, go and take your position in shooting distance of where she passed, and keep a sharp lookout the way she came, and often, in a very few minutes, you will see a buck coming, tracking her. Let him come up near enough for you to get a fair shot, bleat or whistle at him and he will stop. If you are a marksman, then you will have venison. Still-hunting in the months of October and November is the most successful way of hunting. Sportsmen that are good rifle shots are the most successful still-hunting. Shotguns will do for driving, but rifles are the best to use in still-hunting.

Positions at Different Ranges.—At 200 yards, stand up; at 300 yards, kneel or sit down; at all other ranges, sit or lay down, supporting the rifle by your elbows, or a bank, twig, etc.

Read the Game Laws—Of the United States and Canada, and observe them, lest you borrow trouble. Price 25 cents.

Deer and Moonlight.—Where deer are comparatively undisturbed they feed nearly as much in the day as in the night, when the moon is up. If the moon has shone all night they will lie quiet all the next day. When the moon has been up all day they will lie quiet all night. During the last quarter of the moon, when the moon has been down nearly all day, they become very hungry and feed nearly all night, so that is the best time to fire hunt. If you wish to still-hunt, go when the moon rises or is yet up, whether forenoon or afternoon. If you hunt with dogs go at other times, as they will be sluggish and won't run far ahead of the hounds. The best time to fire-hunt is a dark, cloudy night when the moon is up.

Don't Forget to Read Our Other Books—The Complete Camper's Manual or How to Camp Out and What to Do, and the Complete Fisherman's and Angler's Manual; something for the oldest hands to learn. Send for copies at once. Largest circulation of any books published of their kind. Don't miss them.

I Advise the Use—Of scarlet sweaters for deer hunting. I have them.

Use a Water Canteen—As a hot water bottle on cold nights, it equals an extra blanket and will keep you warm all night.

Pull of Twiggers.—Test them for 4 to 4½ lbs. for running game; on rifles about 2 lbs.

Metal for Bullets.—Lead 20 parts, block tin 1 part, for hard bullets; 1 part tin, 30 of lead for average bullets. Have metal and mould both very hot.

A Barrel Head—Makes an excellent moving target for a rifle when bowled like a hoop some distance away

Chalk Your Sight—When hunting at night, smoke it if bright during a sunny day.

Don't (put oil with action parts) of a gun or rifle in cold or freezing weather. If you do the action will stiffen or freeze. Better wipe them dry and clean using no oil whatsoever.

Frosty guns or rifles after use on a freezing day are better left in a cold but safe place. Do not place them near a stove.

Use a Wick Plug—For your rifles or shot guns. It saves cleaning, prevents rust and pitting.

A Savage 303 rifle, 22-inch barrel is splendid for medium or large game.

High Winds and Dry Leaves—Make poor hunting. Light, steady winds after rain is ideal hunting weather.

An All Round Rifle—Is a hard thing to select. A 32-40 Winchester repeater is excellent, especially if express bullets are used for big game hunting or the Winchester repeater Model 1873. A 40 or 45 calibre Rifle is excellent also.

Before Starting Out on a Hunting Trip—Test every cartridge you take along by placing them in the chamber of your gun and closing the action. When a shell sticks discard it and thus be sure of your ammunition that it won't jam.

Holding the Gun—The weapon should be firmly grasped and held to the shoulder; left hand at least 8 inches to the front of the trigger guard.

To Find Water.—If on a plain, select a point that seems below the general level and dig especially where the most growth of vegetation appears. If in a rough country it is easier, as large hills store up water which can usually be dug for at their lowest base.

A Horse—Will drink sparingly of impure water or refuse it. A dog will drink any water no matter how impure. If water smells or tastes bad go without it, unless well boiled first. Prickly pears or bruised cactus leaves will clarify water. It is unwise to drink when overheated. A pebble in the mouth relieves thirst.

Hot Coffee--Is a stimulant far more beneficial before hard work, than the same quantity of whiskey.

For Sharpening—Camp and hunter's knives, axes, etc., use our vest pocket *double* "spit" stone. Its a little wonder. Fits in pocket or carried in camp ditty bag. Price 50 cents, and it is right; by it your cutting and chopping apparatus is right all the time; nothing is so aggravating as a dull knife or axe.

To Dry the Inside of Wet Shoes or Boots.—Soldiers or cowboys heat a pint or so of corn or oats and put them in over night. Small pebbles do as well.

Care of Rifles.—Firearms should always be thoroughly cleaned and oiled before being laid aside, thus keeping the action and barrel in condition. After the day's shooting is done, clean out the barrel bright, th n an oiled rag passed well inside and the outside metal parts to prevent rusting; before using it should be simply wiped off; occasionally the action should be cleaned and slightly oiled, using very good sperm or gun oil; a small cork *with a string to it* placed in the muzzle will often keep dust from entering. Never shoot a rifle or gun that has any obstruction, dirt, piece of cloth, greased rag, etc. in the barrel, for when fired the compression of the air at the point of obstruction will cause the barrel to swell, imparing the accuracy or perhaps rendering it useless forever after.

Don't Wait Until the Last Moment—To order goods that are badly needed. Freight, express, even mail sometimes miscarry. Place your orders in advance as much as possible, then if there is an error, it can be made right without inconvenience all round.

Good Fly Paper for a Tent—Smear common paper with molasses, if too thin add a little sugar and heat it until thick enough.

Always Read Up—On the Game Laws of the U. S. and Canada, and especially of the State where you hunt or trap in, and avoid borrowing trouble. Price 25 cents postpaid.

A Handkerchief—Left in or tied to the carcass of fresh killed game will keep flesh-eating animals away as they scent man.

If You Load Your Own Cartridges—Or own a gun, don't fail to send for the "Ideal Hand Book" of *useful information to shooters* address sending Postage, Ideal Mfg. Co., New Haven, Conn., to whom credit is due for some of the facts quoted herein. It is an invaluable, accurate volume of sterling worth.

Deer and Salt Licks—When you find a salt lick, use at night a reflector light to attract the game. (Read article on Deer hunting "Jacking.") For trapping Deer use No. 4 Newhouse trap. See also Moose hunting.

Say You Are Interested—In "fish and fishing" outfits how to use them to catch fish, send for our book, "The Complete Fisherman and Angler's Manual, or How to Catch Fish." (See title page.) If you ever "camp out," want to know all about clothing, food, cooking, tents and stoves, send for "Complete Campers Manual or How to Camp Out and What to Do." It's money and time well spent. *Each book* has 136 pages, over 200 illustrations.

Don't Forget—That these series of books have been read, studied and used by over *one hundred thousand* sportsmen, hunters and trappers all over the civilized world, for we have even sent them to the interior of Africa and Russia.

Never Go Hunting in the Woods—Without a broken shell extractor, a waterproof safety match box and a reliable pocket compass. These are three essentials for any distant trip.

Don't Use Imported Guns—Be American. (No better guns made.) Put the difference in cost in ammunition and learn to be a good shot.

A Splendid Rifle—One I recommend for large game. A 99 model 303 Savage rifle and Sidle telescope. "It's all right."

For High Power Rifles—Don't fail to provide a *good recoil pad.* It's a thing that insures comfort, accuracy, confidence.

Best Sights for Rifles—Select those of the Lyman grade. If using a shot gun use the detachable shot gun sight (illustrated elsewhere.)

Winchester Rifles—Are all the same quality, material difference in prices vary on account of *exterior finish only.* All parts are interchangeable, so you can easily obtain or replace any part without difficulty.

Outfit For a Tramp Trip.—A pack sack with straps; 1 adjustable handle frying pan; 1 heavy army quart cup, placed in stout coffee pot; 1 fo'ding axe; 1 hunting knife; 1 compass; 1 waterproof matchbox (filled); chunk of bacon; bag of ground coffee mixed with sugar; small sack corn meal and flour mixed; a few ounces of tea, salt, pepper; little baking powder (in waterproof bags); blanket and poncho (rubber) blanket; rifle and ammunition and a fairly full stomach before you start, and a lunch in your pocket; weight about 30 lbs., pack about 24 inches by 18, and you can tramp from New England to Missouri. *Don't forget the book.*

Bake Oven for the Woods.—In a bank of earth dig a fair sized hole, at its farthest *base* dig a vent or smoke hole, have the roof of the hole arch shape and its base flat; sprinkle a little water inside to mud up and plaster the interior. The whole thing need not be over 18 inches square. Start a small fire inside then fill it up with short chunky pieces of good wool and let them burn to an ash; draw out these ashes, and set in your pan or plate of buscuits or small game, to roast or cook; cover up the hole when you draw your ashes, and you have a *practical oven.* You can judge when the interior of the oven is right (hot enough) for the food, by the amount of fuel you burn, and the *heat* by placing your hand in and testing it like the women folks do over at home. Plug up the chimney after the fire is drawn to prevent the loss of heat. Work with your *side* to the wind about fires.

Choose Shoes That Fit—Easily, as dew, moist grass, etc. shrinks and hardens them. Keep them well greased with tallow or fresh meat fat; it softens and helps turn water off.

Cure for "Mountain Fever"—Wild sage brush made into a strong hot tea.

Purify Alkali Water—By using a small lump of crystalized Acetic Acid.

Best Hunting Hounds—Are three-quarter Fox hound and one-quarter Stag hound.

An Excellent Rifle for Large Game—I recommend a '99 model 303 Savage rifle.

How to Cross a Swift Dangerous Stream—
There are four ways to cross a dangerous river or
stream. Pack or Weight fording—Pole fording—Rope or raft fording—Animals must swim
—the outfit (Duffle) won't spoil by a wetting
—the chief point is to get the grub rations
across and keep it dry. (This must be done.)

Pack Fording—Suppose the stream is 30 yards
wide and you find a place where it is swift but
not over waist deep; here your grub will help
for an 80-pound pack will hold you to the bottom, when without it you would be swept away.
This fact is well known, and rocks or gravel
from the bank will be useful if your pack is too
light to hold you down. In this fording your
pack must be well up on your shoulders and ready
to drop quickly, for if you fall down with a
tightly tied or strapped pack, you will not come
up until you have lost interest in the undertak-
ing. Frequently one can find an easy ford, but
on occasions there will be no good crossing for
several miles.

Pole-Fording—If there are three or four in the
party decide on the best ford, usually the widest
stretch. Cut a slender pole between eight and
twelve feet long, and at least three inches in
diameter at the small end. You can find balsams or alders on almost any glacier stream
except in high altitudes, where fording is usually
easy, and the streams are small. It is good to
undress as then there will be less resistance to
the water, and you keep your clothes dry, but
keep on your footgear, or the round glacial
stones will grind your ankles. When all is
ready, stand in line and grasp the pole. The
lightest man (A) should be on the up stream and

489

the heaviest man (B) on the down stream end of the pole. A's pack and clothes should be distributed between the others, as they need weightl and A will be under water occasionally. Now all start across in line, working down stream always keeping the pole parallel with the current. As the water deepens A may be swept from his feet, but he must hold on to the pole for he is making an eddy for the others to walk in. If possible, always pass below rocks, the water is deeper there but less swift than on the up-stream side.

But in all fords remember that it is the fool who never turns back. If the water feels too strong, return while you can, for a glacier stream has no mercy.

If in a timbered Section with the outfit of tools, previously mentioned, raft building is an easy solution of the Problem.

The "Buzzacott" Field Construction Kit.

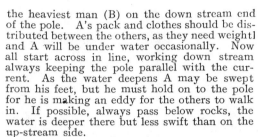

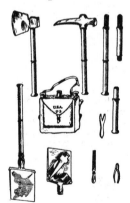

The Military Kit.   Combined Shovel and Axe

Articles designed by the Author for Military Uses.

A Folding Bucket and Wash Basin.

An excellent and really essential article which promotes cleanliness in camps and affords extreme portability; it is undoubtedly the best of its kind, substantially and serviceably made and of 3 gallon capacity

The Bucket is full size, absolutely waterproof and extremely durable; the Wash Basin is separate, but so constructed as to fit snugly *on top of the water bucket* when in use, serving thus an excellent washstand outfit complete, as shown in illustration. When folded together they can almost be carried in your pocket. The metal parts are rust proof spring steel, the canvas heavy brown waterproof duck. and are undoubtedly the best things of its kind ever produced; if desired, funnel and strainer can be furnished.

A Sportsman's Trunk.

Simple Things That Can Be Made in Camp
(with a few tools.)

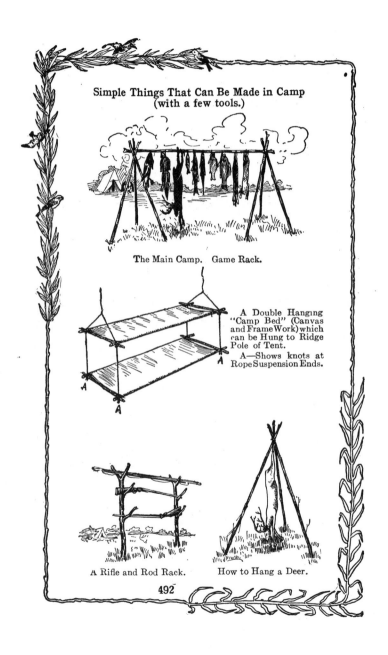

The Main Camp. Game Rack.

A Double Hanging "Camp Bed" (Canvas and FrameWork)which can be Hung to Ridge Pole of Tent.

A—Shows knots at Rope Suspension Ends.

A Rifle and Rod Rack.　　How to Hang a Deer.

492

"Kinks" in Camp Furniture Making
(in the woods.)

The "Bed Tick" Camp Mattress.

"A Rustic Camp Cot, Canvas Top."

For Inside Tent Use.

Larger Size for Two Persons.

"Simple Articles" made right in Camp with aid of a few tools.

THE MOST POWERFUL FIELD GLASS FOR SPORTSMEN.

Approved by the A. & C. S. ct.
(Binocular Telescopes.)

In civil life our knowledge of Field Glasses, Telescopes, etc., is mostly limited to information gained from the use of the small opera glass and the seeing the yard long telescopes displayed in the windows of prominent opticians in our cities, or the binocular field glass (signal glass) nearly a foot long carried by the sight seeing tourist, race track, seaside patrons, or old time sportsmen.

Occasionally, however, we see what appears to be a little opera glass, used on these same occasions, and wonder what can be seen by such a ridiculously small glass, under the circumstances. We would be astonished, however, to see that the little seeming opera glass is far more powerful than both the foot long field glass and the yard long telescope put together, and we, in handling such a small affair, gasp for breath when we hear it cost nearly $40, for it bears the same relation to other field glasses as that of a dollar **watch to a $40 chronometer.** Each, true, has its place in the world, but the place of the Warner & Swasy Prism Binocular Field Glass is strapped to the belt of every sportsman who takes to the woods for pleasure or profit. It is without doubt the most powerful telescope or field glass in the world of its size and almost every government of the world has laid aside its old style glass and adopted the one we illustrate on preceding page. America, England, France, Germany, Russia, Japan and China use the American Prism Glass as illustrated herewith.

Its value to the hunter or sportsman is evident and I know of no one other thing so important in an outfit as one of these small yet powerful glasses. To go big game hunting without one is to be sorely handicapped indeed. I can only liken it to going blind. An occasional five minutes use of a powerful telescope such as this is equivalent to a 5 mile tramp, and I par-

THE CELEBRATED

Warner & Swasey Prism Binocular Telescope

Adopted by LEADING GOVERNMENTS, Signal Service
Etc., of the world.

(See Chapter on "Going
Hunting)"

One-third actual size
Weight 12 ozs.

Closed it occupies 5 ins.
of space and can be
carried in the
pocket.

Field as shown by the best
old style Field Glass of
same power.

Field as shown by the Warner &
Swasey Prism Field Glass.

Small as an
Opera
Glass. More
powerful
than the Best
Field Glass.

The smallest
Most Powerful
Field Glass
in the world.

Each Prism
Field Glass is
provided
with a stout
leather carry-
ing case,
hand sewed &
leather lined,
with straps
complete.

495

ticularly invite the attention of my readers to the chapter (going hunting) elsewhere in the volume. Many and many a time has the author personally turned failure into success by its employment or use, not only this, but I have loaned it to other sportsmen who had repeatededly failed to locate game and it has brought them success. Nowadays it is a most difficult matter to locate game in the woods, the animals themselves take on the colorings of their environments or surroundings and it is almost impossible for the human eye unaided to distinguish or perceive them. Time and time again I could have sworn yonder object was alive and the glass has proven it to be a tree stump, or dead branch. Time and time again has it proved to me that it was alive when I could have sworn it was the reverse. I would no more think of going big game hunting without this glass strapped to my belt, than I would of leaving my cartridge belt behind, its weight complete is but 12 ounces and No. 8 power. I consider the best for general use, its magnifying power corresponds to its No. **8 times.** It is made by the manufacturers of the great Lick and Yerkes telescopes, the gun sight, range , finders, sextents, etc.' used so extensively by the army and navy government of the world. In the mountains, woods, or on the plains, it will pay for itself in moccasin leather saving alone, and by its aid you will find game that you will never see or get without it, ask me what are the most inportant accessories to the successful big game hunter's kit and I will swear by a good field glass, compass, rifle, and the waterproof safety match box, even to dispensing with the experienced guide every time.

The "Buzzacott" Army Field Bakers Oven.

The following is another of the author's invention for military purposes, designed for the baking of bread for troops in the field. When not used for this purpose it can be used for the preparation of foods, which when cooked, or partly so, is placed in the *"Murray system"* of ration cartridges. A device ingeniously arranged whereby the food contiues cooking by *its own heat* and prevents it from cooling.

To illustrate this method we refer to the illustration which shows a metal square canister, the interior of which is *trebly lined* with heat absorbing and retaining material having in its center an inclosed space (circular) into which is slid the *"Ration Can"* which contains food of any kind brought to the boiling point only (when first put in), by its own heat when covered and screw tops in position, the cooking goes on *by its own heat* for 12 to 24 hours, the result is always *cooked hot rations*, ready for immediate issue for an advance of actual needs. These food cartridges are of several gallons capacity and is issued to troops on the firing line, or where the preparation of food would be impossible on campaign service.

Numerous tests have been made and reports indicate unusual success. The Baker's oven has a capacity of 1,000 loaves per day, and can be used either on the ground or in the wagon, illustrated, where is also transported the canvas tent shown; used as shelter by the operators where desired, a feature being that the wagon poles are used as the *tent poles* for the information of the reader is shown a sectional view of the oven with movable shelf, and its fire box and oven ends.

Portable Frame or Military Barrack.

497

The "Buzzacott" Army Field Bakers Wagon, Oven, Etc.

Under Cover. (Wagon Tongues as Tent Poles.)

Showing Constructional Features of Oven.

Ready for the Campaign or March.

498c

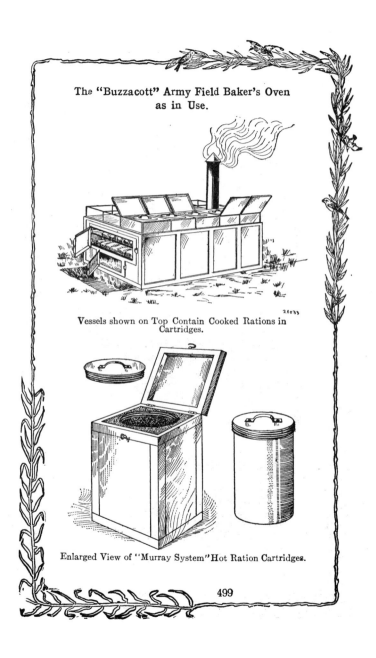

The "Buzzacott" Army Field Baker's Oven
as in Use.

Vessels shown on Top Contain Cooked Rations in
Cartridges.

Enlarged View of "Murray System" Hot Ration Cartridges.

The "Coale and Buzzacott" Military Mess Chests.

(U. S. Government and Military Standard.)

U. S. Medical Hospital Mess Chest Packed.
(100 Men Size.

U. S. Mess Chest (100 Men Size) Showing Contents.

(Officers' 4 to 6 Men Chest and Contents.)

Above Chests are Adopted by the U. S. Government.

500

Going Camping

When is your vacation? How will you spend it? Do you ever stop to think what *a real vacation is?* The short space of time you have eagerly looked forward to is here, or nearly so—how will you spend it? Are your plans laid for a real enjoyable, health-giving trip somewhere? You have been chained down to business, the hum drum life of a restless city, and ceaseless pursuit of the almighty dollar has made your nerves unstrung; you are at times fretful and cross, and despite your business success you feel tired in mind and body; Nature itself seems to tell you to go off and rest somewhere.

Wake up man, go to the woods and forest as did your forefathers before ye, where the pure air laden with the health-giving properties of the woods can brace you, where the air and water is pure, where the sweet grass and wild flowers or leaves fill the very atmosphere with that which your system and sight most craves—*a positive and natural change.* There where apart from a city's ceaseless din and clatter, restful quiet awaits you, there the pure spring water ripples and flows unpolluted by your cities tainted atmosphere and man. Less than fifty miles perhaps from your very desk or bench are the woods and fields, with its cooling shade and waters, green carpeted hills or valleys, and a clear blue sky.

No costly preparation is necessary, the simple outfit made plain by these pages, you already have, or can secure; things that would not do for your vacation at home, suffice your every want here. Gladly too, will your chums accompany you. No elaborate outfit is required, a few hours or days simple selection, preparation, this Manual, and you are ready—off on a trip such as you never took before perhaps. A few hours pleasant ride transports you and your outfit, there you are—woods, waters, trees, privacy are there, and all you ask. Here truly can you begin and breathe life anew. And lo, what a change, and yet the cities distance away can be measured by that smoky sky in the distance. Here a cloudless and almost blue sky, green carpeted hills and fields lie before you,

501

while the very rustle of the leaves and the chirp of the wild birds seem to bid you welcome.

Unconsciously you inhale the aroma of those woods and fields; yonder the lake's cooling waters tempt you to a splash therein anyhow; your pulse beats and your heart throbs quicker, for boyhood days seem before you—you are free again. Look about more, yonder the shade of a mighty tree with its far spreading, shading branches invites you to its cooling shade. There is an ideal spot for your camp, fuel for your fire and light; the ripple of a stream near by tells you water is there in plenty—there is where your camp should be. A few minutes task and your outfit is unpacked, unrolled, while yourself and Dick arrange the tent with comfort and care. Hand the utensil kit to Tom, and the thud of the axe in Jack's hands proclaims that he too, is bent on doing something unasked for; and as the last peg to your tent is driven home, the bright glare of a camp fire shows that Jack has not been idle.

How clean and inviting looks that tent, how soft comfort-giving that canvas floor cloth, how neat in its entirety it all appears, for the Manual tells you and shows you how to make things so; and ere your interest wanes, the appetizing aroma of good coffee greets your nostrils, and soon the cheery voice of Tom proclaims that your first supper in camp awaits you.

And what an appetite—the broiled steak or bacon, the hot buscuit and steaming potatoes, so plainly cooked and served, tastes to you as it never tasted before, for a "camp appetite" is upon you, and this alone is a *relish* for such dishes, that money can't buy. Pass your plate for more if you will, but wait you must; for other appetites have increased prodigiously too, (hence our ample list) while Tom stands amazed, aye complimented; and when ye have satisfied your hunger, fill ye the good old pipe, press down the weed, and as the smoke curls up to meet that of the camp fire, truly do you feel like a boy again; while the stories told around that fire seem doubly interesting for its ruddy, cheerful glow. Your laugh echoes through the woods, and your interest only wanes as the log fire that Jack built goes down.

Glance at your watch and its hands betray that the hour of rest is upon you. Hie to the tent and a pleasant surprise is there for several; the simple camp bed is neatly spread on a soft canvas covered yielding carpet, soft to the touch. Peer under the canvas if you will and the dry leaves or neatly laid brush is shown, and thus the secret of a good camp bed is made plain to all. Turn in boys and tell your stories until restful sleep claims one by one, and as the voices cease, dimmer grows the reflection of the camp fire, and as you reach for the covers of your bed, the pale moon or stars bid you a restful good night. Sleep on ye wearied city mortals, for ye will find that one-half the sleep suffices here, unless perchance impoverished nature bids you rest on, for no cities noise bids you stir.

Two such weeks of daily life such as this, fits a man for a year's hard work again, and when the time comes to break camp and start for home again, regretfully you do so, yet with a clearer eye, a lighter step, a cheerful voice and a rested mind, a body and spirit as of old. A pleasant trip and you find yourself among family and friends again; they comment on that ruddy face, that clearer eye, hardly know ye why, and yet you feel they speak the truth, for you feel as you never felt before.

And now in your old haunts, things that once looked cheerless now seem bright; the knotty problems of the weeks before are solved with ease, your energies are as of old, truly can it be said that camping trip short as it were, did it all.

Last but not least, that which you enjoyed the most, that which has really benefited you so greatly, has actually cost you less than any vacation ever taken before. Figure it up again if you will, and already Tom, Jack and Dick stand ready for that next trip—for you now belong to that *vast army of Campers out.*

It is a peculiar fact that nature supplies most of the things essential to camping out, wood, water, trees, privacy; your own bed furnishes you with covers, your pantry the foods, and perhaps be you handy with rod or gun, luxuries are yours; if not your daily food serves you in camp, your kitchen-your utensils or most of them; while the money you frit a way at home in a single month would

503

supply you with an *outfit* of other essentials that would serve its purpose for many a healthy, enjoyable trip camping in the time to come.

As to the old excuse, married, family, etc. its a poor one. No wife could object did she but know or realize the abstemious effects and resultant benefits that accrue from such an outing, beans to bacon she would want to join you next time. Take your friends along, club together, even the children or the girls. Did you ever see a city bred child or wife that didn't revel and enjoy that day spent in the country fields or even a city park; the echo of the laugh, the romp and the pleasures of that simple bunch of wild flowers plucked by them was equalled by no bouquet your money ever purchased. The butterfly caught, or the fish revived in a camp bucket, will interest that child as no mechanical toy ever did; and the dainty dishes prepared by yourself and the girls, over the simple camp fire, will be relished by an appetite that money or drugs can't buy,

Eat, run, jump, yell, swim, hunt, fish if you will, or paddle those shoe-pinched feet in the saddy creek, and the rest and benefit you obtain will make you feel like a boy again, lasting long in your memory and life.

As to experience—a day or two, and you feel like a veteran. The Manual tells you everything, and should perchance you err, there is even pleasure in it, and no one but your own to criticize or condemn.

Thousands go every year, even children with parties. Once a camper out, always one, shows proof of the resulting benefits received therefrom.

Look at the camp cranks that number your acquaintances, or the thousands of volumes written on it and mark my words, there is reason for it all. That luxurious, costly trip to the seashore does not exceed the benefit of that same period spent in camping out. It matters little where you go, your wants are simple and inexpensive ones; old clothes suffice, your plate, your cup serves you the same, and should you desire other things, the cost is within your reach, be you rich or poor. *Can't do it you say*—then do the next best thing—"Read the Camper's Manual," and our other books. Send for them now.

Portable Folding Camp Furniture (U. S. Standard)

Camp Cot or Bed.

Camp Chair
with Back.

Camp Cot Bed with Mosquito Frame
and Netting Attached.

Camp
Stool.

Enlarged View Showing
Principle of Construction.

Camp Table
with Shelf.

Little
Wonder
Camp
Stool.

Camp Chair with Back
and Head Rest.

Camp Furniture   Adopted by the United
States Government and National Guard.

505

Go ye to the Wild Woods: its Mountains and Streams for "It is good to live thus."

507

The Economical,
Health-Giving,
Enjoyable Vacation

Is a trip to the Green Woods and Valleys, midst the cooling streams and shady nooks, where apart from the conventionalities of the so-called city life—one can secure that positive natural change, that the tired, worn-out system demands. (Mind and Eye crave a positive and natural rest and change.)

Thousands of brainy people in all walks of life are beginning to realize that the fashionable summer resort with its hampering rules of etiquette, is not the place to secure perfect rest, freedom, and genuine comfort.

What the city worked individual needs is a positive and natural change in life and method of living where alone with nature's health-bracing air one can shake off the restraints of home and office and be absolutely free again; independent of walls and atmosphere of inside houses.

The camps by the woods, mountains, lakeside or river bank only can secure to you that which your system most craves; a change in the manners of living—so conducive to perfect health and rest that nothing else can equal, and to-day men, women and children are beginning to realize and love that few days' trip or "Outing in Camp," as the one spot where they can commune with all nature and lay aside the restrictions of a city life and home; and as the world grows wiser the "Army of Campers' out" increase and benefit thereby. Very few can afford that luxurious ocean voyage or a trip to the sea shore, neither of which can compare with a trip to the woods and of a life in camp midst the green fields, and blue waters, where the odor of the forest brings pleasing, healthful, restful sensations for the eye, mind and body—oft enjoyed by you when a boy, now almost forgotten, but yet so essential to you; pictured walls, velvet carpets, fine linen, and silver, can here be dispensed with and the tired mortal that takes a day's resting in the park and enjoys that can best realize what it would be did he but own and transport a simple inexpensive but complete camp outfit in its place; and near the woods or riverside dwell in absolute quiet and comfort, if only for a week, and there midst green carpeted hills and valleys, under a clear blue sunny sky, revel in nature's glories—apart from the harrassing cares of a busy city life, and smoky atmosphere; there where shoe-pinched feet can tread on nature's carpet or paddle in the cooling restful waters of its lakes or streams, where pure air fills the lungs and brings you back to the freedom of boyhood days again—run, jump, laugh, swim, hunt, just as you will or rest, for there no city noises bid you stir.

There where privacy is conducive of comfort and freedom in dress or manners, where the boiled shirt and rigid collar or coat can be thrown aside and absolute comfort and rest be obtained. Every minute of such a life as this fits a man for work again. As to cost, figure it up if you will, elaborate if you choose, and one cannot fail to see that you can own a camp outfit in every detail for the average cost, of your daily life in the city houses while the positive benefits which accure therefrom will be evident long after the cost, pro rata, has been forgotten, for in these days, if judiciously expended, an entire camp outfit for 3 or 4 persons complete, costs but $2.00 or $3.00 per person—per day; everything included; and to those desiring information on the subject the author will cheerfully mail any information desired on receipt of your request and if you kindly give me details as to the size of your party I will tell you exactly what you need and point out or recommend just where to go. As to what to do the Manual covers that I trust satisfactorily, as it has to thousands of others who have so freely consulted me before and profited thereby. I feel that you would not consult a plumber to repair your watch, neither a doctor to adjust your legal troubles. My specialty for a quarter of a century has been camping and camping outfits sent to every quarter of the globe. If then I can be of any service to you in any way command me, for my services are at your disposal be it respecting camps and camp outfits, which is my particular business and life study.

The Author.

509

Scenes from the Wyoming Game and Fish Region.

The Teton Range, Jackson's Lake.

CAMPING KINKS.

Always Camp on a site free from chances of overflow from sudden rains or rise of neighboring creeks and streams. Burn off a clear space if heavy growths of dry grass, brush, etc., prevails, do this carefully lest it get the best of you and a prairie or forest fire result.

Never leave camp without putting out the fire; if no water is at hand use dirt or earth and smother it.

For Mid-Winter Work, a silk or worsted skull-cap should be carried along, and for winter work, in high northern latitudes, a thick knitted woolen cap, large enough to come well down over the ears and neck, is desirable; but never wear a fur cap for hunting, if you value your hair or your health. If you do, your head will get hot when you are walking, the perspiration will run down your neck, you will take off your cap to get relief, and will get a cold in your head that will last you a month.

About Moccasins—When a man whose feet have been cased up in tight-fitting leather boots or shoes, with heavy, awkward, cumbersome soles, and unnatural and ungraceful heels on them all his life, gets out into the woods, and puts on a pair of moccasins for the first time, he feels like the school-boy who has been shut up within brick walls for six months with his books, and is turned out on his uncle's farm for his summer vacation; he feels like a race-horse that has been stabled through a long winter, and in the spring is turned out in a field of green clover; he feels like a bird-dog that has been housed up in his city kennel all summer, and, in the cool, bright autumn days, is turned loose in the country among the quails or prairie chickens. When a man, I say, whose feet have been pinched and whose corns have been cultivated with leather boots or shoes for years, gets out and gets his first pair of moccasins on, he wants to run, leap, sing, dance, shout, whistle —he wants to do anything that will give vent to his joyous feelings. He would shake hands then with his worst enemy, if he were there, and slap him on the back; he would buy his wife a seal-skin sack; he would hug his grandmother.

In ordering them for tender feet specify that *double soles* be provided, and see that they are made of elk or moose skin, the legs of which should extend half way to the knee, so as to serve as leggings as well, there is only two or three good makers of these things in the country, so look out.

To Keep Ants Away from Ration Box—Nail to the four corners of box small legs or wooden uprights. Place these uprights or legs in center of saucers or old tin cans, partly filled with water or oil; ants cannot get to the box.

To Find the North Star—Look for the big dipper the two stars farthest from the handle, are the pointers and the Big star in line with them is the North star.

Don't use old Camping Ground; rather choose a new location in the immediate vicinity. Pitch your tent so that it will be protected in cold weather from prevailing winds, sheltered by some natural shelter, rising ground, bank, clump of trees, bushes, etc.

Trees Poor in Fat are more apt to be struck with lightning than fat trees (the same rule applies in strong winds as branches break.) Poor trees are such as poplars, Willows, Cottonwood, Catalpa, Locust, etc. Fat trees are Bass, Birch, Butternut, Oak, Maple, Beech, Chestnut, etc., etc.

Good Eating When Camping—Pick up or cut a bucketful of the tender leaves of dandelion roots, cut off all portions of the roots, keeping only the tender leaves. Wash them in several waters and strain each time so as to get them thoroughly cleansed. Put them in a cook pot and cover with boiling water and a tablespoonful of salt. Boil for 5 minutes, then strain them well; add fresh boiling water, boil for another 5 minutes, and you have splendid greens (far better than spinach). A bucketful of the uncooked greens will make, when boiled, a good meal for 4 to 6 persons (they are simply delicious), but must be boiled as stated in two waters, season before serving with pepper and salt to taste.

If a pound of bacon cut in very small tiny dice like pieces is added to them when boiling it will make a complete meal—when cold they are elegant fried and served with fried sliced bacon. Always be sure to wash them thoroughly in plenty of water before boiling them. The liquor they are boiled in is good spring blood medicine also.

Mosquito Dope—To three ounces of pine tar add two ounces of castor-oil, one ounce of oil of pennyroyal. This mixture has a good body, an odor like that of a tan-yard, and can be relied on to prevent or cure the bites of any case of mosquitos this side of New Jersey.

One good thorough application of it will usually last three or four hours, and when it gets so thin that the birds begin to bite through it, the victim must paint himself again. It ain't half so bad as the mosquitos, and if you are having plenty of fun, or think you are going to have plenty of it this afternoon or to-morrow, you soon forget all about the smell. The muzzles that are made of mosquito-netting, and intended to be worn over your head, are a failure. I have tried them, and I unanimously pronounce them a failure.

Several times, while wearing one, I wanted to spit, and forgot that I was muzzled until I had gotten myself in a most uncomfortable predicament. When I wanted to eat or drink I had to take the dingus off, and then the mosquitos crawled down my spine and chewed me. Finally while wading a trout-stream, an overhanging limb caught it, tore it off, and flipped it over into Texas. Then I took out the bottle of tar and painted myself, and I have indulged in paint ever since when bucking against mosquitos or any of their relatives. My attention to the receipt was directed by my old friend Shields "Coquina" and I have sworn by it ever since. It will color the face slightly but will soon wear off and leave the skin better, healthier-looking than ever.

It is said by experts that only the female mosquito bites. I don't know whether this is true or not, never having the time to look up

the sex, but I do know that the dope can be relied on to both prevent and cure.

Hang up Birds and Game—Birds by the head, game by the legs.

Pick up Birds—From the water by their heads, shake them and they will come out of the water dry, to pick them up by the wing or leg is to lift up water with them and make them soaking wet and heavy.

A Common Dutch Oven, with cover, is one of the best single allround camping utensils made, in it one can fry, boil, stew, broil, roast, or bake, never use a soldered utensil over a camp fire if you can help it.

To put out Prairie Fires—If coming toward you and serious, fire a streak between yourself and the fire and place yourself and outfit on the burnt portion. If a small fire in camp or _bout it whip or beat it out with wet canvas or a wet gunny sack, green branch of a tree shovel, convas coat, etc.

For a Good Sanitary Rule in Camp—Read Deuteronomy, Chapter 23—10th to 13th verse, and follow the invaluable hint, take a Bible along, its a good instructor on camping.

WHAT TO READ.

If you are down with the blues, read the twenty-seventh Psalm.

If there is a chilly sensation about the heart, read the third chapter of Revelation.

If you don't know where to look for the month's rent, read the thirty-seventh Psalm.

If you feel lonesome and unprotected, read the ninety-first Psalm.

If you find yourself losing confidence in men, read the thirteenth chapter of First Corinthians.

If the people pelt you with hard words, read the fifteenth chapter of John.

If you are all out of sorts, read the twelfth chapter of Hebrews.

To Cure Acute Diarrhoea—Mix and use a tablespoonful of flour in a little vinegar and water or vinegar alone.

THE AUTHOR'S ENTIRE SERIES OF BOOKS — In 8 VOLUMES

The adopted Standards of the American and Canadian Sportsman's Association.
Price, each 50c.   Flexible (Covers).

515.